THE BIBLICAL FLOOD

The Biblical Flood

A Case Study of the Church's Response
to Extrabiblical Evidence

Davis A. Young

William B. Eerdmans Publishing Company
Grand Rapids, Michigan

The Paternoster Press
Carlisle

© 1995 Wm. B. Eerdmans Publishing Co.

Published jointly 1995
in the United States by
Wm. B. Eerdmans Publihing Co.
255 Jefferson Ave. S.E., Grand Rapids, Michigan 49503
and in the U.K. by
The Paternoster Press
P.O. Box 300, Carlisle, Cumbria CA3 0QS

Printed in the United States of America

00 99 98 97 96 95   7 6 5 4 3 2 1

Library of Congress Cataloging-in-Publication Data

Young, Davis A.
    The biblical Flood: a case study of the Church's response
to extrabiblical evidence / Davis A. Young.
        p.   cm.
    Includes bibliographical references and index.
    ISBN 0-8028-0719-4 (pbk.)
    1. Deluge. 2. Bible. O.T. Genesis VI, 9–IX, 17 — Criticism,
interpretation, etc. — History. 3. Bible and geology — History of doctrines.
I. Title.
    BS658.Y68   1995
    222'.1106'09 — dc20   95-1899
                                                            CIP

British Library Cataloguing in Publication Data

A catalogue record for this book is available from the British Library

Paternoster ISBN 0-85364-678-3

To Dottie

For all the years of her friendship, patience,

understanding, and Christian charity

Contents

Preface

As a professor of geology at a self-consciously Christian college with strong denominational ties, I have frequently been asked by various churches, Christian colleges, and theological seminaries to speak about the relationship of geology to Scripture and Christian faith. The majority of my listeners receive my remarks politely and quietly. Usually there are some who express hearty appreciation and enthusiastic agreement. Quite often, however, I encounter those who are disappointed and distressed at what I say. While some know beforehand they will disagree with me, others appear to have expected me to point out how marvelously geology confirms the Bible as they understand it. Perhaps they had hoped to hear evidence for creation, a young earth, and a global deluge. Instead, to their chagrin, they are confronted by my claims that there is abundant evidence for an extremely old earth and that there is no geological evidence to confirm the idea of a universal deluge. Moreover, I ask them to rethink their interpretations of the biblical text in light of geological findings. Such requests are very unsettling to some Christians. Because they (unnecessarily) sense a threat to their faith and to the integrity of the Bible, strong passions are often aroused.

In the discussion periods after my presentations, people have objected to my scientific conclusions, my suggestions for interpreting the early chapters of Genesis, and my philosophy of knowledge. One frequent complaint takes the following general form: "I am sick and tired of letting science determine how the Bible ought to be interpreted." Although they concede that the church rightly changed its interpretation of the Bible in the days of Galileo, they are troubled that the scientists never seem to be satisfied. They want to know why it's always the Bible that is asked to make concessions when there is an alleged conflict between Scripture and science. Why isn't science ever asked to rethink its conclusions in the light of the Bible? Why is the Bible always the loser? Such questions betray a sense of loss on the part of those asking them. Rarely do they perceive a change in interpretation of the Bible as a positive thing. Of course, lurking behind these questions is an ultimate concern about an ultimate loss: "Where will it all end? If I am now asked to yield on the interpretation of Genesis 1 or the flood story, then won't science soon be asking me to give up the resurrection of Jesus Christ? Won't the gospel of God's grace in Christ and my own salvation ultimately have to be abandoned in the face of science?" While I believe that such concerns are unfounded, many Christians seem to fear the slippery slope. With good reason, no Christian, myself included, wants his or her personal salvation or relationship to Christ threatened by anything.

Some people are eager to set me straight. I must not allow science to dictate my understanding of the Bible, they say. The Bible is the infallible Word of God, and Christians ought to take God at his word by accepting the clear and plain teaching of the Bible. I am also told that Scripture is its own interpreter. It should be allowed to speak for itself on its own terms regardless of what science says. It should be interpreted almost as if extrabiblical information did not exist. Thus I am asked to take the statements of the Genesis creation and flood accounts at face value in spite of the evidence that geology and the other sciences may offer to the contrary. I am told that Genesis should control my scientific theorizing, not the other way around. I am encouraged not to trust the unreliable efforts of fallible, sinful human scientists. After all, science has made mistakes and is always changing its mind. Moreover, the world of scientific theorizing is perceived to be dominated by unbelievers. My fellow Christians frequently speak about "secular science" as if science were secular by definition, controlled by those who are opposed to Christ and his Word. There have even been times when I have been told that my attachment to "secular science" and my desire to reinterpret Genesis are sinful. Not a few people have urged me to repent of my sinful intellectual endeavors.

The repeated expression of this sort of genuine concern for my spiritual welfare has caused me to go back again and again to look closely at the Reformed theological tradition to which I belong. Has Reformed theology formally expressed such hostility to the use of extrabiblical information in interpreting the Bible? The Reformation principle of *Sola Scriptura* — Scripture alone — is deeply embedded in the Reformed consciousness. Reformed Christians firmly believe that all our religious knowledge ought to come from the Bible alone. We are not dependent on human opinion or speculation for our knowledge of God or God's relationship to humanity, the created world, morality, or salvation. We derive religious truth from the Bible. The Reformed faith clearly holds to a very high view of the Bible.

Yet this view of the Bible does not rule out the use of extrabiblical information, for Reformed theology has also stressed the value and importance of God's general revelation of himself through his creation. Reformed theology has long held that God's word and works agree and that the Bible cannot be interpreted in a vacuum. Sometimes our knowledge of history, ancient languages, and the created world can help us interpret the Bible correctly. I do not here intend to burden the reader with appeals to Calvin, Kuyper, or Hodge to confirm my contention. One quotation from Dan McCartney, a New Testament professor at Westminster Theological Seminary in Philadelphia, should suffice. He has stated, correctly I believe, that

> if we are to achieve genuine understanding of God's intent in the Bible, we will have to be continually informing our world view both by general revelation and by special revelation. We thus operate in a double hermeneutical circle. It may be disturbing to some to think of general revelation as in any way informing our understanding of special revelation, but it can hardly be otherwise. If nothing else, our knowledge of language and the meaning of words, even the development of concepts such as life, comes about by way of general revelation. We could not even read the Bible without some preunderstanding based on general revelation. Therefore we cannot afford to ignore data from outside the Bible. It too is valid, not by itself, but in relationship to the Bible.[1]

The concerns expressed by those who disagree with my presentations have also caused me to wonder about the actual practice of the Christian church throughout its history. Has the church welcomed or repudiated information from outside the Bible in its task of interpretation? As another Westminster New Testament theologian, Moisés Silva, has written,

---

1. McCartney, "The New Testament's Use of the Old Testament," in *Inerrancy and Hermeneutic*, ed. Harvie M. Conn (Grand Rapids: Baker Book House, 1988), pp. 111-12.

> We should keep in mind that the church has made great advances in scriptural knowledge, and it would be tragic if we were to ignore all of that understanding in our own study. It is actually an illusion to think that we can somehow skip over those centuries and face the teaching of Scripture directly, with a blank mind and without the counsel of those who have gone before us.[2]

Thus stimulated by the challenges of Christians who are "sick and tired of having science dictate the meaning of Scripture" and heeding Silva's warning, I set out to examine just how the church throughout its history has dealt with extrabiblical information in interpreting the Bible.

The scholarly literature on the Bible and extrabiblical sources of knowledge is, of course, vast. To make the project manageable, I had to narrow the focus. Because I am a geologist and because the great flood has played a pivotal role in several centuries of geological theorizing, I selected the interpretation of the Genesis flood narrative as a case study. One remarkable advantage of this choice is that a staggering wealth of extrabiblical data pertains to the narrative. As we shall see, the church has faced relevant information from such diverse sources as deluge traditions, rumors of remnants of the ark, geology, biogeography, paleontology, archeology, anthropology, geophysics, botany, astronomy, and much else. As we will see, the church has rarely ignored and frequently grappled with extrabiblical information in trying to understand the flood story.

I have attempted to sketch the broad outlines of the history of thought in the Christian world regarding the deluge narrative in the light of the extrabiblical data, but I want to stress that I am by profession a geologist, not a historian. While I have profited immensely from the literature on the history of science and from discussions with historians of science, and while I have tried to ground my discussion in historical context, I have scarcely been able to do so as effectively as a professional historian of science. So it may well be that historians will be dismayed at points by the lack of relevant information and issues of considerable historical interest. It was not possible for me to give consistently detailed consideration to all the social, cultural, and ecclesiastical factors that have affected the thinking of theologians and other believers about the biblical record throughout the centuries. My

2. Silva, *Has the Church Misread the Bible?* (Grand Rapids: Zondervan, 1987), p. 21.

hope is that professional historians of the relationship between Christian theology and science can forgive my sins of omission and find this broad-brush survey a sufficient stimulus to fill in some of the details with more expertise than I have at hand.

The project has been a lengthy one, and I have been aided in it by many kind people. I am deeply indebted to the Institute for Advanced Christian Studies for providing generous financial support for three successive summers to facilitate the work. My home institution, Calvin College, has graciously offered me reduced teaching loads for two successive academic years as well as summer financial support under its Calvin Research Fellowship program. Without the extra time made available to me by that program, the project would yet be in its early stages. I am profoundly grateful to the college for its support. Discussions with my anthropologist colleague Donald R. Wilson have clarified my understanding of some of the anthropological issues. Critical evaluations of several chapters by my Old Testament colleagues at Calvin, John H. Stek and Terry L. Eves, and by New Testament scholar Richard B. Gaffin Jr. of Westminster Theological Seminary caught a number of errors and cleared up various misconceptions. I am especially indebted to the historians of science David N. Livingstone of the Queen's University, Belfast, and Ronald L. Numbers of the University of Wisconsin, both of whom read through the entire manuscript and made copious notes and suggestions for improvement. I want to thank them for their expenditure of time and effort in providing invaluable criticisms and comments. Rod Stiling also read the entire manuscript and made helpful comments. The editorial work of Tim Straayer at Eerdmans is much appreciated. Lastly, special thanks are due to my wife and three children, who have for years endured the sight of husband and father engrossed in one more book or article that just had to be perused in order to make this a more successful book.

1. The Flood in Early Jewish Thought

> Pairs of clean and unclean animals, of birds and of all creatures that move along the ground, male and female, came to Noah and entered the ark, as God had commanded Noah. And after the seven days the floodwaters came on the earth. In the six hundredth year of Noah's life, on the seventeenth day of the second month — on that day all the springs of the great deep burst forth, and the floodgates of the heavens were opened. . . . They rose greatly on the earth, and all the high mountains under the entire heavens were covered. The waters rose and covered the mountains to a depth of more than twenty feet. Every living thing that moved on the earth perished — birds, livestock, wild animals, all the creatures that swarm over the earth, and all mankind. Everything on dry land that had the breath of life in its nostrils died. (Gen. 7:8-11, 19-22)

Upon hearing these dramatic words, Sunday School children and mature Christians alike immediately conjure up vivid mental panoramas. Most of us envision a long, orderly parade of animals marching in tandem up a ramp into the ark under the watchful eye of patriarch Noah, adorned with a long white beard and armed with a staff. The animals include, of course, elephants, giraffes, zebras, lions, tigers, and monkeys, and the ark is typically imagined as a stubby double-prowed ship with a large peak-roofed cabin on top.

Turning to the flood itself, most of us imagine the ark in stark

1

loneliness atop a nearly horizonless choppy gray sea. An angry black sky, reverberating with plangent rolls of thunder, hurls spears of lightning and sheets of rain into the abyss. The roiling surface of the water is broken by the summits of a few jagged mountain crags, littered with the corpses of the wicked who sought unsuccessfully to escape the rising waters.

We may ask why so many Christians entertain such perceptions of the flood event when many of these perceptions go beyond what is stated in the biblical text. A few years ago I examined the illustrations of the flood story in several children's story Bibles. Only rarely was the ark portrayed as a floating chest or barge as suggested by the text; it was almost invariably pictured as a double-prowed ship with a cabin atop. The animals were typically depicted entering the ark like well-behaved kindergartners lining up for a fire drill — no Darwinian struggles among the species here — and the emphasis tended to be on the large, exotic African and Asian species that capture the imagination of any young child. Lions, tigers, elephants, hippos, giraffes, and monkeys were almost indispensable components in many portrayals of the animal cargo of the ark. An occasional illustration presented distinctively American fauna, including turkeys, chickens, bears, deer, and raccoons. Three illustrations included pairs of snakes slithering along in the parade; in one case an obviously viperous serpent was distressingly close to the heel of an apparently oblivious Noah. Occasionally turtles, penguins, and kangaroos joined the ranks. Huge flocks of birds were common, and some illustrations included such species as flamingos and hoopoes. Older paintings depicted the flood-waters as a vast ocean on the verge of submerging the highest of rugged peaks. Masses of scantily clad or naked people were draped elegantly over cliff and precipice in some. The message seemed to be that if Noah's neighbors had to perish, they did so with style and grace.

Without question, the understanding that many of us have of the biblical flood story has been significantly shaped by striking visual impressions received during early childhood from such sources as illustrated Bible storybooks and Sunday school lessons enhanced by flannelgraph pictures.[1] It is ironic that Christians today who strenuously object to allowing scientific data to influence our interpretation

---

1. For a stimulating essay on the role of this sort of illustration, see Martin Rudwick, "Encounters with Adam, or at Least the Hyaenas: Nineteenth-Century Visual Representations of the Deep Past," in *History, Humanity, and Evolution*, ed. James R. Moore (New York: Cambridge University Press, 1989), pp. 231-51.

of the Bible are frequently unaware of the extent to which their own views have been molded by influences of this sort external to the text. Throughout church history, Christian commentators, theologians, and scholars have been profoundly affected by various influences from sources outside the Bible in their attempts to interpret the biblical flood text. This book traces the story of how the Christian church through its best scholarship has constantly attempted to understand the history and meaning of the Genesis flood narrative in the light of diverse sources of extrabiblical knowledge.

The Flood in the Old Testament

Our story, however, begins in Old Testament times. The lengthy flood narrative occupies most of the large section of the book of Genesis given over to the account of Noah (6:9–9:29). The intensely dramatic account of a cataclysmic deluge has understandably captured the imaginations of millions of people for thousands of years. The story remarkably demonstrates God's grace penetrating the devastating gloom of his judgment against universal wickedness. Despite its length, dramatic intensity, and theological power, the deluge story made curiously little impression on later Old Testament writers, for there is barely a mention of the catastrophe subsequent to Genesis 9.

The Hebrew word for the flood, *mabbul,* occurs nine times in the deluge narrative. It occurs subsequently in Genesis 10:1 (in reference to Noah's sons, who themselves had sons after the *mabbul*), 10:32 (the nations spread out over the earth after the *mabbul*), and 11:10 (two years after the *mabbul,* when Shem was 100 years old). The only other occurrence of *mabbul* is in Psalm 29:10. Psalm 29 celebrates the awesome power and control that Yahweh exerts over the created order. The psalmist ascribes glory to Yahweh because his voice thunders, is powerful, is majestic, breaks the cedars, strikes with lightning flashes, shakes the desert, twists the oaks, and strips the forests bare. In that context the psalmist wrote that "Yahweh sits enthroned over the *mabbul;* Yahweh is enthroned as King forever." Although this text may allude to the power of Yahweh displayed in the deluge of Noah, it may perhaps better be understood to refer to the primeval waters of Genesis 1:2. Even if Noah's flood was in view, we learn nothing about the event that we did not already know.

The Old Testament refers to other floods, frequently using such terms as *nahar,* "river." Joshua 24:2 (KJV), for example, speaks of Israel's forefathers, including Terah, as living "on the other side of the flood" (i.e., the Euphrates River) and worshiping other gods. Similar biblical allusions to "floods" typically have in view only commonly experienced river floods.[2] Some commentators have seen a reference to the Genesis flood in Psalm 104:5-9 inasmuch as reference is made to great movements of water over the mountains, but in fact the context precludes the flood. Psalm 104 is a psalm of creation, and verses 5-9 "sing of the earth's solid foundations and secure boundaries."[3]

Noah's ark (tebhah) is mentioned twenty-five times in the flood story but nowhere else in the Old Testament. The word tebhah occurs twice in Exodus 2:3, 5, but there it refers to the little reed basket into which baby Moses was placed to escape death at the hands of the Egyptians. Many commentators have suggested that tebhah was an Egyptian loanword and that Noah's ark was a great floating chest. Some surmise that the ark may have been constructed of papyrus reeds like the little "ark" of Moses.[4] Moses resembled Noah in being delivered by an ark that floated on the Nile "flood."

Outside of Genesis, Noah is mentioned only three times in the Old Testament. He appears in 1 Chronicles 1:3 without comment in a genealogy that begins with Adam. In Isaiah 54:9, God speaks of his determination to bring blessing upon the Israelites and recalls the "days of Noah when I swore that the waters of Noah would never again cover the earth." As God had covenanted with Noah and creation at the conclusion of the flood, so he covenants with his people and affirms his unfailing love for them. Finally, in Ezekiel 14:14, 20, Noah, Daniel, and Job are singled out for their exemplary lives. Even so, Noah's righteousness is seen as adequate to save only himself. In these last two texts, the flood story provides the background for object lessons in God's covenant faithfulness and the severely limited efficacy of human righteousness. We learn nothing new about the flood itself.

Whatever impressions the biblical deluge narrative made on the Old Testament authors, they generally did not impart those impres-

---

2. My colleague Prof. John Stek of Calvin Theological Seminary has pointed out that nahar is on occasion used as a synonym for "sea," especially in references to the primordial sea on which the earth is said to be founded (Ps. 24:2) or to the primordial chaos waters that threaten life (Jon. 2:3) or the world order (Ps. 93:3).

3. For relevant comments on Psalm 104, see The NIV Study Bible (Grand Rapids: Zondervan, 1985), p. 895.

4. See, e.g., Derek Kidner, Genesis (Chicago: InterVarsity Press, 1967), p. 88; and Harold Stigers, A Commentary on Genesis (Grand Rapids: Zondervan, 1975), p. 104.

sions in writing.[5] The prophets apparently felt no compulsion to interpret, explain, or defend the flood story.

Other Ancient Flood Traditions

The Babylonian Tradition

In pre-Christian times, Genesis was not alone in depicting a devastating watery cataclysm that drowned virtually all of humanity. Near Eastern archeological explorations during the past two centuries have shown that several versions of a deluge tradition were widely circulated throughout Mesopotamia and other parts of the Near East.[6] Classical Latin and Greek authors also recorded variants of a deluge tradition. Since these traditions were widespread during the Old Testament era and strikingly resemble the biblical narrative, some of them must have been familiar to the Jewish people, although there is little indication that Jewish exegesis of the biblical text was significantly affected by them. The Mediterranean world was surely acquainted with the Mesopotamian flood tradition from *Babyloniaka*, written by the Babylonian priest Berossus (c. 330-250 B.C.). Excerpts have been preserved in the writings of Alexander Polyhistor, Abydenus, and Eusebius. Evidence clearly indicates that Jews living in the centuries immediately before Christ were acquainted with Berossus's version of the deluge, and some Jewish pseudepigrapha may have been influenced by it. Josephus and the early Church Fathers were also acquainted with Berossus's story of the deluge.

In the tradition of Berossus appearing in the writings of Alexander Polyhistor, a first-century B.C. Greek author, Kronos appeared to Xisuthros in a dream and said that mankind would be destroyed by a flood. Kronos ordered Xisuthros to build a boat and to embark with his family and friends. Xisuthros "was to stow food and drink and put

---

5. *The NIV Study Bible*'s notes on Jer. 33:20, 25 suggest, however, that the divine covenant with day and night mentioned in these verses may refer to the covenant with nature established immediately following the deluge.

6. For information on much of the Mesopotamian material, see Alexander Heidel, *The Gilgamesh Epic and Old Testament Parallels* (Chicago: University of Chicago Press, 1946); W. G. Lambert and Alan R. Millard, *Atrahasis: The Babylonian Story of the Flood* (Oxford: Oxford University Press, 1969); and Jeffrey H. Tigay, *The Evolution of the Gilgamesh Epic* (Philadelphia: University of Pennsylvania Press, 1982).

both birds and animals on board and then sail away when he had got everything ready." Xisuthros obeyed. When the flood subsided, "Xisuthros let out some of the birds, which, finding no food or place to rest, came back to the vessel. After a few days Xisuthros again let out the birds, and they again returned to the ship, this time with their feet covered in mud." When the birds were let out a third time, they did not return. Inferring that land had appeared, Xisuthros opened the boat, and, "seeing that it had run aground on some mountain, he disembarked with his wife, his daughter, and his pilot, prostrated himself to the ground, set up an altar and sacrificed to the gods." According to this tradition, part of the boat, which "came to rest in the Gordyaean mountains of Armenia, still remains, and some people scrape pitch off the boat and use it as charms."[7]

The Greek Tradition

The Greek tradition of Deucalion's flood, well established by the time of Christ, must also have been known to the Jews in the late Old Testament period. Herodotus (fifth century B.C.) made passing reference to the reign of Deucalion, but the first mention of Deucalion's flood occurs in the ninth Olympian ode of Pindar (518–c. 446 B.C.), where we read that "Deucalion and Pyrrha, coming down from Parnassos, founded their house at the first and with no act of love established a stone generation to be their folk." In their time "the black earth was awash under the weight of water; but by Zeus' means, of a sudden the ebb-tide drained the flood. And from these came your ancestors." In the *Timaeus*, Plato (427-348 B.C.) recounted how Solon, the wise man of the ancient Greeks, traveled to Egypt and discoursed on the earliest events known to the Greeks, including "how Deucalion and Pyrrha survived the flood and who were their descendants."[8] An expanded version of the legend entailing a floating chest was given by Apollodorus sometime between the first century B.C. and the second century A.D.[9]

---

7. For the complete extract of the Berossus account recorded by Alexander Polyhistor, see Lambert and Millard, *Atrahasis*, pp. 135-36. The similarity of this account to the Sumerian and biblical accounts suggests that Berossus may have been acquainted with the Old Testament story.

8. Herodotus, *The Histories* (Baltimore: Penguin Books, 1954), p. 33; Richmond Lattimore, *The Odes of Pindar* (Chicago: University of Chicago Press, 1947), p. 28; and Plato, *Timaeus* (Baltimore: Penguin Books, 1965), p. 34.

9. James G. Frazer, *Apollodorus: The Library* (London: William Heinemann, 1921), pp. 53-55.

The well-established tradition of Deucalion's flood appears in a greatly embellished form in the work of the Latin poet Ovid (43 B.C.–A.D. 17). Ovid's version of the Deucalion story closely resembles the Old Testament version, suggesting that repeated telling of the Deucalion story and related Greek myths was influenced by contacts between the Greco-Roman civilization and the Old Testament and Babylonian traditions.

Ovid's tale begins with the golden age, "when men of their own accord, without threat of punishment, without laws, maintained good faith and did what was right." The golden age was succeeded by the ages of silver, bronze, and then iron. In the iron age, "all manner of crime broke out." Modesty, truth, and loyalty were replaced by treachery, trickery, deceit, violence, and criminal greed. Even the heights of heaven were unsafe as giants "assailed the kingdom of the gods and, piling mountains together, built them up to the stars above." The resemblance of this narrative to the description of the evil preceding the flood (Gen. 6:1-4) is obvious. Jupiter resolved to send "rain pouring down from every quarter of the sky, and so destroy mankind beneath the waters."

He brought in the south wind, sheets of rain poured from heaven, and Neptune lent the assistance of his waves. The rivers opened their springs, rushed to the sea in frenzied torrents, overflowed their banks, and swept away "in one torrential flood crops and orchards, cattle and men, houses and temples, sacred images and all." People desperately tried to escape by clambering to the hilltops. The ocean overwhelmed the hills, and waves washed the mountain peaks. The greater part of the human race was swallowed up by the waters, and those whom the sea spared died from famine. In the land of Phocis, on the high mountain Parnassus, the little boat carrying the upright Deucalion and his wife ran aground. After landing, the survivors offered prayers to the various deities. Jupiter drove away the storm, and the sea was no longer angry. The floods sank down, the seashore reappeared, the swollen rivers were once more contained within their channels, and the hills reemerged, mud still clinging to the leaves of the trees. Moved to tears by the world's emptiness, Deucalion and Pyrrha threw stones behind them. The stones thrown from male hands took on the appearance of men, while the stones thrown from female hands took on the appearance of women. Different kinds of animals were produced by the earth.[10]

The still later version of Lucian (c. 125–c. 180) shows the clear influence of the Old Testament, Babylonian traditions, and possibly

10. Ovid, *Metamorphoses* (Baltimore: Penguin Books, 1955), pp. 36-40.

Jewish legend. Lucian says that the flood occurred in the lifetime of "Deucalion, called Sisythes." Lucian had heard the Greek account that men of the present did not constitute the original race, for that race had perished and been reconstituted by Deucalion. The original race "were extremely violent and committed lawless deeds," neither keeping oaths nor welcoming strangers nor sparing suppliants. They were punished when "the earth poured forth a flood of water. Heavy rains fell, rivers rushed down in torrents, and the sea rose on high, until everything became water, and all the people perished." Only Deucalion was spared, "because of his prudence and piety," by embarking with his children and wives into a great ark. As Deucalion boarded, "pigs and horses, species of lions, snakes and every kind of creature that grazes on earth came to him, all of them in pairs. He welcomed all, and none harmed him." After the flood had receded, Deucalion built an altar and a temple sacred to Hera.[11]

The Hindu Tradition

A Hindu flood tradition also existed well before the Christian era. The earliest written version of this tradition says that as Manu was washing one morning, a fish warned him to escape a coming flood by preparing and entering a ship. When the flood came, Manu tied the ship to the fish "and by that means he passed swiftly up to yonder northern mountain." The fish then said to Manu, "I have saved thee. Fasten the ship to a tree; but let not the water cut thee off, whilst thou art on the mountain. As the water subsides, thou mayest gradually descend!" Manu gradually descended the slope of the northern mountain. Of all creatures, Manu alone remained. Wishing offspring, he engaged in worship. Eventually a woman was produced from clarified butter, sour milk, whey, and curds that were offered up in the waters by Manu. Through her Manu regenerated his race.[12]

Because there were few significant contacts between the Jews and the Hindu culture during Old Testament times, it is doubtful that the Hindu legend was familiar to the Jews. Yet even apart from the legend of Manu, the people of God in the final centuries of the pre-Christian era were acquainted with recognizable extrabiblical traditions

11. Harold W. Attridge and Robert A. Oden, *The Syrian Goddess (De Dea Syria)* (Missoula, Mont.: Scholars Press, 1976), pp. 19-21.

12. F. Max Muller, *The Sacred Books of the East*, vol. 12 (Oxford: Clarendon Press, 1882), pp. 216-18.

that were potentially relevant to their understanding of the biblical story of the deluge. It was not until around the time of Christ that such traditions were cited as independent testimony to the veracity of the biblical account, however.

Old Testament Pseudepigrapha

The period following the completion of the Old Testament canon in the fourth century B.C. was marked by turmoil and crisis. After their return from exile, the Jews were profoundly affected by the collapse of Persia, the ascendancy of Greek thought and culture, persecution by the Seleucid rulers, and eventual domination by Rome. Several pseudonymous texts written during this period stress the importance of faithful dedication to the religion of the fathers by appealing to the lives of ancient heroes. The Noachian deluge is a frequent theme in such pseudepigraphic literature as *1 Enoch*, *Jubilees*, and *Genesis Apocryphon*.[13]

These writings give clear evidence of Jewish embellishments of the biblical flood narrative. There is no scholarly consensus on whether these embellishments betray the influence of Babylonian flood motifs, but there are no overt references in the pseudepigrapha to the Babylonian tradition, nor are there appeals to any kind of extrabiblical material. Apocalyptic versions of the familiar Old Testament story were simply pressed into service in an effort to urge the Jews to hold fast to the faith of the fathers.

Josephus

Extrabiblical tradition was first employed for apologetic purposes by the first-century Jewish historian Flavius Josephus (c. 37–c. 101). In the third chapter of his *Antiquities of the Jews*, a major work that

---

13. For analysis of Jewish pseudepigrapha and translations, see George W. E. Nickelsburg, *Jewish Literature between the Bible and the Mishnah* (Philadelphia: Fortress Press, 1981); Robert H. Charles, *The Apocrypha and Pseudepigrapha of the Old Testament in English*, vol. 2 (Oxford: Clarendon Press, 1913); and Joseph A. Fitzmyer, *The Genesis Apocryphon of Qumran Cave I* (Rome: Biblical Institute Press, 1971). For a much more detailed review of the treatment of the flood in the Old Testament pseudepigrapha and in Philo and Josephus, see Jack P. Lewis, *A Study of the Interpretation of Noah and the Flood in Jewish and Christian Literature* (Leiden: E. J. Brill, 1968).

recounts Jewish history from the beginning of creation, Josephus retells
the biblical flood story. He writes that Noah was displeased with the
wickedness of his contemporaries but unsuccessful in persuading them
to change their ways. Fearing for the lives of his family and himself,
he departed from the land, but God determined to destroy humanity
and offered Noah a means of escape: the ark. Noah sent his family
into the ark along with all sorts of living creatures. The ark had firm
walls and a roof and was "braced with cross beams, so that it could
not be any way drowned or overborne by the violence of the water."
According to Josephus, the flood began 2,656 years from Adam. When
it was over, "the ark rested on the top of a certain mountain in
Armenia. . . . The ark being saved in that place, its remains are shown
there by the inhabitants to this day." Josephus also maintains that all
the writers of barbarian histories mentioned the flood and the ark,
including Berossus the Chaldean, who reported that there was "still
some part of this ship in Armenia, at the mountain of the Cordyaeans;
and that some people carry off pieces of the bitumen, which they take
away, and use chiefly as amulets for the averting of mischiefs."
Josephus also lists Hieronymus the Egyptian, Mnaseas, and many
others as having referred to the flood. He notes in particular that
Nicolaus of Damascus spoke of

> a great mountain in Armenia, over Minyas, called Baris, upon which
> it is reported that many who fled at the time of the Deluge were
> saved; and that one who was carried in an ark came on shore upon
> the top of it; and that the remains of the timber were a great while
> preserved. This might be the man about whom Moses the legislator
> of the Jews wrote.[14]

In a later part of *Antiquities*, Josephus relates that in a "country called
Carrae . . . there are also . . . remains of that ark, wherein it is related
that Noah escaped the deluge, and where they are still shown to such
as are desirous to see them."[15]

        14. William Whiston, *The Life and Works of Flavius Josephus* (Philadelphia:
John C. Winston, n.d.), pp. 36-38.
        15. Whiston, *The Life and Works of Flavius Josephus*, p. 586. In Lloyd R.
Bailey's thorough study of ancient ideas about landing sites of the ark, *Where Is
Noah's Ark?* (Nashville: Abingdon, 1978), he suggests that Josephus may have
located the ark in two different places. The first reference places the ark in Gordyene,
a mountainous area of the Cordyaeans between the Tigris and Upper Zab rivers,
south and southeast of Lake Van. The second reference places the ark in Adiabene,
between the Tigris and the Lower Zab rivers, southeast of Gordyene.

Josephus specifically identified extrabiblical traditions with the biblical account. He accepted their basic historical trustworthiness, implicitly regarding them as corroborations of the testimony of the biblical story. And, of course, Josephus assumed that the biblical flood was an actual event that occurred as described in the Old Testament account. He assumed without confirmation that relics of the ark survived and that they served to corroborate the biblical account.

Philo

Detailed commentary on the deluge narrative was initiated by Philo of Alexandria (c. 30 B.C.–c. A.D. 45). Philo's views on the flood, expressed in *Questions and Answers on Genesis,* had a profound influence on early Christian writings by way of his pervasive reliance on allegorical exegesis. Although he assumed the historicity of the flood narrative and was interested in the literal surface meaning of the text, Philo's overarching concern was to penetrate to deeper meanings revealed through allegory. Unlike Josephus, Philo paid no attention to extrabiblical flood traditions or reports of ark remnants.

Philo did, however, introduce one extrabiblical observation of a natural phenomenon to settle an exegetical question. He believed that the Hebrew word *ruach* in Genesis 8:1 should be translated "spirit" rather than "wind" because he knew of no instance in which water had been diminished by the wind. He reasoned that if wind could diminish water, then "vast expanses of the sea would long ago have been consumed" inasmuch as wind is constantly blowing across the sea. Therefore the wind could not have been responsible for the diminishing of the deluge floodwaters.

Philo also made the intriguing suggestion that the flood was not "a trifling outpouring of water but a limitless and immense one, which almost flowed out beyond the Pillars of Heracles (the Straits of Gibraltar) and the Great Sea. Therefore the whole earth and the mountainous regions were flooded." It is difficult to know what to make of this. In one breath he characterizes the cataclysm as "limitless and immense" and also appears to limit its extent to the Mediterranean basin.[16]

16. Ralph Marcus, *Philo,* Supplement I: *Questions and Answers on Genesis* (London: William Heinemann, 1953).

Concluding Analysis

The flood narrative was employed by early Jewish writers primarily for
hortatory purposes. It was recast in apocalyptic genre to attack the
enemies of Israel and to rally the Jews to faithfulness to God. It was
allegorized to promote a moral lifestyle. Jewish writers unhesitatingly
assumed that the Old Testament story was literal history. In view of
their very limited knowledge of geography, biology, and geology, the
ancients gave hardly any thought to questions that so sorely vex conservative Christians today about the extent of the flood or the capacity
of the ark. Only Philo remotely suggested a limited flood, one that
"almost" went out beyond the Pillars of Heracles, but for him that was
tantamount to being universal, covering virtually the entire world that
he knew. Early Jewish adherents of the Old Testament cared little
about sources of information external to Scripture. The Old Testament
was regarded as the self-authenticating voice of Yahweh and needed
no independent verification. The only significant concern about extrabiblical information appeared in the limited appeals of Josephus to
the Babylonian deluge tradition of Berossus, the Greek deluge tradition,
and reports of the existence of remnants of the ark and in Philo's
isolated observation about the behavior of wind and water in support
of his interpretation of one verse of the text. Extrabiblical influences
became more important in early Christian centuries.

2. The Flood in Early Christian Thought

The New Testament

New Testament literature commonly links the flood to the theme of final judgment and the return of Christ. In Matthew 24:36-39, Jesus' Olivet discourse on the "signs of the end of the age" provides one such link. Toward the conclusion of the discourse we read that

> no one knows about that day or hour, not even the angels in heaven, nor the Son, but only the Father. As it was in the days of Noah, so it will be at the coming of the Son of Man. For in the days before the flood [*kataklysmos*], people were eating and drinking, marrying and giving in marriage, up to the day Noah entered the ark; and they knew nothing about what would happen until the flood came and took them all away. That is how it will be at the coming of the Son of Man.

Luke 17:26-27 differs little: "Just as it was in the days of Noah, so also will it be in the days of the Son of Man. People were eating, drinking, marrying and being given in marriage up to the day Noah entered the ark. Then the flood came and destroyed them all." Christ used the flood as a model for his return, an event that would suddenly interrupt the routine of daily life. Like the flood, he said, his second coming would unexpectedly create a profound separation between the saved and the destroyed.

In the context of divine condemnation, 2 Peter 2:5 speaks of

13

God as one who "did not spare the ancient world when he brought the flood on its ungodly people, but protected Noah, a preacher of righteousness, and seven others." The flood further serves as a type of the final judgment in 2 Peter 3:3-7:

> First of all, you must understand that in the last days scoffers will come, scoffing and following their own evil desires. They will say, "Where is this 'coming' he promised? Ever since our fathers died, everything goes on as it has since the beginning of creation." But they deliberately forget that long ago by God's word the heavens existed and the earth was formed out of water and with water. By water also the world of that time was deluged [kataklystheis] and destroyed. By the same word the present heavens and earth are reserved for fire, being kept for the day of judgment and destruction of ungodly men.[1]

As in the Olivet discourse, the emphasis falls on the sudden unexpectedness of both the flood and the final judgment. Both passages speak of people blithely assuming that their daily routine will continue mechanically without any possibility of an intrusion of divine judgment. They ignore the fact that the flood broke suddenly on an unprepared wicked world living without God, and so they are not prepared for the fact that Christ will come suddenly in judgment at the end of the age. Both 2 Peter texts regard the flood as a historical event in which God's retribution was displayed.

There is also a reference to the flood episode in 1 Peter 3:18b-21a:

> He [Christ] was put to death in the body but made alive by the Spirit, through whom also he went and preached to the spirits in prison who disobeyed long ago when God waited patiently in the days of Noah while the ark was being built. In it only a few people, eight in all, were saved through water, and this water symbolizes baptism that now saves you also — not the removal of dirt from the body but the pledge of a good conscience toward God.

There are two other New Testament texts that refer to the flood — Luke 3:36 and Hebrews 11:7. In the former, Noah, "the son of

---

1. For a thorough discussion of the references to the deluge in 2 Peter, see Richard J. Bauckham, *Jude, 2 Peter* (Waco, Tex.: Word Books, 1983). Bauckham notes that the verb *kataklystheis* was also used in references to the flood by Josephus and Clement and in the apocryphal book *Wisdom* (p. 299).

Lamech," is one member of the extended genealogy of Jesus' human father, Joseph. In the Hebrews passage, part of the listing of the heroes of faith, Noah is singled out as exemplary: "By faith Noah, when warned about things not yet seen, in holy fear built an ark to save his family. By his faith he condemned the world and became heir of the righteousness that comes by faith."

These New Testament writers clearly assumed the historical existence of Noah and the deluge, and they viewed the deluge as a unique event: they used different terminology to distinguish the Noachic flood *(kataklysmos)* from all other floods *(potamos,* "river"). Probably the most familiar of the texts referring to the latter is Matthew 7:25, which contains the parable of the wise man who built his house on a rock so that it would be spared when the "floods" came.

Although some of the New Testament writers, especially the highly educated Paul, may have known about the Babylonian and Greek deluge traditions and the various reports of the existence of remnants of the ark, no New Testament author appeals to such sources of information to document or defend the Genesis account. For the New Testament writers as for the earlier Jews, the Genesis story was self-authenticating divine Scripture. The story of the flood stood on its own and needed no corroboration.

The Flood in Early Christian Apologetics

The biblical deluge was a common theme in a variety of early Christian literary contexts. Tertullian (160-221), Jerome (c. 345-420), Ambrose (c. 339-397), Cyril of Jerusalem (c. 315–c. 386), and Augustine (354-430) made use of the story of the flood to encourage moral conduct. Origen (c. 185–c. 254), Jerome, Augustine, and others developed Philo's allegorical methods for illustrating Christian principles with the flood narrative.[2] Some writers referred to the flood in surveys of biblical history. And, like Christians to the present day, early Christians had

---

2. New Testament scholar Moisés Silva has argued that Origen viewed literal exegesis as sufficient for the simple believer but maintained that allegory unfolded the deeper things of God for the mature Christian. Origen noted that the New Testament itself uses allegory and that many biblical passages simply cannot be interpreted literally. In Silva's judgment, the allegorizers "perceived their method as a broad approach to Scripture, one that was sensitive to the Bible's many figurative expressions, prophetic announcements, and suggestive associations" (*Has the Church Misread the Bible?* [Grand Rapids: Zondervan, 1987], p. 74).

to defend the faith against philosophical challenges and assaults on the reliability of the Scriptures. The ethical and doctrinal applications of the flood story required no appeals to extrabiblical information, but such appeals did come into play in the sphere of apologetics. Because the church accepted the Old Testament canon, neither the Old Testament in general nor the flood account in particular escaped the attention of hostile critics. Apologists felt compelled to defend aspects of the biblical flood narrative against the challenges of Greek rationalism.[3]

For example, Celsus, a second-century critic of Christianity, challenged the antiquity and originality of the scriptural story by claiming that the Jews had borrowed from pagan traditions. Skeptics also questioned the ability of Noah's ark to contain pairs of all the world's animals. To repel these challenges, early Christian apologists called on their sanctified ingenuity and all available resources, including a range of sources outside of the Bible. This apologetic use of extrabiblical information is not surprising in view of more general attitudes expressed by some writers about the relationship of extrabiblical knowledge to Christian faith. Clement of Alexandria (150-215), for example, stressed the need to bring all kinds of knowledge to bear on the understanding of the Bible. He chided those who thought of themselves as gifted but did "not wish to touch either philosophy or logic; nay more, they do not wish to learn natural science. They demand bare faith alone, as if they wished, without bestowing any care on the vine, straightway to gather clusters from the first." Clement characterized as "truly learned" the Christian who "brings everything to bear on the truth; so that, from geometry, and music, and grammar, and philosophy itself, culling what is useful, he guards the faith against assault. . . . And he who brings everything to bear on a right life, procuring examples from the Greeks and barbarians, this man is an experienced searcher after truth, and in reality a man of much counsel."[4] Clement had no fear of extrabiblical knowledge and urged the study of anything that would contribute to an understanding of God's revelation.

---

3. For exhaustive analyses of all aspects of the interpretation of the flood narrative in early Christian literature, see chaps. 5 and 7 of Jack P. Lewis, *A Study of the Interpretation of Noah and the Flood in Jewish and Christian Literature* (Leiden: E. J. Brill, 1968), and Eugene S. McCartney, "Noah's Ark and the Flood: A Study in Patristic Literature and Modern Folklore," *Papers of the Michigan Academy of Science, Arts, and Letters* 18 (1932): 71-100.

4. Clement, *The Stromata* 1.9, in *The Ante-Nicene Fathers*, 10 vols., ed. Alexander Roberts and James Donaldson (New York: Christian Literature, 1867-1897), 2:309-10.

Augustine likewise appreciated knowledge external to the Bible, encouraging the use of historical and scientific knowledge in biblical interpretation. His attitude is spelled out more specifically in *The Literal Meaning of Genesis*, a book in which he confronts a number of science-related issues. In one lengthy passage, Augustine expresses his deep concern about Christians proposing foolish interpretations of the biblical text that conflict with extrabiblical knowledge:

> Usually, even a non-Christian knows something about the earth, the heavens, and the other elements of this world, about the motion and orbit of the stars and even their size and relative positions, about the predictable eclipses of the sun and moon, the cycles of the years and seasons, about the kinds of animals, shrubs, stones, and so forth, and this knowledge he holds to as being certain from reason and experience. Now, it is a disgraceful and dangerous thing for an infidel to hear a Christian, presumably giving the meaning of Holy Scripture, talking nonsense on these topics; and we should take all means to prevent such an embarrassing situation, in which people show up vast ignorance in a Christian and laugh it to scorn. The shame is not so much that an ignorant individual is derided, but that people outside the household of the faith think our sacred writers held such opinions, and, to the great loss of those for whose salvation we toil, the writers of our Scripture are criticized and rejected as unlearned men. . . . Reckless and incompetent expounders of Holy Scripture bring untold trouble and sorrow on their wiser brethren when they are caught in one of their mischievous false opinions and are taken to task by those who are not bound by the authority of our sacred books. For then, to defend their utterly foolish and obviously untrue statements, they will try to call upon Holy Scripture for proof and even recite from memory many passages which they think support their position, although *they understand neither what they say nor the things about which they make assertion.*[5]

No doubt Augustine would be equally appalled by some of the claims made for the biblical text by modern Christians in the face of modern scientific knowledge.

5. Augustine, *The Literal Meaning of Genesis*, trans. John Hammond Taylor (New York: Newman Press, 1982), pp. 42-43. See also Davis A. Young, "The Contemporary Relevance of Augustine's View of Creation," *Perspectives on Science and Christian Faith* 40 (1988): 42-45.

Augustine provided several examples in which extrabiblical knowledge affected his interpretation of Scripture.

> Let no one think that, because the Psalmist says, *He established the earth above the water,* we must use this testimony of Holy Scripture against these people who engage in learned discussions about the weight of the elements. They are not bound by the authority of our Bible; and, ignorant of the sense of these words, they will more readily scorn our sacred books than disavow the knowledge they have acquired by unassailable arguments or proved by the evidence of experience.[6]

Augustine demonstrated a willingness to adjust his understanding of biblical texts in light of extrabiblical knowledge, secure in the understanding that Scripture and creation have a common author.

Given these views, it is scarcely surprising that Augustine would have been willing to cite relevant extrabiblical knowledge in his defense of the biblical deluge story. And yet neither Augustine nor any other Church Father altered his essential interpretation of the flood text in light of that knowledge or perceived any need for such alteration. All of the early apologists took it as given that the flood narrative was a divine revelation of ancient events. They had neither desire nor grounds for questioning the notion that the flood narrative was literal history down to the finest detail. Hence they appealed to extrabiblical sources strictly to confirm what they already knew about the flood on divine authority. Several sources were widely cited in this regard, including extrabiblical flood traditions and the stories of the contemporary existence of remains of the ark, the same sources used by Josephus. Some also pointed to the existence of fossil remains in mountains.

Pagan Deluge Traditions

The early Christians were familiar with both the deluge legends of Deucalion and Ogyges and the account of Berossus. We might expect that early Christians would have claimed Greek and Babylonian legends as support for the historicity of the biblical deluge, arguing that pagan legends were perverted versions of a reliable biblical original. But the Fathers, believing that the Bible needed no such support, saw little need to follow that course. Unlike Josephus, most early Christian

---

6. Augustine, *The Literal Meaning of Genesis,* pp. 47-48.

writers made little reference to Berossus and took pains to distinguish Noah's flood from Deucalion's, very probably because opponents of Christianity had charged the Bible with having borrowed its story from older legends. Celsus accused the Hebrews of "falsifying and recklessly altering" the Greek legend of Deucalion, for example, and "inventing stories merely for young children." Christian apologists generally countered such accusations by arguing that biblical history was older than pagan tradition and that in any event the floods mentioned in Greek literature were small, localized affairs distinct from the biblical deluge.[7]

Hippolytus (c. 170–c. 236) specifically denied that the Egyptians, Chaldeans, or Greeks had any recollection of Noah's universal flood. The Greek floods of Ogyges and Deucalion, he wrote, "prevailed only in the localities where these dwelt." Julius Africanus (c. 160–c. 240) asserted that the flood of Ogyges was contemporaneous with the Exodus. Lactantius (c. 240–c. 320) alluded in passing to Deucalion's flood but made no connection with the biblical flood.[8]

Theophilus (115-181) sought to establish the authority of scriptural history over Greek speculations about the past by arguing that the Bible was more ancient and true than all pagan authors who had written "in uncertainty." The biblical prophets agreed with one another and foretold what would come to pass, he said, but the Greeks were in error about the deluge. Plato said that the deluge had not extended "over the whole earth, but only over the plains, and that those who fled to the highest hills saved themselves." Some wrote of the preservation of Deucalion and Pyrrha in a chest, and others maintained that Clymenus survived a second flood. Theophilus asserted that those "who wrote such things" were "very profane and senseless persons." In contrast to these Greek speculations, Moses "related in what manner the flood came upon the earth," as well as details of the flood. He told no "fable of Pyrrha nor of Deucalion or Clymenus." Hence the accurate biblical flood account could not be identified with the story of Deucalion. Augustine also briefly noted Deucalion's flood but did not identify it with the biblical flood because, he said, the former did not reach as far as Egypt. The only

---

7. See Origen, *Against Celsus*, in *The Ante-Nicene Fathers*, 4:516.
8. Hippolytus, *The Refutation of All Heresies*, in *The Ante-Nicene Fathers*, 5:149; Julius Africanus, *The Extant Writings of Julius Africanus*, in *The Ante-Nicene Fathers*, 6:132; and Lactantius, *Divine Institutes*, in *The Ante-Nicene Fathers*, 7:59-63.

early identification of Deucalion's flood with the biblical flood appears in the *Recognitions* of Pseudo-Clement.[9]

The Landing Site of the Ark

Belief in the existence of the remains of Noah's ark persisted from the days of Berossus through the early centuries of Christianity. Naturally, remnants of the ark would provide evidence supporting the Old Testament account and refuting the assertion that it was a fabrication or legend based on non-Jewish tradition. Still, all written reports of the ark's existence were based on hearsay: no writer who cited this sort of evidence ever claimed to have seen the ark personally. Moreover, despite substantial discrepancies among various reports of the location of the landing site (see map, p. 33), no writer seems to have doubted the existence of the ark remains or to have puzzled at the thought of a great boat on a mountain.[10]

Theophilus claimed that "the remains are to this day to be seen in the Arabian mountains." He may have had in mind the *Arabia Deserta*, a stretch of land that extended "to the upper limits of the Mesopotamian plain." If so, he would likely have been referring to Mount Qardu in the Gordyaean hills north of Mesopotamia.[11]

Other writers explicitly located the ark in the Gordyaean hills. A fragment from Pseudo-Hippolytus, an expositor of the Targum, states that the ark rested on Mount Kardu (or Mount Godash), in the east "in the land of the sons of Raban." This author maintained that no one had ever been able to reach the summit because of violent storms there and because, "if any one attempts to ascend it, there are demons that rush upon him, and cast him down headlong from the ridge of the mountain into the plain, so that he dies." Given such threats to an inspection of the site, he writes, no one knows what is on top of the mountain — "except that certain relics of the wood of the ark still lie there on the surface."[12]

9. Theophilus, *Ad Autolycus*, in *The Ante-Nicene Fathers*, 2:116; Augustine, *The City of God* 18.10, in *A Select Library of the Nicene and Post-Nicene Fathers of the Christian Church*, ser. 1, 14 vols., ed. Philip Schaff (New York: Christian Literature, 1886-1890), 2:366; Pseudo-Clement, *Recognitions*, in *The Ante-Nicene Fathers*, 8:178.

10. For an extensive review of the ideas of early Christians, Jews, and Muslims about the existence and landing place of the ark, see Bailey, *Where Is Noah's Ark?* (Nashville: Abingdon Press, 1978), pp. 22-46.

11. Bailey, *Where Is Noah's Ark?* p. 24.

12. Hippolytus, *Fragments from Commentaries*, in *The Ante-Nicene Fathers*, 5:198.

Epiphanius (c. 315-403), bishop of Salamis, used the ark as an apologetic device: "Do you seriously suppose," he challenged, "that we are unable to prove our point, when even to this day the remains of Noah's Ark are shown in the country of the Kurds (Gordians)?" He believed that a diligent search at the foot of the mountain would no doubt disclose the remnants of the altar on which Noah sacrificed animals. The ark was alleged to rest "in the mountains of Ararat, in the midst of [the mountains of] Armenia and [of] Gordyene."[13]

Hippolytus asserted that relics of the ark lay "in the mountains called Ararat, which are situated in the direction of the country of the Adiabeni." Julius Africanus acknowledged multiple landing site traditions; he affirmed that the "ark settled on the mountains of Ararat, which we know to be in Parthia; but some say that they are at Celænae of Phrygia, and I have seen both places."[14]

Not all references placed the ark in a specific region of the mountains of Ararat. John Chrysostom (c. 345-407), for example, mentioned Armenia in a challenge to the skeptics:

> Have you heard of the Flood — of that universal destruction? That was not just a threat, was it? Did it not really come to pass — was not this mighty work carried out? Do not the mountains of Armenia testify to it, where the Ark rested? And are not the remains of the Ark preserved there to this very day for our admonition?[15]

At least one early Christian is said to have made a pilgrimage to find the ark. Faustus of Byzantium (fourth or early fifth century) wrote of the efforts of St. Jacob of Nisibis in this regard. Faustus describes Jacob, the bishop of Medzpin, as a venerable saint of God, full of the graces of Christ and having the power to do miracles. He writes that when Jacob arrived "in the principality of Ararat and the canton of Gortouk," he prayed fervently to see the ark. He climbed the mountain but was so thoroughly exhausted when he reached the summit that he fell asleep. An angel of God came to him in his sleep and said, "The Lord gives ear to your prayer and brings to pass what

---

13. Epiphanius, *Panarion*, quoted by John Warwick Montgomery in *The Quest for Noah's Ark* (Minneapolis: Bethany Fellowship, 1972), pp. 72-73, and Bailey, *Where Is Noah's Ark?* p. 28.

14. Hippolytus, *Fragments from Commentaries*, p. 149; Julius Africanus, *The Extant Writings of Julius Africanus*, p. 131. See Bailey, *Where Is Noah's Ark?* p. 25.

15. Chrysostom, "On Perfect Charity," quoted by Montgomery in *The Quest for Noah's Ark*, p. 73.

you desire. That which you find on your pallet is wood from the Ark. There it is: I bring it to you: it comes from the Ark itself. From this moment on you shall cease desiring to see the Ark, for such is the will of the Lord." Jacob awoke praising the Lord and found the plank, "which seemed to have been sliced from a great piece of wood with the blow of an axe." Jacob returned from his pilgrimage, and the people "eagerly accepted the gracious gift of the wood, and it is preserved to this day among them as the visible sign of the Ark of the patriarch Noah." The canton of Gortouk in which Faustus says Jacob sought the ark probably lay in the province of Korcaik, a mountainous region between the Tigris River and Lake Van — the region of the Gordyene hills.[16]

The abundance of reports of remains of the ark doubtless reassured early Christians of the historical validity of the Old Testament story. Modern searchers attracted by these same reports have mostly focused on a peak by the name of Mount Ararat, the Turkish volcano Agri Dagh. This is not the same Ararat referred to in early Christian tradition, however. Modern hunters of the ark appear to be looking in different places than the early Christians did.

The Capacity of the Ark

The early church confronted another challenge that stimulates vigorous discussion to the present day. Skeptics attacked the integrity of the deluge narrative by questioning the ability of the ark to carry all the animals it is said to have carried. Skeptics and apologists alike assumed that the biblical narrative was speaking of the preservation of representatives of all the land animals of the entire world as opposed to just a selected few drawn from a limited region. Although vast portions of the globe were unknown during the early Christian era, the known regions of Europe, Asia, and Africa contained a significant number of familiar and exotic animals. Aristotle was acquainted with about 550 kinds of animals, many of them marine. Herodotus and Pliny mentioned such animals as tigers, elephants, and giraffes that were not found in the Mediterranean region where the early church was concentrated.

Apelles the Marcionite, for one, doubted that the ark was large

---

16. For a complete citation of this account, taken from Faustus's *Historical Library*, see Montgomery, *The Quest for Noah's Ark*, pp. 65-69. For Bailey's evaluation of Faustus's story of St. Jacob, see Bailey, *Where Is Noah's Ark?* pp. 36-43.

enough for its presumed task. He asserted "that in no way was it possible to receive, in so brief a space, so many kinds of animals and their foods, which would be sufficient for a whole year." The ark would not have been capable of holding four elephants, he said, let alone the other animals.[17]

In rebuttal, Origen argued that since at least a hundred years were devoted to the construction of the ark, it would have been most admirable, resembling "an extensive city." He resolved the problem of capacity to his own satisfaction by asserting that the measure of the cubit specified in the biblical narrative was in fact an Egyptian cubit, which is the square of the ordinary cubit. Thus, when the Bible says that the ark was 300 cubits long and 50 cubits wide, it was in fact 90,000 ordinary cubits long and 2,500 ordinary cubits wide. Origen's speculative capacities may have exceeded the carrying capacity of the ark he envisioned. He also asserted that the ark was shaped like a pyramid to provide stability and divert rainfall. Two decks were constructed below and three above. The lower part of the ark was set aside for human and animal excrement. Above that was an area for food storage. The upper decks were devoted to the animals. Of these, the lowermost was the dwelling place for wild beasts and serpents. Then came stables for domesticated animals. The top deck was set aside for the human passengers, since "it is they who excel all in both honor and reason."[18]

Although Augustine also resorted to Origen's use of the Egyptian cubit, his reply to the capacity question was more detailed. Responding to questions about a wide variety of creatures, he suggested that persons with such difficulties should remember that the expression "every creeping thing of the earth" indicated that it was unnecessary to preserve animals that could live in water, such as fish and seabirds. Furthermore, creatures that he believed were born asexually from inanimate things or their corruption, such as flies and bees, did not need to be on the ark, although he favored the idea that they were. If such spontaneously generated creatures were aboard, they might have been present in indeterminate numbers rather than pairs. In any case, Augustine affirmed that God cared for these animals, relieving Noah

17. Origen, *Homilies on Genesis and Exodus* (Washington: Catholic University of America Press, 1982), pp. 75-76.

18. Origen, *Homilies on Genesis and Exodus*, pp. 73-74. For his specifications concerning the size of the ark, see *Origen against Celsus*, in *The Ante-Nicene Fathers*, 4:516.

of that burdensome chore.[19] He suggested that the carnivorous animals miraculously survived on vegetation alone during their stay on the ark, preserving lives of the other animals.

These early defenses of the ark's capacity proved adequate for most Christians because of the relatively small number of known land animals. Origen and Augustine could hardly have foreseen the problems that would confront later Christian scholars as the number of known animals continued to multiply and evidence of fossil animals appeared.

Redistribution of the Animals

Questions about repopulation of the earth by animals after the flood also naturally arose. Thinkers wondered how the postdiluvial animals arrived at distant islands beyond the Mediterranean such as the British Isles, the Azores, and the Canaries, all of which were known in the early Christian era. Ever the man of encyclopedic interests, Augustine wrestled with this problem, too. He postulated a new creation to account for their presence on distant islands.

> There is a question raised about all those kinds of beasts which are not domesticated, nor are produced like frogs from the earth, but are propagated by male and female parents, such as wolves and animals of that kind; and it is asked how they could be found in the islands after the deluge, in which all the animals not in the ark perished, unless the breed was restored from those which were preserved in pairs in the ark. It might, indeed, be said that they crossed to the islands by swimming, but this could only be true of those very near the mainland; whereas there are some so distant, that we fancy no animal could swim to them. But if men caught them and took them across with themselves, and thus propagated

19. Augustine, *The City of God* 15.27, pp. 307-8. Augustine specifically wrote: "For there are some animals which are born out of corruption, but yet afterwards they themselves copulate and produce offspring, as flies; but others, which have no sex, like bees. Then, as to those animals which have sex, but without ability to propagate their kind, like mules and she-mules, it is probable that they were not in the ark, but that it was counted sufficient to preserve their parents, to wit, the horse and the ass" (p. 308). Augustine was naturally drawing on the conceptual biological framework of his own day, which included belief in the spontaneous generation of organisms from both animate and inanimate matter. Contemporary Christians who reject the notion that life could arise naturally from lifeless materials should recognize that early Christians saw nothing intrinsically unscriptural in the idea.

these breeds in their new abodes, this would not imply an incredible fondness for the chase. At the same time, it cannot be denied that by the intervention of angels they might be transferred by God's order or permission. If, however, they were produced out of the earth as at their first creation, when God said, "Let the earth bring forth the living creature," this makes it more evident that all kinds of animals were preserved in the ark, not so much for the sake of renewing the stock, as of prefiguring the various nations which were to be saved in the church; this, I say, is more evident, if the earth brought forth many animals in islands to which they could not cross over.[20]

Augustine's suggestion of a new creation of animals underscores his supposition that no land animals anywhere escaped the deluge. Again, the problem is far more acute for us today.

The Extent of the Flood

Augustine reflected the virtually unanimous opinion in the early church that the flood was geographically universal. Lactantius was content simply to affirm that the water covered all the loftiest mountains, but Augustine responded to specific scientific challenges to diluvial universality with scientific argumentation. He noted, for example, the assertion of skeptics that no flood could have risen fifteen cubits above the highest mountains, since even clouds could not rise above Mount Olympus. Responding to this complaint, as elsewhere, Augustine was content neither with simple appeals to the authority of Scripture nor with assertions that with God all things are possible. He appreciated rational explanations for the events recorded in Scripture. In contrast to some of the earlier Fathers, he accepted the assertion of the skeptics that biblical events ought to be explicable on rational grounds (i.e., in terms of secondary causation), and he answered them on their own terms. On the question of the depth of the flood, Augustine constructed an answer that took account of the accepted science of the day, in this case the Greek physical theory of natural places and the four elements. The critics argued that water, being patently heavier than cloud, could not have risen higher than the clouds now rise around Mount Olympus. Augustine responded that Olympus itself rose higher than the clouds, and it was

20. Augustine, *The City of God* 16.7, p. 314.

covered with earth, the densest of the elements. If earth exists permanently on top of Mount Olympus, why couldn't water, which is "lighter, and more likely to ascend," be raised to that altitude for a brief time?[21]

The most widespread extrabiblical argument for diluvial universality, however, drew on the existence of animal and plant remains embedded in rocks. This evidence was considered to be as persuasive as the relics of the ark. The earliest "geological" opinion may be that of Tertullian. Observing that the mountains and the pathways of streams were constantly changing, he spoke of a time when the face of the whole world was altered by flood waters. "Marine conchs and tritons' horns sojourn as foreigners on the mountain," he said, "eager to prove to Plato that even the heights" had been inundated.[22] Tertullian may well have had the flood in mind in this context, but he makes no specific mention of either Noah or the deluge. His suggestion that marine fossils might constitute proof to Plato, however, is likely an allusion to the philosopher's assertion that the flood of Deucalion was limited rather than universal.

Subsequent references to fossils were more explicitly linked with the deluge. Procopius of Gaza (c. 465–c. 538), for example, wrote,

> It can be shown clearly in many other ways that a universal flood came upon the earth, by which those people are persuaded who believe with difficulty that these things were explained by Moses. For even today in mountains that are lofty and difficult to climb marine remains are found, that is, shells and fragments of tortoise shells and other such things, which even we ourselves have seen.[23]

In discussing the flood, Pseudo-Eustathius wrote,

> Since the waters covered the summits of the mountains, they were covered over and hidden by their flowing. For in these times of ours also, on the summit of Mt. Lebanon, men who cut stone for marking boundaries find various types of marine fishes, which must

21. Augustine, *The City of God* 15.27, p. 307.
22. Tertullian, *On the Pallium*, in *The Ante-Nicene Fathers*, 4:6.
23. Procopius of Gaza, *Commentarii in Genesin*, in Jacques-Paul Migne, *Patrologia Graeca*, 162 vols. (Paris, 1857-1866), 87:286. I am deeply indebted to my colleague Mark Williams of the Department of Classical Languages at Calvin College for his translations of the quotation from Procopius and those that follow from Pseudo-Eustathius and Pseudo-Justin.

have been gathered together in the caves of the mountains when they were caught in the mud.[24]

Thus began a long tradition within Christendom of thinking that the fossil remains contained within rocks were remnants of the universal flood.

At least one Christian voice may have raised the possibility of a more localized flood. Pseudo-Justin, quite probably Theodoret of Cyrus (c. 393–c. 466), wrote,

> If, as many say, there was no flood in every place of the land, but only in those places where humans now live, how is it true that water was raised above the highest mountains to a depth of fifteen cubits? Response. Indeed it does not appear that the deluge did occur in every place, unless perchance the places were low-lying, in which the deluge took place, in certain places of the earth.[25]

The question-and-answer format of this assertion would seem to indicate that concerns about the implications of a universal flood were already significant when it was written and that the concept of a localized deluge was not entirely foreign.

We do not know how widespread the view of fossils as diluvial relics became among the early Christians. Before the time of Christ, the Greeks already had a well-established tradition that fossils were deposited during interchanges of land and sea much more gradual than Noah's flood. Such ideas had been expressed by Xenophanes, Herodotus, Aristotle, Strato, Xanthus, and Strabo, and educated Christians were doubtless aware of their views. Certainly Hippolytus was, for he quoted Xenophanes regarding the entombment of fossils in mud. Acquaintance with the Greek viewpoint may account for the fact that relatively few early Christian writers appealed to fossils as remnants of the flood.[26]

24. Pseudo-Eustathius, *Commentarius in hexaemeron*, in *Patrologia Graeca*, 18:752.

25. Pseudo-Justin, *Quaestiones et Responsiones ad Orthodoxos*, in *Patrologia Graeca*, 6:1282.

26. For a careful look at Greek thinking about fossils, see Adrian J. Desmond, "The Discovery of Marine Transgressions and the Explanation of Fossils in Antiquity," *American Journal of Science* 275 (1975): 692-707.

Analysis and Application

The church today is struggling with how to interpret Scripture in the light of extrabiblical information, particularly that generated by the natural sciences. From its inception the church has been confronted with this issue in some form or other. Early Christians were quickly faced with hard questions about the flood, and, like us today, they had to think about the significance of flood legends, the capacity of the ark, the worldwide distribution of animals, and evidence of a geological nature such as fossils. At the outset, the issue of extrabiblical knowledge was principally associated with attempts to defend Scripture and Christianity against challenges posed by unbelievers. Today many Christians are perplexed by the fact that both friends and critics of the faith seem to make claims on extrabiblical knowledge in defense of their positions. What is its value, then?

Throughout the history of the church, Christian thinkers have responded to extrabiblical knowledge in five basic ways.

1. Some simply ignore extrabiblical knowledge. Confronted with evidence that seems to contradict their reading of Scripture, they dismiss it out of hand with the phrase "Thus saith the Lord." In effect, they broaden a belief in the authority of Scripture to a belief in the infallibility of a given interpretation of Scripture. As a practical matter, individuals who take this route tend not to reject all extrabiblical information, however, but only the information that constitutes a threat to their reading of the Bible; they may happily accept and endorse extrabiblical evidence in support of their position. The risk here is that their judgments of the value of extrabiblical knowledge may be entirely subjective, capricious, and valueless to anyone else.

2. Some people blunt the force of extrabiblical information by appealing in some cases to divine interventions in the natural order. One example of this is Augustine's assertion that some distant islands might have been repopulated after the deluge by a special creative act of God. Conservative Christians in our time have similarly invoked miracles on an ad hoc basis to resolve apparent contradictions between their reading of Scripture and the testimony of physical evidence. This approach essentially undercuts the force of extrabiblical knowledge by subordinating it to an individual's determination of its validity. Those who take this route run the risk of appealing to miracle gratuitously, even when the biblical text gives little ground for making such appeals.

3. Some people seek to discredit the validity of any extrabiblical knowledge they consider to be incompatible with their interpretation

of the biblical text. Christians who reject the theory of biological evolution often adopt this strategy, for instance, disputing all evidence cited in support of the theory. This approach can be very problematic, however. Those who reject a broadly accepted interpretation of physical evidence on flimsy grounds will do little to substantiate their own position and may well saddle the faith they seek to protect with the sort of embarrassment that Augustine warned about so vigorously.

4. Some people make at least a limited effort to accept extra-biblical knowledge and establish its consistency with Christianity and the biblical text. Origen and Augustine adopted this approach when they found ways to argue that all the world's land animals could indeed have been stored on the ark (e.g., by adopting the Egyptian cubit rather than the standard cubit). The early Christian interpretation of fossils as proof of the universality of the deluge also falls into this category. The developing nature of extrabiblical knowledge demands a certain elasticity in this approach, however. For example, given our current knowledge about the nature of fossils, an individual who took up the early Christian claim that fossils are proof of the universality of the deluge would actually be engaging in a rejection of the evidence provided by fossils and hence would fall into the third category.

5. Some people begin with the premise that God reveals himself in both his creation and his inspired Word and conclude that there cannot be any contradiction between the two. Where extrabiblical knowledge appears to undercut a previously held interpretation of Scripture (e.g., when astronomical observations began to undercut the belief that the Bible taught that the sun circled the earth rather than the other way around), such individuals make an effort to reevaluate both the extrabiblical knowledge and the interpretation of Scripture to determine which needs to be readjusted. There is no question that this option can be unsettling, but in the hands of sanctified believers, it can point the way to an improved understanding of the Bible. Augustine endorsed this approach, although he did not always employ it himself.

The relative validity of these five basic approaches depends a lot on the specific issue at hand, the specific biblical text being examined, the specific body of extrabiblical information being confronted, and the historical circumstances in which the confrontation is taking place. A given approach may serve in one set of circumstances but become inappropriate in another. The flood-related extrabiblical information available to the early church was so limited that many Christians were able to accept option four without fear of contradiction. The scant available evidence was easily appropriated in support of the traditional presumption of a universal deluge. In light of the biogeo-graphical, geological, and paleontological evidence available today, how-ever, this approach is a great deal more problematic. Christians who feel the force of this difficulty today are pushed toward one of the other options — either toward a reinterpretation of the Bible based on accep-tance of extrabiblical evidence or toward a reaffirmation of literalistic biblical interpretations and associated attempts either to dismiss or to discredit the extrabiblical evidence. In subsequent chapters we will look at various ways in which the church continued to respond to the growing body of relevant extrabiblical knowledge.

3. The Flood in the Middle Ages and Renaissance

The Middle Ages

As Christianity spread across Europe and western Asia during the Middle Ages, theologians and scholars continued to interpret the fascinating story of the great flood and Noah's ark. There were few significant additions to the body of extrabiblical knowledge associated with the flood throughout this lengthy period, however, and so there were no significant adjustments to traditional interpretations. To the extent that writers interacted with extrabiblical information, they interacted with the traditional information about relics of the ark or fossils in mountains. For the most part, scholars continued to allegorize, to find moral lessons, and to speculate about the construction of the ark.[1]

Islam and the Landing Site of the Ark

One of the major developments of the medieval era was the establishment of Islam in the seventh century. Islamic culture swept rapidly across the Middle East, northern Africa, and parts of southern Europe. The Islamic scriptures were influenced by Hebrew and Christian scriptures, including the Old Testament deluge tradition. In its principal reference to the flood, the Koran states that the ark eventually came to rest on Judi.[2] It is not

---

1. See Don Cameron Allen, *The Legend of Noah* (Urbana, Ill.: University of Illinois, 1949), pp. 75-77.
2. The principal Koranic passage dealing with the flood is 11:4:25-49.

31

known where this might be, although scholars have spoken of two sites as the most likely candidates (see map on p. 33). Suggesting that the Muslims might have borrowed a tradition from Syrian Christians (Theophilus of Antioch claimed that remains of the ark could still be seen in the Arabian mountains), Lloyd Bailey nominated Jabal Judi in the Arabian peninsula as one possibility for the site identified in the Koran. He further noted that the Muslims were more likely to have been influenced by a strong tradition among Nestorian Christians that placed the ark on a mountain just north of the Tigris River at the edge of the Gordyene/Qardu range beyond the Upper Zab River. The 6,800-foot peak here known to modern-day Turks as Cudi Dag was known to Muslims as Jabal Judi. This site may have been the most widely accepted among Christians, Jews, and Muslims during the latter centuries of the first millennium of the Christian era as the landing place of the ark.

The Nestorians built monasteries on Jabal Judi, including one at the summit that was destroyed by lightning in 766. The Muslim historian al-Makin (1223-1274) wrote that Heraclius, emperor of the Eastern Roman Empire from 610 to 641, climbed the mountain to see the ark. Muslims conquered the region in the seventh century and later erected a mosque on the site of the former monastery. Eutychius, a ninth-century bishop of Alexandria, wrote that "the ark rested on the mountains of Ararat, that is, Jabal Judi, near Mosul." The tenth-century Arab geographer al-Masudi (d. 956) wrote that "the ark stood on the mount el-Judi . . . a mountain in the country of Masur . . . eight farsangs from the Tigris. The place where the ship stopped, which is on the top of this mountain, is still to be seen." Another tenth-century Muslim, Ibn Haukal, wrote that "Judi is a mountain near Nisibis. It is said that the ark of Noah (to whom be peace!) rested on the summit of this mountain." The twelfth-century rabbi Benjamin of Tudela wrote that it was "two days to Jezireh Ben 'Omar, an island in the Tigris, on the foot of Mount Ararat . . . on which the ark of Noah rested." He claimed that Omar Ben al-Khatab removed the ark to construct a mosque from it. A thirteenth-century Muslim geographer, Zakariya ben Muhammad al-Kazwine, wrote that wood from the ark was allegedly recovered from the mountaintop to construct a Muslim sanctuary. And the Jewish scholar Bar-Hebraeus (1226-1286) asserted that Mount Qardu (Jabal Judi) was the ark's landing place.[3]

---

3. For sources of the cited material, see Lloyd R. Bailey, *Where Is Noah's Ark?* (Nashville: Abingdon, 1978), pp. 29-30; and John Warwick Montgomery, *The Quest for Noah's Ark* (Minneapolis: Bethany Fellowship, 1972), pp. 299-300.

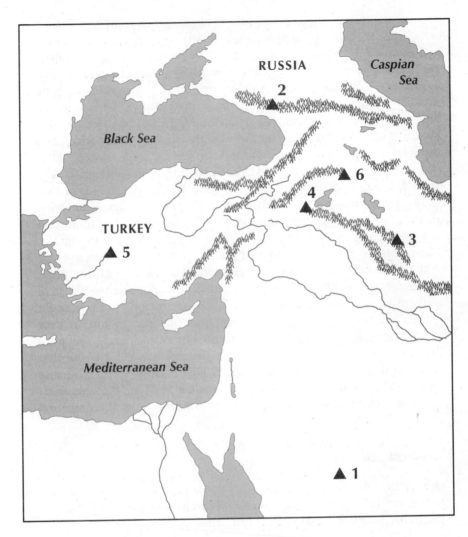

Traditional Landing Sites Claimed for Noah's Ark

1. Jabal Judi of the Koran
2. Baris
3. Adiabene
4. Gordyaean Hills (Mount Qardu, later Jabal Judi)
5. Celaenae in Phrygia
6. Agri Dagh (Mount Ararat)

Other landing site traditions persisted as well, however. Isidore of Seville (c. 560-636) stated simply that the biblical Ararat was a mountain in Armenia and that "to this day wood remains of [the ark] are to be seen there." Only toward the eleventh and twelfth centuries did the focus begin to shift toward the huge volcanic cone Agri Dagh, the modern Mount Ararat in easternmost Turkey, as the final resting place. Vincent of Beauvais (c. 1184-1264) located his Mount Ararat in Armenia in the vicinity of the Araxes River and assumed that that was the mountain ascended by St. Jacob. After that, several late medieval travelers including Friar William of Rubruck (thirteenth century), Odoric (c. 1286-1331), Marco Polo (1234-1324), Friar Jordanus (fourteenth century), and Sir John Mandeville (d. 1372) took it for granted that Agri Dagh was the biblical mountain and recounted local traditions linking the deluge and the mountain. The reports of these explorers commonly mention the immense size of the mountain, the presence of permanent snow high on the peak, and the impossibility of climbing it. Some accounts, such as those of William of Rubruck and Sir John Mandeville, include the tale of St. Jacob's aborted ascent on the assumption that the mountain they were observing was the one St. Jacob climbed. Mandeville even thought he could see the boat high on the mountain. He wrote that on the hill that men call Ararat where Noah's ship rested, the ship may yet "be seen on ferrom [afar off] in clear weather."[4] He doubted those who claimed to have touched the ark because of the perpetual snow.

Medieval Science

During the Middle Ages, some scholars perpetuated the view of Procopius of Gaza by asserting that fossils were remnants of the flood. For example, Michael Glyca (twelfth century) wrote that

> if the water had not reached such a height, birds would hardly have perished. And indeed, that the water of this deluge covered over even the highest mountains, one can consider even from this. When certain men were gathering stone from the mountains of Lebanon for the building of houses, they asserted that they had

4. Mandeville, quoted by Malcolm H. Letts in *Mandeville's Travels* (London: Hakluyt Society, 1953), pp. 106-7. For additional information, see Montgomery, *The Quest for Noah's Ark*, pp. 75-77, 81-91; and Tim F. LaHaye and John D. Morris, *The Ark on Ararat* (Nashville: Thomas Nelson, 1976), pp. 18-22.

found fish petrified in the mire, as Josephus has handed down to memory.[5]

Not everyone agreed that fossils represented dead organisms, however. Many accepted the views of Aristotle on rock formation as modified by the great Islamic thinker Avicenna (980-1037) and accounted for fossils in terms of the action of "petrifying virtues." In his *Meteorologica*, Aristotle stresses the role of "exhalations" in the formation of mineral material. Avicenna developed the concept of these exhalations into the concept of petrifying virtues — that is, fluids capable of transforming liquid into solid, as in stalactites or hot spring deposits. He maintained that these petrifying virtues could operate anywhere: in human beings, they produce gallstones; in the atmosphere, they produce meteorites. And petrifying virtues created fossils by acting on the seeds of plants and animals trapped in cracks within rocks, causing the seeds to grow into petrified shapes resembling mature adults. The action of petrifying virtues was believed to be influenced by heavenly bodies, which caused the growths within the earth to mimic living creatures. Given this explanation, fossils were not thought to convey any useful historical information.

Medieval thinkers generally viewed the cosmos in ahistorical terms. They did not think of the act of creation in terms of a dynamic historical event that could be deciphered independently of Scripture or described in terms of the action of secondary causes. The biblical description of creation sufficed. It was unnecessary and even unthinkable for them to talk about the history of creation in "scientific" terms. Working from what Eugene Klaaren has called the "ontological" view of creation, many medieval scholars believed that the structure and behavior of the cosmos could in part be deduced from the nature of God and the spiritual realm as revealed by Scripture and philosophical inquiry. Empirical observations were commonly interpreted within a conceptual framework that stressed the role of intelligent as opposed to mechanical causes, although Jean Buridan (c. 1295–c. 1358), Nicholas of Oresme (c. 1320-1382), and others favored mechanical explanations. One example of this sort of approach was that minerals were classified in terms of alphabetical catalogs or lists of the occult properties they possessed rather than in terms of their composition or the way in which they were formed.

5. Glyca, *Annales*, in Jacques-Paul Migne, *Patrologia Graeca*, 162 vols. (Paris, 1857-1866), 158:247. I am indebted to Mark Williams of Calvin College's Department of Classical Languages for his translation of this passage.

All of which is to say that medieval attitudes toward creation were not generally conducive to the kinds of discovery that would lead to reevaluation of the flood narrative.[6]

Exploration of the New World

Up through the Middle Ages, the extrabiblical sources that apologists and expositors had paid attention to were for the most part limited to flood traditions, reported sightings of Noah's ark, and sketchy knowledge of the geographical distribution of organisms. Yet forces were at work that would ultimately lead to a more enlarged and fruitful understanding of the behavior of the natural world as Western civilization emerged from the medieval era. Two major developments in particular exercised far-reaching impact on Christendom's treatment of the flood story. The first centered on world exploration and the attendant discovery of new animals, peoples, and lands; the second concerned the rise of a newer scientific outlook.

European explorations of previously unknown areas of the world during the fifteenth and sixteenth centuries had the greater immediate impact, raising at least four major groups of questions that persist to the present day among those who favor a more literal reading of the flood narrative.

1. The voyages of Columbus, Magellan, and others established that the globe was larger than had been commonly imagined.[7] Those who wanted to affirm a global deluge had to tax their imaginations in new ways to find adequate sources and sinks for the even more immense amount of water that would have been required for the task. With the new knowledge of the earth's size, calculations soon disclosed that clouds contained nowhere near a sufficient volume of water with which to drown the entire world.

6. See Eugene M. Klaaren, *Religious Origins of Modern Science: Belief in Creation in Seventeenth-Century Thought* (Grand Rapids: William B. Eerdmans, 1977). For further insight into medieval attitudes toward the study of the earth and cosmos, see Frank Dawson Adams, *The Birth and Development of the Geological Sciences* (New York: Dover, 1954); Herbert Butterfield, *The Origins of Modern Science, 1300-1800* (New York: Macmillan, 1951); N. Max Wildiers, *The Theologian and His Universe* (New York: Seabury Press, 1982); and Eduard J. Dijksterhuis, *The Mechanization of the World Picture* (Oxford: Clarendon Press, 1961).

7. The pre-Christian estimate of the earth's circumference by Eratosthenes (c. 276–c. 194 B.C.) was remarkably accurate, but it was not appreciated until it was confirmed by exploration.

2. The European explorers found indigenous human populations virtually everywhere they landed, even in areas as remote as the mountainous Pacific regions of the New World. How could one account for these peoples and their cultures? If the flood had killed all humanity except for eight people on the ark, then all these indigenous people groups must have descended from the sons of Noah. But how had they gotten to these remote areas, and what accounted for the significant racial and cultural differences among them? Writers such as Laetius and Thomas Thorowgood postulated that Native Americans descended from the ten lost tribes of Israel or from Tartars. The Dutch jurist Hugo Grotius (1583-1645) proposed that Americans were either Norwegians or Germans whose ancestry could be traced to the Viking expeditions. Others postulated the existence of land bridges to the New World and other remote areas that had since disappeared.

3. It was found that many of the indigenous populations had their own flood legends, some of which bore striking resemblances to the biblical story. Some European scholars considered this a signal proof that Native Americans had descended from those who experienced the dreadful cataclysm. So great was the impact of the catastrophe, they said, that it made an indelible impression on the racial memory. Time had dimmed or corrupted the true account but had not managed to erase it completely.

4. The most pressing challenge to a literal reading of the flood account, however, was raised by the discovery of countless new species of plants and animals in the New World that were totally unknown in Europe, Asia, and Africa. Medieval Europe had its royal zoos and illustrated "bestiaries" containing lists of the world's animals, but the number of exotic new additions exploded when the explorers reached the Americas and the Pacific.

Crew members of Columbus's early voyages brought back to Europe descriptions or specimens of alligators, manatees, iguanas, macaws, and various rats. The later voyages of 1498 and 1502 included reports of monkeys, peccaries, and curassows. Macaws and capuchin monkeys rapidly became favorite pets in Europe. Early in the 1500s, the opossum was discovered in Venezuela and returned to Spain by Captain Vincente Pinzon. The Magellan global circumnavigation of 1519-1520 encountered golden marmosets, llamas, rheas, and penguins in various parts of South America. The Spaniard Martin Enciso, traveling to South America in 1510, observed hummingbirds, tapirs, and armadillos. By mid-century a host of other native South American species were known. None of these animals existed in the Old World.

Visits to North America also turned up numerous newly recognized animals. In 1497, Amerigo Vespucci described cougars, wolves, hares, rabbits, and stags from Florida, and John Cabot saw polar bears, caribou, and peregrine falcons in Newfoundland. Álvar Núñez Cabeza da Vaca described the bison in 1532. Jacques Cartier noted auks, puffins, and various small land mammals in 1535. Turkeys were known by 1540 and soon were being exported across the Atlantic. Coronado saw bighorn sheep and pronghorns in 1540.

European explorers and traders reached Australia and parts of the East Indies by the early sixteenth century and found cockatoos, parrots, birds of paradise, cassowaries, fruit bats, and dingoes. Most of the marsupials were not recognized until later, and it was not until the eighteenth century that the existence of wallabies was acknowledged by Europeans. In the meantime many new animals were also being discovered in Africa and India such as the aardvark, gazelle, warthog, civet, dodo, hyena, pangolin, and tarsier. Different varieties of known animals such as the rhinoceros and elephant were also recognized.[8]

The discovery of all these new animals inevitably intensified the questions concerning the capacity of Noah's ark that had earlier captured Augustine's attention. Could the ark possibly have contained all these previously unknown animals? And how could species found only in the New World have traveled to the ark before the flood or returned after the waters subsided? Moreover, what could account for the fact that these species returned to their New World habitats in toto after the flood, without leaving any descendants behind in the Old World? Why were the American species so different from those found in Africa and Asia? Faced with questions such as these, the scholars of the sixteenth and seventeenth centuries could no longer satisfactorily propound the simpler apologetics that had proved adequate for early Christian theologians. Today, with our yet more extensive knowledge of the incredible variety of plant and animal species and their close ties to their physical surroundings, the difficulties associated with such apologetics are yet more acute.

8. For an extended discussion of the discovery of new animals during the years of exploration, see Wilma George, "Sources and Background to Discoveries of New Animals in the Sixteenth and Seventeenth Centuries," *History of Science* 18 (1980): 79-104.

Scientific Developments of the Renaissance

The Problem of Fossils

Interpretation of the flood story was also to be profoundly affected by the study of fossils and the establishment of the mechanical worldview. Although aspects of natural science had flourished during the Middle Ages, relatively little progress was made in understanding the earth. During the Renaissance, however, naturalists increasingly sought to grasp the nature of various stones. Particularly puzzling to some of the finest minds of the fifteenth through seventeenth centuries was the origin of "formed stones" — what we now call fossils.[9] Although fossils were generally considered remnants of the flood or objects produced within the earth by petrifying virtues, a few Renaissance men called both theories into question.

Leonardo da Vinci (1452-1519) offered one early challenge (c. 1508). He expressed doubt that Noah's flood could have been universal, citing the problem of disposing of all the water. He maintained that to remove a spherical, globe-encircling mass of water would require either an unprecedented evaporative action of the sun or some other kind of miracle.[10] But even if there had been a global flood, da Vinci did not see how it could account for the known distribution of fossils. Fossil shells had been found at great heights in the Italian mountains, for instance. But if they had been deposited by Noah's flood, he reasoned, why were they buried within layers of rock rather than lying on the surface of the mountainsides? Nor did he see how flood waters could have carried the shells all the way to the mountains: they were so heavy that they would settle out of even turbulent water long before they could be swept such distances. Moreover, the base of a deep wave moves in the opposite direction of the water at the surface, and flood waters deep enough to cover mountains would have carried the shells away from the mountains rather than toward them. Da Vinci simply could not imagine any construction of the evidence that would make a deluge responsible for the distribution of the fossil shells.[11]

In the early sixteenth century, fossil shells and crabs were discovered in the foundations of buildings in Verona. Gabrieli Fallopio

9. The definitive history of thought on the nature of fossils is Martin J. S. Rudwick's *The Meaning of Fossils* (New York: Science Publications, 1976).
    10. See Edward McCurdy, *The Notebooks of Leonardo da Vinci* (New York: G. Braziller, 1956), p. 316.
    11. See McCurdy, *The Notebooks of Leonardo da Vinci*, pp. 330-40.

(1532-1563) endorsed the medieval view that these fossils were imitations of organic beings brought about by the petrifying virtues latent within the rocky crust. Girolamo Cardano (1501-1576) endorsed the view that the fossils were genuine remains of organisms that were drowned or buried in the great flood. The Calvinist Conrad Gesner (1516-1565) remained noncommittal. Girolamo Fracastoro (c. 1478-1553), on the other hand, asserted that these fossils were the remains of shellfish and that they could be attributed neither to the flood nor to any plastic force within the earth.[12]

Bernard Palissy (1510-1590), a French Calvinist and expert in glass-making, surveying, and ceramics with a knowledge of sand, clay, and soil, was also skeptical of the diluvial theory of fossils. In *The Admirable Discourses*, Palissy notes that his predecessor, Cardano, believed that the "petrified shells scattered about the world came from the sea at the time of the Flood . . . and as the waters covered all the earth, fishes roamed over the world, and that once the sea returned to its bed, it left the fishes behind: and shell-bearing fishes [= shellfish] have turned to stone without changing shape." Palissy dismissed this view as "gossip" and "clumsy error." He could scarcely contain his glee at having the opportunity of "contradicting one so esteemed." He wished that more foreign books had been translated into French so that he could have the opportunity of contradicting them, too![13]

Palissy disagreed with Cardano on the grounds that shellfish cling much too tightly to rocks to be dislodged and transported during a storm. Other marine animals would have been protected from the effects of the wind by the depth of the water. And, chiding Cardano for not having read Genesis, Palissy noted that Moses did not speak of the overflowing of the sea but only of rains and the opening of abysses. Palissy accounted for the existence of the fossil shellfish by arguing that there was a time when "the rocks were but water and mud" in which the animals were living as they do today, but over time both the mud and the organisms hardened into rock together. He also argued that the rock strata had hardened prior to the flood and that they naturally incorporated native species that varied from one location to another. "Just as the earth produces trees and plants, of one kind in one region, and in another region it produces some of another kind

12. See Rudwick, *The Meaning of Fossils*, pp. 40-41.

13. Aurele La Rocque, *The Admirable Discourses of Bernard Palissy* (Urbana, Ill.: University of Illinois Press, 1957), p. 156. See also La Rocque's essay "Bernard Palissy," in *Toward a History of Geology*, ed. Cecil J. Schneer (Cambridge: MIT Press, 1969), pp. 226-41.

... so the sea produces some kinds of fish in one place, which could not live in the other." The softer parts of the animals rotted away before they were petrified, he said, and the mud and the fishes were petrified at the same time.[14]

Debate over fossils intensified in the seventeenth century. The three major views concerning their origin were variously endorsed by the leading naturalists within the British tradition of physico-theology, all of whom were members of the Royal Society of London.[15] John Woodward (1665-1722) argued forcefully that "formed stones" were the remains of the hard parts of animals slaughtered by the Noachian debacle. Robert Hooke (1635-1703) agreed that fossils were organic but was skeptical of a diluvial origin. John Ray (1627-1705) appreciated the evidence for inorganic origin of "formed stones" but persuaded himself that they were likely animal and plant remains, and, like Hooke, he doubted that the flood could account for their distribution. At the other end of the spectrum, Martin Lister (c. 1638-1712) and Oxford's Edward Lhwyd (1660-1709) were representative of a body of competent naturalists who resisted the notion that fossils were real organisms. Lister was troubled by the fact that "formed stones," despite their superficial resemblance to organisms, were composed of the same substance as the enclosing rock and not of shelly material. Others were unable to accept the assertion that the "formed stones" had an organic origin because many of the fossils were significantly different from existing animals and plants. If the stones did have an organic origin, this would imply that the original species had universally passed from the scene, and the notion of the extinction of a species violated the widely held principle of *plenitude* — the notion that God had created a perfect natural order in which each organism had an essential role to play. Extinction would imply that some species were not in fact essential and hence a kind of carelessness or inadequacy on the part of the Creator that many found unthinkable.[16] Furthermore, the fact

14. La Rocque, *The Admirable Discourses of Bernard Palissy*, pp. 155-68.

15. On the physico-theological school, see Clarence Glacken, *Traces on the Rhodian Shore* (Berkeley and Los Angeles: University of California Press, 1967), pp. 375-428. We will examine the views of this school in more detail in Chap. 5.

16. The concept of plenitude was connected with the notion of the great chain of being. Since proponents of the concept assumed that the removal of any living beings from the chain would disrupt its perfection, they viewed the extinction of species as de facto impossible. Their beliefs were sustainable in part because to that point no known living organisms had yet become extinct. Some scholars endorsed both the concept of plenitude and the organic origin of fossils by maintaining that the living counterparts of the fossils had not yet been discovered because

that fossils were found deep in quarries and high in mountains far from the ocean made it seem unlikely that the flood or any other known mechanism could have deposited them there — one more factor that made an inorganic origin for "formed stones" attractive.

Not enough was known about fossils in the seventeenth century to settle the problem of their origin one way or another. Some scholars who believed fossils had been produced inorganically still appealed to them as evidence of the flood on the grounds that only a global flood could account for the deposition of the rocks that enclosed the fossils, and those who disputed the diluvial origin of fossils didn't have enough information to demonstrate the weakness of that hypothesis. By the eighteenth century, however, intense study of fossils had produced a larger and more generally accepted body of evidence that yielded a scholarly consensus that fossils were in fact the remains of living organisms and that the flood could not account for their distribution. Even with that much settled, though, the issue of the extinction of species remained a point of controversy, and there was considerable uncertainty as to what sort of mechanism could account for the deposition of fossils far inland from the sea and high in the mountains.

Much of the difficulty in interpretation was occasioned by fossil shells, bryozoans, corals, crinoids, and other invertebrate hard parts. To heighten the perplexity of naturalists, however, remains of teeth and bones were occasionally encountered in unconsolidated gravel deposits that lay above the stratified shelly invertebrate-bearing rocks. Elephant teeth discovered in English gravels in the seventeenth century and a partial mammoth carcass found in Siberian frozen ground in 1692 were not so easily dismissed as the production of fluids or virtues within rocks. As more finds of this sort were made, pressure increased to develop a satisfactory account of their origins. It is worth noting that even in the face of the difficulties they faced in formulating an explanation, seventeenth-century scholars never adopted the strategy of simply claiming that God miraculously created fossils in place in rocks. Whether the fossils were produced by the deluge or not, these Christian thinkers were convinced that some scientific explanation for their origin could be found.

---

they were living either in the oceans or in remote parts of the world. This belief was plausible enough given the fact that there were considerable portions of the world with which Westerners were still unfamiliar, and a wealth of new species was still being discovered.

The Mechanical Worldview

A second profound scientific development in Renaissance Europe was the rise of a worldview in which physical phenomena were interpreted in terms of mechanical interactions of particles that behaved according to mathematically describable natural laws. Toward the end of the Middle Ages and throughout the Renaissance, scholars gradually broke with the reigning assumption that the surest knowledge of the created world was derived deductively from first principles and turned instead to exploration, investigation, discovery, experiment, and observation for clues to its true nature. Powerful mathematical tools helped observers to explain and predict a broad range of physical motions and helped give rise to a vision of the cosmos as a great machine designed and maintained by God.[17] Explanations of physical phenomena were increasingly cast in terms of rational mechanical and efficient causes. Scholars still appealed to occult, spiritual, and teleological causes as well, but far less often than their medieval predecessors. Generally speaking, the outlook of such fifteenth- and sixteenth-century writers as da Vinci and Palissy, and more particularly such seventeenth-century scholars as Galileo, Kepler, Newton, Hooke, and Boyle, differed radically from that of most medieval scholars.

The new approach affected procedures and results in all of the sciences. During the seventeenth century, the motions within the solar system were deciphered and explained in mathematical terms. Descartes employed mechanical principles in his attempt to explain the formation of the solar system and the globe. Scholars began to entertain mechanical explanations to resolve simple geological problems such as the aqueous deposition of rock strata. Students of creation were generally less content with repeated appeals to miracle to resolve questions about physical events or phenomena mentioned in Scripture. They increasingly supplemented biblical statements about the physical world

17. It has often been suggested that the development of the modern Western scientific outlook was strongly influenced by Christianity and the biblical conception of a voluntaristic creation. See, e.g., Michael B. Foster, "The Christian Doctrine of Creation and the Rise of Modern Natural Science," *Mind* 43 (1934): 446-68; Klaaren, *Religious Origins of Modern Science*; Reijer Hooykaas, *Religion and the Rise of Modern Science* (Grand Rapids: William B. Eerdmans, 1972); and Colin A. Russell, *Cross-Currents: Interactions between Science and Faith* (Grand Rapids: William B. Eerdmans, 1985). Hooykaas has suggested that the seventeenth-century metaphor of the earth as a machine was considerably closer to the spirit of the biblical view of the relationship between God and his creation than was the Greek or medieval metaphor of the world as a self-sufficient or semi-autonomous organism.

with rational explanations in terms of secondary mechanical causes. In doing so, it was not their intent to challenge biblical authority or to diminish God's role in creation. They were simply trying to view the divine creative activity in a new way, premised on the assumption that within the context of the physical world God typically acts in and through describable secondary mechanical causes.[18]

The investigation with the greatest long-range implications for understanding the flood narrative was undertaken by Niels Steensen (1638-1686). Steensen, generally known as Steno, was an interesting study in contrasts. A native of Denmark, he spent much of his adult life in Italy. He was born a Protestant and later converted to Roman Catholicism, and after a very promising early scientific career, he entirely abandoned science to devote his life to theology in a monastery. In his years of scientific endeavor, Steno combined the newer outlook on fossils with the mechanical philosophy. From an early interest in the anatomy of sharks, he turned to the burning issue of the origin of fossils because so many "formed stones" closely resembled the teeth of a great shark that he had dissected.[19] His study of the shapes of various "formed stones" and of their relationships to their enclosing rocks led him to conclude that such objects were not sports of nature that had grown in place but the remains of organisms that had been buried in sediments. Steno was also intrigued by the specific layers of rock in which the fossils were buried. The preliminary results of his thinking were published in *Forerunner to a Dissertation on a Solid Naturally Enclosed within a Solid,* a landmark in the history of geology for its elucidation of several basic principles of stratigraphic reasoning that lie at the basis of modern geology. Steno sensed that rock strata are historical documents from which one could deduce a historical sequence of events. His simplest principle, the principle of superposition, maintained that in a given succession of superposed strata, a layer that underlies other layers must have been deposited earlier. Steno

18. See Richard S. Westfall, *Science and Religion in Seventeenth-Century England* (New Haven: Yale University Press, 1958). Although such seventeenth-century Christian virtuosi as Boyle, Newton, and John Wilkins viewed God's providence as being manifested through secondary mechanical causes, it took some time for this view to be more popularly accepted. In its extreme form, notions of divine providence were effectively supplanted by mechanical explanations, yielding the deistic worldview of a virtually autonomous, self-sustaining cosmic machine.

19. So-called *glossopetrae,* or "tongue stones," smooth triangular objects with serrated edges, were commonly found in unconsolidated surficial sediments throughout Europe. After dissecting a great white shark that had been donated to his laboratory, Steno recognized that *glossopetrae* were actually shark teeth.

went beyond the mere enunciation of general principles to reconstruct a sequence of events from a local succession of strata in the Tuscany region of Italy, and in doing so he laid the foundation for stratigraphic studies that would ultimately undermine the various proposals for a global deluge.

In Steno's day, however, few in the Western world questioned the idea that the earth was only a few thousands of years old.[20] Steno himself did not expect to find evidence of great antiquity in the rocks. Nor did he doubt the reality of the biblical flood. Thus, despite his having initiated geological studies so far-reaching that they would not be fully appreciated for another century, Steno was a child of his time. In his discussion of the relationship of his findings to Scripture, the biblical flood was never far away. Steno launched the enterprise of reconstructing aspects of terrestrial history *independently* of the records of biblical revelation, but he considered it unthinkable that extrabiblical information would lead to theories in conflict with generally received biblical history. Perhaps because of its radically new insights, Steno's book attracted relatively little immediate attention in spite of a brief review in *Philosophical Transactions of the Royal Society of London* and had little impact until the eighteenth century.

Analysis and Application

In dealing with the biblical account of the flood, early Christians focused on deluge legends, reports of remnants of the ark on mountaintops, the capacity of the ark, the postdiluvial distribution of animals, and the significance of fossils. For many centuries the Christian world comfortably accommodated knowledge in these areas into its assumption of a literally historical universal deluge. That easy assumption, however, was sorely tested during the period from the fifteenth century to the seventeenth century as new information accumulated on the number and distribution of animal species and the nature of fossils.

European exploration of the New World produced a new appreciation for the size of the planet and its almost boundless variety of previously unknown plant and animal species. Christians interested in affirming the literal historicity of the biblical flood account had to

20. Walter Ralegh and Thomas Harriot did, however, try to push biblical chronology to its limits.

deal not only with the issue of how so many species could have fit on the ark but, perhaps more critically, how they could have traveled to the ark before the flood and returned to their unique and distant habitats afterward.

In general, the Christians of this period demonstrated a strong inclination to deal with all this new information as valid and significant. They did not always know exactly what to make of the evidence, but few were inclined to dismiss it out of hand as irrelevant. They did not simply invoke scriptural authority and assert that it happened because the Bible said it happened, regardless of what the physical evidence might suggest. Rather, they made efforts in a variety of ways to explain the biblical flood account as they understood it in terms of the physical evidence as they understood it. Concerning the worldwide distribution of animals after the flood, for instance, a number of seventeenth-century scholars postulated that after the flood, animals quickly migrated back to their natural habitats using land bridges that subsequently disappeared into the oceans. Later geological investigation has shown that these postulated land bridges never existed, but the point is that the scholars based their judgments on the best available information of the time and did their best to reconcile the physical evidence with the biblical account.

The same strategy prevailed in efforts to understand the significance of fossils during this period. As evidence mounted that fossils were in fact the remains of living organisms, many seventeenth-century scholars made forthright attempts to reconcile this information with their reading of the biblical account, some quite directly by hypothesizing that all fossils were animals killed by the deluge. Again, the fact that this hypothesis was disproved by subsequent investigation is not the issue. The point is that virtually no scholar of the time took the easy course of simply dismissing the fossil evidence as irrelevant (e.g., by claiming that whatever fossils might be, God must have created them in place in rocks); they all believed that there was a scientific explanation for fossils, and they earnestly sought to uncover it. As long as scholars were convinced that the fossil evidence would prove consistent with the traditional interpretation of a global deluge, they were fearless in searching out new information and grappling with it openly.

4. The Impact of the Exploration of the New World

The exploration of the New World during the fifteenth and sixteenth centuries uncovered a wealth of new information that proved relevant to the interpretation of the deluge narrative. The confirmation of the large size of the globe and the discovery of previously unrecognized animals, new human tribes, and more extrabiblical flood traditions all made previous interpretations more problematic. How did Christian scholars of the era adjust to these new bodies of knowledge? Many church-related scholars (e.g., monastic mapmakers) were obviously aware of the discoveries, but the biblical expositors living at the same time on the whole chose to ignore the discoveries. One would never guess from their writings that the great Protestant Reformers Luther and Calvin knew that the New World had been discovered, for instance. And even a century after Calvin, such noteworthy commentators as John Lightfoot (1602-1675) and John Trapp (1601-1699) seemed oblivious to the importance of the new information.[1] The geographic universality of the deluge was still taken for granted in the sixteenth century.

Luther and Calvin

Martin Luther (1483-1546) devoted nearly two hundred pages of his *Lectures on Genesis* to the flood story. He did not hesitate to appeal

---

1. See Lightfoot, *A Chronicle and Harmony of the Old Testament* (1647; reprint, London: J. F. Dove, 1822); and John Trapp, *A Commentary on the Old and New Testaments* (London: R. D. Dickinson, 1867-1877).

to extrabiblical information, but his comments, published around 1535, ignored the newer discoveries.[2] He invoked extrabiblical arguments based on Aristotelian physics in discussing the sources of flood water. He reviewed the location of various beasts on the ark and asserted that the wild animals, having a "premonition of the wrath of God," must have entered the ark miraculously, because Noah's skill was inadequate "to control animals of such fierceness." Yet Luther made no mention of the discovery of America or how the newly recognized global geography might have affected animal migration.[3]

Luther maintained that paradise was "utterly destroyed and annihilated by the Flood, so that no trace of it is visible any longer." Mountains took the place of fields and plains. The Mediterranean Sea was produced by the flood, and "the area of the Red Sea without a doubt was formerly a fertile plain." He felt that the Persian and Arabian Gulfs, too, were likely remnants of the flood. Luther espoused the long-held opinion that remains of the flood were still to be seen, citing as evidence the fact that in mines "there are commonly found pieces of petrified wood. In the stones themselves there appear various forms of fish and other animals."

After the flood, he wrote, the powers of man were lessened and the wealth of the earth was reduced. He asserted that "before the Flood turnips were better than melons, oranges, or pomegranates were afterwards. Pears were more delicious than spices are today. The strength in a man's finger was probably greater than it is today in his entire arm. In like manner, his reason and wisdom were far superior." He further wrote that the flood drastically eroded the earth's surface and

2. Luther, *Lectures on Genesis Chapters 6–14*, vol. 2 of *Luther's Works*, ed. Jaroslav Pelikan, trans. George V. Schick (St. Louis: Concordia, 1960), pp. 3-186. Luther's discussion of the time of onset of the flood is full of appeals to extrabiblical information. In fact, during the Renaissance and Reformation era it was hotly debated whether the flood began in the spring or fall, and observations from nature were frequently used in such discussions. Luther noted that "fall and winter are better suited for rains" and the flowering olive branch brought back by the dove comported well with a beginning of the flood in October. Even so, he favored springtime on the grounds that it is "the time when the year is most beautiful and the world becomes green again, when the birds sing and the cattle frolic, and the world presents a new face after the raw winter weather. Surely the terror was all the greater, since death and destruction of all things closed in when the beginning of joy and of a new life for all things was being expected" (p. 92). The green olive branch presented no problem for Luther because "some trees are continually green, such as boxwood, fir, pine, cedar, laurel, olive, palm, etc."

3. See Luther, *Lectures on Genesis 6–14*, pp. 67-75.

destroyed the fertility of the soil — in effect introducing a curse that was equal to or greater than the curse attendant on Adam's fall.[4]

He affirmed that the wind mentioned in Genesis 8:1 dried up the moisture. Calling on his knowledge of natural phenomena, he stated that it was nothing new for east winds to dry up moisture. Previous interpreters generally referred the landing of the ark to Armenia, but Luther suggested that the biblical reference was "a designation for the foremost mountain of all, the Imaus, which divides India." Quite probably Luther was working with Ptolemy's map of the world and had the Himalaya range in mind. In any event, he was skeptical of Josephus's claim that remnants of the ark were still to be found in the mountains of Armenia.[5]

Such is the strength of Luther's reputation as a Reformer that even today many contemporary commentators are strongly influenced by his view of the flood despite his dependence on the inaccurate science of his day and his failure to deal with the problematic issues raised by the discovery of the New World.

In striking contrast to Luther, John Calvin (1509-1564) was very cautious in commenting on the flood. He frequently noted varying opinions about details of the narrative without taking sides, and he rarely appealed to any extrabiblical data. He made no reference to fossils, deluge traditions, or other presumed evidences of the event. He was concerned with the practical implications of the flood story without recourse to allegory.

Calvin wrote that the narrative "would be cold, and trifling, and ridiculous" unless replete with miracle that more clearly exhibited the power of God. Taking it for granted that the account should be read literally, Calvin assumed that the flood was universal. Humanly speaking, the ingathering of animals was impossible, but "because Noah, simply trusting the event with God, executed what was enjoined upon him; God, in return, gave power to his own precept, that it might not be without effect." Calvin followed most commentators regarding the landing place of the ark, but, like Luther, he was uncertain about Josephus's claim that remains of the ark were preserved. Unlike Luther, who maintained that the quality of the created order was greatly

---

4. See Luther, *Lectures on Genesis 6–14*, especially pp. 7, 52, 65-66, and 95. See also the commentary on Gen. 2:11-12 in Luther's *Lectures on Genesis Chapters 1–5*, vol. 1 of *Luther's Works*, ed. Jaroslav Pelikan, trans. George V. Schick (St. Louis: Concordia, 1958).

5. Luther, *Lectures on Genesis 6–14*, pp. 107-8.

diminished after the flood, Calvin maintained that everything was restored to its former function afterward.[6]

Extent of the Flood

During this era belief in diluvial universality was hardly restricted to biblical scholars. British savant Sir Walter Ralegh (1554-1618) wrote in his magnum opus, *The History of the World,* that the deluge covered the globe. Both Ralegh and his friend Thomas Harriot (1560-1621) had access to the traditions of Native Americans, which envisioned a world considerably older than that commonly presumed by Christians. Because of such knowledge, Ralegh, Harriot, and their circle were frequently accused of atheism and specific heresies such as pre-Adamism (the belief that human beings lived before the biblical Adam). Yet, if Ralegh entertained such notions as an old earth, pre-Adamism, or a local deluge, none of these ideas found their way into his great work. He spoke of a universal flood, although he did give the traditional view a new twist by proposing that the flood had been placid. Given that Moses so precisely described the location of the Garden of Eden, Ralegh asserted, the flood could not have defaced the original paradise. The fact that the olive leaf was plucked by the dove indicated that olive trees had not been torn up by any torrent. And because the flood had not destroyed a pillar erected by Seth, Adam's son, allegedly still standing in the days of Josephus, Ralegh felt that "it seemeth most agreeable to reason, that the Waters rather stood in a quiet calm, than that they moved with any raging or overbearing violence."[7] He also cited ancient authors as witnesses that a number of ancient cities such as Joppa had been preserved through the flood. Ralegh's arguments were also espoused by such writers as Nathaniel Carpenter (1589–c. 1628), a Dublin academic and friend of Archbishop Ussher.[8] Ralegh noted that some of his contemporaries questioned the universality of the flood, but he rejected their position as an error that started with the Greeks, noting also that some American "soothsayers" had informed him that the flood had also covered the New World.

6. See Calvin, *Commentaries on the First Book of Moses called Genesis,* vol. 1, trans. John King (1847; reprint, Grand Rapids: William B. Eerdmans, 1948).

7. Ralegh, *The History of the World in Five Books* (1614; reprint, London, 1677), p. 24. Of particular relevance is book 1, chap. 3, sect. 5, "Of the Place of Paradise."

8. Carpenter, *Geography Delineated forth in Two Bookes* (Oxford, 1625).

Ralegh held that secondary causes were inadequate to account for the flood fully, that it was a supernatural event in which God gave "strength of influence to the Stars, and abundance to the Fountains of the Deep." Betraying the influence of medieval conceptions, he also wrote that God caused violent eruptions of springs and fountains and condensed "ayr into water by the ministery of his Angels, or whatsoever else best pleased his All-powerfulness."[9] He did not believe that God had to create any waters for the flood, however. He reasoned that since the radius of the earth was 3,500 miles and the highest mountains only 30 miles, enough water could be stored inside the globe to cover its surface to that depth.

As the seventeenth century unfolded, many scholars proved more willing to question the universality of the flood in print. Some of this advocacy of a localized deluge was perhaps born of skepticism, but orthodox Protestants also cautiously adopted a more liberal stance. One of the earliest vocal proponents of a local flood was Isaac La Peyrère (1596-1676), a Jewish convert to Christianity.[10] In *Prae-adamitae*, an electrifying book published in 1655, he advocated the notion that human beings had lived prior to Adam. He was probably emboldened to propose this radical hypothesis by the precedent of Paracelsus (1493-1541), who postulated an origin for Native Americans separate from that of the rest of mankind, but he developed the position from extensive research of his own. As his biographer Richard H. Popkin wrote, "The full pre-Adamite theory of La Peyrère is the consequence of a century of analysis of explorer data," principally concerning the inhabitants of the New World. Maintaining that Paul's discussion of sin and death in Romans makes little sense unless there had been people before Adam, La Peyrère claimed that Adam was not the father of the entire human race but only the first Jew. He also argued that the story of Cain and Abel presumed the existence of an established widespread culture and that a comparison of Jewish and Gentile chronologies indicated that Adam could not have been the first man.

La Peyrère coupled these ideas with the contention that Moses did not write the Pentateuch. He argued that Moses derived his history from earlier writers and that other writers subsequently summarized the first 1,600 years of Jewish history in the first five chapters of

9. Ralegh, *The History of the World in Five Books*, p. 62 (book 1, chap. 7, "Of Noah's Flood").

10. The definitive work on La Peyrère is Richard H. Popkin, *Isaac La Peyrère (1596-1676)* (Leiden: E. J. Brill, 1987).

Genesis. He further argued that the Bible described only events that took place in Palestine — that only Palestine was dark at the crucifixion, for example. And he maintained that many apparently miraculous circumstances were a matter of local appearances rather than actual universal effects. When God turned back the shadow on Ahaz's sundial, he said, the effect was on the sundial and not on the sun. So also with the flood. La Peyrère contended that God sought to destroy only the Jews who had intermarried with Gentiles, not people living in the Americas or China, and hence the flood was limited to Palestine. In support of this assertion, he cited a variety of biblical and extrabiblical evidence. He held that the traditional landing site assigned to the ark — Armenia — indicated that the flood had not ranged beyond a small portion of Asia. He held that the return of the olive branch suggested not a placid rise of flood waters but rather the survival of unharmed trees outside the flood area. Even if the flood waters had risen quietly as Ralegh argued, the trees would have been rotten after having been submerged for months, said La Peyrère. He also stated that Noah's descendants had settled solely in the vicinity of Palestine and not over the whole globe, quipping that they would have had to be extremely fecund to feel it necessary to search out such faraway places as China, Australia, Greenland, and America for room to live.[11]

La Peyrère's advocacy of a local deluge was probably a little less shocking than it might otherwise have been because it more or less fell into the shadows of his even more shocking denial of Mosaic authorship of the Pentateuch and endorsement of the pre-Adamite thesis. In any event, some reputable scholars who thoroughly repudiated what they considered to be La Peyrère's more outrageous proposals were less dismissive of the notion of a localized flood.

One such scholar was Isaac Voss (1618-1689), the son of a Dutch theologian, librarian to the queen of Sweden, and, later in life, a canon in the Church of England. He took note of the various flood traditions around the globe, but doubted that there had been a universal deluge on the grounds that it would have involved too many miracles to accomplish it. There simply was not enough water on earth to have submerged all land, and he characterized as "pious fooleries" any hypotheses that God had miraculously created extra water to fuel the

---

11. La Peyrère, *Prae-adamitae, sive exercitatio super versibus duodecimo, decimotertio and decimoquarto, capitis quinti epistolae D. Pauli ad Romanos. Quibus inducuntur primi homines ante Adamum conditi* (Amsterdam, 1655). An English translation appeared shortly thereafter.

flood and then miraculously eliminated it afterward. Voss also questioned whether the nine generations between Adam and Noah could have produced a population sufficient to overspread the earth, especially given the fact that the first men were "slow and sluggish" in propagating. Voss's computations indicated that many more people could have descended from the eight survivors of the deluge until the time of the construction of the tower of Babel than could have descended from Adam in two thousand years. And since he believed that humans inhabited only a small part of Asia within the borders of Syria and Mesopotamia before the dispersion of Babel, he felt it only reasonable to believe that they would have occupied much less territory before the flood. That being the case, there would have been no need for a universal deluge: why inflict punishment on areas where no man lived? Thus Voss maintained that the deluge was universal only in the sense that the entire *inhabited* world was overwhelmed. He confidently concluded that this perspective put an end to "vain and idle questions" about the flood and removed "all occasion . . . from infidels for doubting the truth of the Sacred History."[12]

Three years later (1662), another ardent critic of La Peyrère's pre-Adamism published *Origines Sacrae*. A highly respected Anglican churchman of unquestioned orthodoxy and reputation as a conciliator with the Nonconformists and holder of numerous ecclesiastical posts including ultimately that of bishop of Worcester, Edward Stillingfleet (1635-1699) sought to demonstrate that there was nothing in the deluge story "repugnant to reason." He granted the validity of the criticism that there was not enough water on earth to submerge all land to any great depth (he calculated that if all the world's clouds were completely drained, only about a foot and a half of water would fall to the surface), but a localized flood would resolve that problem. Stillingfleet saw no biblical imperative for claiming that the flood spread over the entire surface of the earth inasmuch as it was meant only to destroy "all Mankind," and he asserted that at the time all humans resided in the Near East. On the other hand, he apparently also wanted to avoid advocating too small a flood. He asserted that the flood could not merely have covered some small country like Palestine "as some have ridiculously imagin'd" (an apparent swipe at La Peyrère); after all, the flood was sent in response to "universal corruption in the Earth," and it would have had to be sufficient to ensure the destruction of the whole human population.

12. Voss, *Dissertatio de Vera Aetate Mundi* (The Hague, 1659), p. 53.

Stillingfleet did not endorse the notion of the universal destruction of animal populations, however. He believed that animals spread much further throughout the world than humans in the period before the flood, and he reasoned that animal populations living in areas beyond the range of the flood would have been spared. The animals taken on board the ark, then, were needed only to restore local populations after the flood, not to replenish the entire earth. He argued that the survivors of the flood would have needed certain animals to ensure their survival in the immediate aftermath of the flood, and they could not have depended on migrations from distant unravaged areas to meet such needs. They would have needed horses after the flood, for example, and would not have been able to wait for horses to migrate from the Americas back to the Middle East, so it would have been necessary for Noah to take horses along on the ark.

Stillingfleet sensed more acutely than many of his contemporaries the difficulties posed by the discovery of different kinds of animals across the Atlantic. He perceptively noted that some animals cannot live outside the climate to which they are accustomed. Many animals discovered in America had "left no remainders" in the Old World. It seemed strange to Stillingfleet that animals "should propagate into those remote parts of the World from the place of the flood, and leave none at all of their number behind them in those parts from whence they were propagated." He viewed it as additional evidence that the deluge extended only to those areas inhabited by man. With such a view "we need not make so many Miracles as some are fain to do about the Flood; and all those difficulties concerning the propagation of Animals do of themselves vanish and fall to the ground."[13]

Matthew Poole (1624-1679), a well-regarded Nonconformist London minister, may have been the earliest biblical commentator to opt for a localized inundation. Displaying great readiness to look at outside sources for help in illuminating the biblical text, Poole distinguished himself from contemporary British commentators such as Trapp and Lightfoot by uncommon engagement with the issues that were forced on students of the Bible by the voyages to the Americas. He dealt head on with such matters as the capacity of the ark, deluge traditions, sources of water, and animal migrations.

---

13. Stillingfleet, *Origines Sacrae*, 8th ed. (London, 1697), p. 3. More generally, see book 3, chap. 4, "On the Origin of Nations." For further information about Stillingfleet, see Robert T. Carroll, *The Common-Sense Philosophy of Religion of Bishop Edward Stillingfleet* (The Hague: M. Nijhoff, 1975).

Reflecting sentiments widely held among his contemporaries, Poole identified the "fountains of the deep" mentioned in Scripture with an abyss or "sea of waters" held within the bowels of the globe.[14] He did not believe that even this resource would have held sufficient water to submerge all the globe's mountains, however, so he proposed two possible means by which the flooding might have been accomplished: God could have performed a "miracle of Divine power and providence" or he might have spread flood waters "only over all the habitable world, where either men or beasts lived." The latter was all that was required to punish the sins of humanity.[15] He more pointedly endorsed the notion of the limited flood in his *Synopsis;* commenting on Genesis 7:19, he wrote, "It is not to be supposed that the entire globe of the earth was covered with water." It would have been absurd and pointless to overwhelm regions where there were no humans, he said. He agreed with Voss that the human population probably had not extended beyond the limits of Syria and Mesopotamia by the time of Noah. Even if "not so much as the hundredth part of the globe was overspread with water," he wrote, the deluge would still have been universal as long as it affected the inhabited part of the globe. "If we take this ground," Poole insisted, "the difficulties which some have raised about the deluge fall away as inapplicable, and mere cavils; and irreligious persons have no reason left them for doubting the truth of the Holy Scriptures."[16]

Inasmuch as this idea was still widely considered heretical, Poole underscored his belief in the historicity of the event and insisted that there was abundant proof for its having happened in the flood traditions common among such heathens as Berossus, Plutarch, Abydenus, the Chinese, and the Native Americans.

The conceptual stresses exerted by advances of the age of discovery had begun to take their toll. The offhand suggestion of Pseudo-Justin concerning the possibility of a localized flood was now seriously entertained by competent scholars, skeptics, and thoroughly orthodox believers alike. An important benefit to the church was that the extrabiblical discoveries had subtly begun to stimulate more thorough study of the biblical text. Biblical scholars began to recognize, for

14. We will explore the notion of the abyss at greater length in Chap. 5, in the context of diluvial cosmogonies.

15. See Poole, *A Commentary of the Holy Bible* (1679; reprint, London: Banner of Truth, 1979), pp. 16-26.

16. Poole, *Synopsis criticorum aliorumque Sacrae Scripturae Interpretum et Commentatorum* (Ribbius, van de Water, & Halma, 1684-1686).

example, that the Bible often uses universalistic language in reference to localized contexts.

Doubts about the universality of the deluge, however, were hardly universal. The local flood view was still a minority view that met with considerable hostility.[17] Despite the new discoveries, during the latter part of the seventeenth century British scholars still overwhelmingly sought to account for geological phenomena in terms of the action of a global deluge acting in terms of Cartesian or Newtonian mechanical principles. Scholars still struggled to account for animal migrations and to speak of an ark large enough to contain an ever-increasing catalogue of animals. And virtually everyone, whether open to the notion of a local deluge or not, still thought in terms of a literal historical account penned by Moses, the sacred historian.

The Capacity of the Ark

As the list of newly discovered new animal species in the New World and elsewhere grew throughout the sixteenth and seventeenth centuries, Catholic and Protestant scholars used a variety of strategies to update Origen's reply to Apelles concerning the ark's carrying capacity in so that they could answer the "Atheistical scoffers" of their own age.

The first ark of the scientific age was "designed" by Jean Borrel, generally known as Johannes Buteo (c. 1492-1572), a Roman Catholic mathematician, in his *Opera Geometrica* (1554). Buteo provided the basic blueprint for subsequent attempts to deal with the capacity problem by claiming that the dimensions of the ark were divinely provided in terms of the common cubit. Like some medieval "arkitects," Buteo set aside a portion of the ark (in this case, the bottom four cubits) to hold the accumulation of animal waste. Above this were two decks, the lower for the animals and the upper for food. Buteo estimated the usable interior volume of the ark at 350,000 cubic cubits. For purposes of calculation, Buteo converted known animals of the world into the volumetric equivalent of cows, sheep, and wolves. He estimated that all the world's larger animals would occupy a space equivalent to about 120 cows, the world's smaller animals would occupy a space equivalent

17. For a review of rebuttals of the local deluge hypothesis, see Don Cameron Allen, *The Legend of Noah* (Urbana, Ill.: University of Illinois, 1949), pp. 87-89.

to about 80 sheep, and all the world's carnivores would occupy a space equivalent to about 80 wolves. Reptiles, he believed, could easily wrap themselves around rafters and beams.

Buteo estimated that five rows of sixty cow-sized stalls on the bottom deck would hold all the world's animals and yet consume only one-fourth of the ark's space, leaving plenty of storage space for food. Working from an allotment of one cubic cubit of hay per day for a cow, and assuming that all the ruminants on the ark would consume no more than the equivalent of 400 cows, Buteo calculated that a year's supply of hay for all the animals would occupy 146,000 cubic cubits, which he said could easily be stowed on the second deck. Buteo did not bother to calculate the space requirements for birds and human beings, because so much room was available on the upper deck that Noah could even have built a large fishpool if he wanted.[18]

Several similar ark designs followed. During the late sixteenth and early seventeenth centuries, Becanus, Hostus, Gibbeus, and Pererius all introduced modifications into the basic Butean ark.[19] Sir Walter Ralegh believed that the common cubit of Noah's day was larger than at present because, as the Bible reports, there were giants in those days. Ralegh's cubit of "giantly stature" yielded an ark that was 600 feet long, 100 feet wide, and 60 feet high. Although he believed that the animals would have been correspondingly larger as well, Ralegh claimed that they would have had sufficient room in the ark. Because animal classification was not straightforward and the nature of animal species was not well understood, it was by no means easy to say which animals embarked. Ralegh excluded beasts of "mixt" nature like the mule and the hyena (which at the time was thought to be a hybrid between a fox and a wolf) on the grounds that these could have been produced after the flood. He also treated several distinct animals as varieties of the same animal. For example, he considered the wild dog to be a variety of the wolf and hence did not feel that it would have needed to be on the ark. Despite the large number of animals that had been discovered during the preceding century, Ralegh asserted that only about eighty-nine kinds of beasts would have needed to embark. He performed calculations of volume requirements much like those of Buteo and attained virtually the same results.[20]

---

18. Buteo, *Opera Geometrica* (Lyons, 1554). For a summary of Buteo's description of the ark, see Allen, *The Legend of Noah*, pp. 78-79.

19. For details, see Allen, *The Legend of Noah*, pp. 79-80.

20. Ralegh, *The History of the World in Five Books*, pp. 65-66.

Even Poole and Stillingfleet, despite their belief in a local flood, were concerned about the size of the ark. Stillingfleet was generally satisfied with the earlier calculations of Buteo, Ralegh, and Hostus.[21]

John Wilkins (1614-1672), bishop of Chester and warden at Wadham College, Oxford, was one of the driving forces behind the establishment of the Royal Society of London, a friend of Stillingfleet, and a prolific author on scientific and religious subjects. His biographer, Barbara J. Shapiro, claims that in his era "Wilkins was England's single most influential and effective organizer and purveyor of the scientific culture." He had, she wrote, a "firm grasp of the central problem of seventeenth-century English intellectual life" — namely, finding a way to combine knowledge and faith so as to "allow the tentative pragmatic tone of science to soften the dogmatism of English religious life."[22] In 1668, Wilkins published an encyclopedic compilation of various lists of animals, plants, and so on.[23] At the conclusion of a list of animals, Wilkins introduced a digression on the capacity of Noah's ark. He observed that people tended to overestimate the number of kinds of animals in the world and therefore the number that would have had to be on the ark. Wilkins claimed that the numbers of animals "are much fewer than is commonly imagined, not a hundred sorts of Beasts, nor two hundred of Birds."

The solution to the capacity problem, claimed Wilkins, lay not with gimmicks involving abnormally large cubits but in an appropriate calculation of the abundance and sizes of animals. Buteo's thesis needed refinement, because some of his alleged animals were "fabulous," others were not really distinct species, and a few true species had been omitted. Wilkins omitted seals, turtles, crocodiles, and the "senembi" because they could survive in the water. Snakes, lizards, and frogs could find room at the bottom of the ark, whereas rats, mice, moles, and insects could easily occupy nooks and crannies. Wilkins then enumerated the remaining species and classified them, following Buteo and Ralegh, in terms of cow, sheep, and wolf equivalency.[24]

21. Stillingfleet, *Origines Sacrae*, p. 345.

22. Shapiro, *John Wilkins, 1614-1672: An Intellectual Biography* (Berkeley and Los Angeles: University of California Press, 1969), pp. 2, 4.

23. Wilkins, *An Essay towards a Real Character and a Philosophical Language* (London: Gallibrand & Martin, 1668). For a discussion of the life and views of John Wilkins, see Richard S. Westfall, *Science and Religion in Seventeenth-Century England* (New Haven: Yale University Press, 1958).

24. Wilkins's list of animals exemplifies many of the shortcomings of the animal nomenclature and classification of the time. E.g., Wilkins listed only

In making his calculations for food storage, Wilkins made allowances for the dietary requirements of the 40 carnivores aboard, calculating that it would take 1,825 sheep to feed them for the whole year. He estimated that 109,500 cubic cubits of hay would be sufficient to feed the ruminants (including the gradually diminishing stock of sheep) for a year. Evidently Wilkins imagined that the animals would be a good deal less voracious than Buteo had anticipated.[25] Wilkins confidently contended that the measure of the ark, "which some Atheistical irreligious men make use of, as an argument against the Scripture, ought rather to be esteemed a most rational confirmation of the truth and divine authority of it."

A final example of ark calculations was provided by Athanasius Kircher (1602-1680), a German Catholic priest of encyclopedic interests who spent most of his career at the Jesuit College of Rome, first as professor of mathematics and later as an independent scholar. He composed at least forty-four books, many on scientific topics. One, *Arca Noe* (1675), was devoted entirely to a study of Noah's ark. In this comprehensive treatise, Kircher provided detailed illustrations of the inner structure of the ark.[26] The door of the ark was operated by hinges and pulleys, he said. On the lower deck Noah constructed three hundred stalls, each six by six by ten cubits, large enough to house an elephant. Some stalls were partitioned for the smaller animals. Kircher asserted that there were only 130 kinds of animals and 30 species of snakes on the ark, so there was room to spare. The second floor was a granary, and the third floor contained 2,000 cages for about 150 kinds of birds. He held that the animals retained their originally created characteristics, which meant that the carnivores needed meat (specifi-

---

"elephant," even though both African and Indian kinds were known. He listed only "tortoise," even though several kinds must have been known. Certainly more than one kind of "antilope" was known. And he failed to list such animals as the pangolin, hyena, bighorn sheep, hippopotamus, and opossum, even though all were known by the mid-seventeenth century.

25. Because of miscalculation, Wilkins actually overestimated the amount of hay that would be required by a substantial amount — making his case for the capacity of the ark even stronger than he thought.

26. Kircher, *Arca Noe in Tres Libros Digesta, sive de Rebus ante Diluvium, de Diluvio, et de Rebus post Diluvium a Noemo Gestis* (Amsterdam, 1675). For a summary of Kircher's description, see Allen, *The Legend of Noah*, pp. 182-91. For further discussion of Kircher, see chap. 1 of Janet Browne's *Secular Ark* (New Haven: Yale University Press, 1983). For information about Kircher's life and career, see P. Conor Reilly, *Athanasius Kircher, S.J.: Master of a Hundred Arts, 1602-1680* (Wiesbaden: Edizioni del Mondo, 1974).

cally, 4,562.5 sheep, more than twice Wilkins's estimate). Most insects
and reptiles did not need to be on the ark, he insisted, because they
could have spawned after the flood from putrefactions such as rotting
leaves. Hybrids need not have been present either.[27]

Migrations of Animals

The fact that so many sixteenth- and seventeenth-century scholars,
including Roman Catholic and Protestant clerics, were at pains to
defend the adequacy of the ark to hold the world's fauna strongly
indicates a perception on their part that Christian scholarship could
not ignore extrabiblical information. In the face of hostile criticism of
a literal reading of the biblical flood story stemming from the discovery
of so many animals, many Christians felt that they could not continue
simply to assert the adequacy of the ark on the authority of divine
revelation. They felt they had to provide rational responses to the critics
on their own terms — and, indeed, Christian scholars of the era could
rightly congratulate themselves on defending the cargo-hauling abilities
of the ark. But their explanations were successful mostly because
neither they nor their critics genuinely recognized how many animals
had actually been discovered.

But if they were on the whole successful in explaining the
capacity of the ark at the time, they faced far greater problems in trying
to explain how animals could have migrated from such places as the
Americas and Australia to the ark and back again: not only were the
distances considerable but there was the matter of ocean barriers as
well. Kircher hypothesized that the animals swam from island to island.
Poole speculated that the ocean separating the European and American
land masses was smaller in Noah's day — narrow enough to have
permitted many animals to swim across it. Abraham van der Myl
(1563-1637), Lord Chief Justice Matthew Hale (1609-1676), Poole, and
Kircher all suggested that domestic animals might have been conveyed
in boats. Poole specified that the animals might have been transported
by humans in vessels "either for their supply, or profit, or diversion,

---

27. Many other calculations of the capacity of the ark were made throughout
the seventeenth century by such individuals as Augustine Torniellus (1622), An-
drew Willett (1632), Jeremiah Drexel (1644), Louis Capell (1687), and Gaspar
Schott (1677). None of these writers departed from the essential pattern of reasoning
established by Johannes Buteo.

or other ends."[28] Perhaps, it was suggested, some animals escaped from ships that were transporting them to zoos. Gregorius Hornius suggested that animals crossed frozen northern seas during the winter. Hale took care of the bird population by arguing that they could have flown across the narrows between the Old and New World. Waterfowl were not a problem, because they could have flown across the oceans, resting on the water along the way. Van der Myl, however, pointed out that such species as fish, chickens, and pheasants would have had a hard time crossing to America by themselves. The Spanish historian José de Acosta (1539-1600) postulated that animals came to the Americas via a northern land bridge. Richard Simson, a traveler to the South Seas, concurred with Acosta, Justus Lipsius (1547-1606), Hale, and Poole that a land bridge was one possible solution. Lipsius opted for land bridges because he doubted that men would carry rattlesnakes and other unpleasant American species to the New World. Hale likewise assumed that the ferocious beasts would have had to cross land bridges because no one would transport them, they could not swim across the ocean, and deep snows would have prevented them from crossing frozen straits.

Given all the difficulties associated with explanations involving animal migrations from all over the globe, van der Myl endorsed the idea of a limited deluge. He did not think it likely that the descendants of Noah would have transported lions, tigers, bears, dragons, and serpents to distant lands. He also recognized the problem associated with the fact that hundreds of American creatures were unknown in Europe, Asia, or Africa. He regarded America as a primordial world that contained all the plants, birds, and animals originally created by God, whereas Europe, Africa, and eastern Asia contained only a remnant of the original creation because the deluge had affected only that part of the world. In the end, van der Myl urged that the Genesis account not be taken literally: when it says that all living things were destroyed, he held that it really means *almost* all living things.

Matthew Hale adopted a radically different solution by employing a concept of transformation to account for the ostensibly unique American species. He doubted that American animals were aboriginal because they were not found on the islands of the New World. Hale concluded that they must be modified descendants of animals that Noah took on the ark. He proposed that animals could change through interbreeding, natural mutation, and in response to the influences of

28. Poole, *A Commentary of the Holy Bible,* p. 22.

soil and climate. He also argued that Asia and Africa had not yet been explored thoroughly enough to rule out the possibility that American-like species might yet be encountered in the interiors of those continents. Maybe the animals of the New World weren't all that different from the animals of the Old. As we have already seen, Ralegh was inclined to discount the "small" differences among similar animals in different locations. In making his calculations for the capacity of the ark, for instance, he had equated the cat with the Indian snow leopard and the wolf with the wild dog. In essence, he sidestepped the migration problem by considering American animals to be no different from those in Eurasia.

Others dealt with the issue of animal migration by turning to the ultimate solution to the most difficult problems: miracle. Matthew Poole, for example, stated that the God who caused the animals to come to Adam "could afterwards both incline and empower them to go whither he pleased, without the advice of these vain men, who will believe nothing of God which themselves either do not see or cannot do."[29]

Deluge Traditions

If the discovery of the New World created a welter of new problems for the traditional theory of a universal deluge, it also produced at least some evidence to shore it up. Explorers found Native American flood legends similar to those of India and China. Because pagan critics had accused the Christian Scriptures of pilfering the flood story from pagan sources, the Church Fathers had not been much inclined to cite the stories of Deucalion, Xisuthros, or other extrabiblical flood heroes. But as they began to encounter flood traditions around the world, later Christians such as Grotius and Stillingfleet began to reverse the earlier reaction by claiming that the heathen stories were perversions of an inspired flood tradition that was recorded accurately in Scripture.[30] They argued that as the descendants of Noah spread out over the globe, their memories of the cataclysm dimmed and were distorted by paganism. A host of Renaissance scholars identified Noah with a variety of heathen heroes.

29. Poole, *A Commentary of the Holy Bible*, p. 22.
30. See, e.g., Hugo Grotius, *De Veritate Religionis Christianae, Opera Theologica* (London, 1679).

Analysis and Application

The sixteenth and early seventeenth centuries introduced a substantial body of new extrabiblical evidence relevant to the understanding of the biblical flood narrative as Europeans began to explore the New World and report their findings. Among the more important new evidence was a greatly expanded catalogue of animal species, a clearer sense of their distinct and disparate habitats, and a recognition of the great natural barriers to global migration. Christian scholars responded in a number of established ways to the problems that this body of new evidence raised for the traditional reading of the biblical flood story.

Some commentators, such as Calvin, Trapp, and Lightfoot, focused almost totally on textual and theological matters and hence were not drawn into the controversy raised by extrabiblical evidence. Others followed the strategy of Luther, who unhesitatingly exploited extrabiblical evidence to support his assertion of a global deluge and brusquely ignored all such evidence that would have weakened his position. To some extent Luther may be excused for his oversights, because he was living in the first stages of the discovery of the New World, and relevant extrabiblical evidence was by no means secure, but clearly no modern commentator could in good conscience follow this pattern.

Few scholars of the period who did take note of issues of animal migration and the capacity of the ark sought to resolve the problems they raised through appeals to miracle. On the whole, they turned instead to rational argument. Nor did knowledgeable scholars dispute the validity of the evidence, for instance by denying that many new animals were in fact found in the Americas. Rather, those who discussed the capacity of the ark at great length uniformly believed that the new evidence was consistent with the traditional view that the ark had housed all the world's animals. They grossly underestimated the actual number of different species around the globe, but their errors did not violate the scientific standards of the day. Given the level of taxonomic knowledge then available, they gave acceptable accounts of the adequacy of Noah's craft. Once again, however, their strategies are wholly inadequate to bear the weight of our more extensive body of extrabiblical knowledge today.

Even with the more limited evidence available in the seventeenth century, however, not a few scholars began to feel that the traditional interpretation of the biblical flood narrative faced severe challenges. The skeptic La Peyrère and orthodox scholars Stillingfleet,

Voss, and Poole all looked for alternatives to a universal deluge and found, at least to their own satisfaction, aspects of the biblical account that were consistent with the idea of a localized flood. More than three hundred years later, some Christians are still resistant to rethinking their own approach to the flood narrative along these lines, perhaps because they have not felt the weight of extrabiblical evidence as these scholars did.

5. *Diluvial Cosmogonies and the Beginnings of Geology*

By the end of the seventeenth century, intellectual energy that had been devoted to calculating the size of the ark was largely spent. Despite continuing discoveries of new animal species, scholars turned away from considerations of the increasingly intractable problems that these discoveries posed to a traditional interpretation of the biblical flood narrative. Janet Browne has suggested that this change in interest may have been the result of an unconscious disinclination to grapple with problems that had become increasingly more difficult to deal with in an intellectually respectable fashion.[1] In any event, the scholarly community as a whole shifted its interest from the issues of the ark's capacity and animal migration to the geological effects of the flood.

Numerous writers, especially in Great Britain, began to develop scenarios of early earth history in terms of mechanical second causes. Inspired by the new attitude of scientific curiosity about the world and no longer content solely with appeals to the authority of the Bible, many Christian scholars wanted to go beyond the bare biblical statements that God had created the world and then sent a great flood to devastate it. On the whole, they continued to read Genesis as literal, divinely inspired history; they did not want to replace or modify the authority of the Bible but rather to supplement it by fleshing out the outline of events only lightly sketched in Scripture. They began with general attributions of such terrestrial features as mountains, valleys, rocks, strata, and fossils to the effects of creation and the flood. But, captivated by the new understanding of the world developed by Descartes, Galileo, Kepler,

---

1. See chap. 1 of Browne's *Secular Ark* (New Haven: Yale University Press, 1983).

Boyle, and later Newton, these scholars expanded their understanding of the course of creation and the flood in terms of an intricate machine-like earth, attributing its motion, behavior, and history to mechanical interactions among discrete particles. The results of their new learning turned up in numerous global deluge theories published during the late seventeenth and early eighteenth centuries. During this period, the flood was at the center of mainstream theoretical earth science in Europe. In the hands of British scholars particularly, global flood theories became occasions for full-scale exercises in natural theology. The earth's physical features were presented as tangible evidence of the major biblical themes of creation, fall, flood, redemption, and the return of Christ. More specifically, they were presented either as clear evidence of the providential governance of a wise and beneficent God or as clear evidence of a world in decay because of the bondage of sin.

One major difficulty with any universal diluvial theory was finding a source of water adequate to submerge even the tallest peaks of the world. Calculations of the time indicated that a complete exhaustion of all the world's clouds would produce enough rainfall to cover the globe to a depth of only a few inches. Many diluvial theorists identified the source of the additional water as a subterranean abyss — a storehouse of water they associated with biblical references to the "deep." They argued that natural springs provided visible evidence of this underground ocean. Kircher claimed that vast reservoirs of water were released from the center of the earth when the flood began and that the ensuing devastation eliminated several land bridges. Matthew Hale appealed to the ancient belief that the antediluvian earth was smoother than it is now so that less water from the abyss would have been needed to submerge the entire surface. Even Matthew Poole spoke of a subterranean water source in his commentary on Genesis.

Most writers wanted to describe the physical means by which the abyss was tapped when the fountains of the great deep were broken up, and so was born a tradition of theories of the earth featuring the deluge. British theories of the earth were initiated by a Cambridge divine, Thomas Burnet (1635-1715), with his controversial volume *The Sacred Theory of the Earth*.[2] Burnet's grand vision encompassed the entire

---

2. The original title was *The Theory of the Earth Containing an Account of the Original of the Earth, and of all the General Changes Which It Hath Already Undergone, or Is to Undergo Till the Consummation of All Things.* The work was first issued in Latin in 1681, and the first English translation appeared in 1684.

   For a summary of the views of Burnet and several other diluvialists discussed

sweep of earth's physical history from the creation to the consummation of all things. He believed that the present globe differed from the original earth; he maintained that mountains, "great ruines," and ocean basins were evidences of a disordered, imperfect world, a result of the fallenness of humanity and the judgment of God. He asserted that the transformation from order to disorder occurred during Noah's deluge.

For Burnet the key question was the source of the water. Previous attempts to identify an adequate source in terms of second causes had failed, and Burnet agreed that the problem should not be avoided by asserting that God had created and annihilated the flood waters ad hoc. He found his solution in the hypothesis of a subterranean abyss. He believed that the original globe had developed into a layered structure out of the "chaos" of Genesis 1:2. Following Descartes's *Principles of Philosophy,* Burnet argued that the original chaos settled out with the help of gravity, the heavy particles sinking and the lighter particles floating.[3] The end result, he wrote, was a concentrically stratified earth the central core of which was surrounded by a subterranean abyss of waters in turn covered by the inhabited rocky shell. Burnet read Psalm 24:2 ("He founded the Earth upon the Seas, and establish'd it upon the Floods") and 136:6 ("He stretched out the Earth above the Waters") as clearly endorsing the existence of such an abyss.

After humanity sinned, the sun gradually warmed the globe, causing expansion, said Burnet. The pressure of the abyss produced

---

in this chapter, see Davis A. Young, "Scripture in the Hands of Geologists (Part One)," *Westminster Theological Journal* 49 (1987): 1-34; Don Cameron Allen, *The Legend of Noah* (Urbana, Ill.: University of Illinois, 1949), pp. 92-112; Marjorie Hope Nicolson, *Mountain Gloom and Mountain Glory: The Development of the Aesthetics of the Infinite* (Ithaca, N.Y.: Cornell University Press, 1959), pp. 184-270; Gordon L. Davies, *The Earth in Decay: A History of British Geomorphology, 1578-1878* (New York: American Elsevier, 1969); Clarence Glacken, *Traces on the Rhodian Shore* (Berkeley and Los Angeles: University of California Press, 1967), pp. 375-428; Roy Porter, *The Making of Geology: Earth Science in Britain, 1660-1815* (Cambridge: Cambridge University Press, 1977), chap. 3; Richard Huggett, *Cataclysms and Earth History* (Oxford: Clarendon Press, 1989), chap. 4; Evelyn Stokes, "The Six Days and the Deluge: Some Ideas on Earth History in the Royal Society of London, 1660-1775," *Earth Science Journal* 3 (1969): 13-39; and David C. Kubrin, "Providence and the Mechanical Philosophy" (Ph.D. diss., Cornell University, 1969).

3. See René Descartes, *Principles of Philosophy,* trans. Valentine R. Miller and Reese P. Miller (Boston: Kluwer, 1983). Part four of the *Principles* is devoted to a discussion of how the earth and similar bodies could develop by means of the interaction of various kinds of particles. Descartes included cross-sectional diagrams illustrating his speculations that the earth's internal structure comprised a series of layers.

fissures on the underside of the solid crust. The propagation of these cracks was perfectly timed by divine providence so that the climax of the process coincided with the peak of human wickedness. At that moment, the earth's crust was disrupted and an enormous volume of waters rushed from the abyss, completely overflowing the surface. Huge slabs of crust tilted and foundered into the abyss. Mountains were formed by the uptilted edges of these slabs, and the depressed areas became ocean basins. Burnet saw scriptural evidence for this activity in Job 38:8 ("Or who shut up the Sea with doors when it brake forth, as if it had issu'd out of a womb?") "Who can doubt," wrote Burnet, "but this was at the breaking open of the *Fountains of the Abysse?*" The beginning and ending of the deluge were marked by repeated "goings and comings" of the waves.[4]

Burnet went on to explain that at the conclusion of the flood, the waters settled into the newly formed ocean basins and ultimately drained back into the subterranean abyss, which was connected to the ocean floor by channelways and cavities that had been formed by the collapse of the crust. The existence of such cavities was abundantly proved, he said, by the existence of caves, volcanoes, and earthquakes. He argued that the Mediterranean and Caspian Seas would overflow were they not connected to the oceans by means of underground passages, since they have no significant surface outlets.[5] Burnet made no effort to incorporate fossils into his theory.

Prior to publication Burnet had solicited Isaac Newton's advice. While suggesting alternatives on a number of points, Newton wrote to Burnet that he considered the theory "most plausible" — indeed, more probable than his own conjectures.[6] And Burnet's theory impressed others for decades to come. Virtually everyone characterized *The Sacred Theory* as a literary masterpiece. But the volume also drew a firestorm of criticism from a range of British clerics and natural philosophers. Herbert Croft (1603-1691), the bishop of Hereford, was convinced that Burnet had done severe injustice to the Word of God by failing to pay sufficient attention to the details of the biblical text. John Beaumont, a student of fossils and member of the Royal Society,

4. Burnet, *The Sacred Theory of the Earth* (London: Centaur Press, 1965), pp. 77-78.

5. For Burnet's views on underground passageways, see *The Sacred Theory of the Earth*, pp. 98-99.

6. See letters of Newton to Burnet dated January 1681, in *The Correspondence of Isaac Newton*, vol. 2, ed. Herbert W. Turnbull (Cambridge: Cambridge University Press, 1960), pp. 329-34.

was critical of Burnet's science. Others tried to improve on his explanation of the deluge.[7]

Among the more irenic critics was Robert Hooke (1635-1703), the great British scientist whose accomplishments were overshadowed only by those of the greater Newton. Like his contemporaries Lhwyd, Ray, Lister, and Steno, Hooke sought a sensible explanation for the existence of apparently organic remains in mountains far from the sea. In a 1688 lecture, Hooke indicated that Burnet's version of the flood was inadequate to account for either fossils or rock strata. Hooke contended that the flood did not last long enough to produce the effects that Burnet described. Hooke attributed the location of fossils to the upheaval of the seabed by successive earthquakes. In a world in which mountains were clearly being denuded by rivers and streams, he reasoned, everything would have been leveled by now if there were not some mechanism at work re-elevating the hills.[8]

Hooke argued that the fossil shells found on mountainsides were the remains of marine animals that had lived in seas before the time of the flood and that this ancient sea bottom was elevated during the violence of the flood. His view of the structure of the earth was largely similar to that of Burnet except that he envisioned antediluvian seas. He maintained that God created *two* different firmaments — the firmament of heaven (i.e., the earth's atmosphere) and a firmament of earth separating the waters above (i.e., the primordial seas) from the waters below (i.e., the waters of the abyss). When Genesis speaks of the Spirit of God brooding over the waters at the time of creation, said Hooke, the reference is to the waters above.

Hooke argued that the flood produced great changes to the surface of the earth. The waters of the subterranean abyss thrust up the overlying shell, elevating the primordial seabeds along with their accumulated sediments and the remains of dead animals preserved as fossils. At the same time, the primeval continental landmasses sank and were deluged by water from the displaced ocean basins. Thus, according to Hooke, the present continents are uplifted remnants of antediluvian seafloors, while the present ocean floors are the submerged remnants of antediluvian landmasses.[9]

7. See, e.g., Herbert Croft, *Some Animadversions upon a Book Intituled the Theory of the Earth* (London, 1685), and John Beaumont, *Considerations on a Book Entituled the Theory of the Earth, publisht by Dr. Burnet* (London, 1693).

8. See Davies, *The Earth in Decay*, pp. 39-40, 86-91.

9. See Hooke, *Lectures and Discourses of Earthquakes and Subterraneous Eruptions* (1705; reprint, New York: Arno Press, 1978). Although many of Hooke's

Burnet received a more hostile treatment from Erasmus Warren (d. 1718), the rector of Worlington. In a 1690 book entitled *Geologia*, Warren launched a devastating broadside. Although Burnet professed belief in a literal creation, paradise, fall, and universal deluge, Warren was convinced that he did not advocate a sufficiently literal interpretation of the Bible on these points and charged that "the *Theorist* has assaulted *Religion*, and that in the very *foundation* of it."[10] Burnet's chaos was too chaotic and formless for Warren's tastes. Moreover, contrary to Burnet's assertions, Warren believed that Genesis 1 clearly implied that the antediluvian earth had both mountains and seas. And he stated that Burnet had misinterpreted Psalm 24:2 and 136:6: these verses speak not of the superposition of land on water but of the juxtaposition of land by the sea, said Warren; when the Bible speaks of "the great deep," it is not describing a subterranean abyss.

Warren did agree with Burnet that God had not created new quantities of water at the time of the flood, though he had his own reasons: (1) the initial act of creation was complete in itself, and any further creation would imply that it was originally imperfect and unfinished; (2) God reveals in Scripture the agents he used to produce the flood, and he does not specify any miraculous superadditions; and (3) there was in any case no need for additional waters, miraculous or otherwise. Burnet had greatly overestimated the amount of water required for the flood. Warren argued that the deluge could not have involved the total destruction of the world, for if it had, the rivers of the Garden of Eden would have been completely obliterated, and Moses would not have bothered to mention them. He argued that Burnet had misinterpreted Genesis 7:20 when he said that the summits of all the world's mountains had been covered with at least fifteen cubits of water, and he then proceeded to indulge in some rather pointedly nonliteral interpretation of his own, asserting that the text actually meant to say only that the general landscape was submerged to a depth of fifteen cubits. At their peak, the floodwaters covered only the lower flanks of the foothills, said Warren, and the mountaintops were un-

---

ideas about fossils and the deluge predate the issuance of Burnet's book, *Lectures and Discourses* also contains some later material in which Hooke evaluates Burnet's hypothesis.

10. Warren, in the preface to *Geologia; or, A Discourse concerning the Earth before the Deluge, Wherein the Form and Properties Ascribed to It, in a Book Intituled 'The Theory of the Earth,' Are Excepted against and It Is Made Appear, That the Dissolution of that Earth Was Not the Cause of the Universal Flood* (1690; reprint, New York: Arno Press, 1978).

touched. He suggested that the waters had come from caves in the primeval mountains that God had used as a stronghold since the beginning of the world. God produced the flood by opening these caves and allowing the long-trapped waters to rush down the mountainsides and cover all the low-lying territory.[11]

A more influential treatment appeared in *An Essay toward a Natural History of the Earth* by John Woodward (1665-1722), professor of physick in Gresham College.[12] As a leading naturalist, Woodward wished to put his thoughts about terrestrial history on a firmer observational basis than Burnet offered. Through extensive examination of rock outcrops in Britain and voluminous correspondence with naturalists around the world, Woodward had become more familiar than either Burnet or Warren with the layered structure of the earth's rocks. He had studied fossils as well and concluded that they were the remains of organisms that had perished in the deluge. More generally, Woodward's natural theology grew out of a perspective that was fundamentally different from Burnet's. Gordon Davies has observed that Burnet viewed God as a judge who ordained "a progressive, punitive decay of the entire universe" and so he envisioned the flood "as merely one terrible episode in this universal degeneration of Nature." In contrast, says Davies, Woodward's teleological interpretation impelled him "to seek the divine benevolence even in the tumult of the Flood." In Woodward's view of the deluge, the element of judgment was secondary to the idea that God used the flood to reorder the world for the benefit of human beings.[13]

Woodward was more concerned with the effects of the flood than with its mechanism. He simply proposed in passing that the flood was caused by the overflow of the subterranean abyss and moved on to describe in more detail what happened once the earth was submerged. He theorized that the surface soil and rocks of the earth were "dissolved" into fine constituent particles or "corpuscles" by the surging waters. Because of the "dissolution," the flood consisted of a mixture of water, fine particles of rock, and suspended organic remains.

11. Warren, *Geologia*, pp. 300-303.
12. Woodward, *An Essay toward a Natural History of the Earth and Terrestrial Bodies, Especially Minerals, as Also of the Sea, Rivers, and Springs, with an Account of the Universal Deluge and of the Effects That It Had upon the Earth* (1695; reprint, New York: Arno Press, 1978). For background on Woodward, see Joseph M. Levine, *Dr. Woodward's Shield* (Berkeley and Los Angeles: University of California Press, 1977).
13. Davies, *The Earth in Decay*, pp. 79-80.

Toward the end of the flood period, the suspended matter settled out
— first the heaviest particles and then increasingly lighter particles.
After the floodwaters returned to the abyss, the earth's surface was
covered with layers of different kinds of particles — strata of sandstone,
limestone, coal, and other rock types. Because Woodward started with
the assumption that the heaviest particles in the flood mixture would
have settled out first, he reasoned that in any given geological formation, the bottommost strata would have the highest density and the
topmost would have the lowest density. The remains of plants and
animals that were trapped in the accumulating strata should presumably also have drifted into their resting places in order of specific
gravity before hardening there to become fossils.

Despite long-lived influence on biblical commentators, Woodward's interpretation of the biblical flood was subjected to as much
criticism as Burnet's theory. Edward Lhwyd dismissed the *Essay* as a
romantic theory full of whimsy and absurdity. John Ray objected to
Woodward's "presumptuous manner." John Arbuthnot (1667-1735), a
satirist skilled in mathematics and experimental philosophy who eventually became a member of the Royal Society, the College of Physicians,
and the Scriblerians, was not impressed by Woodward's efforts either and
took him to task in a pamphlet, concluding that his "Alternations of the
Earth" were all "contrary to the Laws of Nature, and consequently
exclude the Philosophy of Second Cause."[14] He accused Woodward of
having conveniently sidestepped several pressing questions: What
brought the water from the abyss to the surface? What substance took
the place of the abyssal water that had abandoned the internal cavity of
the earth? What force could at the same time be potent enough to
dissolve rock and gentle enough to spare animal and vegetable tissue?
Why didn't the dissolved matter fall into the cavity of the abyss when it
began to settle out? How were the strata solidified? And what brought
about the disruption of strata? Arbuthnot convincingly demonstrated
that Woodward had indeed breezed past some critical issues. Of particular importance was Arbuthnot's claim that observation did not support
Woodward's sweeping assertion that rock strata and fossils are arranged
on the basis of specific gravity. After describing a 232-foot-deep pit in
Amsterdam in which individual strata showed considerable variation in
specific gravity, Arbuthnot tartly concluded,

14. Arbuthnot, *An Examination of Dr. Woodward's Account of the Deluge,
etc. with a Comparison between Steno's Philosophy and the Doctor's, in the Case
of Marine Bodies Dug out of the Earth* (London, 1697).

It is strange that the Laws of Gravity, which have been violated in so many Particulars, in raising the Water of the Abyss, and making a lighter Body, descend in its Room; in sustaining Minerals in Water, and stopping them in their Descent before they reach'd the Centre; in placing the heaviest solids in the upper Strata, etc. I say, it is strange the same Laws of Gravity should place a few Shells with as much Nicety, as the Doctor does in his Collection, not transgressing so far as a fifteenth Part.[15]

Arbuthnot allowed that he much preferred the treatises of Moses and Steno to Woodward's *Essay*.

Naturalist Fettiplace Bellers of the Royal Society of London also made the telling point that rock strata do not follow the order of specific gravity as Woodward asserted but that denser strata commonly lie above lower-density rocks. Despite the evident flaws in Woodward's arguments, however, he was defended by such individuals as John Harris and was for many years cited by both naturalists and theologians as having established the case for a universal deluge.[16]

Subsequent to the 1687 publication of Isaac Newton's landmark *Principia*, a number of scholars, including Edmund Halley (1656-1722) and William Whiston (1667-1752), grounded their diluvial conceptions on his sound mathematical and physical principles. In 1694 Halley (for whom the famous comet was named) addressed the Royal Society of London on the subject of the flood. He judged that fossil remains "far and above the Sea" constituted proof that the flood had indeed been universal, and he dismissed the presumption of a special creation and annihilation of waters as the most difficult hypothesis of all. God generally used natural means to bring about his will, noted Halley. And since forty days of rain could not begin to cover the earth, the Genesis narrative must be referring to some extraordinary fall of water in one great mass. Halley proposed that the shock of a closely passing comet could have caused a catastrophic overflow of the ocean onto land and an alteration of the earth's axial alignment. The shock from such an encounter would have caused the sea to run violently toward

15. Arbuthnot, *An Examination of Dr. Woodward's Account of the Deluge*, pp. 213-14.

16. See Bellers, "A Description of the Several Strata of Earth, Stone, Coal, &c. Found in a Coal-Pit at the West End of Dudley in Staffordshire," *Philosophical Transactions of the Royal Society of London* 27 (1710): 541-44; and Harris, *Remarks on Some Late Papers Relating to the Universal Deluge and to the Natural History of the Earth* (London, 1697).

the point "where the Blow was received," said Halley, dragging along with it the seabottom and piling it up into mountains on the land. Then the "Heap of Waters would return towards the opposite Parts of the Earth," moving successively in one direction and then another until the material it transported at last came "to settle in such a Manner as we now observe in the Structure of the superficial Parts of the Globe."[17] Halley delayed publication of his lecture for three decades, no doubt fearing controversy. Burnet's experience could not have been lost on him, and he must have known that the Church of England was not yet prepared to dismiss the role of miracle in the deluge.

William Whiston was, like Isaac Newton, an anti-trinitarian who harbored strong millenarian hopes. Much influenced by Newton's physics, Halley's work on comets, and Woodward's studies on strata and fossils, Whiston published *A New Theory of the Earth* in 1696. Prior to publication Whiston had sent the manuscript to Newton for his perusal. Newton was so impressed that he used his influence to have Whiston appointed as his successor as Lucasian Professor of Mathematics at Cambridge, a position from which Whiston was later dismissed. He also later fell out of favor with Newton. Whiston placed the global deluge within the framework of the very latest developments in physics, emphasizing the major role that comets likely played at the beginning of terrestrial history, at the time of the fall, and during the deluge.

Whiston hypothesized that the earth originally formed from a large comet and that this is what Genesis 1:2 is referring to when it speaks of "the great deep." He believed that the comet differentiated into a layered earth in the fashion proposed by Descartes and Burnet — the settling process of particles of different specific gravities produced a planet made up of a central core surrounded by a subterranean watery abyss which in turn was surrounded by a rocky shell. He asserted that the primitive earth rotated only once a year on an upright axis, citing several biblical texts in defense of this radical assertion. Earth's original condition was irreversibly changed by the flood, which, Whiston specified, took place on Thursday, November 27, the seventeenth day of the second month from the autumnal equinox, when the planet passed through the atmosphere and tail of another great comet for a period of "about 10 or 12 hours." This passage had the effect of opening

17. Halley, "Some Considerations about the Cause of the Universal Deluge," *Philosophical Transactions of the Royal Society of London* 33 (1724): 118-23. He delivered the lecture to the Royal Society on 12 December 1694.

the floodgates of heaven, as tremendous torrents of rain from the comet's atmosphere fell to earth. The passage of the comet also distorted the shape of the earth from spherical to elliptical by creating enormous tides in both the subterranean abyss and the outer rocky shell. Because of its greater rigidity, the rocky shell was unable to deform as readily as the abyss. Severe stresses caused extensive fissuring of the shell, and where it was pushed downward onto the abyss, subterranean waters were forced up through the fractures onto the surface. The combination of torrential cometary rains and the outflowing of the abyss redistributed surface features. As floodwaters drained, said Whiston, strata and fossils were redeposited in essentially Woodwardian fashion.[18]

Oxford's Savilian Professor of Astronomy John Keill (1671-1721) was critical of the rationalistic approach of a number of the flood theorists, including Burnet and Whiston.[19] Gordon Davies has characterized Keill as "a deeply religious Newtonian, who was convinced that many Scriptural events are not amenable to scientific explanation." He was generally disinclined to "import science into religion" and specifically wanted to keep the deluge solely within the domain of theology. Keill argued against Whiston that a passing comet would have no effect on the subterranean abyss even if it did produce great oceanic tides. He also argued that there would not be sufficient pressure in a comet's tail to convert it into rain. He dismissed Burnet's theory as fanciful and insufficiently empirical, pointing out the weaknesses in his theories of the mechanics of external crust formation, an originally vertical axis of rotation, antediluvian rivers, and the origin of mountains. Keill showed mathematically that Burnet's external crust could never form because the solid particles would not float on liquid like clay flakes but would sink as soon as they coagulated. Genesis 4 spoke of antediluvian human beings using iron tools, noted Keill, so the original crust must have contained iron — and yet if Burnet were correct, the heavy iron particles would have quickly sunk through the subterranean abyss and could not have been preserved in the external crust. Davies notes the irony that "Keill, the scientist, was eager to invoke supernatural forces in explanation of events in Earth-history,

18. Whiston, *A New Theory of the Earth* (1696; reprint, New York: Arno Press, 1978). For background on Whiston, see James E. Force, *William Whiston: Honest Newtonian* (Cambridge: Cambridge University Press, 1985).

19. See Keill, *An Examination of the Reflections on the Theory of the Earth, Together with a Defence of the Remarks on Mr. Whiston's New Theory* (Oxford, 1699).

while Burnet, the cleric, was equally eager to demonstrate the entire sufficiency of natural processes."[20]

Although largely a British enterprise, diluvialism was not restricted to England. In Zurich, for example, the Swiss doctor, mathematics instructor, and student of natural history J. J. Scheuchzer (1672-1733) had been strongly influenced by Woodward's diluvial views.[21] During his early career he believed that fossils were sports of nature, but after his conversion to Woodward's position, he penned a clever treatise entitled *The Fishes' Complaint and Vindication* (1708) in which he ridiculed the medieval view that fossils were inorganic mimics of living creatures. He presented his position using fossilized fish as proponents of the view that fossils were remains of once-living organisms. Scheuchzer's fish complained about being treated by many thinkers as mere freaks of nature. They insisted that they be recognized as true animals that had died during the deluge. The fish claimed to have suffered along with mankind during the great flood and asked to be accorded some dignity on that account. In support of his fish story, Scheuchzer described some large vertebrate fossils that he claimed might be the remains of one of the human sinners who perished in the waters of Noah. A few years later, Scheuchzer submitted a letter to *Philosophical Transactions* announcing the discovery of fossilized humans, and shortly thereafter (1726) he published a brief treatise describing a fossil skeleton found in a German quarry that he believed to be human. Here at last were the remains of an entire individual giant who had perished in the debacle, he said. Long after his death, Scheuchzer's identification ultimately proved to be the debacle, for the skeleton was properly identified by anatomist Georges Cuvier as an extinct giant salamander. The human witness of the deluge had been exterminated once again![22]

Diluvial cosmogonies continued apace in the British Isles during the early eighteenth century. John Hutchinson (1674-1737), who served for a time as an assistant of John Woodward, was concerned that contemporary empirical science was too rationalistic and was

20. Davies, *The Earth in Decay*, p. 73.

21. See Melvin E. Jahn, "Some Notes on Dr. Scheuchzer and on *Homo diluvii testis,*" in *Toward a History of Geology,* ed. Cecil J. Schneer (Cambridge: MIT Press, 1969), pp. 193-213.

22. See Scheuchzer, *The Fishes' Complaint and Vindication* (Zurich: Gessner, 1708); *Homo Diluvii Testis* (Zurich: Burkli, 1726); and "Sceleton duorum Humanorum petrefactorum pars," *Philosophical Transactions of the Royal Society of London* 34 (1726): 38-39.

gradually replacing biblical authority. To counter this trend, Hutchinson tried to establish his own version of a "biblical physics" that could compete on equal footing with Newtonian physics.[23] Self-consciously setting his views over against those of Newton, he issued a book entitled *Moses' Principia* that presents a view of the flood somewhat similar to that of Burnet.

Despite the work of Hutchinson and others, however, by the middle of the eighteenth century flood cosmogony was waning as mainstream theoretical earth history. Perhaps the last competent treatment of the deluge as the principal causative agent for the world's geological strata was *A Treatise on the Deluge*, published in 1761 by Hutchinson's disciple Alexander Catcott (1725-1779).[24] Catcott argued that the worldwide deluge traditions, including those of India, China, and America, were evidence for the universality of the biblical account. He rejected the idea that fossiliferous sedimentary rocks were deposited in a series of partial deluges on the grounds that the pyramids of Egypt, which he believed dated back to the time of Noah, before the time of known limited deluges, were constructed of fossil-bearing rocks. Catcott went on to develop a theory of the deluge that included flooding from the abyss and Woodward's thesis that the world's fossil-bearing strata had settled from suspended material in the floodwaters. He claimed that pyramidal mountain peaks were formed when draining floodwaters rushed through thick stacks of soft layered sediments, cutting out valleys and leaving peaks composed of stratified material. Catcott's topographic theory received experimental support when he successfully reproduced small-scale mountain topography in a large box of layered sediments through which streams of water were allowed to flow.

But Catcott also addressed a variety of problems associated with a global flood. As a competent field worker, he was bothered by the occurrence of steeply tilted rock layers and the existence of certain kinds of rock that had plainly experienced a complex history.[25] He

23. See Hutchinson, *Moses' Principia* (London, 1724-1727), p. 57. See also G. N. Cantor, "Revelation and the Cyclical Cosmos of John Hutchinson," in *Images of the Earth: Essays in the History of the Environmental Sciences,* ed. Ludmilla Jordanova and Roy Porter (Chalfont St. Giles: British Society for the History of Science, 1979), pp. 3-22; and Michael Neve and Roy Porter, "Alexander Catcott: Glory and Geology," *British Journal for the History of Science* 10 (1977): 37-60.

24. See Catcott, *A Treatise on the Deluge,* 2d ed. (London: E. Allen, 1768).

25. Neve and Porter discuss in detail the concerns and reservations that Catcott had about the deluge theory as indicated by his unpublished field notebooks ("Alexander Catcott: Glory and Geology").

avoided facing these geological problems in his *Treatise*, although he was willing to deal with some of the issues raised by the discovery of the Americas. He agreed with Lipsius and Hale that no one would have transported dangerous animals such as rattlesnakes and lions from the Middle East to distant habitats, so he concluded that such species must have migrated overland shortly after the flood. Then there was the question of human populations in America. Catcott suggested continental splitting as the solution. He read Genesis 10:25 as indicating "that the Earth was *split* or *divided asunder* for a very great extent, and the *Sea came between*, in the days of *Peleg*." Surely on viewing the situation of America, disjoined from the Old World by an immense sea, said Catcott, one would "not be backward in allowing, that *This* was the *grand Division* intended by the Passage under consideration." He suggested that the Greek legend of the sinking of Atlantis probably reflected a memory of this division of the earth. Africa and America were once joined by a very narrow gulf, he said, and about three hundred years after the flood the earth was divided by means of an earthquake and the middle land sunk beneath the ocean.[26]

Analysis and Application

From the mid-seventeenth to the mid-eighteenth century, a range of British mathematicians, naturalists, and clerics from the Church of England attempted to demonstrate that belief in a global biblical deluge was perfectly compatible with extrabiblical knowledge and the latest theoretical developments in mechanistic science. They maintained that the fact that such a deluge had occurred could now be established not only on the basis of biblical authority but also on mathematical and scientific grounds. Their various theories reflected different conceptions of natural theology, the roles of science and theology, and the bearing of Scripture on the interpretation of nature. Their diluvial cosmogonies provided a mainstream scientific paradigm that stimulated hard thought, biblical exegesis, widespread geological observation, and some of the earliest geological experiments.

But if these seventeenth-century cosmogonies were on the whole plausible given the limitations of the geological science of the day, they were nevertheless seriously flawed in other ways — perhaps most notably by the fact that their proponents based them on relatively small

26. Catcott, *A Treatise on the Deluge*, pp. 140-45.

bodies of favorable evidence and tended to ignore damaging evidence. The cosmogonists generally avoided the insurmountable problems of animal distribution and migration, for instance, and resisted determinations that geological strata are not arranged in order of specific gravity. On the other hand, the theorists were for the most part committed to providing honest scientific accounts of physical processes associated with the flood, and they resisted making appeals to miracle in order to resolve difficulties in those accounts.

In the end, the old diluvial cosmogonies fell victim to their own success. The genuine spirit of scientific inquiry that they engendered and stimulated gradually produced a wealth of geological discoveries that undercut the premises of diluvialism. All manner of different field observations indicated that geological strata could not be the remains of layers of soft sediments deposited together at the same time. Furthermore, the plethora of exegeses of the deluge account raised doubts in many scholarly minds about whether the Bible was being properly used in trying to settle questions of geological history. By the middle of the eighteenth century, few competent proponents of diluvialism remained.

The basic pattern of the attempts to accommodate extrabiblical information during this period is by now familiar. Scholars began with the assumption that the biblical flood narrative describes a literal universal deluge and then sought evidence of that event using the best scientific tools and evidence available to them. As evidence accumulated, however, their theories became increasingly untenable, and when that happened, all those who were dedicated to the truth of the matter — scientists and theologians alike — abandoned the discredited hypotheses and began to look elsewhere.

6. *The Collapse of Diluvial Cosmogonies and the Beginnings of Modern Geology*

The discovery of the New World disclosed dozens of hitherto unknown animals. Despite the serious problems raised for the concept of a global deluge by this new knowledge, Christian intellectuals of the sixteenth and seventeenth centuries continued to seek ways to explain the deluge in scientific terms. Even though some orthodox scholars such as Voss or Stillingfleet proposed a more restricted flood, the church at large felt little need to adjust its long-held view of a strictly literal universal flood. Christians rested secure in the belief that the calculations of respected scholars established the point that the ark could hold all known animals including those of the New World. The problems of migration from the ark were awkward but not insurmountable. There was no evidence to dispute the existence of former land bridges or to show that animals could not rapidly diversify because of environmental factors.[1] Moreover, some held out the hope that animals that had been found living only in the Americas might yet be discovered closer to the Middle East in still unexplored areas of Africa or Asia. All of which is to say that at the end of the seventeenth century, there was still not enough biological evidence to convincingly challenge traditional views of the capacity of the ark.

The same was the case with geological evidence. Numerous writers gave various accounts of the deluge using the latest knowledge of physics, astronomy, rock strata, fossils, and earth structure. Al-

---

1. Of course, the proposal of rapid diversification of animals after their emergence from the ark posed significant problems in its own right, since it presumes a rate of change vastly more accelerated than that presumed by any conventional evolutionary theory, and quite unaccountable in terms of any accepted understanding of biology.

though this evidence was adequate to uncover flaws in the details of various flood theories, it proved insufficient to challenge the basic thesis of a global deluge. Global diluvialism represented mainstream scientific thought in the late seventeenth and early eighteenth centuries.

Eighteenth-Century Commentary

Many outstanding British biblical commentators of the eighteenth century gave little hint of any awareness of the difficulties attendant on the discovery of the Americas. They showed even less inclination to modify their conception of the flood as derived by biblical exegesis. Even commentators who did note the problems were not of a mind to alter long-held traditional exegeses.

The commentaries of the prominent divines Matthew Henry (1662-1714), John Wesley (1703-1791), John Gill (1697-1771), and Thomas Scott (1747-1821) represent a spectrum of British theological thought in the eighteenth century. For example, in his classic *Commentary on the Holy Bible* (1706), the English Nonconformist minister Matthew Henry stated that the flood came 1,656 years after creation, that Noah did not need to collect the animals since they came of their own accord, and that secondary causes were probably used to supply floodwater.[2] Likely aware of calculations showing that rainfall alone could not have produced the requisite floodwater and possibly acquainted with the widely held views of the diluvialists, Henry wrote that the flood came from the abyss. During the flood the normal hostility between animals ceased, but afterward they reverted to true character. Henry also suggested that the tops of mountains may have been washed down somewhat by the waters and that the heat of the sun helped to dry up the waning waters. On the whole, he paid scant attention to extrabiblical evidence or to the problems that had plagued scholars during the previous century. Henry intended his commentary to be devotional and practical, and he expressly left the critical questions to Poole's *Synopsis*.

The great founder of Methodism, John Wesley, omitted virtually all dialogue with relevant authors and current debates about the nature of the deluge in his exegesis of the text. He simply asserted the universality of the flood, the preservation of all species aboard the ark,

---

2. Henry, *Commentary on the Holy Bible*, vol. 1 (1706; reprint, New York: Fleming H. Revell, n.d.).

and the ability of waters of the deep and rains to cover the earth fully. Once the flood was over, he said, the heat of the sun exhaled some of the water, and subterranean caverns soaked up the rest.[3] Several years later in his journal for 1770, Wesley expressed great admiration for Burnet's *Sacred Theory,* commenting that its account of the flood was "highly probable."[4]

In contrast, John Gill, the Baptist divine who pastored one church in Horsleydown for fifty-two years, displayed considerably more awareness of contemporary discussions. Gill believed that the flood legends of the Arabs, Chinese, Mexicans, Peruvians, and Brahmins confirmed the universality of the flood. He cited calculations by Buteo and Wilkins as establishing the point that the ark was spacious enough to have held the requisite animals and food. He maintained that plenty of source water was hiding in subterranean passages beneath such places as the Caspian and Black Seas as well as in the air. He specifically referred to one writer's assertion that "thick air is easily turned into water" and that the atmosphere might well extend as far as the moon. Gill calculated that if rain fell toward the earth at a rate of 250 miles per day, then in the allotted time of 40 days, "all the watery particles, which were 10,000 miles high, might descend upon the earth; and this alone might be more than sufficient to cover the highest mountains." Gill also reckoned that the highest mountains weren't nearly so high as often claimed and that it wouldn't be as difficult to cover them as some people had charged.[5]

Gill responded to concerns about animal migration by appealing to the ability of wild creatures to swim across narrow seas and to the notion that humans might have brought them across larger bodies of water in boats. And if these explanations would not suffice, he offered a backup argument: "What is it the power and providence of God cannot do, who could not be at a loss for ways and means to replenish a world in all the parts of it he had made desolate, when it was his pleasure?"[6]

The Anglican commentator Thomas Scott affirmed that unnamed "learned men" had shown that the ark was more than adequate

3. Wesley, *Explanatory Notes upon the Old Testament,* vol. 1 (Bristol: William Pine, 1745).

4. See the journal entry for January 1770 in *The Works of John Wesley,* vol. 3 (Grand Rapids: Zondervan, 1958), pp. 385-86.

5. Gill, *An Exposition of the Old Testament,* vol. 1 (London: W. H. Collingridge, 1852), pp. 42-45.

6. Gill, *An Exposition of the Old Testament,* p. 49.

to contain all the animals and their provisions. He further asserted that the ark was even large enough to have accommodated as many sinners as might have repented at the last moment. Scott dismissed as presumptuous attempts to explain the flood in terms of second causes. Yet despite his reluctance to discuss the mechanisms of the flood, he did suggest that at the conclusion of the debacle, the waters were in part evaporated "and in part ran off into the lower countries and the bed of the ocean, or sunk into caverns in the bowels of the earth." He insisted that despite the contentions of some learned men, the deluge was strictly universal and that even in his day, "traces of the deluge are found in all parts of the earth." Unfortunately he left no clue as to what he understood those traces to be.[7]

Generally speaking, eighteenth-century biblical commentators, like Luther and Calvin before them, made relatively little effort to engage either extrabiblical data or scientific discussions. They evidenced little sense of the difficult problems posed by the discovery of the New World and were willing to make confident assertions about the universality of the deluge on essentially textual grounds. They uncritically accepted diluvialism because it reinforced traditional conceptions of the deluge.

As the eighteenth century proceeded, however, the community of natural philosophers found it more difficult to sustain a belief in diluvialism. Despite Catcott's late efforts, mounting evidence was undermining attempts to account for all the earth's fossiliferous strata by means of a flood theory. Eventually diluvialism collapsed for both theological and scientific reasons. The stress on the theological side accumulated as individual texts of Scripture were used to support a variety of competing theories and speculations about earth history.[8] The fountains of the great deep (Gen. 7:11), for example, had been variously understood to refer to the abyss, comets, the ocean, and water from caves. These diverse interpretations and conflicting applications of the relevant texts to scientific problems of earth history led to a growing suspicion that the texts were being used improperly, that they were being pressed into answering categories of questions they were not meant to answer. Theologically oriented naturalists began to wonder openly if the inspiration of the Bible

---

7. Scott, *The Holy Bible* (New York: Collins & Hanny, 1832).

8. For an extended review of the interpretations of selected texts relevant to the deluge that were adopted within the diluvialist tradition, see Davis A. Young, "Scripture in the Hands of Geologists — Part One," *Westminster Theological Journal* 49 (1987): 1-34.

extended to the sphere of science. Did God give Scripture as a source of scientific information, they asked, or was it a book of redemption, theology, and morals? As the sense grew that Scripture provided no single, incontestable, infallible diluvial scenario, scholars began to back away from grandiose "biblically based" flood cosmogonies.

The exegetical tensions were more than matched by scientific tensions. Many thinkers sensed that diluvialism grew too much out of speculation and too little out of empirical evidence. Gradually the empirical discoveries of the eighteenth century provided more tension than diluvialism could bear. Important developments in the study of rock strata, spectacular fossil finds, and new knowledge about animal species and their relationships to their environment all fatally undermined diluvialism.

The Rise of Stratigraphy and Geomorphology

At first, the recognition that the earth's outer skin is typically stratified was readily integrated into theories of global diluvialism. John Woodward had stressed that stratification was widespread, and he, Hutchinson, Catcott, and others explained the strata as deposits of the receding deluge. As the eighteenth century progressed, however, stratigraphy increasingly became a stumbling block for diluvialism.

Despite Steno's important work on stratification, it was not until Woodward had emphasized the significance of layering that a number of people began to describe stratified outcrops and quarries in the *Philosophical Transactions of the Royal Society of London*. For example, in 1710, Fettiplace Bellers described strata in a coal pit at Dudley, Staffordshire, and included a table of specific gravities of the strata. John Strachey (1671-1743) contributed papers in 1719 and 1725 on strata in coal mines at Mendip in Somersetshire, and John Michell (1724-1793) discussed stratification in connection with earthquakes.[9] Occasionally, brief letters

9. Bellers, "A Description of the Several Strata of Earth, Stone, Coal, &c. Found in a Coal-Pit at the West End of Dudley in Staffordshire," *Philosophical Transactions of the Royal Society of London* 27 (1710): 541-44; Strachey, "A Curious Description of the Strata Observ'd in the Coal-Mines of Mendip in Somersetshire," *Philosophical Transactions of the Royal Society of London* 30 (1719): 968-73; Strachey, "An Account of the Strata in Coal-Mines, etc." *Philosophical Transactions of the Royal Society of London* 33 (1725): 395-98; Michell, "Conjectures concerning the Cause and Observations upon the Phaenomena of Earthquakes," *Philosophical Transactions of the Royal Society of London* 51 (1760): 566-634.

describing unconsolidated strata in surficial deposits were also published.[10] By mid-century, naturalists had begun to describe and map successions of rock strata on a large scale and to classify mountains on the basis of their groups of strata. Much of that work was done in continental Europe, where scholars were considerably less constrained by the demands of natural theology or the desire to produce biblical-scientific cosmogonies than were scholars in Great Britain.

In Italy, Antonio Vallisnieri (1661-1730), a physician, professor at the university in Padua, and fellow of the Royal Society of London since 1705, concluded from his examination of Alpine strata that the marine-looking strata were too widespread to be the product of Woodward's deluge. He suggested that water would need to cover the globe for a much longer time than the year of the deluge in order to lay down all the observed strata.[11] In 1740, Anton-Lazarro Moro (1687-1764), a Roman Catholic priest and naturalist, described mountains in terms of the presence or absence of stratification. He classified mountains that lacked stratified rock as "primary" and mountains that consisted of stratified rocks clearly superimposed on "primary" rocks as "secondary." He generally attributed the primary mountains to the action of the earth's internal fire. Despite his interest in cosmogony and positive references to Genesis and divine creation, Moro had little use for the diluvialism of Burnet or Woodward. According to Moro, "the deluge ought to be believed according to the Scripture, as a miracle, and not to be proved by natural rules."[12] A mining inspector and professor of mining in Venice, Giovanni Arduino (1714-1795) further developed Moro's classification in northern Italy by recognizing four different divisions. Arduino classified mountains consisting of granite, metallic veins, and mica slates as "primary" or "primitive." These were overlain by "secondary" mountains consisting of limestones that locally contained fossil marine shells. Above those strata were "tertiary" materials such as gravel, sand, clay, and marl containing abundant

---

10. E.g., James Kelly, "An Account of the Strata Met with in Digging for Marle, and of Horns Found under Ground in Ireland," *Philosophical Transactions of the Royal Society of London* 35 (1726): 122-23.

11. Vallisnieri, *Dei Corpi Marini che sui Monti si Trovano* (Venice, 1721). For a useful summary of the historical development of various classifications of mountains, see Frank Dawson Adams, *The Birth and Development of the Geological Sciences* (New York: Dover, 1954), and Rachel Laudan, *From Mineralogy to Geology: The Foundations of a Science, 1650-1830* (Chicago: University of Chicago, 1987).

12. Moro, *Dei Crostacei e Degli Altri Corpi Marini che si Trovano sui Monti Libri Due* (Venice: Ceremia, 1740).

marine remains. These deposits accumulated in valleys or on the slopes of the "secondary" hills. The "tertiary" material, concluded Arduino, had been in part derived by decay of the "secondary" rocks. Some volcanic layers were also interlayered with "tertiary" strata. The fourth category contained surface materials eroded from the mountains by the action of running water.[13]

German-born scientist-explorer Pierre Simon Pallas (1741-1811) occupied the chair of natural history in the Imperial Academy of St. Petersburg. At the request of Empress Catherine II he led an expedition to Siberia and described primitive, secondary, and tertiary mountains based on the efforts of previous investigators and his own explorations of the Ural and Altai mountains. Pallas believed that the classification of mountains was applicable to the Alps, the Apennines, the Caucasus, and several other ranges.[14]

Johann Gottlob Lehmann (1719-1767), a physician, copper producer, and professor of chemistry in St. Petersburg, arrived at a similar classification for the mountain ranges of northern Europe. Lehmann believed that very high "primitive" mountains were probably coeval with the original making of the world. Surrounding these mountains were "secondary" mountains that consisted of *Flötzgebirge* — flat layers of rock formed from water-borne sediments and exhibiting abundant quantities of fossils. Superimposed on these were local "accidents." Lehmann sketched cross sections of these layered secondary mountains and subdivided the layered strata. A Swedish chemist at Uppsala, Torbern Bergman (1735-1784), followed Lehmann's classification, and Georg Füchsel (1722-1773), a royal physician and devotee of mining, published detailed maps and cross sections of Lehmann's strata.[15]

The classification of Lehmann and Bergman was further developed and elevated to quasi-canonical status by Abraham G. Werner (1749-1817), an outstanding teacher at the Mining Academy of Freiberg, Saxony.[16] Like his predecessors, Werner used the terms *primary* or

13. Arduino, *Osservazione sulla Fisica Constituzione delle Alpi Venete* (1759).

14. Pallas, *Observations sur la Formation des Montagnes et les Changements arrives au Globe, particulierement de l'Empire Russe* (St. Petersburg, 1777).

15. Lehmann, *Versuch einer Geschichte von Flötzgeburgen* (Berlin, 1756). Füchsel, "Historia Terrae et Maris ex Historia Thuringiae per Montium Descriptionen Erecta," *Acta, Acad. Elect. Moguntinae zu Ehrfurt* 2 (1762): 44-209.

16. On Werner, see Laudan, *From Mineralogy to Geology*; Alexander M. Ospovat, "The Distortion of Werner in Lyell's *Principles of Geology*," *British Journal for the History of Science* 9 (1976): 190-98; and Mott T. Greene, *Geology in the Nineteenth Century* (Ithaca, N.Y.: Cornell University Press, 1982).

primitive for the oldest mountains *(Urgebirge).* He also employed Lehmann's term *Flötzgebirge.* However, he introduced a new category of "transition" strata *(Übergangsgebirge)* that included steeply inclined, unfossiliferous stratified slates and graywackes that lay above the primitive rocks but below the *Flötz* rocks. The *Flötz* rocks included limestone, gypsum, salt, coal, sandstone, and basalt. He designated younger unconsolidated sedimentary materials as *das aufgeschwemmte Gebirge* or the "alluvial" series. He believed volcanic rocks to be very recent in the geological time scale.[17]

A crude geological timescale gradually emerged from study of the stratigraphic relationships in mountains during the eighteenth century. Naturalists agreed that primitive rocks were the oldest because they lay beneath all others, that transition rocks (if they used that term) were a little younger, that secondary or *Flötz* rocks were younger yet because they lay atop primitive rocks, and that tertiary or alluvial rocks were younger still because they lay atop secondary formations. Individual strata could be distinguished within the various groupings, and their relative ages were determined by their position in a succession of strata. The irregular boundaries that separated primitive from secondary and secondary from tertiary rocks implied that deposition had not been continuous. The discontinuities between groupings of strata implied periodic interruption by uplifts and deposition by causes other than the flood. Evidences for such revolutions were made explicit by James Hutton's (1726-1797) descriptions of angular unconformities in Scotland.[18]

Naturalists and mining engineers involved in the classification schemes measured the thicknesses of strata, determined their lateral extent, and noted the regularity with which the various strata succeeded one another. Lehmann, Füchsel, and Pallas discovered that rock strata occurred in orderly sequences, that European sequences were commonly thousands of feet thick, and that in many instances individual

17. Werner, ed., *Brief Classification and Description of the Various Rocks*, trans. Alexander Ospovat (New York: Hafner Press, 1970).

18. Hutton, *Theory of the Earth*, vol. 1 (Edinburgh: Creech, 1795). At Siccar Point on the Scottish coast east of Edinburgh, at Jedburgh, and on the Isle of Skye, Hutton pointed out the phenomenon of the angular unconformity, a situation in which relatively horizontal rocks overlie the evidently eroded edges of steeply tilted layers. Hutton argued that such phenomena were evidence for important revolutions in earth history. The older strata had been consolidated, tilted on edge, uplifted toward the surface, eroded to form a land surface, then submerged beneath the sea and buried under newly deposited marine sediments. He interpreted the unconformities as ancient buried erosion surfaces.

formations could be traced for tens or hundreds of miles. The thickness, extent, and orderliness of stratigraphic successions, unrecognized in the heyday of diluvial cosmogonies, were increasingly difficult to account for in terms of a catastrophe presumed to have been marked by chaos, confusion, and turbulence. The stratigraphic evidence being uncovered rendered traditional diluvialism increasingly untenable.

Attempts were also made to explain the surface features of the landscape. It had been widely accepted for some time that rivers eroded mountainsides, and yet there were many mountain valleys throughout northern Europe that contain no rivers or at most small streams that scarcely seemed capable of having produced any major excavation. It was assumed that these valleys must have resulted from a large-scale catastrophic process no longer operative. Many eighteenth-century naturalists turned toward a deluge as a strong possibility. Surface deposits of gravel and sand found far from any existing river system were also considered by many to be evidence of a large inundation at some point in the past. Geological evidence was thus used to push the site of the flood's action from the strata to the earth's surface.

The Advent of Neptunism

Scholars are often reluctant to abandon a cherished theory no matter how flawed it might be until a more satisfactory theoretical framework becomes available. The demise of diluvial cosmogony during the eighteenth century was facilitated not only by the collection of new stratigraphic data but also by the emergence of neptunism as an alternative way of viewing the earth's history. Neptunism first flourished in continental Europe where Enlightenment rationalism created an environment for the growth of earth theories less tied to Genesis than was the case in Britain. Only later did neptunism catch on in Great Britain and America.

The fundamental thesis of neptunism was that the bulk of the earth's geological features could be accounted for in terms of the gradual diminishing of an ocean that covered the infant globe at creation. The theory had roots in the speculations of Descartes and the classical Greeks, but it did not begin to enjoy widespread acceptance until the eighteenth century, following the publication of a volume entitled *Telliamed* by a well-traveled French diplomat named Benoit de Maillet (1656-1738). Geological observations he made during his frequent travels in the Middle East and throughout the Mediterranean led de Maillet to postulate that rock formations had been laid down in a gradually lowering ocean over the course of millions of years.[19] French savant and director of the botanical garden in Paris Georges Louis Leclerc, Comte de Buffon (1707-1788), linked the theory of the recession of the ocean together in one grand cosmogony with his comprehensive explanation of biological and geological phenomena in terms of the gradual cooling of the globe from an originally incandescent state over a period of tens of thousands of years.[20] The suspicions that the British naturalists Lhwyd, Ray, and Hooke entertained in their letters that the earth was more than six thousand years old were made shockingly explicit by de Maillet and Buffon. And the Swedish botanist and taxonomist Carl Linnaeus (1707-1778) viewed both the occurrence of fossils far inland from the sea and the raised marine terraces along the Scandinavian coasts as evidence of a past diminution of the ocean.[21]

The neptunist theory received a definitive treatment by Werner. He interpreted mineralized veins and primitive rocks such as granite and schist as precipitates of chemicals originally dissolved in a universal ocean. Most neptunists agreed that primitive rocks were chemical precipitates, but Werner also believed that many of the stratified rocks, particularly those of a crystalline nature such as basalt, were also chemical in origin. He further maintained that the transition and *Flötz* rocks were a combination of chemical precipitates and mechanically

19. De Maillet, *Telliamed; or, Conversations between an Indian Philosopher and a French Missionary on the Diminution of the Sea,* ed. Albert V. Carozzi (Urbana, Ill.: University of Illinois Press, 1968). Although the work was written between 1692 and 1718, de Maillet delayed publication until 1748. Perhaps to avoid censure, he published the work anonymously and attributed his argument to a fictitious Indian philosopher named Telliamed (de Maillet spelled backward). See also Albert V. Carozzi, "De Maillet's *Telliamed* (1748): An Ultra-Neptunian Theory of the Earth," in *Toward a History of Geology,* ed. Cecil J. Schneer (Cambridge: MIT Press, 1969), pp. 80-99.

20. Buffon's global cooling hypothesis can be found in *The Natural History of Animals, Vegetables, and Minerals, with the Theory of the Earth in General* (London, 1976) and *Les Epoques de la Nature* (Paris: Editions du Museum, 1962).

21. For a brief discussion of Linnaeus, see chap. 1 of Janet Browne's *Secular Ark* (New Haven: Yale University Press, 1983). For detail on Linnaeus's life, see Tore Frangsmyr, *Linnaeus: The Man and His Work* (Berkeley and Los Angeles: University of California, 1983). Of special interest is a chapter on Linnaeus as a geologist. Both Linnaeus and his contemporary Anders Celsius had been somewhat influenced by Immanuel Swedenborg in their neptunist leanings. Linnaeus postulated that the receding ocean had been clogged with sargasso weed, thus damping wave action, calming the sea, and permitting sedimentation. The Scandinavian terraces that so impressed Linnaeus and fellow Swedish scientists are now known to have risen after the removal of glacial ice.

produced sediments. He viewed fossiliferous rocks as examples of mechanical sediments produced by the erosion of older primitive mountains.[22] Other neptunists regarded most of the layered *Flötz* rocks as mechanically derived sediments deposited on the surface of primitive mountains and subsequently tilted. Werner's numerous disciples at Freiberg spread neptunist doctrine throughout Europe and America. Neptunism boasted such prominent defenders as Jean Andre Deluc (1727-1817), Jean François d'Aubuisson (1769-1819), Leopold von Buch (1774-1852), Robert Jameson (1774-1854), and famed geographer Alexander von Humboldt (1765-1859).

Although neptunism largely replaced diluvialism as an explanation for the formation of layered rocks, interest in the Noachian flood was hardly dead. Diluvialism may have been dying out, but many scholars continued to believe that there was scientific evidence for the flood. Diluvialists such as Woodward, Whiston, Hutchinson, and Catcott had maintained that the biblical flood deposited the rocks now categorized as secondary and tertiary, or transition, *Flötz*, and alluvial. Neptunists variously attributed the formation of at least secondary and some tertiary deposits (or at least transition and *Flötz* deposits) to the action of a shrinking ocean that predated the biblical flood, but some of them still attributed tertiary or alluvial materials composed of gravel, sand, clay, and peat to the flood. Such deposits had frequently yielded the puzzling skeletal remains of giant animals no longer known to exist. Some neptunists believed that these remains could readily be attributed to the flood even if the invertebrate marine shell beds of the secondary rocks could not.

Discoveries of Vertebrate Remains

In 1728, Hans Sloane (1660-1753), the president of the Royal Society of London, summarized several of these peculiar animal finds.[23] Issues of the *Philosophical Transactions of the Royal Society of London* frequently contained notices of "strange bones," teeth, or horns that had accidentally been encountered during the digging of wells or ex-

---

22. Werner, *Brief Classification and Description of the Various Rocks*.
23. Sloane, "An Account of Elephants' Teeth and Bones Found Underground," *Philosophical Transactions of the Royal Society of London* 35 (1728): 457-71; and "Of Fossil Teeth and Bones of Elephants: Part the Second," *Philosophical Transactions of the Royal Society of London* 35 (1728): 497-514.

cavation for building foundations.[24] Particularly intriguing were a growing number of discoveries of teeth, tusks, and bones belonging to a strikingly elephant-like creature.[25] Some of the discoveries were in Europe, but reports of remains of an elephant-like creature kept trickling in from the frozen expanses of Siberia. In a 1692 Siberian expedition, Ysbrand Ides, Peter the Great's envoy to China, not only encountered tusks and bones but saw remnants of a partially preserved carcass embedded in frozen ground. Ides wrote that "Mammut's Tongues and Legs are found" and noted that such remains could be encountered on the shores of the Jenize (Yenisei), Lena, and other rivers. One of his companions found a head when a frozen piece of riverbank collapsed. Most of the flesh was rotten. Ides recounted an old native belief that the mammoths "continually, or at least by reason of the very hard Frosts, mostly live under Ground, where they go backwards and forwards," and they died when they came in contact with air. In contrast, said Ides, the Russians believed that there were elephants in the area when the climate was warmer before the deluge. After the flood, the air became cold enough to freeze them, and their "bones have lain frozen in the Earth ever since, and so are preserved from Putrefaction till they thaw." Ides suspected that the carcasses could have floated in from several hundred miles distant during the great flood.[26]

Additional Siberian mammoth finds were reported in the early eighteenth century. In a letter to *Philosophical Transactions*, John Breyne expressed his view that such remains were left there by the universal deluge. When several large bones and a tooth were dug up in the Hudson River valley of North America, Puritan leader Cotton Mather attributed them to an antediluvian giant. In 1739, elephant tusks, molars, and bones were discovered in a marsh near the Ohio River in Kentucky. A 1765 expedition to the site now known as Big

---

24. E.g., "Chartham News; or, A Brief Relation of Some Strange Bones There Lately Digged Up, in Some Grounds of Mr. John Somner's in Canterbury," *Philosophical Transactions of the Royal Society of London* 22 (1701): 882-93.

25. For more extended discussions of the early discoveries of vertebrate remains in surficial deposits and the ways in which they were interpreted, see chap. 4 in John C. Greene's *The Death of Adam* (Ames, Iowa: Iowa State University Press, 1959); chaps. 1-6 in Robert W. Howard's *The Dawnseekers* (New York: Harcourt Brace Jovanovich, 1975); and Evelyn Stokes, "The Six Days and the Deluge: Some Ideas on Earth History in the Royal Society of London, 1660-1775," *Earth Science Journal* 3 (1969): 13-39.

26. Ides, *Three Years Travels from Moscow Over-land to China* (London: W. Freeman, 1706).

Bone Lick turned up huge amounts of skeletal material, and two years later an account of some of the tusks and grinders was presented to the Royal Society of London. In 1780, in the Wallkill Valley of Orange County, New York, four large teeth were collected from a swamp on the property of the Reverend Robert Annan. Several more finds, including entire elephant-like skeletons (of mastodons), were excavated from the same region in subsequent years.

In 1796, Thomas Jefferson acquired remains of a huge skeleton with claws that had been recovered from a cave in western Virginia. Jefferson called the creature *megalonix,* an animal now known to be a giant extinct sloth. In the meantime, Siberia continued to yield frozen carcasses of rhinoceros and mammoth, some of which were studied by Pallas. One of the more impressive finds was made by Shumakhov in 1799 in the delta of the Lena River when he noticed a strange looking mass within the frozen ground. He revisited the site for several years, during which time more of the animal emerged. During the fifth year, the carcass thawed completely and slid down to the river bank. The tusks were chopped off and sold. Drawings of the creature came into possession of M. F. Adams, a zoologist member of the Russian Academy of Sciences, who hustled off to the Lena delta in 1806 to see the carcass for himself. The trunk, tail, and one ear were gone, but one eye still kept its color. Soft parts, except for the skin on the head, one foot, and the side on which the animal lay, had been completely destroyed by wild animals and dogs. The animal, a male, had been well fed and fat. The hide preserved on the ground was covered with thick hair.[27] Remnants of the beast were returned to the St. Petersburg museum.

In the long run, the discovery of most far-reaching significance took place in 1797 at Hoxne, England, when a series of flint implements were found in a layer of gravelly soil. The discoverer, John Frere (1740-1807), reported that the implements "lay in great numbers at the depth of about twelve feet, in a stratified soil" and were associated with "some extraordinary bones, particularly a jaw-bone of enormous size, of some unknown animal." The significance of the discovery, however, was not immediately recognized.[28]

27. I. P. Tolmachoff, "The Carcasses of the Mammoth and Rhinoceros Found in the Frozen Ground of Siberia," *Transactions of the American Philosophical Society,* n.s., 23 (1933): 23-24.

28. Frere, "Account of Flint Weapons Discovered at Hoxne in Suffolk," *Archaeologia* 13 (1800): 204-5. For an exhaustive discussion of the early discoveries of human artifacts and their significance, see Donald K. Grayson, *The Establishment of Human Antiquity* (New York: Academic Press, 1983).

Neptunism and the Flood

Despite the growing belief that primitive, secondary, and most tertiary rocks must have formed prior to the deluge, perhaps during long ages of creation, neptunists nonetheless had room for the deluge. After all, the fossil remains of most of the monstrous animals discovered during the seventeenth and eighteenth centuries had come from swamps, marshes, and gravels that formed subsequent to most tertiary formations. Not all neptunists worked out specific deluge theories, but predictably closer links between neptunism and Scripture (and particularly the Noachic flood) were forged in the British Isles. The ideas of Richard Kirwan (1733-1812) are illustrative. Kirwan, a chemist and mineralogist, Inspector of Mines for Ireland, and eventually long-time president of the Royal Irish Academy, discussed the topic of the deluge in a lengthy article.[29] He suggested in neptunist fashion that the original sea had retreated through rifts in the crust until a few centuries before the deluge, an amount of time necessary for the rocks formed from the universal ocean to become sufficiently hardened to withstand the shocks they would undergo during the ensuing catastrophe.

What, asked Kirwan, were the geological proofs of the deluge? Having "proved" that at the time of the creation, no mountains reached higher than 8,500 feet, he argued that shells found at higher elevations than that could only have been left there by a subsequent inundation. He found further evidence for a flood in the fact that the fossil remains of organisms that dwell in widely disparate and distant climates were mixed promiscuously with each other in the rocks. Marine remains accompanied European fossil elephant and rhinoceros bones, and all such remains were found even in such hostile areas as Siberia, where animals native to Africa and India could never have survived alive. Kirwan argued that the remains must have been swept into the harsher regions over great distances from their native habitats by an enormous inundation.

Kirwan rejected previous explanations of a universal deluge. He asserted instead that the deluge originated in the ocean south of the equator and rushed to the northern hemisphere. It was forceful enough, he said, to carry the carcasses of animals such as elephants from the

---

29. Kirwan, "On the Primitive State of the Globe and Its Subsequent Catastrophe," *Transactions of the Royal Irish Academy* 6 (1797): 233-308. For a general look at neptunism and the flood, see Colin Russell, "Noah and the Neptunists," *Faith and Thought* 100 (1972): 143-58.

southern countries and marine species from southern seas to high latitudes beyond 45° N, where their remains can now be found in surficial deposits. The force of the flood must have traveled northward, he reasoned, because no remains of animals native to the north are found in the southern lands. Moreover, he contended that traces of a violent shock or impression from the south were perceptible in the shapes of the mountains. Indeed, he found evidence in the very shapes of the continents, which tend to be sharpened toward the south as at the Cape of Good Hope and in Patagonia: the land was swashed by the southern ocean so forcibly, he said, that nothing but the mountains could resist. Finally, an inundation from the southeast would also have been necessary to drive the ark northwesterly toward Armenia.

Kirwan envisioned the great southern ocean surging northward with irresistible impetuosity against a continent that at one time likely united Asia and America. This material was torn up and swept away as far as latitude 40° N, he said, leaving only scattered islands. The progress of the surge was checked by the mountains of China, Tartary, and the west American coast. Sweeping into China, the torrents picked up the soil covering what is now the Gobi Desert and pressed on toward the north polar regions. Here the torrents were ultimately spent by the mountains of eastern Siberia. But on the way these huge torrents dashed over the mountains "bearing over them the vegetable and animal spoils of the more southern, ravaged or torn up continents" to the plains of western Siberia, where the remains were deposited.

The bed of the Atlantic Ocean was also scoured by the water. As evidence, Kirwan called attention to the similarities in shapes of coastlines on the opposite sides of the Atlantic and asserted that "the depression of such a vast tract of land cannot appear improbable when we consider the shock it must have received, and the enormous load with which it was charged."[30] The concussion of water also rent the basaltic masses along the Scottish and Irish coasts into pillars, he said.

Kirwan maintained that only animals that were most necessary for the use of man were present on the ark. Since the "ravenous animals" would have posed a threat to the immediate survivors of the deluge, Kirwan proposed that carnivores were probably created after the flood and after the "graminivorous" animals had greatly multiplied. He likewise attributed the animals of America and of the torrid and frigid zones to a subsequent creation. Kirwan further suggested that

30. Kirwan, "On the Primitive State of the Globe and Its Subsequent Catastrophe," p. 288.

prediluvial vegetables gave off such vast quantities of oxygen that the atmosphere before the flood was much purer than now, perhaps explaining the greater longevity of the antediluvians. After the flood, however, the surface of the earth was covered with putrefying animals and fish which absorbed oxygen and supplied only "mephitic" and "fixed" air, thus bringing the atmosphere to its present state. He conjectured that domestic disturbances within Noah's family induced him to move, along with those closest to him, to "the regions he inhabited before the flood, in the vicinity of China, and hence the early origin of the Chinese monarchy."[31]

The widespread opinion that the world's stratified, fossiliferous rocks could be accounted for in terms of the action of a biblical global deluge had faded. Nonetheless, nearly a century later, orthodox Christian naturalists were still largely committed to a universal flood, a flood that accounted only for surficial phenomena, including surface gravels, vast deposits of marine shells, and graveyards of vertebrates. The hardened stratified deposits were now generally regarded as having formed much earlier than the flood, in all likelihood at the time of creation. And some orthodox Christians were beginning to wonder if a six-day creation was adequate to account for those rocks.

Developments in Biogeography

Further adjustments were also being forced by growing knowledge about animal and plant distribution. The eighteenth-century expeditions such as Captain Cook's voyages to the Pacific were continuously adding to the list of organisms, pushing it well beyond the 500 birds, 150 quadrupeds, and about 10,000 invertebrates that had been catalogued by John Ray in the seventeenth century. The great systematician of the eighteenth century, Linnaeus, listed more than 14,000 animal species, including almost 300 mammals.

Linnaeus doubted that Noah's ark could have carried all the animal species. Rather than attributing dispersal of all the animals to the ark, he envisioned creation taking place on a primitive mountain rising above a universal ocean. "Each pair of animals was created in a particular climatic belt in association with the other species designed for such conditions." Reindeer and arctic lichens existed at

31. Kirwan, "On the Primitive State of the Globe and Its Subsequent Catastrophe," p. 293.

the summit; tropical palms and monkeys lived at the base. Every plant had its proper soil and every animal its proper climate, and "the mountain was an entire world in miniature."[32] In standard neptunist fashion, Linnaeus had the animals spread out to their ultimate environments and latitudes as the universal ocean shrank and exposed more land.

Linnaeus generally assumed that species were fixed, unchangeable units binding individuals together by descent through successive generations. He argued that the number of individuals in a species is constantly increasing, so if we work backward, we can trace each species to one set of primeval parents created by God. Linnaeus further stressed the notion that the function and structure of an organism is indissolubly linked to the environment for which it was adapted. Every species inhabited its own definite place. Linnaeus objected to the notion of a universal deluge on the grounds that it would have upset the God-ordained stability of creation. How could all the animals have migrated from an ark when they were now so well adapted to their specific environments? For example, how could a reindeer, so well adapted to the bitter cold of the far north, survive a trek from the ark to the tundra of Scandinavia?

Buffon accounted for animal distribution in terms of his theory of the cooling of the globe. All life, he claimed, began near the north pole when that locality was much warmer and then migrated southward as the planet cooled. The southward movement of organisms into the Americas, Europe, Asia, and Africa led to increased isolation as animals were cut off from one another by wide oceans.[33]

In the first detailed review of mammal distribution, a little-known zoologist, Eberhardt A. W. Zimmermann, a late eighteenth-century professor of mathematics and physics in Brunswick, dispensed altogether with the concept of a common dispersal center. He dismissed Linnaeus's idea of original created pairs existing in the same place on the ground that the first pair of lions would quickly have devoured the first pair of sheep, goats, and other species, and would ultimately have starved because they had eaten the first pair of everything else. Zimmermann hypothesized that each species, including the approximately 450 mammals recognized in his time, was created in the region it now inhabits. The climate that prevails now in each region would

32. See Browne, *Secular Ark*, pp. 16-23; and Frangsmyr, *Linnaeus: The Man and His Work*.

33. Browne, *Secular Ark*, pp. 23-25.

also have prevailed at the time of species creation. Thus whole environments were created at once.[34]

Analysis and Application

Despite the considerable body of scholarship pertaining to the capacity of the ark, the worldwide distribution of animals, and diluvial cosmogonies, some of the more important biblical commentators of the eighteenth century failed to interact significantly with that scholarship. Henry, Scott, and Wesley gave little attention to extrabiblical information and were generally content to support traditional views with naive, sweeping, unsubstantiated assertions or by invoking miracle. Gill often knowledgeably interacted with extrabiblical knowledge more than others, but, when faced with the difficulties posed by animal migration to and from the ark, even he ultimately fell back on miracle.

Discoveries made after these commentators wrote rendered the case for a global deluge still weaker. For example, eighteenth-century scholars increasingly came to appreciate the very close dependency of species on their habitats. Ultimately this awareness exposed a fatal flaw in theories depending on any sort of natural migration of animals over long distances. It is possible for only a very few species to migrate over long distances; the absence of appropriate food, water, and climate renders such journeys impossible for most animals.

Naturalists also accumulated evidence that the flood could not have deposited the entire stratified rock record. They increasingly concluded that if the flood left behind geological evidence, it must have been confined to various surface features and deposits. Coupled with this shift in understanding of the deluge's effects was a growing sense that the earth must have experienced a history longer than the traditionally supposed six thousand years. As significant quantities of physical evidence accumulated, many of those who grappled with it felt a need to reconsider traditional interpretations of the biblical texts relevant to earth history.

---

34. Zimmermann, *Specimen Zoologiae Geographicae Quadrupedum Domicilia et Migrationes Sitens* (Leyden: T. Haak, 1777). For an analysis of Zimmermann's work, see F. S. Bodenheimer, "Zimmermann's *Specimen Geographicae Quadrupedum*: A Remarkable Zoogeographical Publication at the End of the Eighteenth Century," *Archives Internationale d'Historie des Sciences* 8 (1955): 351-57.

7. Early Nineteenth-Century Developments in Geology

The Rise of Diluvial Catastrophism

By the beginning of the nineteenth century, the interpretation of the geological strata had changed radically. Virtually no established geologist thought that the thick sequences of stratified sedimentary rocks so evident in quarries, cliffs, and mountains had anything to do with the flood. Neptunists attributed stratification to deposition of sediments from a shrinking primeval ocean. Others suspected that rock strata represented deposits laid down in successive interchanges of land and sea, possibly over long periods of time before the advent of human beings. Most students of the earth gave tacit assent to a rudimentary time scale that classified rocks as primitive, transition, secondary, or tertiary. Great thicknesses of strata, many evidently deposited on the sea bottom, strongly implied that the earth's prehuman history extended far beyond a few thousand years. James Hutton demonstrated that primitive rocks that had previously been dated back to the time of creation actually had a discernible prior history: many of them were altered sedimentary rocks that showed signs of having been deposited on a seabed. Geological unconformities gave evidence of extensive histories involving the consolidation of strata, uplift and tilting, and severe erosion of the tilted rocks before deposition of the next sequence of strata. Discoveries of several unconformities within thick stacks of sedimentary rocks and various other observational and experimental findings accumulated to suggest that the earth was really quite ancient. The vast majority of naturalists readily agreed with John Playfair's

1802 assessment that "though there be in it no *data*, from which the commencement of the present order can be ascertained, there are many by which the existence of that order may be traced back to an antiquity extremely remote."[1]

Students of geology were now mapping secondary and tertiary strata in detail. In southern England, for example, the engineer of the British canal system, William Smith (1769-1839), worked out the stratigraphy of much of the secondary sequence during the last decade of the eighteenth century. In the first decade of the following century, Georges Cuvier (1769-1832) and his colleague Alexandre Brongniart (1770-1847) at the French Museum d'Histoire Naturelle in Paris did the same with tertiary strata in the Paris basin. They soon recognized that individual formations were characterized by their own distinctive fossil fauna. And Cuvier recognized that the Paris basin sequence contained alternating marine and terrestrial deposits, the former containing fossilized invertebrate shells and the latter containing fossilized vertebrate quadruped remains. Both the regular distribution of fossils and the alternations between marine and terrestrial remains made it difficult to reason that the deluge could have produced the earth's consolidated fossiliferous sedimentary rocks.

Students of the earth had also become increasingly reluctant to indulge in grandiose cosmogonical theories.[2] Even so, the presumption of a vast deluge was still common among late eighteenth-century naturalists. Leading geologists of the early nineteenth century on the Continent, in Britain, and in America still had no difficulty in attributing many surficial geological features to catastrophic diluvial action.

Recognizing the tentative, incomplete state of knowledge about the earth, the multitude of important unanswered questions about the earth's past, and the need for a reasonable theory of the earth at the close of the eighteenth century, Alpine geologist Horace Benedict de Saussure (1740-1799), professor of philosophy at the Academy of Geneva, published an agenda for future research to provide a "foundation for a theory of the earth." Among the matters he felt should be

---

1. Playfair, *Illustrations of the Huttonian Theory of the Earth* (Edinburgh: William Creech, 1802). For an overview of late eighteenth- and early nineteenth-century geological thought, see Charles C. Gillispie, *Genesis and Geology* (New York: Harper, 1951).

2. For a review of the transition from cosmogony to geology, see Martin J. S. Rudwick, "The Shape and Meaning of Earth History," in *God and Nature*, ed. David C. Lindberg and Ronald L. Numbers (Berkeley and Los Angeles: University of California Press, 1986), pp. 296-321.

addressed were "historical monuments," including "the deluges or great inundations; their epochs and extent." In a section on "rolled pebbles," de Saussure suggested that a study of high elevation pebbles and rolled blocks "foreign to the soil which bears them" and of the large valleys nearby could yield "some indications of the direction, size and force of the currents produced by the grand revolutions of the earth." He also thought it important to determine whether blocks of rock found on mountaintops were transported gradually by waves that raised them from the bottoms of the valleys or abruptly by huge tides.[3] De Saussure spoke for the geological community when he identified the role and effects of past floods as a significant geological issue. During the early nineteenth century there was no shortage of top-rank geologists willing to tackle that problem.

Georges Cuvier, scientist-administrator extraordinaire who firmly established the disciplines of both vertebrate paleontology and comparative anatomy, was a professor of zoology at the College de France who also held an influential post in the Museum d'Histoire Naturelle.[4] He was also a nominal Protestant who, according to his biographer Dorinda Outram, viewed Protestantism as "a series of opportunities rather than as a body of belief." His handling of the issue of the flood, says Outram, was not motivated by any deep spiritual attachment to Scripture. In his *Essay on the Theory of the Earth*, an introduction to his monumental multivolume work on fossil vertebrates, Cuvier proposed that the secondary and tertiary strata had been formed during successive sudden catastrophes caused over long ages by "repeated irruptions and retreats of the sea."[5] The idea of multiple catastrophes was suggested by fragmented and overturned strata, the presence of heaps of debris and rounded pebbles found among the solid strata, and the carcasses of large quadrupeds that had been partially

3. De Saussure, "Agenda; or, A Collection of Observations and Researches the Results of Which May Serve as the Foundation for a Theory of the Earth," *Philosophical Magazine* 3 (1799): 33-41, 147-56. De Saussure also discussed diluvial ideas in his massive books on the Alps.

4. See William Coleman, *Georges Cuvier, Zoologist* (Cambridge: Harvard University Press, 1964), and Dorinda Outram, *Georges Cuvier: Vocation, Science and Authority in Post-Revolutionary France* (Manchester: Manchester University Press, 1984).

5. Cuvier, *Essay on the Theory of the Earth*, ed. Claude C. Albritton Jr., trans. Robert Kerr (1878; reprint, New York: Arno Press, 1978). The essay was first published as a *Discours Preliminaire* to Cuvier's great work *Recherches sur les Ossemens Fossiles* and subsequently issued separately as *Discours sur les Revolutions de la Surface du Globe*.

preserved in surface deposits of the northern regions. Cuvier maintained that natural catastrophes had caused the permanent extinction of several large mammals such as the mammoth.

Cuvier asserted on zoological grounds that the most recent of these catastrophes could not have been very ancient, consistent with the existence of many traditions, including that of Moses, that the globe had suffered a recent catastrophe. Cuvier fully agreed that

> if there is any circumstance thoroughly established in geology, it is, that the crust of our globe has been subjected to a great and sudden revolution, the epoch of which cannot be dated much farther back than five or six thousand years ago; that this revolution had buried all the countries which were before inhabited by men and by the other animals that are now best known; that the same revolution had laid dry the bed of the last ocean, which now forms all the countries at present inhabited; that the small number of individuals of men and other animals that escaped from the effects of that great revolution, have since propagated and spread over the lands then newly laid dry; and consequently, that the human race has only resumed a progressive state of improvement since that epoch, by forming established societies, raising monuments, collecting natural facts, and constructing systems of science and of learning.[6]

Cuvier stopped just short of an explicit identification of this recent catastrophe with the Mosaic flood.

George Bellas Greenough (1778-1855), a student of Werner, member of Parliament, and one of the founders and first president of the Geological Society of London in 1807, also stopped short of such an identification. In *A Critical Examination of the First Principles of Geology*, issued in 1819 when he was president of the Geological Society, Greenough addressed the problem of the great displaced blocks that were scattered across the face of Europe. He maintained that if seas, rivers, or collapsing lakes could not transport such exotic blocks, then "the only remaining cause, to which these effects can be ascribed, is a Debacle or Deluge."[7]

To account for the bones and tusks of elephants found in Siberia, Pallas proposed that the deluge had swept over the Alps and the mountains of Tartary during a period of tremendous eruptions that he believed

---

6. Cuvier, *Essay on the Theory of the Earth*, pp. 171-72.
7. Greenough, *A Critical Examination of the First Principles of Geology* (London: Strahan & Spottiswoode, 1819).

produced the Moluccas, the Philippines, and other volcanic islands in the Indian Archipelago. Greenough had difficulties with Pallas's hypothesis, however. He doubted that the bones could have traveled from the Indian Ocean to Siberia without fracture or abrasion, for instance. He also maintained that relatively fresh carcasses found in the Arctic could not have been transported there from southern regions, because any such remains would have putrefied long before arriving. Moreover, the bones of the elephants were mixed with the bones of such decidedly northern species as the ox, buffalo, elk, and horse. Greenough also wondered why volcanic eruptions would have caused deluges to take a northern rather than southern course, and he questioned whether the volume of water involved would have been adequate to produce the presumed disruption. "The rising of these islands could displace only a quantity of water equivalent to their bulk," wrote Greenough, and such a quantity would not have been able to surmount the mountains of Asia. Greenough also rejected a proposal of Sir James Hall (1761-1832), early geological experimentalist and good friend of James Hutton, to account for the granite blocks dispersed over the Jura mountains by a debacle.[8]

Despite problems with the various hypotheses, Greenough believed that the widespread distribution of alluvial sand and gravel proved that the same inundation had affected all countries, as did the universal occurrence and distinctive symmetry of mountains and valleys. Moreover, he maintained that the direction in which the waters of the deluge flowed could be ascertained by an examination of the orientations of "bowlder-stones, mountains, valleys, promontories, and escarpments."[9] The timing of the geological deluge was a crucial issue, however, for identifying the deluge that Greenough believed had left its mark on the earth's surface features with the biblical deluge. He found no evidence that might help to determine whether the geological deluge occurred before or after the creation of man. There existed only the negative evidence that no human skeletal remains nor "implements of art" had been discovered either in the regular strata or in the diluvian surficial deposits.[10]

---

8. Greenough, *A Critical Examination of the First Principles of Geology*, pp. 151-54.

9. Greenough, *A Critical Examination of the First Principles of Geology*, p. 155. For Hall's ideas about the deluge, see James Hall, "On the Revolutions of the Earth's Surface," *Transactions of the Royal Society of Edinburgh* 7 (1815): 139-212.

10. Greenough, *A Critical Examination of the First Principles of Geology*, p. 186.

A more difficult matter was the cause of the deluge. Greenough suggested that a transitory cause foreign to the solar system, "capable of inundating continents, and giving to the waters of the deep unexampled impetuosity, but without altering the interior constitution of the earth, or deranging the sister planets" was needed. Greenough recalled Halley by looking favorably on the possibility of a cometary or meteoritic shock to the earth.[11]

Diluvial catastrophism was firmly established when William Buckland (1784-1856) was inaugurated as professor of geology at Oxford in 1819. Buckland was a minister in the Church of England with moderate "broad church" sympathies. As indicated by his advocacy of the gap theory for Genesis 1 (i.e., the belief that a long period of time occurred between Gen. 1:1 and 1:2, between the initial creation and the state of formlessness of the earth), he did not insist on strict biblical literalism. Buckland was very sensitive to two matters: (1) the flood played a much smaller role in reconstructions of geological history than it had a century earlier despite the considerable attention still paid to it, and (2) geology was increasingly charting its own course and paying less heed to theological assertions about the alleged demands of scriptural texts. In his landmark Oxford inaugural lecture, Buckland sought to allay the suspicions of the theologically conservative university authorities that geology might be hostile to revealed religion by painstakingly demonstrating the compatibility of geology and religion, particularly with regard to the flood. Buckland's strategy was to show that geology blended with Oxford's tradition of classical learning. As Nicolaas Rupke observed, in Buckland's inaugural "the diluvial theory became the linchpin by which modern geology attached itself to the carriage of the Anglican tradition of learning and the clerical purpose of an Oxford education."[12]

Buckland conceded some slight difficulties in efforts to harmonize geology and Christian faith, but he maintained that there was harmony on the most essential points, including the deluge. He virtually equated the hypothesized geological inundation with the deluge of Moses and optimistically pronounced that

> the grand fact of *an universal deluge* at no very remote period is proved on grounds so decisive and incontrovertible, that, had we

11. Greenough, *A Critical Examination of the First Principles of Geology*, p. 196.

12. Rupke, *The Great Chain of History: William Buckland and the English School of Geology, 1814-1849* (Oxford: Clarendon Press, 1983), p. 60.

never heard of such an event from Scripture, or any other, authority, Geology of itself must have called in the assistance of some such catastrophe, to explain the phenomena of diluvian action which are universally presented to us, and which are unintelligible without recourse to a deluge exerting its ravages at a period not more ancient than that announced in the Book of Genesis.[13]

Just what were those "decisive and incontrovertible" grounds? Buckland argued that the shape and position of hills and valleys as well as the confluence of streams into a main trunk favored the flood. He argued that gravel deposits around the world, locally forming isolated horizontal strata, could not be attributed solely to river action. Moreover, the unfossilized organic remains of animals identical to species now in existence found deposited in the gravels pointed to a deluge. The two great points of the relatively late appearance of the human race and the universality of a recent deluge, said Buckland, were "satisfactorily confirmed by every thing that has yet been brought to light by Geological investigations." Young Professor Buckland, however, had no doubt whatever that the thick successions of stratified, fossiliferous rocks underlying surface gravels were *not* produced in the deluge but were rather deposited in a slow and gradual manner during successive periods of both tranquillity and great disturbance. In some cases, said Buckland, these strata had been produced from the destruction of more ancient consolidated rocks and then violently uplifted prior to the deposition of the more modern strata. Although the deluge had sculpted and destroyed the consolidated strata, the strata themselves could not have been formed in "the single year occupied by the Mosaic deluge." According to Buckland, the antediluvian continents were fundamentally the same as those of the present.

Buckland's inaugural address exerted considerable influence on a variety of geologists, including his friend William Conybeare (1787-1857) and William Phillips (1775-1828), coauthors of the highly respected *Outlines of the Geology of England and Wales.* Conybeare was an early member of the Geological Society of London, one-time fellow at New College, Oxford, and dean of Llandaff. Like Buckland, he was an Anglican minister with centrist affinities, a readiness to look kindly on nonliteral scriptural interpretations, and a willingness to cooperate in matters of science with those outside the Church of England such

13. Buckland, *Vindiciae Geologicae; or, The Connexion of Geology with Religion Explained* (Oxford: Oxford University Press, 1820), pp. 23-24.

as his coauthor Phillips, a Quaker. Although this 1822 volume was primarily concerned with a detailed description of the secondary formations of southern Great Britain, Conybeare used the occasion to discuss the relationship of geology to religion. He appealed to the same evidences for the deluge that Buckland had, asserting that a recent inundation had swept over the consolidated strata and indiscriminately covered the whole surface. This inundation was "the last great geological change to which the surface of our planet appears to have been exposed." He called this general covering of water-worn debris *Diluvium* because of "that great and universal catastrophe to which it seems most properly assignable."[14]

In the meantime, in 1821, a bone-filled cave was discovered at Kirkdale in Yorkshire. As one of the cave's first explorers, Buckland found what he took to be further confirmations of a universal deluge.[15] The exploration of caves for fossils had recently taken on considerable importance. Buckland had already examined a few, but the remains of Kirkdale provided the occasion for compiling a vast catalogue of physical evidence in support of a recent global flood. Buckland placed on a sound empirical, systematic basis the flood catastrophism expressed by Cuvier and implicit in the thought of many contemporary geologists. Following the publication of a synopsis of his findings in *Philosophical Transactions*, Buckland published his great work *Reliquiae Diluvianae* in 1823. Not quite identifying his universal deluge with that of the Bible, Buckland's dedicatory letter to the Lord Bishop of Durham observed that the conclusions of his work afforded the "strongest evidence of an universal deluge" and expressed the hope "that it will no longer be asserted, as it has been by high authorities, that geology supplies no proofs of an event in the reality of which the truth of the Mosaic records is so materially involved."[16] Also included was a brief

14. Conybeare and Phillips, *Outlines of Geology of England and Wales* (London: William Phillips, 1822), p. xxvii. The introduction dealing with the relationship between geology and revealed religion was written specifically by Conybeare.

15. For a reproduction of Conybeare's caricature of Buckland entering Kirkdale cave and confronting a group of live hyenas, see Martin Rudwick, "Encounters with Adam, or at Least the Hyaenas: Nineteenth-Century Visual Representations of the Deep Past," in *History, Humanity, and Evolution*, ed. James R. Moore (New York: Cambridge University Press, 1989), p. 245.

16. Buckland, *Reliquiae Diluvianae; or, Observations on the Organic Remains Contained in Caves, Fissures, and Diluvial Gravel and on Other Geological Phenomena Attesting the Action of an Universal Deluge*, ed. Claude C. Albritton Jr. (1823; reprint, New York: Arno Press, 1978), p. iii.

chapter containing evidence showing that the inundation had occurred at high elevations. Buckland argued that "granite blocks drifted from the heights of Mont Blanc to the Jura, and the bones of diluvial animals found by Humboldt on the elevated plains of South America" showed that all the high hills and the mountains under the whole heavens were covered when the last great physical change affected the surface of the whole globe.[17] Buckland came as close as possible without specifically identifying the geological and biblical floods.

In *Reliquiae Diluvianae* Buckland summarized the results of the discoveries at Kirkdale and several other British and European caves. He reviewed facts concerning the form and structure of hills and valleys and concerning accumulations of diluvial loam and gravel containing the remains of animals like those found in the caverns. All of these facts, said Buckland, cast light on the earth's state prior to the "last great convulsion" affecting its surface and "affording one of the most complete and satisfactory chains of consistent circumstantial evidence I have ever met with in the course of my geological investigations."[18] In Kirkdale cave, Buckland had discovered a great abundance of hyena bones and excrement as well as bones of tigers, bears, wolves, foxes, weasels, elephants, rhinoceroses, hippopotamuses, horses, oxen, deer, hares, rabbits, water-rats, mice, ravens, pigeons, larks, ducks, and snipes. The bones, some of which had been gnawed, were embedded in crystalline material on the cave floor and in red mud overlying the crystalline material. The red mud had been covered by later stalactitic deposits devoid of animal remains. Buckland concluded that the gnawed bones were those of animal carcasses that had been dragged into a lair of hyenas. He contended that the red mud covering the assemblage of extinct vertebrate species had been washed into the cave by the deluge and hence he maintained that the stalactitic material covering the mud was postdiluvial. Buckland cited the limited stalactite deposits over the mud and the presence of undecayed bones as evidence that the mud layer was introduced no earlier than the time inferred by Cuvier — that is to say, the time that had "elapsed since that great and universal inundation which has overwhelmed the earth" was about five or six thousand years.[19]

In the latter part of the book, Buckland discusses the dispersion of the bones of extinct elephants, deposits of loam and gravel, and

---

17. Buckland, *Reliquiae Diluvianae*, p. 223.
18. Buckland, *Reliquiae Diluvianae*, pp. 1-2.
19. Buckland, *Reliquiae Diluvianae*, p. 51.

diluvial evidences around the world. The book also carries an appendix in which he argues that the flood was responsible for the excavation of river valleys. Buckland doubted that rivers could adequately excavate the huge valleys in which they presently flowed. Unlike Kirwan and Pallas, however, Buckland insisted that the great deluge must have swept out of the north, since boulders on the surface and in gravel deposits of Europe and North America had been transported from identifiable sources to the north.

As the years passed, Buckland backed away from the views he so eloquently set forth in *Reliquiae Diluvianae*. In a footnote in his contribution to the Bridgewater Treatises, Buckland observed that subsequent discoveries showed that many of the animals he had previously described had existed

> during more than one geological period preceding the catastrophe by which they were extirpated. Hence it seems more probable, that the event in question, was the last of the many geological revolutions that have been produced by violent irruptions of water, rather than the comparatively tranquil inundation described in the Inspired Narrative. It has been justly argued, against the attempt to identify these two great historical and natural phenomena, that, as the rise and fall of the waters of the Mosaic deluge are described to have been gradual and of short duration, they would have produced comparatively little change on the surface of the country they overflowed.[20]

Although he still endorsed the notion of great deluges, Buckland pointedly distanced himself from identifying the geological and biblical deluges, and he also attributed the extinct cave animals to a time prior to the creation of man. Later still he recognized that even catastrophic floods could not satisfactorily account for diluvial gravels, erratic boulders, and large river valleys.

During the years in which Buckland's catastrophic deluge dominated much geologic discussion, particularly in Great Britain, important field investigations were conducted in the Auvergne region of central France, a region previously explored by Guettard, Desmarest, Montlosier, von Buch, and d'Aubuisson. Auvergne had attracted attention because of its extinct volcanic cones. The nature of these volcanoes and their associated rocks became a major problem because of contro-

20. Buckland, *Geology and Mineralogy Considered with Reference to Natural Theology*, Bridgewater Treatise series, no. 6 (London: William Pickering, 1837).

versies over the nature and origin of basaltic rock. Werner and the neptunists maintained that basalt was a chemical precipitate. Hutton, Playfair, Hall, and others who belonged to the vulcanist party suspected that basalt might be a volcanic rock. Naturalists were eager to compare the Auvergne rocks with basalts of disputed origin in Scotland and Ireland. They began to recognize that there had been a long succession of volcanic events in Auvergne, including eruption of basaltic lava flows from the cones. Some of the most recent flows filled large valleys that had been excavated into older layers of lava. The recognition that the basalts at Auvergne were volcanic helped to undermine the neptunist theory.

In his early field investigations of the Auvergne area, Oxford's professor of chemistry Charles Daubeny (1795-1867), another associate of Buckland and enthusiastic advocate of the diluvial origin of valleys, classed different lava flows as either postdiluvian or antediluvian. He suggested that if Buckland was correct in attributing the excavation of valleys to the Mosaic deluge, then "the modern volcanoes of Auvergne must all have been posterior to the latter event," since valleys in the older lava flows (presumably scoured by diluvial waters) were filled with more recent lava flows.[21]

Diluvial catastrophism also spread to America. The outstanding chemist and mineralogist Benjamin Silliman (1779-1864) of Yale, a devout Congregationalist, contributed greatly to the establishment of American geology through his teaching, public lecturing, personal research, and founding in 1818 of the *American Journal of Science*, a still-thriving periodical that is devoted almost exclusively to geology.[22] Among other things, he brought out an American edition of a textbook by British geologist Robert Bakewell to which he appended a lengthy essay on the consistency of geology with sacred history.[23] Silliman flatly rejected the old idea that the bulk of stratified rocks could have been

21. Daubeny, "On the Volcanoes of Auvergne," *Edinburgh Philosophical Journal* 3 (1820): 361-62. For more on the geology of Auvergne, see Kenneth L. Taylor, "Nicolas Desmarest and Geology in the Eighteenth Century," in *Toward a History of Geology*, ed. Cecil J. Schneer (Cambridge: MIT Press, 1969), pp. 339-56.

22. On the early life of Silliman, see Chandos Michael Brown, *Benjamin Silliman: A Life in the Young Republic* (Princeton: Princeton University Press, 1989). See also John F. Fulton and Elizabeth H. Thomson, *Benjamin Silliman, 1779-1864: Pathfinder in American Science* (New York: H. Schuman, 1947).

23. Bakewell, *Introduction to Geology*, 2d ed. (based on the fourth British edition), ed. Benjamin Silliman (New Haven: Hezekiah Howe, 1833); pp. 404-13 and 458-66 in Silliman's addendum are specifically relevant to the issue of the deluge.

the work of a global deluge. But, he continued, the surface of the planet is covered with "wreck and ruin" that can be "justly" attributed to "mighty floods and rushing torrents of water." Nor were these surface phenomena restricted to Europe; "we must charge to moving waters the undulating appearance of stratified sand and gravel, often observed in many places, and very conspicuously in the plain of New Haven, and in other regions of Connecticut and New England," wrote Silliman. He attributed to "diluvial agency" both "bowlder stones" and the vast deserts of sand in South Africa, the Sahara, Arabia, Germany, Russia, and at the foot of the Rocky Mountains.

Silliman maintained that denuded valleys, fossilized bones and skeletons of extinct species, and many beds of oyster shells were probably the result of diluvial action. He believed that the tusks of the extinct elephant that had been found in northern Asia were deposited there by a deluge that drowned and buried the bodies of whole races of animals. Nothing could be more violent, destructive, and over-whelming than the universal deluge of Genesis, he said, and "certainly upon the face of the earth are every where recorded, in legible characters, the necessary physical effects of such a debacle." But there were some difficulties. Silliman suggested that some gravel deposits could have been produced by local floods, and he suspected that the universal flood would have been much too short to accomplish the rounding of boulders. Like Cuvier and Buckland, Silliman did not explicitly equate the geological with the Noachic deluge, but he did claim that it was legitimate to compare the two. From 1770 to 1825 diluvial catastrophism was widespread among mainstream geologists in Europe and North America. Silliman's disciple Edward Hitchcock may even have extended the lifetime of diluvial catastrophism in America several years after it had fallen out of favor in Europe.

The Collapse of Diluvial Catastrophism

Despite its popularity among geologists and a British and American lay public eager to see biblical revelation corroborated by science, diluvial catastrophism began to crumble upon closer inspection. As already noted, Buckland gradually abandoned his early views. Perhaps the most perceptive of those taking a closer look at the approach was John Fleming (1785-1857), a capable naturalist who ultimately became professor of natural history in Aberdeen in 1834 and an evangelical, Calvinistic pastor of the Church of Scotland who participated in the disruption of 1843 to join the Free Church of Scotland. In a series of articles published during the 1820s in the *Edinburgh Philosophical Journal*, Fleming advanced several arguments against diluvial catastrophism.

In an initial poke at current diluvial speculations, Fleming criticized the tendency of naturalists to blur the distinction between the *genus* and *species* of fossil remains. "We are so impatient to speculate," he charged, "that we do not stop to inquire, whether the bones found in a fossil state belong to the living *species*, or to a member of the same *genus* only, now extinct."[24] Assuming that many fossil remains resembling modern tropical animals must themselves have lived in tropical regions, naturalists got into trouble by speculating that "these organic remains must have been brought into their present situation, by some violent means, from tropical regions, or that our country once enjoyed the warmth of a tropical climate." Fleming argued that the "unbroken state" of the remains rendered the violent transportation idea absurd, and astronomy ruled out the climate change hypothesis. An example of the speculative tendency concerned the fossil elephants of Europe, Asia, and America. As amply demonstrated by the anatomical studies of Cuvier and others, these extinct elephants were a different species from those now living and could well have been native to northern countries. In fact, the Lena River delta carcass discovered in 1799 was covered with more than thirty-six pounds of thick, lengthy hair, which certainly seemed to suggest that it was "not a native of a tropical climate, but an inhabitant of a cold region." This particular species of elephant was suited to live in Siberia, said Fleming, and the Siberian climate was basically the same when the mammoth lived there as it is now. Where was the need for a cataclysm?

Fleming also trained his critical guns on Buckland's Kirkdale cave. While defending Buckland's identification of the cave as the den of an extinct species of hyena, Fleming questioned his identification of the red mud as a diluvial deposit. Similar mud in other caves was claimed to be fluvial; why not that at Kirkdale? Fleming also wondered why the deluge was so selective in drowning the hippopotamus but allowing the ox and horse to survive. The subdivision of strata into diluvian and postdiluvian

24. Fleming, "On the Revolutions Which Have Taken Place in the Animal Kingdom, as These Are Indicated by Geognosy," *Edinburgh Philosophical Journal* 8 (1823): 110-22. See also Fleming's "Remarks Illustrative of the Influence of Society on the Distribution of British Animals," *Edinburgh Philosophical Journal* 11 (1824): 287-305.

could not be sustained, he argued, because the vertebrate remains occurred in both alleged diluvian clay and "acknowledged *post-diluvian* marl." The flood should have indiscriminately consigned all British quadrupeds to a "watery grave" but instead targeted precisely those animals that "in all ages must have been most eagerly sought after by the huntsman, and such as his efforts would, long before this period, have annihilated." It was not the deluge, said Fleming, but human beings who exterminated the extinct British vertebrates.

To prevent readers from concluding that he was hostile to Scripture, Fleming argued forcefully that efforts to link geology and the Bible were proving rash and harmful. Of course, the works and the words of God must give consistent indications of his government, "provided they be interpreted truly." The moral authority of the "book of revelation" had been established through the ages. But interpreters of the book of nature, said Fleming, "have been few in number, their field of observation too limited, and their prejudices too obvious, to permit any high value to be attached to their theoretical deductions." Geology would fare better, he thought, if its practitioners were "more disposed to examine the structure of the earth, and the laws which regulate the physical distribution of its inhabitants" and less eager to identify their conjectures with popular truths. Furthermore, he asserted that the interests of revelation would be better served if believers would not exhibit such "morbid earnestness" to gain support for their creed from the sciences but would rather calmly acknowledge the fact that

> geology never can, from its very nature, add the weight of a feather to the moral standard which he has embraced, or the anticipations of eternity in which he indulges, even should he fancy that it has succeeded in disclosing the dens of antediluvian hyaenas, in exhibiting the skeleton of a rhinoceros drowned in the flood, or in discovering the decayed timbers of the ark. This indiscreet union of Geology and Revelation can scarcely fail to verify the censure of Bacon, by producing *"Philosophia phantastica, Religio haeretica."*

Fleming intensified his assault in 1826 when he wrote "The Geological Deluge, as Interpreted by Baron Cuvier and Professor Buckland, Inconsistent with the Testimony of Moses and the Phenomena of Nature."[25] Fleming was concerned that Buckland in particular, with his high view of Scripture, had allowed his imagination to become

25. Fleming, "The Geological Deluge . . . ," *Edinburgh Philosophical Journal* 14 (1826): 205-39.

overactive in his desire to find evidence for the flood. Fleming reminded Buckland that he had attributed the extinction of many species of quadrupeds to the deluge, whereas Scripture spoke of the preservation of at least a pair of every kind. Buckland contended that the flood was sudden, transient, virtually universal, and simultaneous, rushing about with overwhelming impetuosity, but Moses mentioned only the universality of the flood, and if anything the biblical evidence suggested that the flood was slow and gradual, inasmuch as it took forty days for the waters to rise. If the flood had been as violent as Buckland suggested, it is hard to imagine how the ark could have survived, much less landed relatively close to the point from which it first lifted off the ground as the Bible reports. Buckland said that the flood excavated deep valleys by tearing up solid rock, which would imply that prediluvian geography must have been radically different from what it is now, and yet Moses implied that the countries had the same appearance before and after the flood. If one took the biblical reference to the olive leaf seriously, one would have to conclude that the Mosaic flood was not violent enough to have disturbed the soil or trees; and the fact that Noah was able to plant a vineyard shortly after the flood further indicated that the soil had not been washed away.

Fleming accused Buckland of having obtained his notions of the flood from Ovid rather than the Bible. Himself endorsing the biblical description of a slowly accumulating, nonviolent flood, Fleming disposed of all forms of flood geology, saying that he was "not prepared to witness *in nature* any remaining *marks* of the catastrophe, and I feel my respect for the authority of revelation heightened, when I see on the present surface no memorials of the event."

Buckland and his fellow catastrophists habitually attributed the existence of river valleys and canyons, gravel beds, mud in caves, and extinct animals to the action of the flood. The diluvialists said that river valleys had been carved by the tremendous power of the flood as it drained off the surface of the earth, but Fleming, like Hutton and Playfair before him, argued that the sinuous shapes of canyons and valleys and the fact that they gradually widen owing to the existence of tributaries mirrors the shapes of modern stream channels, which we know were produced solely by the streams themselves. It was clear to Fleming that ancient canyons and valleys were carved out by the long-continued action of running water rather than by a stupendous but brief flood. Flood waters might erode loose soil and loosen boulders, said Fleming, but there is no way they could have carved deep valleys out of solid bedrock.

Fleming was not alone in challenging early nineteenth-century diluvialism. Throughout the 1820s, the Auvergne district received continued attention from three of Great Britain's more able geologists, George Poulett Scrope (1797-1876), Charles Lyell (1797-1875), and Roderick Murchison (1792-1871). Upon careful investigation of the valleys and lavas, all three of them concluded that the action of rivers and streams over a long period of time was perfectly capable of excavating the valleys. Bucklandian deluges were unnecessary. Indeed, if a great torrent had swept over that part of Europe, then the cinder cones from which some of the older lava flows had emanated should have been disrupted or even swept away altogether, and they had not been.[26]

By 1830, many geologists were having second thoughts about a single universal deluge and were taking another look at the physical evidence. Authorities began to issue public recantations. Cambridge's Adam Sedgwick (1785-1873), like his friends Buckland and Conybeare a "broad church" Anglican with perhaps stronger evangelical leanings, had also been an early advocate of diluvial catastrophism. Yet, upon retiring from the presidency of the Geological Society of London in 1831, Sedgwick announced his abandonment of the deluge theory:

> There is, I think, one great negative conclusion now incontestably established — that the vast masses of diluvial gravel, scattered almost over the surface of the earth, do not belong to one violent and transitory period. It was indeed a most unwarranted conclusion, when we assumed the contemporaneity of all the superficial gravel on the earth. We saw the clearest traces of diluvial action, and we had, in our sacred histories, the record of a general deluge. On this double testimony it was, that we gave a unity to a vast succession of phaenomena, not one of which we perfectly comprehended, and under the name diluvium, classed them all together. . . . Our errors were, however, natural, and of the same kind which led many excellent observers of a former century to refer all the secondary formations of geology to the Noachian deluge. Having been myself a believer, and, to the best of my power, a propagator of what I now

<hr>

26. See George P. Scrope, *Memoir on the Geology of Central France, Including the Volcanic Formations of Auvergne, the Velay and the Vivarais* (London, 1827), and Charles Lyell and Roderick I. Murchison, "On the Excavation of Valleys, as Illustrated by the Volcanic Rocks of Central France," *Edinburgh New Philosophical Journal* 13 (1829): 15-48. For a valuable discussion of the Auvergne volcanoes, see Martin J. S. Rudwick, "Poulett Scrope on the Volcanoes of Auvergne: Lyellian Time and Political Economy," *British Journal for the History of Science* 7 (1974): 205-42.

regard as a philosophic heresy, and having more than once been quoted for opinions I do not now maintain, I think it right, as one of my last acts before I quit this Chair, thus publicly to read my recantation.[27]

Sedgwick suggested that geologists had been too hasty in referring all superficial gravel to the action of the Mosaic flood, on the grounds that no trace of humanity had been recovered from those deposits. Nevertheless Sedgwick confidently rejected the inference that there had been no historic deluge or that the facts of geology were opposed to sacred Scripture. Not a word in the Bible or the traditions justified looking to mere physical monuments as the intelligible records of the event, he said. Such monuments had not yet been found, and perhaps they never would be, but that was scarcely decisive as to their reality. To cover all bases, Sedgwick affirmed that, although certain traces of a great diluvian catastrophe within the human period had not been found, it had been shown that "paroxysms of internal energy, accompanied by the elevation of mountain chains, and followed by mighty waves desolating whole regions of the earth, were a part of the mechanism of nature." Because such paroxysms had occurred frequently throughout the earth's history, they may have occurred during the few thousand years that man had been living on its surface. Sedgwick triumphantly concluded that "we have therefore, taken away all anterior incredibility from the fact of a recent deluge; and we have prepared the mind, doubting about the truth of things of which it knows not either the origin or the end, for the adoption of this fact on the weight of historic testimony."

Greenough issued a similar recantation in 1834, acknowledging that he once held the "not hastily formed" opinion based on the best available geological data that the entire globe had been covered by a general deluge.[28] But now, better acquainted with "physical and geological nature," he had been convinced otherwise. He acknowledged his debt to Lyell for bringing together a vast mass of evidence suggesting

27. Sedgwick, "Address to the Geological Society," *Proceedings of the Geological Society of London* 1 (1831): 313-14. Sedgwick's early ideas about the flood may be found in his essays "On the Origin of Alluvial and Diluvial Formations," *Annals of Philosophy* 9 (1825): 241-57, and "On Diluvial Formations," *Annals of Philosophy* 10 (1826): 18-37. On Sedgwick's life, see Colin Speakman, *Adam Sedgwick, Geologist and Dalesman: A Biography in Twelve Themes* (Heathfield, U.K.: Broad Oak Press, 1982).

28. Greenough, "Anniversary Address to the Geological Society," *Proceedings of the Geological Society of London* 2 (1838): 42-70.

that if a deluge had swept over the entire globe five thousand years earlier, its traces could "no longer be distinguished from more modern and local disturbances." Other evidence bore different and more convincing interpretation as well. What he had viewed as "diluvial" elephants and other animals could probably be better referred to two or three distinct epochs, he granted, and the stone blocks found in the Jura Mountains, northern Germany, northern Italy, and England "are not the waifs and strays of one, but of several successive inundations."

What had Lyell said to convince Greenough of his error? In the final volume of his epochal *Principles of Geology* issued between 1830 and 1833, Charles Lyell, a deist, poured plenty of cold water on current diluvial thinking. In a chapter on the geology of the Eocene Epoch, he reviewed the geology of the Auvergne region and then took up a discussion on the "supposed effects of the flood."[29] Lyell noted that contemporaries who used the terms *antediluvian* and *postdiluvian* with respect to the volcanoes of Auvergne assumed "that there are clear and unequivocal marks of the passage of a general flood over all parts of the surface of the globe." He rejected that view as incompatible with the evidence, but he did leave the door open for a localized deluge. He contended that a flood extending to the whole of that part of the earth inhabited by human beings might have occurred had there been both "extensive lakes elevated above the level of the ocean" and "large tracts of dry land depressed below that level" in a given region. Lyell postulated that if the waters of Lake Superior, situated six hundred feet above sea level, were to be set loose "by the rending or sinking down of the barrier during earthquakes," the entire valley of the Mississippi, with its huge population, would be deluged. A similarly catastrophic flood might be induced by the depression of part of Asia, he suggested. The "great cavity" of western Asia has an area of 18,000 square leagues, and a "considerable population." The lowest parts in the vicinity of the Caspian Sea are three hundred feet below the level of the Black Sea. In that area floodwaters could cover hills rising three hundred feet above the plain, and if deeper depressions had existed at some earlier time, then even loftier mountains might have been covered in a flood of the region.

Although Lyell recognized that the majority of older commentators held to the geographical universality of the flood and that both

29. Lyell, *Principles of Geology*, vol. 3 (London: John Murray, 1833), pp. 270-74. See also James R. Moore, "Charles Lyell and the Noachian Deluge," *Evangelical Quarterly* 45 (1973): 141-60.

Deluc and Buckland had eloquently and zealously supported the notion
of a great flood that "worked a considerable alteration in the external
configuration of our continents," he expressed agreement with Fleming
that the biblical narrative did not "indicate the impetuous rushing of
the waters, either as they rose or when they retreated." For Lyell as for
Fleming, the survival of the olive branch seemed a clear indication that
vegetation had not been destroyed in the deluge.

     Lyell confessed reluctance to talk about the flood at all because
of the sensitive nature of people's feelings about the subject. He concluded his "digression" by asserting that he had always considered both
the causes and effects of the flood to be in the preternatural category
"beyond the reach of philosophical inquiry." And he warned those who
were anxious to point out "the coincidence of geological phenomena
with the occurrence of such a general catastrophe" that they must
neglect "no one of the circumstances enumerated in the Mosaic history,
least of all so remarkable a fact as that the olive remained standing
while the waters were abating." Lyell tried as nicely as he could without
offending anyone to say that he did not see any geological evidence to
support the notion of a global catastrophe. Indeed, he found that "the
strictest interpretation of the scriptural narrative does not warrant us
in expecting to find any geological monuments of the catastrophe," a
conclusion consistent with the preservation of the volcanic cones of
Auvergne.

Analysis and Application

Naturalists of the early nineteenth century accumulated a great deal
of information that led to changes in their view of earth's history and
the role of the Noachic deluge in it. They all paid scrupulous attention
to the full spectrum of available geological information and adjusted
their ideas in response to that information. Many of them were orthodox Christians, and yet they felt no need to distort the evidence
they encountered in order to sustain their belief in the biblical deluge.
One finds no appeal to miracle on the part of even the most ardent
advocate of the deluge, William Buckland. The premier geologists were
persuaded that existing geological evidence supported the notion of a
global or at least continental deluge. Every one of them rejected the
old diluvialism which attributed the deposition of fossiliferous secondary and tertiary strata to the flood, however. They identified only
surface deposits as the effects of the deluge.

Even that view collapsed, however, because of the importance that these men placed on extrabiblical evidence. Buckland, Sedgwick, and others ultimately abandoned nineteenth-century diluvialism when it became clear that gravels, valleys, polished rocks, cave deposits, and the like could no longer be satisfactorily understood as the result of a giant deluge. Because the Christian naturalists of the era were unafraid of God-given evidence, they recognized that extrabiblical information provided a splendid opportunity for closer investigation of the biblical text in order to clear up earlier mistakes in interpretation. Biblical expositors of the period were more reluctant to grapple with extrabiblical data in so forthright a manner, as we will see in Chapter 8.

8. Advance and Regression in Geological Thought

The Coming of the Ice Age — the Frozen Flood

The diluvial explanation of gravels, boulders, and wide river valleys had suffered a fatal setback by 1840. Although James Hutton and John Playfair had described before 1800 the effects of glaciation, their work attracted little attention. Unaware of their contributions, Ignatz Venetz (1788-1859), a civil engineer, and Jean de Charpentier (1786-1855), a mining engineer whose father had been a professor at Werner's Freiberg Academy, undertook careful investigations of glacial phenomena in the Alps during the 1820s and 1830s. Charpentier recognized that erratic boulders, gravels, and sandy drift in the mountains had been deposited by melting glaciers and that broad U-shaped valleys were excavated by advancing ice. He also realized that Swiss glaciers had been larger in the past.

In 1836 a brilliant young Swiss naturalist, Louis Agassiz (1807-1873), a student of Cuvier and professor in the College of Neuchâtel who was already renowned for pioneering studies on fossil fish, was given a guided tour of glacial phenomena in the Rhone River valley by Charpentier. Aware that Charpentier explained Swiss erratics and gravels as glacial deposits, Agassiz was skeptical at first but quickly became an enthusiastic convert. He immediately undertook extensive field research throughout Europe and the British Isles and had already gleaned sufficient information by the summer of 1837 to create a sensation with a lecture before the Swiss Society of Natural History announcing that vast ice sheets had covered the northern continents all the way to the Mediterranean Sea during the Pleistocene epoch.[1]

Not unexpectedly, William Buckland was extremely interested in Agassiz's startling hypothesis. Hoping to discount Agassiz's new ideas, Buckland participated in one of the most significant field trips in history in October 1838. Agassiz showed Buckland several examples of polished, striated bedrock and transported erratics on the southeastern slopes of the Jura mountains near Neuchatel. Together they examined glaciers in the Alps. Buckland received a firsthand lesson in the capabilities of flowing ice and was convinced that alpine glaciers had once been much more extensive. He informed Agassiz that he had seen similar phenomena in Scotland and England and had attributed them to diluvial action, but he now realized that flowing ice accounted for such features much more satisfactorily than an aqueous catastrophe ever could. Buckland had become a glacialist. Lyell soon followed.

Agassiz issued a full-scale work in 1840 entitled *Études sur les Glaciers*. He, Buckland, and Lyell also gave important papers in late 1840 before the Geological Society of London on the evidence that glaciers had covered Scotland, Ireland, and England in the distant past, pointing out the widespread occurrence of moraines, shoreline terraces of ancient lakes, and striated and polished bedrock. General skepticism reigned. Many believed that the action of icebergs swept over land accounted for some of the features more effectively than the action of glaciers. In a few years, however, Agassiz's theory of a great continental ice sheet prevailed because it explained so much about the erratics, polished rocks, gravels, and wide valleys that had been previously puzzling in the context of the deluge hypothesis. A scant two decades after his inaugural lecture, Buckland had completely repudiated diluvial catastrophism and had warmly embraced the concept of a great ice age. In Rupke's words, Buckland "saw glaciation as the 'grand key' to the diluvial phenomena." Many of his contemporaries eventually followed.[2]

---

1. The term *Pleistocene epoch* was used to refer to the time when the latest surficial deposits were deposited on top of older rocks.

2. For more detailed discussion of the first proposals concerning the effects of glaciation and an ice age, see Horace B. Woodward, *The History of the Geological Society of London* (London: Geological Society, 1907), pp. 136-45; Edward Lurie, *Louis Agassiz: A Life in Science* (Chicago: University of Chicago Press, 1960), pp. 96-106; and Nicolaas Rupke, *The Great Chain of History: William Buckland and the English School of Geology, 1814-1849* (Oxford: Clarendon Press, 1983), pp. 96-107.

Development of the Geological Time Scale

While the great debates over the flood and glaciation were going on, geologists were also occupied with detailed mapping and subdivision of the simple geological time scale inherited from the eighteenth century. By the mid-1800s, the time scale had become highly refined.[3] The subdivisions were worked out primarily in the British Isles and western Europe, where thick successions of fossiliferous strata abounded. The secondary rocks of England were fruitfully subdivided. These rocks consisted of a very thick series of strata that had first been mapped by William Smith. In a book issued in 1822, William Conybeare and William Phillips carefully described, refined, and extended the sequence and lumped the strata into groups of related units. For example, they defined the succession of strata including a prominent formation in Scotland and western England known as the Old Red Sandstone and the overlying formations including the Coal Measures as the *Carboniferous* Order because of the abundance of coal in the succession. During the latter 1830s, Adam Sedgwick and Roderick Murchison mapped and described a terrane of rocks that lay beneath the Old Red Sandstone in Devonshire and labeled it *Devonian*.[4] Sedgwick and Murchison also mapped the "transition" rocks of Wales over a period of years.[5] Despite bitter disputes about how to classify these strata, the geological community ultimately recognized a *Cambrian* and *Silurian* system in these strata. Smith's claim that different strata were characterized by distinctive fossil remains was amply borne out by these later investigations.

Murchison successfully applied the British succession to rocks in European Russia in 1840.[6] There he recognized rocks that he assigned to the Silurian, Devonian, and Carboniferous systems on the

---

3. For a good overview of the historical growth of the geological time scale, see William B. N. Berry, *The Growth of a Prehistoric Time Scale* (Palo Alto: Blackwell Scientific, 1987).

4. For detail on Sedgwick and Murchison and the establishment of the Devonian time period, see Martin J. S. Rudwick, *The Great Devonian Controversy* (Chicago: University of Chicago, 1985).

5. For further detail on Sedgwick and Murchison and the establishment of the Cambrian and Silurian periods, see James A. Secord, *Controversy in Victorian Geology* (Princeton: Princeton University Press, 1986).

6. On Murchison's contributions, see Robert A. Stafford, *Scientist of Empire* (Cambridge: Cambridge University Press, 1989). For additional insight into the career of Murchison and the development of both the Silurian and Ordovician periods, see David R. Oldroyd, *The Highlands Controversy* (Chicago: University of Chicago Press, 1990).

basis of their fossil content. Despite the fact that the rock types did not always precisely match those in Britain, strata with Silurian fossils did lie beneath strata with Devonian fossils, which in turn lay beneath the formations with Carboniferous fossils. On another trek toward the Urals the following year, Murchison found another group of strata with unfamiliar fossils above the Carboniferous units. He named this series *Permian* after the nearby town of Perm.

Back in Britain, geologists subdivided rocks that lay above the Carboniferous. Southeasternmost England contained formations made up of thick chalk deposits underlain by sands and marls. These chalks were traced across the English Channel into France and Belgium, where they had been designated the *Cretaceous Terrane* in 1822 by Jean Baptiste Julien d'Omalius d'Halloy (1783-1875). Beneath the British chalk and marl are various limestones. Because of the abundant spherical pellets known as oolites in many of the limestones, the entire series was first known as the Oolitic, but eventually the term *Jurassic* was applied because the rocks contained similar fossils and occupied the same stratigraphic position as limestones in the Jura mountains. Rocks beneath the limestones and overlying the Carboniferous rocks correlated with so-called Trias strata in Germany and were eventually identified as the *Triassic*.

Even tertiary strata were subdivided. In the third volume of his *Principles of Geology* (1833), Lyell described rocks of the *Eocene*, *Miocene*, and *Pliocene* epochs. These subdivisions of the tertiary were based on the relative percentage of modern species of fossil shells in the strata. The term *Quaternary* was employed by 1829 to describe alluvial, lacustrine, and volcanic material overlying consolidated Tertiary beds in France. The term *Pleistocene* also was applied to Quaternary deposits to describe formations overlaying Pliocene deposits — what Lyell had earlier termed *later* Pliocene deposits.

By the early 1840s, a detailed geological time scale had been worked out on the basis of successions of superposed sedimentary strata distinguished by characteristic fossils. The primitive, transition, secondary, and tertiary gave way to the Precambrian, Cambrian, Silurian, Devonian, Carboniferous, Permian, Triassic, Jurassic, Cretaceous, Tertiary, and Quaternary, and the Tertiary was subdivided into Eocene, Miocene, and Pliocene strata.[7] These rock sequences could be traced

---

7. For recent overviews of the geological time scale, see N. J. Snelling, *The Chronology of the Geological Record* (Oxford: Blackwell Scientific, 1985), and Walter B. Harland, *A Geologic Time Scale 1989* (New York: Cambridge University Press, 1990).

all across Europe and were always found to occupy the same relative order. Although strata of a given system might be missing locally, rocks were never found out of sequence where the strata were clearly in a right-side-up position. Rocks containing Triassic fossils were always found lower than rocks containing Jurassic fossils, for example, and rocks containing Silurian fossils were always found lower than rocks containing Devonian fossils.

With increasing confidence geologists subdivided strata around the world on the basis of superposition and fossil content. They also found that rocks belonging to different periods were often separated from one another by erosional surfaces known as unconformities, indicating that periods of uplift, tilting, and erosion had occurred several times during the deposition of a given sequence of sedimentary rocks. Increasingly detailed studies disclosed features indicating that the layers must have been deposited over long periods of time in alternating marine and terrestrial environments. In the face of the wealth of new data, no reputable geologist any longer attributed the consolidated fossiliferous strata to the action of the flood.

New Paleontological Discoveries

While they were engaged in their detailed mapping and subdivision of strata and expansion of the geologic time scale, naturalists were also discovering spectacular fossilized "dragons," monstrous marine and terrestrial vertebrates that made the extinct elephants appear tame by comparison. Some of the most impressive remains were encountered in the Jurassic and Cretaceous beds of southern England by Mary Anning (1799-1847), who at the age of eleven found a skeleton of an *Ichthyosaurus*, a sleek, sharp-toothed, fast-swimming marine reptile. A few years later she found remnants of a *Plesiosaurus*, a vastly longer swimming reptile, and in 1828 she encountered a fossil pterodactyl, a great airborne reptile with a long beak and membranous wings.

Cuvier also described finds of Jurassic and Cretaceous vertebrates, including a pigeon-sized pterodactyl and a fierce fifteen- to twenty-foot-long marine lizard that Conybeare had named *Mosasaurus*. Remains of a variety of extinct species were discovered in the Stonefield Slate not far from Oxford. Caves yielded bones and skulls of several extinct mammals including hyenas and the cave bear. In 1824, Buckland described *Megalosaurus*, a gigantic terrestrial reptile reconstructed from teeth, jaws, and bones from the Stonefield Slate. Cuvier estimated that the creature had been about forty feet long. Not to be outdone, Gideon Mantell (1790-1852), an outstanding British amateur paleontologist, found a more complete specimen whose thigh bones prompted his estimate that it had been sixty feet long. Mantell had also collected crocodile and plesiosaur teeth and bones. In 1822, Mantell's wife found the earliest specimens of *Iguanodon*, and years later, Mantell described another extinct lizard, *Hylaeosaurus*.[8] One of the great collectors of the era was anatomist Richard Owen (1804-1892) of the Royal College of Surgeons, arguably England's premier paleontologist of the mid-nineteenth century.[9] Owen described and reconstructed skeletons of several great extinct lizards and in 1841 proposed the establishment of a new "suborder of Saurian Reptiles, for which I would propose the name of Dinosauria."[10] He also described several extinct South American mammals.

By 1850 numerous small extinct land animals had also been described. Fossil kangaroos were found in Australia. Fossil sloths were found in the Americas. The rapidly expanding list of newly recognized extinct land animals inevitably raised a variety of questions in connection with the biblical account of the flood. The first major issue concerned the contents of the ark. By this point, it had really ceased to be an issue for established geologists, who were altogether convinced by a weight of evidence that seemed both incontrovertible and compelling. They were accustomed to interpreting Jurassic and Cretaceous strata as deposits that had been formed millions of years before the advent of human beings. But for laypeople, theologians untrained in the physical sciences, and nonprofessional "scriptural" naturalists who worked from outdated geological theory or otherwise continued to think of fossiliferous strata as flood deposits, the issue was extremely problematic. Those who insisted that all species of all land animals had been preserved on the ark now had to include among them not only lions and bears but also mastodons, mammoths, giant sloths, pterodactyls, megalosaurs, iguanodons, hylaeosaurs, and a host of other

8. Brief accounts of some of the major vertebrate discoveries can be found in Woodward's *History of the Geological Society of London*, pp. 114-33; chap. 1 of Adrian J. Desmond's *The Hot-Blooded Dinosaurs* (New York: Warner Books, 1975); Rupke's *Great Chain of History*, pp. 130-48; and J. B. Delair and W. A. S. Sarjeant's "The Earliest Discoveries of Dinosaurs," *Isis* 66 (1975): 5-25.

9. See Adrian J. Desmond, *Archetypes and Ancestors: Paleontology in Victorian London, 1850-1875* (Chicago: University of Chicago Press, 1984).

10. Owen, quoted by Robert W. Howard in *The Dawnseekers* (New York: Harcourt Brace Jovanovich, 1975), p. 136.

extinct mammals. The prospect of an ark with pairs of forty-foot-long monsters aboard stretched the limits of credulity. The most obvious way to avoid the problem was to assume that God had eliminated such beasts in the catastrophe, but that involved a departure from a strict literal interpretation of the biblical account, which states that God preserved at least two of *every* kind of beast in the ark. To this day, this problem is not faced squarely by proponents of flood geology.

A second issue related to animal migration. Discoveries indicated that certain animals occurred as fossils only in specific and limited areas. Fossil kangaroos, for example, were found only in Australia, and fossil sloths were found only in the Americas. The problem of migration thus became doubly severe for those who wished to preserve a literal reading of the biblical text: they not only had to argue that kangaroos found the means to migrate from the ark to Australia after the flood but they also had to argue that kangaroos had found a way to migrate from Australia to the ark before the flood. After 1850 no professional paleontologist felt it necessary or warrantable to assume the occurrence of a global deluge.

"Scriptural Geology"

Despite the unceasing deluge of discoveries in the early decades of the century that devastatingly annihilated the global deluge theory, a few writers resisted the tendency of geologists to develop theories apart from a recognition of Mosaic history. Some objected to Buckland's restricted brand of diluvialism. Some sought to update the diluvialism of Woodward and Catcott. For the most part, as James R. Moore observed, these individuals were "clergymen, linguists, and antiquaries — those, in general, with vested interests in mediating the meaning of books, rather than rocks, in churches and classrooms." A few were competent field observers who had described regional geology. In any event, reflecting an undying attachment to biblical literalism, England spawned a reactionary movement of "scriptural geologists."[11] The "scriptural geologies" of such people as Granville Penn, George Young,

11. See Moore, "Geologists and Interpreters of Genesis in the Nineteenth Century," in *God and Nature*, ed. David C. Lindberg and Ronald L. Numbers (Berkeley and Los Angeles: University of California Press, 1986), pp. 322-50; Milton Millhauser, "The Scriptural Geologists: An Episode in the History of Opinion," *Osiris* 11 (1954): 65-86; and Rupke, *The Great Chain of History*, pp. 42-50.

George Bugg, Joseph Sutcliffe, George Fairholme, Sharon Turner, and William Kirby were typically marked by a strict adherence to literal readings of the flood narrative — until they chose to make exceptions.[12] They typically proceeded by forcing selected geological data into the historical framework they believed to be supplied by a literal interpretation of Genesis; along the way, they typically ignored a sizable amount of problematic geological and paleontological data.

Perhaps pride of place among the scriptural geologies belongs to *A Comparative Estimate of the Mineral and Mosaical Geologies*, published in 1822 by Granville Penn, a toweringly self-assured and prolix writer. He argued at some considerable length that, contrary to the assertions of the neptunists, primitive rocks could not have formed by precipitation and crystallization from an initial chaos; rather, as Moses taught, they had been created *in situ* by God. "We would be sure to reason unphilosophically and falsely," Penn asserted, if we were to conclude that a piece of granite had formed by aqueous solution or igneous fusion simply because it looked as though it had been formed by water or fire. Primitive formations were made "in *correspondence* with the laws which [God] was then *about to establish*," said Penn, "and in *anticipation of effects and appearances* which were thenceforward to be produced only by the operations of those laws."[13]

Penn also spoke directly to the issue of the flood. The problem with "mineral geology," he said, was that it rejected the Bible's revelation of "a great universal revolution" that God had brought about "by the operation of *water*." On the third day of creation, a first revolution suddenly deepened the ocean bed, violently allowing water to rush in. A second revolution 1,656 years later depressed the exposed land area

12. Among the writings of the scriptural geology school were George Young and J. Bird's *Geological Survey of the Yorkshire Coast, Describing the Strata and Fossils Occurring between the Humber and the Tees, from the German Ocean to the Plain of York* (Whitby, 1828); George Bugg's *Scriptural Geology* (London, 1826-1827); Sharon Turner's *Sacred History of the World, as Displayed in the Creation and Subsequent Events to the Deluge* (London, 1832); Joseph Sutcliffe's *Short Introduction to the Study of Geology, Comprising a New Theory of the Elevation of the Mountains and the Stratification of the Earth, in Which the Mosaic Account of the Creation and the Deluge Is Vindicated* (London, 1817); and Joseph Sutcliffe's *Geology of the Avon* (Bristol, 1822).

13. Granville Penn, *A Comparative Estimate of the Mineral and Mosaical Geologies* (London: Ogle, Duncan, 1822), pp. 76-77. Penn gave evidence of a similar certainty about God's strategy in creating and ordering the world in his earlier work *A Christian's Survey of all the Primary Events and Periods of the World, from the Commencement of History to the Conclusion of Prophecy* (London, 1811).

and raised the former sea bed, submerging what had formerly been dry land and rendering the former seabed habitable. This was the Noachic flood.

True Mosaic geology allowed for these two revolutions only, said Penn. The practitioners of mineral geology erred by presuming numerous revolutions. Scripture provided a true chronological order of geological events consisting of a first formation, a first revolution on the third day of creation, a long period of relative calm, and a second revolution during the flood. Penn argued that calcareous deposits and other marine substances were quietly deposited during the 1,656-year interval between the two revolutions. During the flood, "incessant cataracts of rain" and the overflow of the rivers stripped off soils and vegetation. Vertebrate remains and the bulk of stratified rocks were distributed by eddies, tides, and the continuous flux and reflux of currents. Equatorial animals were transported to northern sites by the flood. Human beings, on the other hand, would have been clustered together and drawn "into the *vortex* created by the *conflux* of the two seas meeting from the opposite hemispheres on the subsidence of the last intervening land; and would thus have been immediately carried downward with violence, into the profundity of the *new sea.*"[14]

Despite insisting on strict adherence to the Bible concerning other points, Penn asserted that the ark had not in fact carried representatives of all the earth's animals. He stated that the extinction of animals such as the mastodon was divinely ordained as part of God's plan of renovation. He also affirmed that since vegetation could not have survived a devastating year-long flood, God must have created postdiluvial vegetation just like the original vegetation.[15]

Penn recognized that his thesis had other difficulties as well. He wondered, for example, why the rivers of the garden of Eden had familiar names if the surface of the postdiluvian earth were wholly new. His solution was to resort to the exegetical subterfuge of postulating that the description of the rivers was a "parenthesis" inserted into the direct thread of the history for the purpose of illustration. "The fluvial description introduced into the *four verses,* cannot therefore be regarded, critically, as any part of the Mosaical history," he wrote, and so had "no weight" to affect the strong evidence of the Mosaic history of the

14. Penn, *A Comparative Estimate of the Mineral and Mosaical Geologies,* p. 336.

15. Penn, *A Comparative Estimate of the Mineral and Mosaical Geologies,* pp. 341-46, 399-417.

destruction of the primitive earth by the deluge. Even the most enthusiastic biblical literalist found it increasingly difficult to devise scientific theories without abandoning literalism at key points.

Another reactionary effort was tucked in an appendix to the Bridgewater Treatise written by William Kirby, a biologist of modest accomplishments and one-time president of the Royal Society.[16] He admitted that his knowledge of geological science was limited, and his work bore it out. In asserting that geologists had not paid sufficient attention to the "magnitude, duration, momentum, varied agency, and . . . consequences" of the biblical flood, he betrayed an apparent ignorance of the fact that the field had been dominated by various flood theories during the previous 150 years but that all reputable professionals had long since abandoned diluvialism. His assertions were all badly dated — he named abyssal waters, torrential rain, and volcanoes as sources for the flood, for instance, and cited the abundant fossils in stratified rocks as clear evidence of the action of the diluvial waters — and in general he sought to attribute far more effects to the flood than any geologist was prepared to.

One of the most influential scriptural geologists was George Fairholme, whose masterwork *New and Conclusive Physical Demonstrations Both of the Fact and Period of the Mosaic Deluge* was issued in 1837. Fairholme lamented the fact that belief in a universal deluge was vanishing and that such scholars as Sedgwick and Buckland had recanted their earlier diluvialism. Despite the growing body of evidence to the contrary, Fairholme optimistically announced that evidences of a general deluge had recently assumed "the character of *complete demonstration* . . . by a mass of exclusively *physical* testimony." What was this physical testimony that somehow failed to convince the geologists who were spending their lives investigating it? Undaunted by the widespread knowledge of the existence of unconformities, conglomerates, and steeply tilted strata of constant thickness, Fairholme forwarded the untenable claim that the sedimentary rocks contained no evidence of great age and were deposited rapidly and continuously in a moist state so that each individual stratum was unconsolidated when the next layer was deposited on top of it.

Ignoring countless reported observations of geologists, Fairholme further claimed that he had not personally seen a single instance

16. Kirby, *On the Power, Wisdom, and Goodness of God as Manifested in the Creation of Animals and in Their History, Habits, and Instinct*, Bridgewater Treatise series, no. 7 (London: William Pickering, 1835).

of a well-defined ancient valley on the subterranean surface of any individual formation, and on this basis he proceeded to conclude that secondary strata could not have been formed by causes in existence today.[17] To support his assertion that the deluge occurred only a few thousand years ago, Fairholme calculated from the rate of recession of Niagara Falls that the river began to flow there only five thousand years ago. Since North America is underlain by aqueous sedimentary rocks that now form dry land, he said, the continent must have emerged from the sea at that time. When the land rose, Lake Erie began to overflow its basin, and the Niagara River began to carve out the falls.[18] Such assertions were quite unsupportable on the basis of the science of the day, much less thereafter.

Early Nineteenth-Century Theological Responses to Scientific Developments

How did leading theologically conservative commentators assess the accumulation of geological, biogeographical, and geomorphological evidence in the early nineteenth century? In commentaries on Genesis and dictionary articles on the flood, we encounter a broad spectrum of approaches ranging from those of Charles Simeon to Edward Robinson. At one extreme, Charles Simeon (1759-1836), founder of the low church party in the Church of England, completely avoided all the thorny problems and all interaction with other writers in his *Expository Outlines on the Whole Bible* (1833). Assuming the universality of the flood to be unproblematic, Simeon was concerned only with the moral and spiritual applications of the flood story to the lives of individual believers and to the life of the church. At the opposite extreme was Edward Robinson (1794-1863), founder of the journal *Biblical Repertory* and professor of biblical literature at Andover and Union Theological Seminaries. Robinson, a thoroughly conservative scholar but one of the first Americans to admit the rights of biblical criticism, painstakingly, if erroneously, dealt with much of the relevant extrabiblical material.[19]

17. Fairholme, *New and Conclusive Physical Demonstrations Both of the Fact and Period of the Mosaic Deluge* (London: James Ridgway, 1837), pp. 408-10.
18. Fairholme, *New and Conclusive Physical Demonstrations Both of the Fact and Period of the Mosaic Deluge*, pp. 186-97, 228-37.
19. On Robinson, see Jerry Wayne Brown, *The Rise of Biblical Criticism in America, 1800-1870: The New England Scholars* (Middletown, Conn.: Wesleyan University Press, 1969).

Deluge Chronology

Most nineteenth-century commentators continued to assume the literal historicity and universality of the deluge. Some assigned a date to the deluge by extrapolating from genealogies and other chronological markers in the biblical text. Methodist commentator Adam Clarke (1762-1832) put the flood at 2468 B.C., while Robinson put it at 2348 B.C. Courses on the chronology and history of the biblical books formed an important component of American seminary curricula of the period, and William Hales's massive multivolume work *A New Analysis of Chronology and Geography, History, and Prophecy* filled an important niche as a resource. Hales (1747-1831) was an Irish chronologist, a professor of Oriental languages at Trinity College, Dublin, and later the rector of Killashandra. His work originally appeared in three volumes between 1809 and 1812, and a second four-volume edition appeared in 1830 just prior to his death. Hales's study included a table of suggested dates for the onset of the deluge ranging from the Septuagint's 3246 B.C. to the 2104 B.C. of the Vulgar Jewish Computation. He preferred 3155 B.C. himself.

The Capacity of the Ark

Discussions of the ark's capacity, frequently based on appeals to seventeenth-century calculations, were often stunningly out of touch with the latest knowledge. Adam Clarke was justly famed throughout England as an outstanding Wesleyan preacher, scholar, and churchman, and it has been said that the scholarship in his massive Bible commentary is "marked by an amazing openness" regarding difficulties and points of detail in the biblical text. He gives evidence of some acquaintance with the science of his day as well, although he appealed to John Arbuthnot's calculation of ark capacity and adopted the common argument that the number of animals was much less than commonly perceived. He acknowledged that later discoveries had established a greater number of species than were known to Arbuthnot or John Wilkins (whose calculations he also warmly approved), but he blithely proceeded to state without demonstration that "the whole of these would occupy but little room in the ark." He failed to deal in any way with the issue of the larger number of extinct animals that had turned up in the fossil record, in the end simply affirming confidently that the "capacity of the ark, which has been made an objection against Scripture, ought to be esteemed a confirmation of its Divine authority."[20]

Edward Robinson made his observations concerning the ark's capacity in his updated 1832 American edition of the *Dictionary of the Holy Bible*, a massive work originally compiled in 1730 by eighteenth-century French Roman Catholic scholar Augustin Calmet (1672-1757). Robinson, according to Jerry Wayne Brown "the one American scholar to achieve an international reputation in biblical studies before the Civil War," was especially careful to bring material on philology, interpretation, and geography up to the highest standards of contemporary scholarship. Yet in the matter of the flood narrative, Robinson apparently relied on Calmet's antiquated arguments, for, like Clarke, he wrote that the number of animals on the ark was not so great as generally believed, used outdated estimates of the number of known species, and made no mention of extinct mammals. His estimates were scarcely larger than those of Ralegh and Wilkins despite the explosion of knowledge about the world's animals. Although acknowledging that "modern discoveries have augmented the variety of species of beasts and birds," he claimed that "the number of them is not sufficiently great to annul the argument he has adduced." He went on to endorse the outdated argument that the number of species increased substantially after the flood as well: "The innumerable varieties of species now known, are greatly the effect of climate, of food, of habit, whether roving or domesticated, and these would allow for considerable deductions from the general mass of creatures in the Ark."[21]

Hales claimed that the ark could have carried 20,000 men with provisions for six months plus 1,800 cannons and associated military stores. Could we then doubt its ability to contain eight people and 250 pairs of four-footed animals? Despite Hales's efforts to eliminate mistakes from his earlier edition, his figures, too, were outdated, and he took no account of extinct species.[22]

Methodist minister Joseph Sutcliffe had not only written books on scriptural geology but also published a commentary on the entire Bible. Offended by a lecture suggesting that the ark would not have

20. Clarke, *Commentary on the Holy Bible* (New York: G. Lane, 1846), pp. 66-82.

21. Robinson, *Calmet's Dictionary of the Holy Bible: American Edition* (Boston: Crocker & Brewster, 1832), s.v. "ark."

22. Hales, *A New Analysis of Chronology and Geography, History, and Prophecy*, vol. 1, 2d ed. (London: Rivington, 1830), p. 323.

been able to hold pairs of all the world's creatures, Sutcliffe responded by opting for a cubit not less than thirty inches long, forgetting that an enlarged cubit solved nothing if all the animals were correspondingly larger.[23] The ark, he thought, "must have been equal to ten or twelve first-rate ships of war." Although claiming John Wilkins as one of the best writers on the capacity of the ark, Sutcliffe himself made no estimate of the number of known species.

The German evangelical Lutheran Heinrich A. C. Hävernick (1811-1845), a theologian at the University of Konigsberg who endorsed E. W. Hengstenberg's conservatism on questions of Old Testament authorship and unity, confidently asserted that "excellent mathematicians" had shown that the ark could contain more than 6,600 kinds of animals: "this fact has remained till now unrefuted, as from its nature it cannot be otherwise."[24]

Animal Migration

While Clarke accounted for the ark's capacity in naturalistic terms, he appealed to miracle to account for how the pairs of animals were brought in an orderly fashion to the ark and how the carnivores lived in peace with the other animals for a year. Robinson granted that a quick migration of animals to the ark from the extreme heat of Africa or the coldest parts of the North might well have proved fatal to them but argued that they could have escaped that fate had they migrated by "insensible degrees" or been bred there. Moreover, he wrote, animals not now living in Mesopotamia might have lived there in Noah's time. Hävernick wanted to solve the problem the same way. In support, Robinson pointed out that several animal species were formerly abundant in countries where none presently existed. He knew that fossils of the hippopotamus, wolf, and beaver had been recovered from England, and he knew that cranes and storks had formerly bred in England as well as Holland. Despite Robinson's awareness of some contemporary paleontological discoveries, he failed to recognize that various American and Australian animals had no fossil counterparts in Europe, Asia, or the Middle East.

23. See Sutcliffe, *Commentary on the Old and New Testament* (London: John Mason, 1838).

24. Hävernick, *An Historico-Critical Introduction to the Pentateuch* (Edinburgh: T. & T. Clark, 1850). This volume is an English translation of the 1837 German edition.

Theories of the Flood

Several commentators believed that physical evidence plainly pointed to the flood, but virtually all were acquainted at best only with outdated science. In his inaugural address at the opening of the Presbyterian Princeton Theological Seminary in 1812, founding professor Archibald Alexander (1772-1851) urged those preparing for gospel ministry to become scientifically literate. Noting that "natural history, chemistry, and geology have sometimes been of important service in assisting the Biblical student to solve difficulties contained in Scripture," Alexander stressed the importance for the "advocate of the Bible" to attend to truth in all its forms. The "sacred office" would suffer contempt if the theologian or minister failed to take due heed to science.[25] We should not be surprised, then, to find that in his teaching about the biblical flood, Alexander appealed to both tradition and physical evidence. The tradition of the flood "has been handed down through successive generations in almost every country," he said, and is attested in the physical record as well: "We find traces of the deluge in every part of the world, such as marine substances on the highest mountains." The fact that bones and relics of sea and land animals are "promiscuously mingled together in many parts of the earth . . . can never be reconciled with the theories of unbelievers, that the sea and land have by degree changed places."[26] Alexander quoted no sources, so we do not know where he received his ideas. His writing suggests that he thought that fossils in stratified rocks on mountaintops were the result of the flood, however, which would have put him decades out of touch with the best geological thinking, but he may have had in mind the geomorphological and paleontological evidence in surficial deposits to which some late eighteenth-century and early nineteenth-century naturalists had appealed.

25. Alexander, *The Sermon Delivered at the Inauguration of the Rev. Archibald Alexander, D.D., as Professor of Didactic and Polemic Theology, in the Theological Seminary of the Presbyterian Church, in the United States of America, to Which Are Added the Professor's Inaugural Address and the Charge to the Professor and Students* (New York: J. Seymour, 1812). Most of the inaugural address has been reprinted in Mark Noll's book *The Princeton Theology, 1812-1921* (Grand Rapids: Baker Book House, 1983).

26. Alexander, "Theological Lectures: Nature and Evidence of Truth, October 1812" (manuscript of a classroom lecture). The cited material appears in an excerpt from the lecture in Noll's *Princeton Theology*, pp. 61-71. On Alexander's life, see Lefferts A. Loetscher, *Facing the Enlightenment and Pietism: Archibald Alexander and the Founding of Princeton Theological Seminary* (Westport, Conn.: Greenwood Press, 1983).

Adam Clarke contended that an immense quantity of water occupied the center of the antediluvian earth. As this burst forth at God's command, "circumambient strata" sank and filled the "vacuum occasioned by the elevated waters." God could have used lightning to convert the whole atmosphere into water had he wished to do so. As it was, the "incessant glare of lightning" and the "continual peals of thunder" added "indescribable horrors" to the scene. The rain and the abyss together were sufficient to overflow the earth and "to *dissolve* the whole terrene fabric" as "judicious naturalists" had supposed. Clarke appealed to the outdated works of John Ray and John Woodward, who, he said, had "rendered it exceedingly probable that the whole terrestrial substance was amalgamated with the waters, after which the different materials of its composition settled in beds or strata according to their respective gravities." He was not concerned with long-standing objections that existing strata are not ordered in anything like ascending specific gravities; he maintained that any such anomalies could be attributed to disruptions introduced by earthquakes and volcanic eruptions. As Woodward had shown, every part of the earth bore "unequivocal evidence of disruption and violence." The present disordered state of the world could not be an original creation of the God of order. The globe everywhere bore the "marks of the crimes of men, and of the justice of God." The most recent geologist to whom Clarke referred was Richard Kirwan, apparently unaware of the fact that Kirwan disagreed with Woodward's assertion that all sedimentary rocks could be attributed to the flood; he completely overlooked the work of such recent geologists as Buckland, Sedgwick, and Fleming.

Chronologist William Hales specifically adopted Kirwan's idea that the main current of deluge waters came from the south and cited as evidence the deep indentations in the southern coasts of Asia, Africa, America, Ceylon, and Madagascar. He argued that the universality and northerly course of the deluge were also evidenced by the abundant fossils in the Alps and Pyrenees, bivalves high in the Andes, skeletons of rhinoceroses and hippopotamuses in Siberia, and frozen mammoths in Siberia. Despite Buckland's compelling argument for a northerly source of the deluge, Hales concluded that "we have no longer room to doubt of the northerly progress of the cataracts of the deluge from high southern regions." The fact that Hales cited invertebrates in stratified rocks as examples of flood relics shows that he, too, was appealing to substantially outdated theory.[27]

27. Hales, *A New Analysis of Chronology and Geography, History, and Prophecy*, p. 326.

Isaac Voss's local flood hypothesis bothered Edward Robinson. He wondered how Voss could know that parts of the world outside the Near East were uninhabited at the time of the flood. Why would such a "prodigious ark" need to be built? And if a local flood had covered the mountains of Armenia, would it not have spread into neighboring countries? But Robinson was also aware of the difficulties of universality. The greatest problem as he saw it was the quantity of water needed, and he resolved it with an appeal to the subterranean abyss. But what of the cold that would have affected Noah and the animals at the great heights to which they would have been elevated by the waters? Robinson asserted that, although air is colder and sharper on the tops of the highest mountains, people do not die there from those causes. In any event, he thought it likely that the colder air would have been raised yet higher by the rising envelope of flood water, so that the ark's passengers probably "breathed nearly, or altogether, the same air as they would have ordinarily breathed a thousand or twelve hundred paces lower, that is, on the surface of the earth." Robinson liked Burnet's theory but wished that he hadn't gone to such extremes. He thought it credible that the state of the globe before the deluge was different from that of the present. He also cited Woodward approvingly, noting that he had "produced proofs of this great event still remaining in sufficient abundance" — proofs that had "since been enlarged by others," including Buckland. Like Clarke, Robinson seemed unaware that Woodward's views had long since been discredited and he failed to grasp the fact that Buckland's flood was totally different from Woodward's.

Sutcliffe theorized that God increased the powers of gravitation at the time of the flood, causing the seas to rush onto the land in increasingly high tides until the mountains were washed and "the latent rocks presented their shaggy cliffs." Sutcliffe was evidently familiar with the views of Whiston and Halley, because he specifically rejected them, arguing that the waters that overflowed the mountains were held there neither by the laws of gravity nor by the approach of a comet. He was probably more comfortable with the views of Woodward, Catcott, and Penn, as suggested by his repeated references to the flux and reflux of tides that stratified the earth and left the "world of plants and trees, which once grew in the warmer climates, deposed in our coal-fields" along with numberless "plants of which botany is now ignorant."[28] Hävernick asserted that "re-

28. Sutcliffe, *Commentary on the Old and New Testament*, pp. 20-21.

mains and traces of a deluge" indicated its universality, but he failed to identify those remains.[29]

The Landing Site

Discussions of the landing site continued to be important. While agreeing that the ark landed in Armenia, Clarke disputed claims that the ark remained on Mount Ararat, because nothing of the kind was to be seen there. Contradicting his comments elsewhere, Robinson expressed skepticism that Mount Ararat was the landing site for Noah on the grounds that the cold would have destroyed any person who "should have the hardihood to persevere." He adopted the older tradition that the ark came to rest in the mountains of Kurdistan. Sutcliffe observed that the existence of the ark was attested in antiquity by Abydenus, Berossus, and Herodotus and suggested that the ark finally came to rest on Mount Ararat, the elevation of which he estimated at eight thousand feet above sea level.[30]

Analysis and Application

Early nineteenth-century Christians had an obvious desire to claim the support of science or natural history for their understanding of the biblical flood story. While the exact relationship of the deluge to surface deposits was still being debated, there was no doubt among leading geologists that the sedimentary rock pile was caused by interchanges of land and sea acting over long periods of time, not by a single brief deluge. Geologists knew that sedimentary layers had consolidated prior to deposition of succeeding layers, and they recognized that deposition had been interrupted by episodes of uplift and erosion. The discoveries of the remains of mammoths, giant sloths, and various terrestrial dinosaurs in the late eighteenth and early nineteenth centuries made it clear that the world had formerly been populated by a large number of now extinct animals. The difficulty of imagining how all these beasts (and especially the many enormous ones among them) could have entered the ark and survived there for a year presented further chal-

---

29. Hävernick, *An Historico-Critical Introduction to the Pentateuch*, p. 113.
30. Clarke, *Commentary on the Holy Bible*, p. 74; Robinson, *Calmet's Dictionary of the Holy Bible*, s.v. "Ararat"; and Sutcliffe, *Commentary on the Old and New Testament*, p. 21.

lenges to a literal reading of the biblical flood narrative. In addition, the explosion of knowledge of new species of animals and their fossil distribution militated against the assumption that they could all have migrated across the globe to and from the ark.

The "scriptural geologists" had to ignore a vast amount of compelling evidence in order to sustain the traditional view of the flood. Whether in ignorance or by design, many commentators cited as authoritative the writings of naturalists a century or more out of date. Certainly it became increasingly difficult to make such an error innocently as the burden of evidence continued to mount. And, in fact, as the nineteenth century wore on, "scriptural geology" and flood geology schemes in general began to disappear from the scene as Christians began to face the growing extrabiblical evidence honestly and to seek ways in which they could affirm both the truth of the physical record and the truth of the biblical narrative.

9. The Popularizers of Geology

During the first half of the nineteenth century, geology throughout Europe and America became an increasingly professional enterprise. Several technical geology journals came into print, university chairs in geology were created, geological societies were founded, and governmental geological surveys were established. Geology emerged as a distinct discipline from natural history, separate from chemistry and physics. Students of the earth came to be identified as geologists rather than natural philosophers or natural historians. Geology developed its own methods of investigation and became less tied to the demands of biblical exegesis and the interests of orthodox Christian theology. In Martin J. S. Rudwick's words, geologists gradually "excluded as unscientific almost all that had previously made the earth rich in cosmological meaning: the origin of the earth, its ultimate fate, and, above all, the origin and early history of mankind."[1] Technical literature evidenced little concern to relate geological discoveries or theories to biblical texts. Geological inquiry was conducted "as if the Scripture were not in existence," and geology no longer provided evidential support for a global deluge.

Because of the increasingly technical character of geology, few biblical scholars or clergy had either access to or time to read such professional journals as the *Edinburgh Philosophical Transactions* or the *Geological Society of London Quarterly*, or presidential addresses of the Geological Society. The failure of individuals such as Clarke or

---

1. Rudwick, "The Shape and Meaning of Earth History," in *God and Nature*, ed. David C. Lindberg and Ronald L. Numbers (Berkeley and Los Angeles: University of California Press, 1986), pp. 296-321.

Robinson to grapple with the latest geological knowledge is thus partly understandable. At the same time, ordinary Christians seemed to know enough about developments in the field to realize that contemporary geologists were abandoning support for a global deluge. Indeed, many British clergy in particular, including the "scriptural geologists," came to view geology as an "infidel science" dedicated to undermining Christian orthodoxy. In this unsettling context, an invaluable service was performed by theologically orthodox popularizers of geology. Several Christian geologists, professional and amateur, as well as some geologically knowledgeable theologians, wrote eloquently for the Christian community to introduce them to earth history and to convince them that, far from posing any threat to Christianity, recent discoveries harmonized beautifully with Scripture properly understood. These writings, presented in a manner accessible to Christian clergy and theologians, exerted a profound influence among theological conservatives.[2] In what follows we will examine the opinions of three major popularizers — England's John Pye Smith, America's Edward Hitchcock, and Scotland's Hugh Miller.

John Pye Smith

John Pye Smith (1774-1851), a divinity tutor in the dissenting Homerton College in London, established his conservative credentials early in his career by challenging German biblical criticism. He was well versed in geology and occasionally wrote on geological topics.[3] A landmark set of Smith's lectures was issued in 1840 under the title *On the Relation between the Holy Scriptures and Some Parts of Geological Science.* Smith was persuaded that contemporary geologists were dis-

2. James R. Moore has argued that the interval between 1832 (the date of the publication of Lyell's *Principles of Geology*, which arguably marked the point at which the field of geology was professionalized) and 1860 (the date of the publication of *Essays and Reviews*, which arguably marked the point at which the field of Old Testament scholarship was professionalized) witnessed the "efflorescence" of scriptural geologists and the harmonizers. He remarked that in Germany an older division of labor had left the reconciling of the findings of geologists and biblical scholars to a few conservative theologians, whereas in Great Britain and America it was the geologists who did the harmonizing. See Moore, "Geologists and Interpreters of Genesis in the Nineteenth Century," in *God and Nature*, pp. 322-50.

3. On Smith's life see J. Medway, *Memoirs of the Life and Writings of John Pye Smith* (London, 1853).

covering genuine truths. He maintained that geologists were honorable and that Christians were wrong to accuse them of being heretics simply because their claims seemed to contradict traditional interpretations of some Scripture passages. Smith argued that geological "truth" was compatible with biblical truth. He devoted much of his book to showing the compatibility of geology and the Genesis 1 creation account using a novel version of the restitution or gap interpretation, but he also devoted two chapters to the flood.

Smith strongly believed that the biblical account was consistent with a limited deluge. Adopting an argument that would become a staple of local flood advocates, Smith wrote, "It is evident that 'the earth' is put, by a frequent scriptural metonymy, for the inhabitants of the earth; whence it is reasonable to infer that the universal terms in our text have their proper reference to mankind, the subjects of guilt, whose flagitious character cried for a condign manifestation of Jehovah's displeasure."[4] Smith was convinced of the historicity of the flood, citing the "histories and traditions" of all nations as adequate proof that the cataclysm was "indelibly graven upon the memory of the human race." But he was surprised that so many scholars saw some logical connection "between the universality of historical tradition, and a geographical universality of the deluge itself." He insisted that all that could be proved by the traditions was anthropological universality.

Smith discussed examples of British drift that had often been cited as evidence of the deluge and asserted that such formations had probably been deposited before the creation of man. Writing before acceptance of the glacial hypothesis, Smith suggested that the rounding of pebbles and boulders in drift required "a very long time of rubbing and grinding by currents, eddies, and tides at the bottom of the sea." He attributed the blocks of Alpine rocks now found in the Jura mountains as well as gravels and grooves on outcrop surfaces in North America and Europe to several local deluges. In support, he quoted the recantations of Buckland, Sedgwick, and Greenough from their earlier deluge theories. Smith inferred that the occurrence of most diluvial phenomena in the northern hemisphere was "adverse to the admission of a deluge simultaneous and universal for every part of the earth's surface." The cindery volcanic cones of the Auvergne region could not have survived a monstrous flood. Either the Auvergne volcanoes had

---

4. Smith, *On the Relation between the Holy Scriptures and Some Parts of Geological Science* (New York: D. Appleton, 1840), p. 98.

formed since the deluge, which he doubted, or else the "deluge did not reach to this part of the earth."

Regarding biogeography, Smith conceded that past calculations of the capacity of the ark worked so long as the number of animal species was on the order of four hundred, but he rightly charged that recent calculations generally showed "the most astonishing ignorance of every branch of Natural History"; the catalogue of known species at that time included more than a thousand mammals, five thousand birds, and two thousand reptiles.[5] There was no way that pairs of all these animals could have fit on the ark, said Smith. And then there was the yet greater problem of accounting for the transportation of the animals to and from the ark. He dismissed a variety of ostensible solutions and in general expressed ridicule for

> the idea of their being brought into one small spot, from the polar regions, the torrid zone, and all the other climates of Asia, Africa, Europe, America, Australia, and the thousands of islands; their preservation and provision; and the final disposal of them; — without bringing up the idea of miracles more stupendous than any that are recorded in Scripture, even what appear appalling in comparison. The great decisive miracle of Christianity, the RESURRECTION of the LORD JESUS, — sinks down before it.[6]

He denounced as fanciful the "scriptural geologies" of Penn, Fairholme, Young, and Kirby.

What then, asked Smith, should we make of the flood? The idea of creation and annihilation of the waters was ruled out by the language of Scripture, and "we are not at liberty thus to invent miracles," since the Bible had already assigned two natural causes. Smith suggested that the biblical terms excluded "the idea of a sudden and violent irruption" and presented the idea of a gentle elevation and later subsidence "so that the ark was lifted, floated, and borne over the awful flood" in a "calm and quiet" manner.

Smith assumed that the human race had not spread far from Eden. The human population was small and "in a course of rapid progress towards an extreme reduction, which would have issued in a not very distant extinction." Adopting an essentially Lyellian subsi-

5. Smith, *On the Relation between the Holy Scriptures and Some Parts of Geological Science*, pp. 136-37.

6. Smith, *On the Relation between the Holy Scriptures and Some Parts of Geological Science*, pp. 252-53.

dence hypothesis, Smith located the antediluvian population in central Asia considerably below sea level. In addition to tremendous rain, he supposed an elevation of the floor of the Persian Gulf and Indian Ocean or else a subsidence of the inhabited land of central Asia. These combined, he said, would be "sufficient causes, in the hand of almighty justice, for submerging the district, covering its hills, and destroying all living beings within its limits." Drainage would be effected by a return of the seabed to its previous level or by uplift of some tracts of land. Finally Smith reminded his readers that the orthodox seventeenth-century clerics Poole and Stillingfleet had concluded that the Bible spoke of a localized flood on biblical grounds without the benefit of any geological findings.

Edward Hitchcock

Very influential on American attitudes toward the flood was Edward Hitchcock (1793-1864), student and friend of Benjamin Silliman, a Calvinistic Congregationalist theologian, president of Amherst College, founding member of the National Academy of Sciences, and expert on New England geology.[7] On numerous occasions, the geologist-theologian took up his pen to elucidate the bearing of geology on Christian faith. According to Stanley Guralnick, Hitchcock saw it "as his task to assure the world, especially any skeptics of science, that every finding of geology could then be corroborated in revelation, so that there was never any contradiction between the two accounts of nature."[8] Because Hitchcock wrote for theological and ecclesiastical journals, he had a major impact on the thought of theologians and pastors. In one of his early efforts, Hitchcock irritated theologian Moses Stuart of Andover Theological Seminary by noting the unsettled character of the exegesis of Genesis 1 and asking whether geology might not "put into the interpreter's hand the clue that will disentangle all difficulties." Eager to guard an increasingly professionalized exegesis against any infringe-

---

7. For analyses of Hitchcock's thought, see Philip J. Lawrence, "Edward Hitchcock: The Christian Geologist," *Proceedings of the American Philosophical Society* 116 (1972): 21-34; and Stanley M. Guralnick, "Geology and Religion before Darwin: The Case of Edward Hitchcock, Theologian and Geologist," *Isis* 63 (1972): 529-43. For Hitchcock's views on the flood, see Rodney Lee Stiling, "The Diminishing Deluge: Noah's Flood in Nineteenth-Century American Thought" (Ph.D. diss., University of Wisconsin-Madison, 1991), pp. 51-101.

8. Guralnick, "Geology and Religion before Darwin," p. 530.

ment of its rights by science, Stuart said that he was unable "to see how the discoveries of modern science and of recent date, can determine the meaning of Moses' words." Undeterred, Hitchcock addressed the topic of the flood in a lengthy article that appeared in *The American Biblical Repository*, an organ of Congregationalist Andover Seminary, in three parts in 1837 and 1838.[9]

In the first part, Hitchcock reviewed the biblical story and extrabiblical flood traditions. Although some of his contemporaries regarded many of the traditions as unrelated, Hitchcock believed that they all originated in the deluge of Noah because many of the gods and demigods resembled Noah and his sons, the ark was alleged to have been involved in heathen worship, and the dove, raven, and rainbow were all featured in ancient mythology.

In the second part, Hitchcock reviewed the history of ideas regarding the historical and geological deluges. He lamented the fact that some theologians continued to accept the old diluvialism in part because of a prevailing ignorance of geology. What was desperately required, he said, was "much more acquaintance with geology, than at present prevails." He rejoiced that at least some advances toward the truth had been made in the previous fifty years. Hitchcock understood why people once believed that fossiliferous stratified rocks were the product of the deluge, but he failed to understand how Kirby, Penn, and Fairholme could continue to espouse such discredited views. "That such opinions should be advanced" by so able a scientist as Kirby, said Hitchcock, simply confirmed the fact that he knew very little geology. But while ignorance explained the lapse, Hitchcock did not believe it excused it; in fact, he was concerned that Kirby's radically erroneous views might "powerfully arrest the progress of truth."

Hitchcock dismissed the work of Penn and Fairholme as "physico-theology modernized." He was not impressed by their presumed

---

9. Hitchcock's initial contributions to his exchange with Stuart included the following articles: "The Connection between Geology and Natural Religion," *The Biblical Repository and Quarterly Observer* 5 (1835): 113-38; "The Connection between Geology and the Mosaic History of the Creation," *The Biblical Repository and Quarterly Observer* 5 (1835): 439-51 and 6 (1835): 261-332; and "Remarks on Professor Stuart's Examination of Gen. 1 in Reference to Geology," *The Biblical Repository and Quarterly Observer* 7 (1836): 448-87. Stuart wrote "Critical Examination of Some Passages in Gen. 1; with Remarks on Difficulties That Attend Some of the Present Modes of Geological Reasoning," *The Biblical Repository and Quarterly Observer* 6 (1836): 46-106. Hitchcock's later three-part treatment of the issues appeared under the title "The Historical and Geological Deluges Compared," *The American Biblical Repository* 9 (1837): 78-139; 10 (1837): 328-74; 11 (1838): 1-27.

geological knowledge or unwarranted self-confidence. Mincing no words, he charged that their knowledge of geology was obtained mostly by reading. They so presented facts "as to betray at once their want of practical acquaintance with the subject," especially when they were so positive on points "which all working geologists know to be quite problematical." He vehemently objected to the practice of accusing geologists of atheism simply because they "imputed the changes in the earth's condition to secondary causes." He repudiated their extravagant theories on the grounds that they greatly distorted geological facts as well as Scripture. Hitchcock flatly rejected the view that primary rocks were created "just as we find them," that secondary rocks were deposited between the creation and the deluge, and that tertiary and diluvial strata were deposited by the deluge.

> None but a geologist can know what absurdities must be received, and what distortions made of facts, before such opinions can be embraced. They answered well enough for the times when phys-ico-theology was in its glory; because then it was only a few gener-alities, and these very misty, that were known: and at this day they can be embraced, without a suspicion of their absurdity, by those who know but few of the details of geology. Yet to the geologist they appear a thousand times more extravagant and opposed to facts than any opinions that have been entertained by the cultiva-tors of this science, and which Penn and Fairholme so violently oppose.[10]

Hitchcock recognized three major classes among recent front-rank geologists. The first denied any universal or general deluge, the second believed a general deluge had taken place before the creation of man and believed that the Mosaic deluge was probably a more restricted event, and the third believed that traces of several extensive deluges could be found and that the last of these might have been the Noachic deluge. Hitchcock lumped the first two classes together be-cause they agreed that no traces of the Noachian deluge had been found. He argued that their position did not necessarily conflict with revelation, because the Mosaic account did not require that traces of the deluge remain permanently. It would in fact be unreasonable to expect to find traces of the Mosaic deluge among the fossiliferous secondary or tertiary rocks. For one thing, a tumultuous deluge would

10. Hitchcock, "The Historical and Geological Deluges Compared," p. 109.

have torn up the earth's surface, sweeping detritus elsewhere, but the fossiliferous rocks generally appear to have been deposited in quiet water and are arranged with great regularity. For another, a year-long flood could not have produced the immense numbers of fossils that had been found. Furthermore, most fossils were not identical to existing species of animals and plants, and "organic remains become more and more unlike living beings" as we go deeper in a pile of strata. If all animals except those spared on the ark had been killed and "entombed by the agitated waters of a deluge," the "existing races" should be found "as often at the bottom as at the top of the fossiliferous rocks." Hitchcock saw no escape from the force of the evidence unless one maintained that there was an entirely new creation of species that were mostly different from those destroyed by the deluge.

Hitchcock went on to argue that deluge currents would have removed softer parts of the surface, abraded the harder parts, and produced thin deposits. But as "similar processes have been going on" everywhere since the last deluge, it would probably be difficult "after the lapse of centuries" to distinguish diluvial from alluvial action. Traces of Noah's deluge might easily be obliterated. If so, however, "the fact argues nothing against the scriptural account." The absence of traces of the biblical flood should cause no alarm, said Hitchcock, because geology furnished presumptive evidence in favor of the occurrence of such a deluge — the view of the third class of geologists. Hitchcock marshaled three lines of evidence to support the Bucklandian conclusion that "the phenomena of diluvium prove a powerful rush of water from the north over the northern hemisphere." First, "boulders and diluvial gravel are found almost uniformly in a southerly direction from the rocks from which they have been detached." He described a host of occurrences of boulders and gravel throughout New England, the Great Lakes region, Europe, Asia, and Africa. Although not yet a convert to the ice age theory about to burst on the scientific world, Hitchcock granted that masses of ice might have participated in the diluvial transport by carrying larger boulders to their present locations. After all, would not "a rush of water over our continent from the Arctic regions" have swept along icebergs? But he maintained that the vast accumulations of diluvial sand and gravel bore "the marks of the action of water." Hitchcock attributed the rounding of the boulders to the action of streams that existed prior to the last cataclysm.

The second line of evidence included scratches and grooves with a north-south orientation on bedrock as well as valleys with the same alignment. Hitchcock asserted that these features, with which he had become thoroughly acquainted in his study of New England's topography, had led most intelligent men to "feel as if there could not be much doubt respecting the occurrence of a general deluge in the northern hemisphere in comparatively modern times." Hitchcock's third line of evidence focused on the animal remains found in caverns and fissures. Relying heavily on *Reliquiae Diluvianae*, Hitchcock could not "explain the phenomena in any other way, than by admitting the occurrence of such a catastrophe."

But then he raised the big question. Was this alleged deluge identical with that described by Moses? He listed three major reasons not to equate the two floods. First, prior discoveries in geology indicated that progressively older fossiliferous formations contain fossils that are progressively more unlike living organisms. Thus the great preponderance of extinct species among the fossils in the diluvium implied some degree of antiquity. Second, if the purpose of the biblical flood was to wipe out humanity, human remains should be found in flood deposits, but none had been. The only way to escape the force of that argument was to limit antediluvians to central Asia, a region "whose diluvium has been as yet little explored." Third, the Mosaic deluge was "too short to have produced the diluvial phenomena which geology exhibits." Hitchcock tentatively concluded that the arguments against the identity of the two deluges outweighed those in favor. Even so, he insisted again, "no presumption is derived from geology against the truth of Moses' history of the deluge." To the contrary, there was a presumption "in its favor even on the most unfavorable supposition."

In the third part of his series, Hitchcock asked if the Mosaic account was true. After reviewing six major objections to the Mosaic chronology, including the argument from biogeography, he argued that the biblical account was true and that a localized deluge sufficiently satisfied the demands of the text. He maintained that appeals to miracle solved no problems associated with the flood, and commented that God generally didn't operate through miracle anyway. Hitchcock cautiously endorsed the theory of French geologist Élie de Beaumont (1798-1874) that the sudden catastrophic uplift of mountain chains generated great waves that washed over the continents and that tremendous volcanic eruptions simultaneously triggered torrential rains.[11] If such conclusions were admitted, "every reasonable man will

11. On Beaumont, see Mott T. Greene, *Geology in the Nineteenth Century* (Ithaca, N.Y.: Cornell University Press, 1982).

allow, that the Mosaic account of the deluge stands forth fairly and fully vindicated from all collision with the facts of science." Realizing that some people wanted to claim more positively that "geology strikingly confirms the Mosaic history," Hitchcock urged his readers to consider the matter unsettled.

In 1851 Hitchcock again tackled the flood in *Religion of Geology*, a work that included a condensation of his three articles with slight shifts in emphasis and a conclusion in which he summarized arguments in favor of a local flood. Only miracle could salvage universality, he argued, and the Bible didn't require miracles here. The problems with universality included the sources of such a vast quantity of water, the difficulty of providing for the animals in the ark, the distribution of the animals and plants on the globe after the flood, and the probability that vegetation would have been destroyed. No provision was made for seeds on the ark, and so presumably a new plant creation would have been required, a point to which the biblical text did not speak at all. Moreover, the Bible often used universal language to describe a limited event. Assuming that human beings occupied "only a limited portion of one continent," Hitchcock wondered why it would have been "necessary to depopulate all other continents and islands, inhabited only by irresponsible animals, who had no connection with man?" He called on Bishop Stillingfleet, Matthew Poole, and John Pye Smith for support. Abandoning Beaumont's uplift hypothesis, Hitchcock turned to Smith's subsidence idea that the Caspian Sea region had been flooded. He speculated that volcanic eruptions caused by vertical movements of the Indian Ocean seabed might have condensed enough water vapor to yield forty days of rain.

Hitchcock concluded that even though newer interpretations of the biblical narrative did not seem to be "the most natural meaning," yet if geological facts "unequivocally require such an interpretation to harmonize the Bible with nature," then "science must be allowed to modify our exegesis of Scripture." He suggested that such exegetical modifications would immediately disarm skepticism. And he insisted that the Bible still stood as an immovable rock amid the "conflicting waves" even though no trace of the deluge event remained in nature. Hitchcock had not completely swung over to Moses Stuart's point of view, but, despite his continued allegiance to natural theology and harmonization, his catastrophism had become more placid and he was less concerned about a literal match between Scripture and geological details.

Hugh Miller

Surpassing both Smith and Hitchcock was Hugh Miller (1802-1856), a highly respected and devout Presbyterian who was gifted with an elegance, grace, wit, and clarity of written expression matched by few. In his capacity as editor of *Witness,* the voice of the evangelical wing of the Church of Scotland that ultimately formed the Free Church of Scotland during the Disruption of 1843, Miller gained a reputation as a zealous, eloquent, and trusted defender of Christian orthodoxy.[12] In earlier years, Miller had been a stonemason, and he honed his talents for geological observation during years in the quarries. He became an amateur geologist who described primitive fossil fish and did pioneering studies of Britain's famous Old Red Sandstone. Miller was highly respected by leading scientists including Agassiz, who wrote a long commendatory introduction to the American edition of Miller's *Footprints of the Creator.* Miller was indeed an effective popularizer of geology. His reputation for theological soundness and his facility with the pen enabled him to reassure Christian believers that geology posed no threat to orthodoxy. Among the harmonizers, Hugh Miller may have been first among equals.[13]

Like Hitchcock, Miller attributed the deluge traditions to a historical flood event that was burned into the consciousness of the race. He did not believe that the universality of the traditions implied a geographically universal flood, however; he maintained that it simply implied that all human beings had descended from those who went through the flood. Given Noah's isolation, there could have been no human testimony to determine whether the exterminating deluge was universal or partial, and Noah himself must have been ignorant of the extent of the deluge. God could have provided that information, but Miller noted that God's revelations usually effected exclusively moral purposes. More generally, Miller asserted that "those who have perilously held" that the Bible imparted "definite physical facts, geo-

12. On Miller, see Peter Bayne, *The Life and Letters of Hugh Miller* (London: Strachan, 1871); Charles D. Waterston, *Hugh Miller: The Cromarty Stonemason* (Edinburgh: National Trust for Scotland, 1966); and George Rosie, *Hugh Miller — Outrage and Order: A Biography and Selected Writings* (Edinburgh: Mainstream, 1981).

13. Among his geological writings are *The Old Red Sandstone; or, New Walks in an Old Field* (Boston: Gould & Lincoln, 1858), *Footprints of the Creator; or, The Asterolepis of Stromness* (New York: Hurst, n.d.), and *The Testimony of the Rocks* (Boston: Gould & Lincoln, 1858).

graphic, geologic, or astronomical" along with moral facts "have almost invariably found themselves involved in monstrous error." Because the extent of the deluge was a physical question that had no more moral implications than the shape or the age of the earth or the motions of the heavenly bodies, there was no need to reveal such information. Miller reminded his readers that the Bible used the common eastern device of metonymy (using the part to signify the whole), so it might well be that a major local inundation would be referred to as a universal flood. He also reminded his readers that Poole and Stillingfleet had adopted a local flood on solely biblical grounds.

In a clear appeal to extrabiblical data, Miller asserted that with respect to the flood as with respect to other biblical references to matters of physical science, "the limiting, modifying, explaining facts and circumstances must be sought for in that outside region of secular research, historic and scientific." He believed it essential that the church stay as well acquainted with such research as the enemies of the faith did. From research "much valuable biblical illustration" had been derived. He warned against ignorance of extrabiblical data, chided those who were content to solve scientific problems with the Bible alone, and showed that extrabiblical data had frequently corrected erroneous interpretations of the Bible. "Plain men who set themselves to deduce from Scripture the figure of the planet" had little doubt that the earth was flat "until corrected by the geographer"; "plain men who set themselves to acquire from Scripture some notion of the planetary motions" thought that the sun moved around an earth at rest "until corrected by the astronomer"; "plain men who have sought to determine from Scripture the age of the earth" were confident that the earth was about six thousand years old "until corrected by the geologist." In sum, plain men quite properly learned the way of salvation from the Bible, but every time they "sought to deduce from it what it was *not* intended to teach, — the truths of physical science, — they have fallen into extravagant error."[14] And if such error is casually or, worse, boldly or even belligerently endorsed, it must necessarily mar the overall credibility of the church.

To account for the apparently universal biblical language, Miller asked his readers to think about the impressions an observer would receive during sudden subsidence of the land or uplift of the seabed. An observer on a boat would be unaware of the cause of what was happening. If subsidence occurred, an intelligent witness could testify

14. Miller, *The Testimony of the Rocks*, pp. 305-6.

to "the persistent rise of the sea, accompanied mayhap by rain and tempest." The witness would testify that "it had been flood without ebb, as if the fountains of the great deep had been broken up" for many days. But the observer would "depart perilously from his position as a witness-bearer" if he claimed, when his boat floated above a hill eight hundred feet in elevation that all hills with the same elevation everywhere were also covered. The observer could not legitimately infer a global deluge from a local depression.

Miller joined Smith and Hitchcock in discounting the old diluvialism. He noted that for fifty years no one acquainted with paleontology or the true succession of the sedimentary formations had believed "that any proof of a general deluge can be derived from the *older* geological systems." Geologists had looked for traces of the deluge in surficial deposits, but John Fleming had clarified the difficulties of that endeavor, and many diluvialists had recanted. Miller also discounted Granville Penn's assertion that the flood had swept mammoth carcasses across the globe on the grounds that the mammoths were now known to have been native to the areas in which their remains were found. The remains of many extinct species that were once thought to have been transported great distances before being deposited in caves were likewise later determined to have been native to Europe.

Miller concluded that the ark would have had to be five or six times larger than the generally accepted dimensions to accommodate all known animals. Not only had there been many discoveries of new species but naturalists had also come to recognize that many different kinds of animals that had formerly been classified as a single species were in fact distinct species. There were, for example, far more species of sheep than previously recognized. Miller also reminded his readers that the Bible spoke of at least seven of each clean animal being on the ark, a fact overlooked in many of the older calculations.

Miller laid out the biogeographical evidence in more detail than anyone else had before. The migration of the wild animals to the ark would have involved "a miracle nowhere recorded," he maintained, and the burden of proof for such a miracle lay on those who asserted a universal deluge. Setting aside the issue of whether carnivores could have ceased being carnivorous during the flood time, Miller noted that of "the creatures that live on vegetables, many are restricted in their food to single plants, which are themselves restricted to limited localities and remote regions of the globe." Many insects had no wings and feeble locomotive powers, some gnats could live for only a few hours or days after losing their wings, and other insects lived only upon single plants. Getting all the animals to the ark posed staggering difficulties, and getting them all back after the flood posed equally staggering difficulties. How would the insects have returned, for instance? As wingless grubs? Miller warned his opponents that "the expedient of having recourse to supposititious miracle in order to get over a difficulty insurmountable on every natural principle, is not of the nature of argument, but simply an evidence of the want of it."

Vastly expanded knowledge of the fossil record made the bio-geographical argument far more persuasive than it had been only a century earlier. Animals in various parts of the world had been preceded by similar animals. The sloths of South America had been preceded by the extinct megatherium, known only from fossil remains. The kangaroos and wombats of Australia had been found as fossils only in that region. The birds of New Zealand were found as fossils only in New Zealand. The problem of the migration of species to and from the ark could not be evaded by recourse to an interchange of land and sea. Miller claimed with devastating logic spiced with biting humor that, on the supposition that a continuous tract of land stretched between South America and Asia,

> it is just possible that, during the hundred and twenty years in which the ark was in building, a pair of sloths might have crept by inches across this continuous tract, from where the skeletons of the great megatheria are buried, to where the great vessel stood. But after the Flood had subsided, and the change in sea and land had taken place, there would remain for them no longer a roadway; and so, though their journey outwards might, in all save the impulse which led to it, have been altogether a natural one, their voyage homewards could not be other than miraculous.

One would need miracles for even less well-traveled species. How could Great Britain and Ireland have been restocked with their original inhabitants? While "the red deer and the native ox *might* have swam across the Straits of Dover or the Irish Channel," such an effort would have been "far beyond the power of such feeble natives of the soil as the mole, the hedgehog, the shrew, the dormouse, and the field-vole."[15] But the biological distribution problem was even more serious. Freshwater fish and mollusks would have been killed. Given the spawning habits of salmon and trout, would not the flood have

15. Miller, *The Testimony of the Rocks*, pp. 347-48.

destroyed them? Invertebrates of the shores would be destroyed. Few of the more than 100,000 species of plants or their seeds could survive submersion in water for a year. Without another miracle, three quarters of the globe's vegetation would necessarily have perished.

Miller professed puzzlement that learned, respectable theologians would accept "any amount of unrecorded miracle" rather than admit a partial deluge. Could they not see that the controversy was not between Moses and the naturalists but between the readings of different theologians? Since all of natural science was arrayed against the theologians who held a global deluge, and inasmuch as "there has been always such a marked economy shown in the exercise of miraculous powers," Miller concluded that theologians who held that the deluge was coextensive with its moral purpose were on the right track. His quarrel lay "not with Moses or the truth of revelation . . . but with the opponents of Stillingfleet and of Poole." Chastising those who ignored geology as baseless speculation, Miller vigorously insisted that Christians had to pay attention to the discoveries of the *science* of geology. Individuals unacquainted with geology placed themselves "in positions greatly more perilous than they seem to think, when they enter on the field of argument with men who for many years have made it a subject of special study." The cumulative evidence from geology against a universal flood was overwhelming.

Where did Miller locate his partial flood? Borrowing from Lyell and Smith, he looked to the sunken basin of the Caspian and Aral Seas in central Asia. He supposed that if a trench-like strip between the Caspian Sea and the Gulf of Finland were depressed, "it would *so open up the fountains of the great deep* as to lay under water an extensive and populous region." The vast plains around the Caspian, laden with salt and sea shells, "show that the Caspian Sea was at no distant period greatly more extensive than it is now." If "the land began gradually to sink," Miller speculated, "slowly and equably for forty days together, at the rate of about four hundred feet per day," a rate less than twice the rate at which the tide rose in the Straits of Magellan, such a rise would render itself only as "a persistent inward flowing of the sea." One could further envision "some volcanic outburst coincident with the depression" that would affect the atmosphere, causing "heavy drenching rains" to descend the whole time. Although the rains would add little to the volume of the flood, they would appear to an observer as one of the flood's main causes and would add to the terror by swelling the rivers. By the end of the fortieth day, an "area of about two thousand miles each way" would have "sunk in its centre to the depth of sixteen thousand feet — a depth sufficiently profound to bury the loftiest mountains of the district." As "the contours of its hills and plains would remain" as before, "the doomed inhabitants would see but the water rising along the mountain sides, and one refuge after another swept away, till the last witness of the scene would have perished, and the last hill-top would have disappeared."[16]

Analysis and Application

The contemporary church would benefit immensely from a rediscovery of the compelling writing of Smith, Hitchcock, and Miller. The specific exegeses of Genesis espoused by these individuals may be open to criticism, but it is to their credit that they viewed the growing body of extrabiblical evidence devastatingly opposed to the traditional ideas of the deluge not as a threat to faith but as an occasion for reaching a better understanding of Genesis. Their considerable success in influencing late nineteenth-century conservative theology can probably best be attributed to the fact that they were very evidently committed to truth in both the realm of science and the realm of faith. On the one hand they had practical experience in geology and were familiar with the leading geological scholarship of the day, and on the other hand they had impeccable orthodox credentials and made good use of formats that were readily accessible to theologians. Hitchcock reached the theologians through frequent contributions to theological journals, while Smith and Miller gave lectures and wrote popular books for an era that was fascinated by the issues of science and religion. Altogether they made it difficult for their contemporaries to remain ignorant of the fundamentals of geology or to evade its implications for their reading of the biblical narrative.

16. Miller, *The Testimony of the Rocks*, pp. 356-59.

10. Theology in the Mid-Nineteenth Century

The Rise of Higher Criticism

Orthodox Bible commentators in the mid-nineteenth century faced challenges other than those posed by the natural sciences. Biblical criticism had become an increasingly dominant theological force as German scholars in particular began analyzing the Bible critically like any other book. Study of the Old Testament in Germany, increasingly an academic pursuit divorced from vested ecclesiastical interests, was undertaken "with a critical intensity and professionalism matched only by that of the sciences in Britain and America." As James R. Moore commented, "Genesis in the one land was being studied in the manner of geology in the others."[1] Critical scholars began to question traditional views of inspiration, revelation, and authorship of biblical books. They suspected that sizable parts of the Old Testament were collations of oral and written sources rather than direct revelations from God. The Mosaic authorship of the flood narrative and historicity of the flood were challenged. Assuming that perceived "moral crudities" in the Old Testament were unworthy of God and open to the possibility that ostensibly supernaturalistic elements might have a naturalistic basis, many scholars suggested that the text had been altered on many occasions by writers with different theological conceptions. The

---

1. Moore, "Geologists and Interpreters of Genesis in the Nineteenth Century," in *God and Nature*, ed. David C. Lindberg and Ronald L. Numbers (Berkeley and Los Angeles: University of California Press, 1986), pp. 322-50.

sequence of events in the narrative history of the Old Testament was no longer considered to be quite so straightforward. The very nature of the Bible was at stake. More particularly, the traditional conception of Genesis as a unified, original, divinely inspired document composed by Moses, the "sacred historian," came under sustained attack. Given the meager archeological and literary materials available in the early nineteenth century, many hypotheses about sources and dates of authorship were necessarily based on internal textual evidence and philosophical predilection rather than on extrabiblical evidence. No one had found any extrabiblical versions of source documents in Near Eastern excavations. In general, conservative orthodox writers of the era were more likely than critical writers to adjust textual interpretation on the basis of extrabiblical concerns.

Although the beginnings of biblical criticism can be traced to such seventeenth-century thinkers as La Peyrère, Richard Simon, and Spinoza[2] (and even further back, to Porphyry in the patristic era), modern criticism began in 1753 when the Roman Catholic scholar Jean Astruc (1684-1766) claimed that Moses must have received information from written documents that he assembled into the book of Genesis. Astruc suggested that variations in the divine names and repeated accounts of the same event in Genesis provided keys for dividing the text into distinct documents. Apparent repetitions of events and variations in the divine names Elohim and Yahweh were especially striking in the flood narrative. Was the biblical flood story actually a composite account?

Subsequent scholars, particularly in Germany, modified Astruc's original hypothesis. Johann Gottfried Eichhorn (1752-1827), professor of Oriental languages at Göttingen, suggested that Moses had taken advantage of ancient Yahwist and Elohist sources in compiling the book of Genesis. According to Eichhorn, these sources provided "authentic records of the experience of the earliest human beings."[3] In 1800 Alexander Geddes (1737-1802), a Scottish Roman Catholic priest, rejected Mosaic authorship altogether and claimed that the

2. On skepticism and criticism, see Richard Popkin, "Bible Criticism and Social Science," *Boston Studies in the Philosophy of Science* 14 (1974): 339-60. Popkin's paper examines the approaches to criticism adopted by La Peyrère, Spinoza, Simon, and Pierre Bayle.

3. For a synopsis of Eichhorn's views in the context of a valuable overview of important aspects of biblical criticism, see John Rogerson, *Old Testament Criticism in the Nineteenth Century: England and Germany* (London: Society for Promoting Christian Knowledge, 1984), p. 17.

Pentateuch was compiled and edited between the reigns of David and Hezekiah from various fragments composed before and during the time of Moses. He identified some passages as "interpolations." Geddes was also skeptical of the traditional view of biblical inspiration and wanted to remove what he referred to as "supernatural crudities" from the text.[4] Similar views were further developed and advanced during early decades of the nineteenth century by the Hebraist H. F. Wilhelm Gesenius (1786-1842), professor of theology at the University of Halle, and Wilhelm M. L. de Wette (1780-1849), who argued that the pentateuchal documents were compiled around the time of the exile. De Wette doubted that any valid historical information could be extracted from the Pentateuch.[5] Still later, Heinrich Ewald (1803-1875) of the Universities of Göttingen and Tübingen published an elaborate reconstruction of the history of composition of the Old Testament that entailed repeated revisions of blocks of material. He envisioned the early chapters of Genesis as part of a "great book of origins" that had been written by a Levite during the first third of Solomon's reign. He postulated that subsequent writers modified this composition until the fall of Jerusalem.[6] In 1853 Hermann Hupfeld (1796-1866), Gesenius's successor at Halle, distinguished two Elohist sources within the Pentateuch. Thus began the documentary hypothesis that postulated a combination of three originally distinct sources in contrast to earlier views which envisioned a Yahwist editor interpolating material into a single Elohist document.[7]

For most of the first half of the nineteenth century, biblical criticism was essentially a German enterprise. In Britain criticism caught on only among Unitarians and Deists. The orthodox scholars kept a wary eye on German criticism. John Pye Smith, for example, wrote a lengthy attack on German criticism several years before he wrote his book on geology.[8] American theological scholarship lagged in its reception of criticism, although Moses Stuart and Edward Robinson both used some critical insights within an orthodox theological

---

4. On Geddes, see Rogerson, *Old Testament Criticism in the Nineteenth Century*, pp. 154-57.

5. On De Wette, see Rogerson, *Old Testament Criticism in the Nineteenth Century*, pp. 28-57.

6. On Ewald, see Rogerson, *Old Testament Criticism in the Nineteenth Century*, pp. 91-103.

7. On the documentary hypothesis, see Rogerson, *Old Testament Criticism in the Nineteenth Century*, pp. 130-37.

8. Smith, *Scripture Testimony to the Messiah* (London, 1821).

framework.[9] In contrast, the young American theologian from Princeton Theological Seminary Charles Hodge (1797-1878) spent a couple
of years in Germany during the 1820s and was alarmed by what he
viewed as rationalistic, soul-chilling tendencies in German criticism
and moved in reaction toward the warm piety and biblical fidelity of
the confessionally orthodox German school of Tholuck and Hengstenberg, which staunchly opposed the higher critical movement.[10]

Bishop Colenso

German higher critical views significantly spilled over into Great Britain with the 1860 publication of a controversial volume popularly
known as *Essays and Reviews*, which included a strong challenge to
the harmonizing strategies of such traditionalists as Hugh Miller,[11]
and with Anglican bishop John William Colenso's massive multivolume broadside against traditional interpretation of the Pentateuch.
Colenso (1814-1883), the mission-minded bishop of Natal in southern
Africa, who was trained in traditional biblical scholarship, found himself asking questions of the text for which he could find no adequate
answers. He turned to critical scholarship and was profoundly influenced. The ultimate result was a vast work, *The Pentateuch and Book
of Joshua Critically Examined*, published between 1862 and 1879. The
fourth volume, dealing with Genesis 1–11, appeared in 1864.

Influenced by higher critical perspectives and by developments
in geology and biogeography, Colenso concluded that the flood story
was not historically true. For one thing, he inferred from the description of the Garden of Eden that the biblical writer believed the face
of the earth was much the same before and after the flood. He also
took into account the severe problems posed by biogeography for
animal migrations to and from the ark. He noted that both freshwater

---

9. See Jerry Wayne Brown, *The Rise of Biblical Criticism in America,
1800-1870: The New England Scholars* (Middletown, Conn.: Wesleyan University
Press, 1969), and John H. Giltner, *Moses Stuart: The Father of Biblical Science in
America* (Atlanta: Scholars Press, 1988).

10. For a discussion of the conservative German confessional school and
its opposition to criticism, see Rogerson, *Old Testament Criticism in the Nineteenth
Century*, pp. 79-90.

11. The challenge to harmonizing strategies was mounted by C. W. Good-
win in an essay entitled "On the Mosaic Cosmogony," in *Recent Inquiries in
Theology by Eminent English Churchmen, Being Essays and Reviews*, ed.
Frederic H. Hedge (Boston: Walker, Wise, 1860), pp. 233-78.

animals and vegetation would have died in a universal flood and noted that a single pair on the ark would have been insufficient to ensure the survival of insects and animals that live in herds or large groups, such as buffalo and bees. He was quite convinced that the ark could not have held representatives of all the world's animals. The biblical narrative indicates that Noah was commanded to provide their food, implying that he must have known beforehand what food each animal needed and would have been able to obtain it, which Colenso dismissed as impossible given the vast differences in habitats around the globe. He concluded that "if the people are to be required to believe" that the ancient story was "historically true, — as if this were necessary to salvation, — as if 'all our hopes for eternity,' 'all of our nearest and dearest consolations,' depended upon our believing this," then all these questions about animal migration and the ark would have to be reckoned with until it was "recognised that they cannot be answered."[12]

Colenso invoked Hugh Miller to dismantle John Wilkins's calculation of the ark's capacity. He debunked the idea that all modern animals descended from a few primitive types that had disembarked from Noah's craft, citing representations of animals on Egyptian monuments that were recognizably identical to modern animals. Colenso also doubted that Noah and his family could have waited atop Agri Dagh for two months as the waters receded because the air there would scarcely have supported their respiration and the freezing temperatures there would have killed all the survivors even if they had been able to breathe.[13]

Lyell and Miller provided support for Colenso's view that geology offered no evidence of a universal deluge. But Colenso was not inclined to endorse the idea of a partial deluge either. He doubted that Noah could have handled the needs of even a population of local animals for a year on the water. There would not have been sufficient air and light on the ark to sustain the health of the passengers. Filth and disease would have abounded. Could local worms have crawled onto the ark? And couldn't local birds simply have flown out of the area? Moreover,

12. Colenso, *The Pentateuch and the Book of Joshua Critically Examined*, 7 vols. (London: Longman, Green, 1862-1879), 4:176-229. His discussion of inhabitants of the ark appears on pp. 176-84.

13. Colenso, *The Pentateuch and the Book of Joshua Critically Examined*, p. 196. Although Colenso's argument was valid, he was largely dispatching a straw man: relatively few contemporary commentators held that the ark landed on modern-day Agri Dagh.

Colenso argued that the language of Scripture couldn't be more emphatic in implying a universal flood. As far as he was concerned, science was in obvious conflict with the biblical text.

He objected to appeals to miracle as a way out of the difficulties on the grounds that the Bible gives not "the slightest intimation" of miracles. "The whole tenor of the story" excluded miracle. Above all, Colenso failed to see that "multiplying miracles *ad infinitum*" was a more "*reverent* mode of dealing with Scripture" than the course of criticism on which he had embarked. The real issue, he believed, was historicity. To teach that the account of Noah's flood was "a statement of real historical matter-of-fact, merely because the Bible records it as such" was to sin against God and the truth and make an idol of the Bible! The only way to stress the lasting religious value of the Bible was to recognize its human frailties and errors. Colenso maintained that it was the mixture of "human frailty, ignorance, mistake" in the Bible "with the Divine Truth which is the Eternal Word of God" that gave Scripture its "special value as a true, natural, history . . . of the progress of human life and religion."

If we endorse the reasoning that deluge traditions imply a great flood, Colenso argued, should we not also endorse the reasoning that legends of humans arising from stones imply that at some point stones actually were transformed into people? Colenso maintained that many deluge legends developed as primitive explanations of fossils in mountains. Similarly, the bones of giant extinct animals might have given rise to legends of giants. He did concede, however, that the biblical flood legend could "rest upon a reminiscence of some tremendous inundation of the ancient fatherland of the Hebrew tribes, — possibly . . . resulting from geological changes, connected with the formation of the present Caspian Sea, mixed up with recollections of some more recent catastrophe in the lower plains of Mesopotamia."[14]

Colenso shared with contemporary conservatives an appreciation of the difficulties that science posed for a literal interpretation of the flood text. Conservatives tried to preserve the historicity of the text by assuming that the biblical text was a record of a local flood described through the eyes of an observer, but Colenso rejected harmonization and asserted that the biblical account contained factual errors deriving from the outmoded conceptions of the world held by the biblical writers.

14. Colenso, *The Pentateuch and the Book of Joshua Critically Examined*, p. 219.

Scholars Open to Critical Ideas

Other British commentators who were mildly sympathetic to critical views were far less drastic about rejecting the historicity of the deluge. John James Stewart Perowne (1823-1904), Anglican vice principal of St. Davids' College in Lampeter, for example, contributed a lengthy article on Noah to William Smith's *Dictionary of the Bible*. Noting the different usages of Elohim and Yahweh in the text, he suggested that Moses might have consulted a different narrative while putting together the flood story, but he was more interested in the bearing of scientific data on the nature of the flood than in pushing critical views.[15] He dismissed the notion of a universal flood on the grounds that the ark would have been inadequate to hold the huge number of known species and because of "the manner in which we now find these animals distributed over the earth's surface." And in any event, said Perowne, "the narrative does not compel us to adopt so tremendous an hypothesis." Recourse to miracles was unnecessary, extravagant, and "utterly unsupported by the narrative." Although the text sounded universal, the language was framed with "poetic breadth." Rather than all the globe's mountains being submerged, "as far as the eye could sweep, not a solitary mountain reared its head above the waste of waters." Some lower mountain range was probably intended as the ark's landing site. Perowne suggested that the flood "extended over the whole valley of the Euphrates, and eastward as far as the range of mountains running down to the Persian gulf, or further." Any sudden subsidence of the land could have been the cause of the biblical flood.

Discounting seventeenth-century diluvialism and the catastrophism of Cuvier and Buckland and following Hugh Miller, Perowne agreed that scientific considerations compelled belief "that the Flood of Noah . . . extended only over a limited area of the globe" unless a "stupendous miracle" had been wrought. Unlike Colenso, Perowne insisted on the reality of the deluge in light of New Testament evidence and tradition, but he admitted that it was not always clear whether the traditions pointed back "to a common centre . . . or whether they were of national growth, and embody merely records of catastrophes, such as especially in mountainous countries are of no rare occurrence."

Henry Alford (1810-1871), dean of Canterbury, claimed more decisively than Perowne that the flood narrative was of mixed Yahwist

15. Perowne, "Noah," in *A Dictionary of the Bible*, ed. William Smith, vol. 2 (Boston: Little, Brown, 1863), pp. 562-76.

and Elohist character.[16] "Contradictions" pointed to different sources, but harmonizing of discrepancies was "evident by the fact of the insertion of the two accounts in immediate contiguity by the sacred writer." Despite this challenge to the literal accuracy of the text, Alford did not reinforce the claim with appeals to extrabiblical scientific information — a surprising omission in view of the fact that conservatives had historically proved willing to alter strictly literalistic readings of the flood narrative in order to accommodate such information. Also striking is that despite Alford's sympathies for critical ideas, he wrote as if he believed that there was a literal universal flood in which a real ark landed on Mount Ararat, 16,254 feet high. Would he have spoken thus if he knew the scientific data well?

Conservative Commentary

In the 1860s, British, German, and American conservative commentators from several ecclesiastical traditions were openly hostile to views that challenged the Mosaic authorship of the flood narrative or posited the incorporation of partly conflicting sources in the text. Nevertheless conservatives were frequently more zealous than critical scholars in allowing extrabiblical knowledge to shape their interpretations of the text, and they were generally equally ready to abandon literal interpretations. After Smith, Hitchcock, and Miller had spelled out the realities of science for the theological world, orthodox commentators in droves adopted a local deluge concept, and most showed some acquaintance with the scientific data. Many explicitly referred to one or another of the three scholars, while others showed implicit awareness of their Caspian basin hypothesis.[17] Some commentators, including Robert S. Candlish (1806-1873), pastor of St. George's church in Edinburgh and a leader of the Free Church of Scotland, continued to ignore extrabiblical data and concentrate solely on the ethical applications of the text, but the majority were concerned with relevant scientific matters.[18]

16. Alford, *The Book of Genesis and Part of the Book of Exodus* (London: Daldy, Isbister, 1871), pp. 29-43.

17. Many theologians and commentators became aware of the works of Smith and Miller through reviews in the theological journals. E.g., a lengthy and cautiously favorable review of Smith's book by Matthew Boyd Hope appeared in *Biblical Repertory and Princeton Review* 13 (1841): 368-94.

18. See Candlish, *Commentary on Genesis* (1868; reprint, Grand Rapids: Zondervan, n.d.), pp. 122-50.

Many leading conservatives in the 1860s explicitly endorsed the idea of a localized deluge. James G. Murphy (1808-1896), professor of Hebrew at the Presbyterian College in Belfast and a vigorous critic of Colenso, wrote that only "the portion of the earth's surface known to man" was flooded, that Scripture said nothing about distant parts of Europe, Africa, America, or Australia.[19] Robert Jamieson (1802-1880), conservative Church of Scotland minister of St. Paul's church in Glasgow and author of the material on Genesis in the influential Jamieson, Fausset, and Brown commentary, viewed the flood as a historical event transcending a destructive Nile inundation or a snow melt in the Armenian mountains that might have been exaggerated in the excited imaginations of terrified inhabitants but that was nonetheless only regional in scope.[20] Charles H. Hitchcock, the geologist son of Edward Hitchcock, wrote in John Kitto's *Illustrated History of the Holy Bible* that the flood was "probably not co-extensive with the earth's surface. It would have been unnecessary if the descendants of Adam occupied a limited portion of the continent of Asia, as has generally been supposed."[21] John Duns (1820-1909), John Fleming's successor as professor of natural science at the Free Church of Scotland's New College in Edinburgh, wrote that he was aware of no physical evidence of a universal deluge.[22] And Franz Heinrich Reusch (1825-1900), Roman Catholic professor of Old Testament exegesis at the University of Bonn, claimed to be in good company in adopting the geographically localized flood.[23] No conservative, however, was ready to abandon an anthropologically universal flood.

Deluge traditions were still viewed as remembrances of a real destruction. In his massive commentary on Genesis, Johann Peter Lange (1802-1884), a Reformed professor of dogmatic theology at the University of Bonn, attributed flood traditions to the heathenizing of the sacred tradition by the nations.[24] E. Harold Browne (1811-1891), a Cambridge scholar and Anglican bishop of Ely and Winchester,

19. Murphy, *Commentary on the Book of Genesis* (1866; reprint, Andover: Warren F. Draper, 1887), pp. 176-216.

20. Jamieson, *A Commentary Critical, Experimental and Practical on the Old and New Testaments*, vol. 1 (1864; reprint, Grand Rapids: William B. Eerdmans, 1945), pp. 87-109.

21. Hitchcock, in Kitto's *Illustrated History of the Holy Bible* (Norwich, Conn.: Henri Bill, 1866), pp. 70-84.

22. Duns, *Biblical Natural Science* (London: William MacKenzie, n.d.).

23. Reusch, *Nature and the Bible*, vol. 1 (Edinburgh: T. & T. Clark, 1886), pp. 376-461. This edition was a translation of the fourth German edition of 1876.

24. Lange, *Genesis* (New York: Scribner, 1868), pp. 279-343. The original German edition appeared in 1864.

challenged those like Colenso who had abandoned the historicity of the narrative by asking why so many nations had retained a recollection of the same calamity. Browne claimed that the universality of traditions was intelligible only if "such an event actually did occur." The Genesis account had been "variously distorted and disguised in the legends of the heathen world." Reusch also insisted that the legends could be explained only by derivation from a common source.[25]

Conservatives naturally entertained varying conceptions of the deluge. Following John Fleming, Donald Macdonald claimed that the flood was "certainly of a comparatively tranquil character." The rise and subsidence of the water was gradual, and the "floating of the ark with its precious cargo" would certainly not indicate "violent tumultuous agitation." The tranquil nature of the flood was especially indicated by "the fact that vegetation, to some extent at least, survived, as proved by the newly plucked olive-leaf."[26] Jamieson also suspected that the deluge was tranquil, but Lange still thought in terms of violence. He spoke of a "roaring and rocking of the waters" that brought about a "benumbing torpor" on many of the animals, causing them to hibernate and hence need less food during their stay on the ark.

Arguments for a restricted deluge necessitated a special reading of the biblical text. Murphy cautioned against demanding "an inflexible literality to such terms as *all*" in regard to the flood, and Macdonald, Jamieson, and Browne underscored the point that universal terms are used elsewhere in the Bible in connection with more limited events. Tayler Lewis (1802-1877) of the Reformed Church in America was a linguistics scholar at Union College in New York who frequently wrote on the relationship of science and theology, and he gained some notoriety in an exchange with geologist James Dwight Dana that was reminiscent of the earlier debate between Edward Hitchcock and Moses Stuart.[27] Lewis noted that properly substituting the word *land* for the word *earth* immediately reduced the scale of the event.[28] Jamieson

25. Browne's commentary on Genesis appeared in vol. 1 of *The Holy Bible*, ed. Frederic C. Cook (London: John Murray, 1871), pp. 64-82.

26. Macdonald, *Introduction to the Pentateuch*, vol. 1 (Edinburgh: T. & T. Clark, 1861), pp. 387-92.

27. See Morgan B. Sherwood, "Genesis, Evolution, and Geology in America before Darwin: The Dana-Lewis Controversy, 1856-1857," in *Toward a History of Geology*, ed. Cecil J. Schneer (Cambridge: MIT Press, 1969), pp. 305-16.

28. The American translation of Lange's commentary includes copious notes by Tayler Lewis. Of particular interest is a lengthy "excursus on the partial extent of the flood, as deduced from the very face of the Hebrew text" (Lange, *Genesis*, pp. 314-22).

similarly showed that the term *earth* is commonly used in the Bible in reference to regions, countries, and similarly limited portions of the globe. Failure to translate the text correctly, he said, had led earlier commentators to incorrect conclusions about the extent of the debacle.

The approach most widely adopted by this group of commentators was to assert that the flood had been described from the vantage point of an observer. Lewis stressed that this observer would have experienced emotional distress as a result of the calamity. The narrative style was adapted to produce an impression of an actual spectacle that spoke "to the soul's eye" of the reader — and hence "to reconcile this with any scientific correctness is worse than trifling." The narrator spoke "according to his conception as grounded on the state of his knowledge," using the ancient idea of waters above the firmament. "This precious subjective truthfulness" of the account counted as evidence for its great antiquity. "One all-absorbing image of power" lay before the observer, who saw a shoreless waste everywhere, but "what he may have *thought*, we know not." According to Jamieson, the flood story was "the testimony of a spectator" recording what he witnessed, and therefore the hills mentioned were "those within the range of his visible horizon." If so, the expression "under the whole heaven" should not be taken in the literal sense "but must be understood with limitation." Browne went so far as to claim that "we have in Genesis the very syllables in which the Patriarch Shem described to the ancestors of Abraham that which he himself had seen," presumably a plain like the region around Babylon with only a few low hills. In that case, "a moderate depth of water would have sufficed to cover all the highest hills under the whole canopy of heaven." Quite possibly vapors hiding the mountains cleared off so that the summits of the hills at last became visible. Browne conceded that the biblical words could mean that the deluge overwhelmed the globe, but, had the flood inundated only the inhabited world, "the effect would have been the same to Noah, and would, most likely, have been described in the same words." Reusch considered direct revelation about the deluge unnecessary since Noah and his family were eyewitnesses who handed down the narrative of their experiences to their descendants. Moses had only to write down verbatim "the tradition which had come down to him from Noah." In any case, the flood was universal only from the point of view of eyewitnesses, and only local mountains were actually covered. Duns agreed that the high hills were those seen by Noah. He was eager to call attention to some important textual facts that were "universally overlooked" in efforts to find physical traces of the flood: the flood neither obliterated the Edenic rivers nor uprooted olive trees.

While these commentators had biblical grounds for adopting a local deluge interpretation, extrabiblical information, much of which had been gleaned secondhand from Smith, Hitchcock, or Miller, played a crucial role. There were, of course, exceptions. James Murphy made no overt appeals to biogeography or geology, and Tayler Lewis bent over backward to dissociate the interpretation of the text from scientific issues. In contrast, Macdonald's *Introduction to the Pentateuch* included a section on the credibility of the Pentateuch in relation to modern science, and Robert Jamieson claimed that "considerations suggested by various branches of science compel us to view the language of Moses as . . . restricted in this narrative." Other commentators freely discussed the implications of the scientific data, and most hesitated to invoke miracles to evade the force of that data.

According to Macdonald, the congregating of the animals for a long time "and their subsequent dispersion to their appropriate climates, from the equator to the poles" was one such problem. Browne was also struck by the animal distribution problem but maintained that animals did migrate to the ark, that they had sensed the impending catastrophe and become "perfectly tame and tractable." Jamieson noted that every region was distinguished by its own indigenous fauna and flora and that different species had their native countries and special habitats "where their proper food abounds, and their constitutions are adapted to the temperature." Acknowledging his indebtedness to Hitchcock, Jamieson argued that the animals could not have migrated from polar or torrid zones "unless they had been miraculously preserved." To get to their respective homes after the flood, "years would be spent in crossing seas and continents, in traversing mountains and plains," and they could not have reached the precise regions they were destined to inhabit without another miracle. Reusch argued that Noah would have had to make long journeys to a wide variety of climatic zones to collect the animals and that he could not have done so without "a knowledge of zoology wonderfully in advance" of his time.

Closely related was the issue of the inhabitants of the ark. "Only the animals necessary to man" needed to be on the ark, said Murphy. If so, the number preserved was unknown and the space required could not be compared with the recorded dimensions of the ark. Duns, Jamieson, and C. H. Hitchcock noted that the number of known species was far too great to have been fully represented on the ark and proved "the traditional calculations of the old commentators . . . as totally inadequate." Jamieson estimated that pairs of all known species would have constituted a passenger list of more than a million animals. Hitchcock cleverly observed that even the British Museum did not contain representatives of all known species. Browne suggested that if the ark contained insects, they would have been present as larvae or eggs rather than full-grown adults. Reusch asserted that the biblical narrative referred primarily to animals that had attracted the "attention and sympathy" of man; there was no need to heap up miracles, because it was "the preservation of the animal world as it was known to the men who then existed, that is meant." Lange was the rare conservative who held out hope that the ark included animals from around the globe.

Jamieson recognized that a global flood would have killed all vegetation, requiring a new creation of most plants. River and lake fish would have "perished by the prevalence of a salt sea, or brackish water," and ocean creatures would have died because the sea would have been diluted by the copious descent of fresh rain. Reusch agreed and did not want to rule out a new creation of animals after the deluge.

On the geological side, Macdonald, Jamieson, C. H. Hitchcock, and Browne were all aware of the argument that Auvergne volcanoes should have been severely eroded by a deluge sweeping over France. Macdonald accepted the notion of a tranquil flood and the associated point that there would not then be any unequivocal traces of the historical deluge. Still the shadow of Edward Hitchcock fell on these writers: they believed that geology had established the point "that the supposition of a deluge involves no natural impossibility, by showing not only that any region, however elevated, may by subsidence be submerged under the waters of the ocean" and that "traces of floods in various lands and of great height, discovered by geology, show at least that inundations took place which were comparatively general, and which are analogous to the Deluge, if not identical with it." Although geology had found little compelling evidence for the deluge, they believed that what had been found indicated that it was reasonable to suppose that some sort of tremendous widespread flood might have occurred. Several writers, including Macdonald, Reusch, Murphy, Jamieson, C. H. Hitchcock, and even Lange, appealed directly or indirectly to the Lyell-Smith-Miller hypothesis of Caspian basin subsidence as a possible scenario for the cataclysm.

Scholars who discussed the landing of the ark in any detail were skeptical that Mount Ararat was the site, because a landing on that mountain would simply pose further difficulties for a global flood.

Jamieson, for example, wondered how eight people and a "motley group of the inferior animals, could safely descend" from Mount Ararat, a 17,750-foot-high mountain, in view of the fact that only "a very few adventurous persons in modern times" had successfully scaled the peak. His conclusion was that "the traditional Mount Ararat is supported neither by evidence nor probability."

German Conservatism

After mid-century the most conservative views came from Germany. If Lange hesitated to break completely with the notion of a universal deluge, Keil insisted on a universal deluge in the face of extrabiblical evidence. In the line of Hengstenberg, Hävernick, and von Gerlach, the great conservative Lutheran expositor Johann Friedrich Karl Keil (1807-1888) trained a generation of confessional preachers during his twenty-five years as professor of Old Testament and New Testament exegesis and Oriental languages at the University of Dorpat. He claimed that the flood must be considered universal whether or not scientists could "conceive of a universal flood of such a height and duration in accordance with the known laws of nature,"[29] for such an event can always be produced by the omnipotence of God. Despite his swipe at science, Keil did not hesitate to appeal to selected extrabiblical evidence in support of his interpretation. There were flood legends "found in nearly every nation," for example, and there was the fact that "the earth presents unquestionable traces of submersion in the fossil remains of animals and plants, which are found upon the Cordilleras and Himalaya even beyond the limit of perpetual snow." On this point he appealed to Buckland and Cuvier, failing to recognize that they both excluded fossils in stratified rocks as diluvial evidence. Keil sensed that recent interpretations of geological evidence weighed against the historicity of the flood, but, not wishing to see scientific arguments favoring his ideas discredited, he dismissed this "latest phase of geology," asserting that there was no force to its claims.

Keil discounted conclusions hostile to global diluvialism and "drawn from the successive order of the various strata, with regard to the periods of their formation" on the grounds that geology had not yet "advanced beyond mere opinion and conjecture, with regard to the

29. Keil, *Biblical Commentary on the Old Testament* (Edinburgh: T. & T. Clark, 1864-1901).

mode in which the rocks were formed and their positions determined." Keil's use in the 1860s of the terminology of Werner and Jameson implied that he understood neptunism still to be the dominant theory in geology, whereas it had of course been laid to rest decades earlier.

Keil also rejected basic conclusions long established by geologists. He regarded as untenable on the basis of "continued geognostic [a Wernerian term] researches" the idea that each fossiliferous formation contained plants and animals distinctive to itself, that the fossil organisms are so completely different from existing plants and animals that the latter could not have sprung from them, and that there were no fossil human remains as old as fossil animals. He further doubted that the transition rocks (another Wernerian term) contained only fossils of the lower orders of plants and animals and that mammals first occurred in Triassic, Jurassic, and Cretaceous formations. Clearly Keil's doubts about geology were not based on recent knowledge.

Keil repudiated objections to the suitability of the ark for carrying the animals as "groundless fancy." Here, too, he attempted to buttress his claim by undercutting the authority of natural science to present evidence to the contrary on the grounds that it was still too primitive to make any firm conclusions relating to the ark; it was "still in the dark as to the formation of species, and therefore not in a condition to determine the number of pairs from which all existing species are descended." Despite Keil's vast influence on subsequent generations as a commentator, his views concerning the flood ran counter to the prevailing conservative opinion of the time that the deluge was a local event.

Analysis and Application

The work of Smith, Hitchcock, and Miller led scholars from several countries and theological traditions to abandon traditional notions of the deluge. Despite their deep commitment to the authority of Scripture, orthodox commentators rightly recognized the crucial role of extrabiblical knowledge for a proper understanding of the Word. They showed a remarkable willingness to face scientific issues and a great reluctance to resort to appeals to miracle in order to solve difficult exegetical problems. With the major exception of Keil, commentators were inclined to accept the conclusions of competent scientific authorities and to avoid ludicrous theories at the fringes of science that sounded biblical but lacked substance. These writers unflinchingly acknowledged that the evidence from volcanoes, rock strata, and fossils all strongly indicated that a universal flood could not have occurred and that in any event it was not rationally conceivable that pairs of all the world's animals could have trekked to and from the ark, much less that they could have been accommodated aboard. Confidently assuming that science could serve as a God-given tool to reach a more accurate understanding of the text, they probed the text more thoroughly and uncovered details consistent with a local deluge. It is especially noteworthy that orthodox students of Scripture tended to pay closer attention to extrabiblical knowledge than did their more liberal colleagues who engaged in biblical criticism. Their reevaluations of the text on the basis of the best science of their day led neither to a denial of the historicity of the deluge nor to unwarranted speculations about the history of the biblical text.

11. New Discoveries and Deluge Theories of the Late Nineteenth Century

Traditions

The Discovery of the Mesopotamian Epics

No sooner had conservative and critical biblical scholars begun vigorously defending a geographically limited deluge than further discoveries requiring new adjustments were made. For example, great advances were made in archeology during the nineteenth century. European scholars, explorers, and diplomats described ruins throughout Mesopotamia. Decipherment of cuneiform writing was under way, and in the 1840s the first excavations at Khorsabad, Nineveh, Nimrud, and other Assyrian sites uncovered a wealth of texts. Biblical scholars had long justifiably concluded that Berossus's legend was a corrupted version of the biblical story because they believed that Genesis was much older. That view changed irrevocably when George Smith (1840-1876), a young assistant in Assyriology at the British Museum, spoke about new findings in ancient Near Eastern studies in an address before the Society of Biblical Archaeology in 1872.[1]

---

1. The text of Smith's address was published as "The Chaldean Account of the Deluge" in *Transactions of the Society of Biblical Archaeology* 2 (1873): 213-34. Smith updated his work in subsequent publications, including "The Eleventh Tablet of the Izdubar Legends: The Chaldean Account of the Deluge," *Transactions of the Society of Biblical Archaeology* 3 (1874): 530-96; and *The Chaldean Account of Genesis* (New York, 1876). For some discussion of the history of Middle Eastern excavations, see H. V. F. Winstone, *Uncovering the Ancient World* (New York: Facts on File, 1985).

169

While sorting through thousands of clay fragments, Smith pieced together twelve tablets of a lengthy epic, the eleventh of which described a flood strikingly like that of the Bible. Recovered at Nineveh around 1853, these tablets from the library of the Assyrian monarch Ashurbanipal purported to be copies of flood epics belonging to the city of Erech during an earlier era. Smith believed that he had found portions of three different versions written in an older script and containing marginal commentary. The original deluge text, he said, could not have been composed later than the seventeenth century B.C. and might have been written much earlier. The text described events during the reign of a monarch whom Smith provisionally called Izdubar.[2] Izdubar, the hero of the epic, lived shortly after the flood, and his exploits concerned the Babylonian cities Erech (Warka), Babel, Surippak (Shuruppak), and Nippur. The tale said that "Izdubar, the conqueror of kings and monsters, the ruler of peoples, fell into some illness and came to fear death, man's last great enemy." He sought out Sisit, the heroic survivor of the flood who had presumably attained immortality.[3] Smith's translation told about a warning of a coming flood, a command to construct a ship which the hero then built and caulked with bitumen, the loading of the ship with animals and birds, and floating on a raging flood. After seven days the ship came to rest on Mount Nisir, from which the hero successively sent out a dove, a swallow, and a raven. After disembarking, Sisit offered sacrifices to the gods.

Smith asserted that "the events of the Flood narrated in the Bible and the inscription are the same, and occur in the same order," but the Mesopotamian story was that of a maritime people, as evidenced by the fact that the ark was called a ship, was launched, made a trial voyage, and had a pilot. The biblical story, on the other hand, gave evidence of having been composed by an inland people: the ark was described as a simple box, and it made no mention of a trial voyage or a pilot. In a monumental understatement, Smith observed that "this account of the Deluge opens to us a new field of inquiry in the early part of the Bible history." He suggested that the two stories represented two distinct traditions of the flood.

2. Izdubar eventually came to be known as Gilgamesh as the scholarly understanding of the language on the tablets improved: the Izdubar epic is identical to the Gilgamesh epic.

3. Sisit corresponds to the flood hero Utnapishtim in the Gilgamesh epic. Smith linked Sisit with Xisuthrus in Berossus's legend.

During succeeding summers Smith returned to Nineveh and recovered more fragments that were part of another deluge tradition the hero of which was named Atrahasis. Further versions were discovered at Nippur and Sippar within a few decades. In light of Smith's spectacular discoveries, scholars could no longer facilely claim that the Mesopotamian version was derived from an accurate tradition faithfully reproduced in the Bible, for here was evidence of a written version that was older than the Mosaic account. The question naturally arose: Who borrowed from whom?

Flood Traditions

Jacob Bryant (1715-1804) and George Stanley Faber (1773-1854) had earlier discussed flood legends in the context of comprehensive mythological studies and concluded that such legends derived from the biblical event.[4] Conservatives of the nineteenth century generally agreed, but doubts arose about the hypothesis of common origin, and many scholars scrutinized anew the entire corpus of flood traditions. Of special importance were extensive surveys by François Lenormant (1837-1883) and Richard Andree.[5]

Lenormant noted that the deluge tradition appeared among all races except "among the African tribes or the dusky populations of Oceanica." He believed that the principal traditions agreed with the biblical account, reinforcing their "original unity" in a "real and well-defined event." He maintained that the Mesopotamian and Hebrew traditions were the same before Abraham's migration to Canaan and that India's legend of Manu was a Semitic importation. He believed that the Hindus adopted the Chaldean form of the deluge tradition on the grounds that "commercial relations between the two countries" would have made their exposure to the tradition "historically quite natural." In contrast, he asserted, the Greeks mingled the ancient tradition with memories of more recent river floods or other local catastrophes. Although American deluge traditions were "infinitely more like that of the Bible and of the Chaldaean religion than among any nation of the Old World," he doubted that these

4. See Bryant, *A New System; or, An Analysis of Ancient Mythology*, vol. 3 (London, 1774); and Faber, *The Origin of Pagan Idolatry* (London, 1816).

5. Among the earliest comprehensive collections of myths were Andree's *Die Flutsagen: Ethnographisch Betrachtet* (Braunschweig: Friedrich Vieweg, 1891) and Lenormant's *The Beginnings of History*, which first appeared in English as a translation of the second French edition (New York: Scribner's, 1883).

traditions had passed to the New World during migrations from Asia by way of the Aleutian Islands because no hint of the traditions had been found among Mongolian or Siberian peoples. Still, he noted that legends from Mexico, Guatemala, Nicaragua, Peru, and elsewhere differed sufficiently from the biblical story to remove the suspicion of influence by Christian missionaries; they were embedded in a mythological framework that outlined four primitive ages of man, like that of India. Lenormant postulated that the American deluge tradition might have been a foreign importation from an epoch earlier than the crossing of the Bering land bridge and Aleutians. Certain features of the Fiji Island narrative sounded to him like references to some local phenomenon such as a tidal wave. But the Polynesian traditions were almost identical in widely separated localities, suggesting that a corrupted Hindu form of the deluge narrative had found its way into Malaysia and was picked up from there by the Polynesians.

Setting aside the elements of local origin and issues of importation, Lenormant concluded that the diverse legends "must necessarily be the reminiscence of an actual and terrible event" that occurred "near the primitive cradle of mankind." Finally, he wrote,

> three great races are left, whose assured inheritance it is, who did not borrow it from one another, but among whom the tradition is incontestably primitive, dating back to the most ancient memories of their ancestors. And these three races are precisely those, and those alone, connected by the Bible with the descent from Noah, whose ethnic filiation is given in the tenth chapter of *Genesis*. This observation . . . gives a singularly exact and historic value to the tradition recorded by the sacred book. . . . We need not hesitate to state that the Biblical Deluge, far from being a myth, was an actual and historic fact, which overwhelmed at the very least the ancestors of the three races of Aryans or Indo-Europeans, Semites or Syro-Arabians, and Chamites or Kushites.[6]

Despite concluding that flood legends provided evidence for the reality of the deluge, Lenormant raised serious challenges to the notion of anthropological universality. By attributing a few legends to local events, calling attention to the absence of legends among some peoples, and raising the possibility that legends were imported into already

---

6. Lenormant, *The Beginnings of History*, pp. 487-88. Lenormant's attitude of racial superiority is common in writings of the nineteenth century.

inhabited regions, Lenormant implicitly asserted that not all of humanity had perished in the deluge.

Richard Andree drew slightly more radical conclusions. From a compilation of nearly ninety deluge traditions, he categorized twenty-six as having been influenced by the Babylonian tradition and another forty-three as original and independent. He drew attention to the apparent lack of deluge traditions in Arabia, China, Japan, northern and central Asia, Africa, and much of Europe, lending credence to the notion that not everyone had descended from survivors of a single deluge. Critical scholars assimilated Andree's notion of an anthropologically restricted deluge with considerably more ease than conservatives.

Paleontology and Anthropology

Major discoveries continued in paleontology. Not only were there further finds of dinosaurs and South American mammals but the great plains of North America yielded a treasure trove of hitherto unrecognized extinct mammals. During the latter decades of the century, several exploratory parties made forays into the badlands of the western Dakotas, Nebraska, and Kansas as well as fossil-rich sites in Wyoming and New Mexico. Several great American vertebrate paleontologists made important contributions to the field: Joseph Leidy (1823-1891) of the University of Pennsylvania; Edward Drinker Cope (1840-1897), a Philadelphian of independent means; Othniel Charles Marsh (1831-1899) of Yale University; Henry Fairfield Osborn (1857-1935), first of Princeton and later of Columbia University and the American Museum of Natural History; Charles H. Sternberg (1850-1943) of Kansas; William Berryman Scott (1858-1947) of Princeton University; and John Bell Hatcher (1861-1904), who excavated under the auspices of various universities and museums. They uncovered the remains of extinct varieties of rhinoceros, camel, and deer as well as more exotic species such as titanotheres, uintatheres, oreodons, creodonts, plesiosaurs, mosasaurs, and pterodactyls. Marsh also found remains of such now familiar dinosaurs as Triceratops, Stegosaurus, Apatosaurus, Diplodocus, and the fearsome Tyrannosaurus. The wealth of material these scholars uncovered began to fall into some interesting patterns. The fossil record seemed to indicate quite clearly, for instance, that horses had progressively enlarged from the size of a small dog to the great steed of today, that the convolutions on the surfaces of their teeth had increased in complexity, and that the structure of the foot had gradually changed from four small toes on the front foot and three on the hind foot to the large single hoof on each foot of the modern horse. Several other mammals displayed similar changes through successively younger deposits.[7]

By 1870 numerous human bones and stone tools had been found at Hoxne, Kent's Cavern, and Brixham Cave in England, at St. Acheul and Moulin Quignon in France, and at several other European sites in clear association with extinct Pleistocene animals. Thanks in no small part to the persistent work of Jacques Boucher de Perthes (1788-1878), a lifelong French customs official and amateur aficionado of antiquities, students of the ancient past gradually came to recognize the great antiquity of the human species. Boucher de Perthes's carefully documented stratigraphic studies conclusively refuted assertions that human remains came to be associated with the remains of extinct animals by accident or later burial or the like: human beings did in fact live alongside various now-extinct species. In 1856, the first skeletal Neanderthal remains were found. By the 1880s, several such finds had been made throughout Europe. Distinctive stone tools found at the sites gave clues to human cultural development. Anthropologists began talking about paleolithic, or old stone age man, and neolithic, or new stone age man. Because paleolithic bones and tools were sometimes found with the remains of extinct Pleistocene animals, some scholars began to characterize them as the remains of humans who perished in the great deluge and to characterize neolithic bones and tools as the remains of humans who had descended from the occupants of the ark.

Other scholars rejected the notion that all human beings descended from the three sons of Noah — or even from Adam. For example, Alexander Winchell (1824-1891), professor of geology at the

---

7. For a helpful overview of some of the important American paleontologists of the latter nineteenth century and their discoveries, see Url Lanham, *The Bone Hunters* (New York: Columbia University Press, 1973). See also Robert W. Howard, *The Dawnseekers* (New York: Harcourt Brace Jovanovich, 1975), and Adrian J. Desmond, "The Discovery of Marine Transgressions and the Explanation of Fossils in Antiquity," *American Journal of Science* 275 (1975): 692-707. On the career of Henry Fairfield Osborn, see Ronald Rainger, *An Agenda for Antiquity: Henry Fairfield Osborn and Vertebrate Paleontology at the American Museum of Natural History, 1890-1935* (Tuscaloosa: University of Alabama Press, 1991). On Sternberg, see C. H. Sternberg, *Life of a Fossil Hunter* (New York: Holt, 1909), and Katherine Rogers, *The Sternberg Fossil Hunters: A Dinosaur Dynasty* (Missoula, Mont.: Mountain Press, 1991).

University of Michigan, asked rhetorically in his massive volume *Preadamites* whether the table of nations in Genesis 10 implied that regions beyond the limits of the Middle East were vacant immediately after the deluge. Had the "black tribes of Africa and Australia and Melanesia, and the brown nations of Asia and America and Polynesia, been produced from the posterity of Noah during the interval which separates us from the flood?" Winchell knew that most Christians gave an affirmative answer.

> Yes, says the catechism, which, under cover of religious instruction, assumes to indoctrinate our children in ethnological science. Yes, yes, says the commentator, who experiences no difficulty in swallowing the exegetical and indigestible crudities which have been the heirlooms of the church for two thousand years. Yes, yes, yes, exclaims, too unanimously, the modern teacher of "divine truth," all unconscious that the science of ethnology has made visible advances since Jerusalem was the center of the world.

Winchell clearly disagreed with the catechism, the commentators, and the modern teachers of divine truth — and this despite the fact that he was a conservative Methodist. He attempted to demonstrate that all humans were not derived from Noah by pointing to passages in Genesis implying the existence of peoples contemporary with the descendants of Noah. On linguistic and ethnological grounds he argued that the Mongoloid and other peoples could not have descended from Noah. "The descendants of Noah found them in every new country, and could give no account of their origin." In Winchell's judgment, the deluge did not destroy all humans "but only all the people which fell within the purview of Semitic history and tradition." He thus added his voice to the growing chorus of those endorsing a local flood.[8]

---

8. Winchell, *Preadamites; or, A Demonstration of the Existence of Men before Adam*, 5th ed. (Chicago: S. C. Griggs, 1890), p. 89. For details on the history of discoveries pertaining to human antiquity, see Donald K. Grayson, *The Establishment of Human Antiquity* (New York: Academic Press, 1983). On Neanderthal discoveries in particular, see Frank Spencer, "The Neanderthals and Their Evolutionary Significance," in *The Origins of Modern Humans: A World Survey of the Fossil Evidence*, ed. Fred H. Smith and Frank Spencer (New York: Alan R. Liss, 1984). For further reading on nineteenth-century anthropology in general, see Thomas R. Trautmann, *Lewis Henry Morgan and the Invention of Kinship* (Berkeley and Los Angeles: University of California, 1987), and George W. Stocking Jr., *Victorian Anthropology* (New York: Free Press, 1987).

New Geological Theories of the Deluge

The discovery of the Izdubar epic lent further credence to the notion that a real historical event lay behind all forms of the Near Eastern deluge story, and efforts to find a scientific basis for the event continued. As the Lyell-Smith-Miller hypothesis of a sinking Caspian Sea basin failed to capture the allegiance of most geologists, new explanations surfaced in the latter nineteenth century. Because some geologists had no interest in corroborating an infallible Bible or advancing the cause of orthodox Christianity, they regarded the quest for geological evidence of the deluge as a purely scientific venture, but Christian geologists had apologetic reasons for explaining the event on scientific grounds.

Eduard Suess

A novel flood scenario was proposed by Eduard Suess (1831-1914), a skilled Alpine geologist from the University of Vienna. Between 1883 and 1909, Suess published a massive three-volume work on global structure entitled *Das Antlitz der Erde*. Older geological texts written by such Christian geologists as Hitchcock often concluded with a discourse on the relationship between Christianity and geology. In a remarkable turn of events, at a time when geology texts were increasingly marked by professionalism, respect for the boundaries of the discipline, and avoidance of religious matters, Suess *began* his magnum opus, a work devoid of orthodox apologetic concerns and sympathetic to higher criticism, with a lengthy discourse on the flood.[9] According to historian Mott Greene, Suess achieved several aims by discussing the flood: he made the point that the debate about the flood had to be settled on the basis of evidence, and he substantiated his mastery "of the widest spectrum of materials," establishing his authority to expound a comprehensive theory of the crust's dynamic history. He took on extreme uniformitarians who denied any flood catastrophe and catastrophists who made a universal phenomenon of it.

Suess suggested that the structure of mountains hinted at the "occasional intervention . . . of episodal disturbances of . . . indescribable and overpowering violence." The most stupendous dynamic

---

9. Suess, *Das Antlitz der Erde*, 3 vols. (Vienna, 1883-1909). The work appeared in an English translation in five volumes as *The Face of the Earth*. For discussion of Suess's ideas on tectonics see Mott T. Greene, *Geology in the Nineteenth Century* (Ithaca, N.Y.: Cornell University Press, 1982).

natural event for which human testimony existed was the deluge. As great floods often owe their power to violent hurricanes and earthquakes, he suggested that many flood legends might owe their origin to such events. Seismically generated floods typically occurred along low coastal regions or the lower courses of river valleys. When seismic vibrations occurred in alluvial regions, the brittle upper layer above the water-saturated ground would split open "in long clefts, and from these fissures the underground water, either clear or as a muddy mass, is violently ejected, sometimes in great volumes, sometimes in isolated jets several yards high." Suess asserted that the biblical flood was caused by the simultaneous occurrence of a cyclone and a seismic convulsion in a broad river valley. "The fact that the vessel was driven inland from the sea against the course of the rivers" was decisive, he wrote: any flood caused solely by rain "would certainly have carried the ship from the Lower Euphrates to the sea." After describing examples of recent events in the lower courses of the rivers of India, he attributed the biblical flood to "great atmospheric disturbances, vast falls of rain, storm, and darkness" accompanied by earthquakes, probably within the Persian Gulf. The darkness was caused by a cyclone "which had broken over the land." Suess's hypothesis struck a sympathetic chord with several higher critics. They saw in his scenario a satisfactory natural explanation for the features of the biblical account, which most of them believed must have had some historical event behind it.

Sir Henry Howorth

Like Suess, Sir Henry Howorth (1842-1923) had no Christian apologetic motivations, but he nonetheless produced what amounted to a modernized version of the cataclysms of Kirwan and Buckland based on the large accumulations of vertebrates entombed in surface deposits.[10] Howorth did not believe that Genesis carried any weight with respect to specifically geological investigations beyond the extent to which he believed that biblical and other traditions suggested the reality of a physical event that science should not ignore. He was more worried about scientific than theological dogma: he complained that some scientists, reacting nega-

10. See Howorth, *The Mammoth and the Flood* (London: Sampson Low, 1887). Howorth was an active participant in scientific debate in Great Britain toward the end of the nineteenth century. He wrote on a number of topics that concerned the Pleistocene Epoch.

tively to the assertions of biblical literalists, were refusing to give appropriate credence to the biblical flood tradition.

Howorth also complained about the reigning dogma of uniformity, the belief that the processes at work in the geological past could not have been different from those now in operation. He maintained that it was "indefensible to plead that Nature's workshop has always contained precisely the same tools and no others, and that we are bound to have recourse to normal and existing causes only in explaining all the effects we find." He argued that certain geological features could only have been produced by causes no longer in operation. For example, he maintained that the destruction of the mammoth and its contemporaries and the deposition of their remains under loam or gravel was properly attributed to a diluvial cataclysm that overwhelmed a vast part of the earth's surface. He further asserted that the catastrophe was accompanied by a sudden change of climate that froze animals living in a formerly temperate Siberia and accounted for the gap between paleolithic and neolithic man.

Howorth tried to establish his hypothesis with endless descriptions of massive burials of mammoths and other large mammals around the world. He claimed that the mammoths could not have lived in the tundra like that of present-day northern Siberia, which is "swept by terrible icy winds, and covered with moss, sprinkled with a few humble flowers." It would have been physically impossible for elephants and rhinoceroses to exist on such a feeding ground, he said. They need trees and long grasses that are unavailable in climates that are ruled by winter ten months of the year. Howorth argued that the mammoth and its contemporaries lived where their remains are now found but that, while they lived, this region was temperate enough to support trees. "The *debris* of vegetation and of the freshwater and land shells found with the Mammoth's remains," he argued, confirmed "that the climate of Northern Siberia was at the epoch of the Mammoth much more temperate than now" — much like present-day *southern* Siberia — and "the larch, the willow, and the alnaster were probably the prevailing trees." He suggested that woods extended as far north as the Arctic Sea, and winters were temperate. He asserted that frozen mammoth flesh was as fresh "as if recently taken out of an Esquimaux cache or a Yakut subterranean meat-safe," indicating that the mammoths must have been frozen immediately at death and remained continuously frozen since they were first entombed. The mammoths must have been buried in a region of comparatively genial climate with soft ground, and the ground must have been frozen suddenly during the cataclysm.

Howorth further argued that paleolithic human beings were contemporaries of the mammoth, but he knew of no single instance in which the remains of a mammoth or rhinoceros had been found with the remains of a neolithic human or a domesticated animal with the remains of a paleolithic human. One category of fauna had apparently completely replaced another. A single sudden, widespread, and potent cause "swept away" the mammoth, the rhinoceros, the cavebear, the European hyena, and paleolithic man, he argued. Bone graves in the Americas, Australia, and New Zealand also pointed to animals having been entombed together. The scientific evidence converged "with irresistible force," said Howorth, "to the conclusion that the period during which the Mammoth lived came to a close in many latitudes with a catastrophe on a great scale" that extinguished the mammoth, many of its contemporaries, and paleolithic man over very wide areas. He did claim, however, that many people descended from groups untouched by the spectacular deluge. One need not have been on the ark to have survived Howorth's flood.

Sir Joseph Prestwich

Speculation about large-scale catastrophic floods was not restricted to the thought world of amateurs like Howorth lurking around the fringes of the geological community. Sir Joseph Prestwich (1812-1896), one of the finest British geologists of the latter half of the nineteenth century, had spent his early life as a wine merchant doing geology in his spare time, but his contributions to the science were so highly regarded that he became president of the Geological Society of London during the early 1870s. In 1874, at the age of sixty-two, he became professor of geology at Oxford University. His geological expertise concerned surface deposits associated with the ice age and early man. He was the first geological authority to confirm the findings of Boucher de Perthes regarding the antiquity of man. Toward the end of his career, Prestwich, intrigued by the deluge question, issued a series of strictly scientific papers on the subject.

His first paper (1892) documented the rubble drift of southern England, a coastal accumulation of locally derived angular rock fragments deposited on top of raised beaches.[11] The rubble drift he ex-

11. Prestwich, "The Raised Beaches, and 'Head' or Rubble-Drift, of the South of England: Their Relation to the Valley Drifts and to the Glacial Period; and on a Late Post-glacial Submergence," *Quarterly Journal of the Geological Society*

amined contained bone fragments of several extinct animals and of paleolithic humans. These bones were fractured, but they had not been abraded or gnawed by carnivores. Prestwich never found whole skeletons in the deposits. Although the shells of land mollusks showed up in the deposits, there were no marine or river shells: the deposits displayed no obvious relationship to river or stream systems. Prestwich also described loess, a fine loamy material that blankets large parts of the British and European interior, and he documented steep fissures filled with angular rubble cemented by calcite. Several of these fissures were filled with shattered bone fragments of recent mammals. Prestwich sought to explain all these phenomena in terms of a slow postglacial submergence of southern England. He postulated that land animals retreated to higher ground as the water rose and eventually drowned and that some corpses drifted but others settled where they died. Later "the submerged land was again raised . . . by a succession of uplifts more or less rapid, with intervals of rest or of slow movement." This emergence produced "divergent currents which swept down the loose surface-debris with varying rapidity and for varying distances," over old sea cliffs onto beach terraces. Prestwich reasoned that the uplifts were short and rapid because the rubble was free from erosional wear and the fractured fragments retained their sharp angles. Since he found rubble drift at elevations of up to 1,300 feet, he envisioned submergence to that depth.

The following year Prestwich extended his argument to the Mediterranean area, focusing especially on rubble drift in France, Gibraltar, and Sicily.[12] He described fissures and caves on the level summit of Montagne de Santenay in southern France that contained the remains of various large mammals. He argued that the submergence of the land would naturally have driven the animals to seek refuge near the summit. "Flying in terror and cowed by the common danger," carnivores and herbivores would have perished together if they had fled to an isolated hill too low to top the rising water. If subsidence were slow, the animal carcasses would have decayed in place and their limbs

---

of London 48 (1892): 263-343. The raised beaches can generally be identified by their terrace-like character, the result of wave action either when the beach was lower or the sea level was higher. In either case, the terraces are found at higher elevations than present-day beaches.

12. See Prestwich, "On the Evidences of a Submergence of Western Europe, and of the Mediterranean Coasts, at the Close of the Glacial or So-called Post-glacial Period, and Immediately Preceding the Neolithic or Recent Period," Philosophical Transactions of the Royal Society of London 184 (1893): 903-84.

would have been "scattered and dispersed irregularly on the submarine surface." When the submerged land rose up again, the bones, detached limbs, and detritus would have been "carried down by divergent currents to lower levels," or they would have fallen into "fissures of the rock over which the detrital matter passed, or else, when facing the coast, over the ledges of the old cliffs rising above the Raised Beaches." The bones would have been smashed by the accompanying loose rocks, said Prestwich.

He also described fissures in the Rock of Gibraltar containing bones of bears, hyenas, big cats, horses, rhinoceroses, deer, oxen, wolves, and other animals. He maintained that only submergence could have brought together such an unlikely group of animals.

On the north coast of Sicily a ring of cliffs forms an amphitheater overlooking a flat plain that extends to the Bay of Palermo. Caves just above the junction of the plain and the cliffs contained an abundance of fragmented hippopotamus bones, as did breccia deposits in front of the caves. Prestwich hypothesized that the animals fled to the amphitheater during submergence and were trapped there as the waters rose, the cliffs proving "impassable to the larger and heavier animals." He painted the picture of animals "thronged in vast multitudes, crushing into the caves and swarming over the ground at their entrance, where they were eventually overtaken by the waters and destroyed."

Prestwich noted that rubble drift and bone-bearing breccias were rarer at the eastern end of the Mediterranean. The ossiferous fissures were "uncertain in Syria, and seem to be wanting in Cyprus and Palestine." Prestwich inferred that the eastern Mediterranean area was less affected by the submergence and re-elevation of the land than was the west.

Prestwich failed to link the submergence hypothesis to the biblical deluge in either of these papers, but he did make the link explicit in 1894 in a paper presented to the Victoria Institute, a British association of those deeply interested in the relationship between the Bible and science.[13] Now he claimed that his hypothesis provided "a more

13. Prestwich, "A Possible Cause for the Origin of the Tradition of the Flood," *Transactions of the Victoria Institute* 27 (1894): 263-305. Prestwich was prevented by illness from presenting the paper himself; it was read by Prof. T. Rupert Jones. Before his death two years later, Prestwich issued one more important summary of his views in a small book entitled *On Certain Phenomena Belonging to the Close of the Last Geological Period and on Their Bearing upon the Tradition of the Flood* (London: Macmillan, 1895). The Victoria Institute was founded specifically to defend Scripture against the claims of false science.

adequate cause for the Tradition of the Flood than any local river or land flood," for his submergence was "an inundation of continental dimensions, and destructive to large populations of men and animals." Prestwich also left room for a flood that was not anthropologically universal by suggesting that in each area there were a few survivors who might have looked upon the flood as universal because for them "the only visible sign must have been the slow encroachment of the waters over their visible land."

J. William Dawson

J. William Dawson (1820-1899), longtime professor of geology at Canada's McGill University, was a strongly orthodox Christian who endorsed the concept of large-scale flooding and eschewed evolution.[14] In *The Meeting Place of Geology and History*, Dawson wrote that the Berossus legend, the Chaldean deluge tablets, and the traditions summarized by Lenormant all provided testimony to the occurrence of a deluge in the Babylonian plain.[15] Geology and archeology had revealed the remains of prehistoric human beings who were alive when animals and climatic conditions were different from what they are today. Dawson believed that an extreme uniformitarian view had arisen in reaction against the "convulsive geology of an earlier period" and was wrongly entertaining the idea that the age of "palaeocosmic" human beings was of vast duration and had "passed only by slow gradations and a gradual transition into the new conditions of the modern period." Dawson felt compelled by recent findings to assert to the contrary that there were "two distinct human periods . . . characterised by differences of faunae and of physical conditions, as well as by distinct races of men" and specifically that a transient postglacial submergence had extinguished "palaeocosmic men" and their companion animals. Dawson thought it probable that this "greatest of all revolutions in human affairs" might have formed the basis of all the various deluge traditions. The biblical deluge need not have been limited to a single year: local subsidence might already have been in progress for a long time, and Noah might have experienced only the culmination of the submergence in the central district of human residence. Dawson thus allowed that

14. On Dawson, see Charles F. O'Brien, *Sir William Dawson: A Life in Science and Religion* (Philadelphia: American Philosophical Society, 1971).

15. Dawson, *The Meeting Place of Geology and History* (Chicago: Fleming H. Revell, 1894); see also *The Historical Deluge in Its Relation to Scientific Discovery and to Present Questions* (New York: Fleming H. Revell, 1895).

Noah's flood might have been local and yet still have destroyed paleo-lithic man of the mammoth age. Geological theorizing about the deluge was by no means finished.

Reaction to the Deluge Theories

The Suess hypothesis immediately captured the fancy of the higher critical school, while the catastrophic scenarios of Howorth, Prestwich, and Dawson appealed to biblical conservatives.[16] In general, most geologists were not convinced by speculations about grand submergences. In the spirited discussion following Prestwich's paper at the Victoria Institute, Dawson, Howorth, and a few others waxed enthusiastic over his hypothesis, but serious questions were also raised. Professor T. M. Hughes stated that it was not clear that the bone fragments in the rubble deposits were contemporaneous and that any of a number of agents could have moved the rubble downslope. Hughes also questioned the assertion that rising water would have swept large numbers of hippopotami into fissures. Could not such good swimmers have ridden out any wave? Professor E. Hull thought it odd that a marine subsidence would have left no marine shells in the ossiferous fissures. Warren Upham (1850-1934), a glacial geologist with the United States Geological Survey, was troubled by the postulated rate of emergence. According to Upham, a total emergence of around a thousand vertical feet would have little more effect than the flow of a powerful river current on its banks. An emergence occurring at the rate of an ebbing tide (one or two feet per hour) for a month or more would "be quite inadequate to form the rubble drift," he wrote. A minister put his finger on the most glaring flaw in Prestwich's scheme: "The chief difficulty," noted the Reverend J. M. Mello, "is the apparent limitation in area of the submergence indicated by the beds which he has described." Mello pointed out that physical evidence should be greatest in the Babylonian area if that was the center of the flood, but in fact Prestwich's evidence lessened from west to east along the Mediterranean coastline, and there was little evidence at all to indicate submergence along the coasts of Asia Minor and Palestine. If the rubble drift evidence did in fact point to some sort of generalized flood, it

---

16. Included in this group was George Douglas Campbell (1823-1900), the eighth duke of Argyll, who, like Henry Howorth, was an amateur who enjoyed involvement in late Victorian-era scientific discussion. He contributed a small book entitled *Geology and the Deluge* (Glasgow: Wilson & McCormick, 1885) in which he adopted views very similar to those of Howorth.

would appear to have had little effect on the region described in the biblical story.

Geologist Thomas George Bonney (1833-1923) challenged the scenarios of Dawson, Howorth, and especially Prestwich in an article published in 1903.[17] Bonney was an ordained priest who later became a fellow of St. John's College, Cambridge. In 1877 he became professor of geology in University College, London, and between 1884 and 1886 was president of the British Association. Recognized as an authority on igneous and metamorphic rocks, Bonney was nevertheless a geologist of wide-ranging interests, including glacial theory. He argued that the sharp gap between the Paleolithic and Neolithic periods that Dawson attributed to the deluge was in fact only a comparative break. Moreover, the Mediterranean area was precisely where the best evidence for the break should be expected "if primaeval man and the contemporaneous fauna had perished in a deluge." Against the submergence hypothesis, Bonney contended that the "conflict of rushes" in any sudden uplift from beneath a shallow sea would rapidly blunt the transporting forces so that rocks and boulders would not travel very far. He suggested that Prestwich's rubble drift resembled Alpine and Himalayan mud avalanches and noted that loess might easily have been transported by wind. He also noted that the animal remains at Santenay differed from one cave to another, and he suggested that over an extended period of time spring floods might have trapped local denizens of the caves. Bonney argued that such floods would have occurred during snow melting seasons, "when pasturage is scanty, and the animals most likely to perish. Rivulets of waters, swollen by the heavy rains and melting snow, would wash the plateau and carry carcasses into fissures, which might even serve as traps when covered by snow." Furthermore, some of the fissure deposits were stratified, implying sequential rather than one-time cataclysmic deposition. In addition, the quagmires at Kentucky's Big-bone Lick, the imperfectly frozen surface of the Siberian tundra, drought in South Africa, and frost in Patagonia all suggested means other than flood by which large numbers of animals might perish. Bonney was also troubled by the selectivity of Prestwich's flood. Why did the lion, brown bear, lynx, wolf, bison, and reindeer escape the submergence while others did not?

17. Bonney, "Science and the Flood," *The Expositor* 7 (1903): 456-72. On Bonney's life, see William W. Watts, "Thomas George Bonney, 1833-1923," *Proceedings of the Royal Society*, series B, 99 (1925-26): xvii-xxvii; and Thomas G. Bonney, *Memories of a Long Life* (Cambridge: Metcalfe, 1921).

In the end he maintained that the idea of a universal or large-scale deluge could claim no real support from geology.

George Frederick Wright

The glaring weaknesses of late nineteenth-century diluvial hypotheses did not prevent George Frederick Wright (1838-1921) from espousing similar ideas. Wright pastored a Congregationalist church in Andover, Massachusetts, and in 1881 became professor of New Testament language and literature at Oberlin Seminary in Ohio. Throughout his career, Wright traveled widely, was active in scientific organizations, conducted research in geomorphology, and wrote several books about the ice age.[18] Early twentieth-century evangelical thinking was strongly influenced by Wright. Like Smith, Hitchcock, and Miller, he imparted the latest geological knowledge to theological conservatives in books and theological journals. During his time, Wright was probably the most knowledgeable defender of the idea that the biblical narrative of the flood had scientific support.

Heavily influenced by Prestwich and Miller, Wright suggested that the biblical flood might be explicable in terms of rapid postglacial vertical land movements in Europe, Asia, and possibly North America. In 1902, Wright published a series of three important articles in *Bibliotheca Sacra* entitled "Geological Confirmations of the Noachian Deluge."[19] He adopted the now-familiar strategy of arguing that the language of the flood story described what appeared to the senses of the participant, that it did not go beyond the visible phenomena, and that it did not try to "settle minute extraneous questions." He suggested that the Bible "represents the Flood as caused not so much by the rising of the water, as by the sinking of the land." In addressing the scientific aspects of the deluge, Wright contended that the depressed basins of Lake Baikal, the Aral Sea, and the Dead Sea were the result of comparatively rapid movements probably no more than 40,000 years ago. He suggested that a sea occupied the Gobi Desert until recently, citing extensive shore-line deposits there and early Chinese records to

---

18. For a review of Wright's life and thought, see Ronald L. Numbers, "George Frederick Wright: From Christian Darwinist to Fundamentalist," *Isis* 79 (1988): 624-45. Elsewhere Numbers suggests that Wright represents the link between nineteenth-century and modern creationism (*The Creationists* [New York: Alfred A. Knopf, 1992]).

19. Wright, "Geological Confirmations of the Noachian Deluge," *Bibliotheca Sacra* 59 (1902): 282-93, 537-56, 695-716.

that effect. He maintained that ice sheets depressed underlying land during the glacial period and that other portions of the earth's surface rose commensurately, an effect that was exaggerated by the lowering of the sea level that resulted from the general transfer of water from the oceans to the ice sheet. When warmer temperatures came, he argued, ice melted and the previously glaciated areas rose, the previously elevated land dropped, and the oceans rose again. Wright believed that disturbances in elevation of this sort during the glacial period "produced such an abnormal temporary instability of conditions that the story of the Flood, when reasonably interpreted, is not encompassed with any more *a priori* geological improbabilities than is any of the other great facts of geological history."

In his concluding article, Wright reviewed physical evidence for the flood. He acknowledged his debt to Prestwich for the European evidence of rubble drift, ossiferous fissures, and widespread loess and pointed out that loess also covered much of China. Acknowledging that wind helped produce the loess, Wright nevertheless asserted that a great body of standing water had to be involved. He also argued that the presence of the Arctic seal in the Caspian Sea and in Lake Baikal and the beach gravels and raised shorelines in southern Russia were produced by a postglacial deluge.

Four years later Wright published *Scientific Confirmations of Old Testament History*, a work containing an expanded version of his earlier articles. The new material consisted of a discussion of Mesopotamian flood traditions, a section on the recency of the glacial epoch, additional examples of physical evidence from Europe and Asia, and a totally new section on evidence for the deluge in North America. Wright set out to link the biblical flood to the ice age by demonstrating the recency of the ice age. Summarizing material from his earlier book *The Ice Age in North America*, Wright stated that water first began to cascade over the Niagara Falls when the North American ice sheet retreated to the north. Assuming an erosion rate of five feet per year, he calculated that the falls must have started around 5000 B.C., "contemporaneous with a high civilization in Egypt and Babylonia." Citing corroborating evidence from other waterfalls, lakes, and ponds in glaciated areas as well as postglacial stream erosion and such special formations as limestone boulders set atop pedestals in areas of slightly acid groundwater in the eastern United States, Wright argued that the ice age must have ended relatively recently.

Wright also contended that the vast sheets of loess in the central states were the result of wind action and floods released by melting glaciers. A human skeleton found at the base of undisturbed loess indicated that humans once occupied the Missouri River valley, he said, and were probably exterminated by glacial floods that preceded the biblical flood. The biblical flood would not have had to be global to destroy all living human beings, Wright claimed, because the inhabitants of the New World had already been wiped out by earlier catastrophes; the human population at the time of the flood was essentially limited to a comparatively small area in Central Asia. He did concede, however, that some people in North America might have escaped both the glacial floods and the biblical deluge.

Wright sketched his flood scenario as follows:

> In connection with the instability of the earth's crust accompanying, and probably caused by, the accumulations of ice during the Glacial epoch and its subsequent melting, with the return of the water to the ocean bed, there was a wide-spread depression of Europe and of Northern, Central, and Western Asia, which, though gradual at first, culminated in a catastrophe of more rapid subsidence, followed by a still more rapid emergence of the continents, with numerous successive sudden uplifts over various portions of the submerged area. Such a continental subsidence, amounting to about fourteen hundred feet in Western Europe and about three thousand feet around the heaviest continental masses of Central Asia, would fill the Jordan Valley with oceanic water; would temporarily convert all European Russia, except the Ural Mountains, in company with the great Aral-Caspian depression and all Western and Northwestern Siberia, into a sea; would make Lake Baikal an arm of the ocean, and would let oceanic water through the Sungarian depression, southeast of Lake Balkash, into the Desert of Gobi, and there fill a basin in the center of Asia larger than the Mediterranean Sea. Corresponding results would naturally follow in the entire valley of the Euphrates and about the borders of Armenia.[20]

According to Wright, the evidence for such events included the ossiferous fissures, rubble drift, recent silting of the Jordan River valley, accumulation of widespread beach gravel several hundred feet above sea level around the Black Sea, gravel beds containing mammoth bones in the Lena River valley, the dispersal of tribes and races from central Asia as a result of population pressure, and findings of human remains

20. Wright, *Scientific Confirmations of Old Testament History* (Oberlin, Ohio: Bibliotheca Sacra, 1906), pp. 359-60.

associated with the remains of extinct animals of the glacial epoch. Wright continued to espouse these views for years to come.

Analysis and Application

The amazing paleontological discoveries of the latter nineteenth century constituted yet more compelling evidence that fossiliferous rocks could not have been deposited by a single flood event. Biblical scholars who took serious account of these discoveries generally owned up to the fact that neither the Bible nor the extrabiblical evidence supports in the least the idea that sedimentary rocks were formed during a deluge. The only place one might hope to find evidence for the biblical flood is in surface deposits. Those who want to search for that evidence would far better follow the lead of geologists like Dawson, Suess, Prestwich, or Wright. Although their ideas have been discounted by subsequent geological investigation, they at least avoided wild speculation based on careless interpretation of the biblical record and evasion of valid extrabiblical data. Unlike many proponents of flood geology, these geologists displayed technical competence and scientific integrity as well as realistic assessments of the implications of the deluge traditions.

12. Biblical Scholarship until the Fundamentalist-Modernist Controversies

Higher Criticism

Higher critical conceptions of the Old Testament had long dominated academic biblical scholarship in Germany and continued to do so into the twentieth century. Scholars who offered reconstructions of Israelite history at variance with the traditional understanding often held the idea that Old Testament religion was a progressive development of religious consciousness rather than a response to divine revelation. Hegelian philosophy, evolutionary worldviews built on Darwin's biology, German romanticism, and studies of the biblical text all contributed to these reconstructions, which were typically based on the documentary hypotheses of Kuenen, Graf, and Julius Wellhausen (1844-1918). Holder of several professorial positions in Germany, including the Universities of Marburg and Göttingen, Wellhausen taught that the earliest parts of the Pentateuch were derived from two independent sources, which he identified as the Yahwistic and Elohistic documents. He argued (1) that the two documents were compiled into a single continuous narrative; (2) that another author composed the book of Deuteronomy, incorporated it into the Yahwist's narrative, and revised the whole in the time of Josiah; and (3) that another editor later revised the entire Pentateuch. Wellhausen worked this scenario into an evolutionary reconstruction of Israel's history which he characterized as the spontaneous expression of a natural religious impulse.

A few scholars such as Christian Friedrich August Dillmann

(1823-1894) and Franz Delitzsch (1813-1890) espoused the documentary hypothesis within the context of more traditional orthodox theology.

Dillmann, professor of theology in Berlin, accepted the hypothesis that the flood narrative had been derived from two different sources but remained convinced that an obscure reminiscence of a frightful devastation lay behind both sources.[1] The devastation, said Dillmann, was universal only to the extent that every living thing on "earth" was destroyed — "earth" being confined to that "narrow geographical range of vision possessed by the ancient Hebrews" embracing only parts of Asia, Africa, and Europe. Dillmann agreed with Suess that Lower Babylonia was the original home of the flood legend and "that an experience of cyclonic inundation was its foundation." He considered the Izdubar (Gilgamesh) epic to be much older than the biblical accounts but nonetheless denied that the biblical accounts had been constructed on the basis of Babylonian representations on the grounds that the Jews would have no reason for appropriating a deluge legend unless they already knew about a flood that had destroyed mankind. Dillmann maintained that flood legends from other parts of the world yielded no evidence for a global Noachian flood. Reports of such legends were very recent, he said, and, in the case of the Mexicans, Peruvians, and Cubans, did not always provide "a thoroughly satisfactory guarantee"; he suggested that many such legends might have been spontaneously produced by experiences of great local inundations or might have spread by migration and diffusion during the past two thousand years.

Delitzsch, a confessionally orthodox Lutheran scholar who served as a professor at Rostock, Erlangen, and Leipzig, was even more conservative.[2] He considered the flood to be "a total judgment" almost on the order of the final judgment. He argued that mythologizing the flood would effectively reduce the history of redemption to a moral commonplace. Although accepting the historical trustworthiness of the Pentateuch, Delitzsch conceded that the flood narrative appeared to

---

1. Dillmann, *Genesis Critically and Exegetically Expounded* (Edinburgh: T. & T. Clark, 1897). This edition was translated from the sixth German edition of 1892. Dillmann's original commentary was actually a revision of an earlier book by August Knobel.

2. Delitzsch wrote often on Genesis. His earliest comments were originally published in 1852 in *Die Genesis*. Subsequent German editions appeared but were not translated into English. His writing took a somewhat more critical turn in his later *Neuer Commentar über die Genesis* published in 1887 (ET, *New Commentary on Genesis* [Edinburgh: T. & T. Clark, 1887]).

be composed of closely interwoven Elohistic and Yahwistic narratives, which in turn were based on a primitive flood legend. He also attributed both Israelite and Babylonian forms of the legend to a common origin. As the flood tradition spread toward Greece and India, he said, the narrative acquired "fresh national colouring." He maintained that the diverse traditions provided confirmation of the "historical unity of the human race."

Delitzsch granted that a flood covering the highest peaks was "inconceivable" and that too many animals would have perished in a mixture of fresh and salt water. It would have required unprecedented miracles to accomplish or circumvent such difficulties, and the narrative mentioned no such miracles. In any event, he wondered, why would it have been necessary to drown the Himalayas and Cordilleras when water only a few feet deep would suffice to kill everything? In the end, Delitzsch affirmed that Noah preserved only "the animal world by which he was surrounded." He did not believe that any animal remains of the flood survived as evidence; fossil remains belonged to prehistoric epochs. Delitzsch, too, looked kindly on the hypothesis of Eduard Suess.

After the publication of *Essays and Reviews* and Colenso's monumental work on the Pentateuch, higher criticism became more fashionable in the academic circles of England, Scotland, and North America. Scholars such as W. R. Smith in Scotland, S. R. Driver in England, and C. A. Briggs in the United States became increasingly comfortable with Wellhausen's documentary hypothesis.[3] In Britain, Wellhausen's source division was adopted in Presbyterian and Anglican circles by such scholars as John Skinner (1851-1925), Thomas Kelly Cheyne (1841-1915), and Herbert E. Ryle (1856-1925). Ryle, who had served variously as Hulsean Professor of Divinity at Cambridge, bishop of Exeter and Winchester, dean of Westminster, and president of

---

3. William Robertson Smith was professor of Oriental languages and Old Testament exegesis at the Free Church College in Aberdeen, a position from which he was suspended because of his defense of critical ideas. On Smith and criticism in the Free Church, see Richard A. Riesen, *Criticism and Faith in Late Victorian Scotland: A. B. Davidson, William Robertson Smith, and George Adam Smith* (Lanham, Md.: University Press of America, 1985). Charles Augustus Briggs (1841-1913) held a variety of professorial positions at Union Theological Seminary in New York. After acquittal from heresy charges by the Presbytery of New York, Briggs was suspended in 1893 by the General Assembly of the Presbyterian Church in the U.S.A. for his views on inspiration. A few years later Briggs was ordained as a priest in the Protestant Episcopal Church. Briggs was a coeditor, along with Driver and Alfred Plummer, of the *International Critical Commentary*.

Queens' College, Cambridge, claimed that "compositeness of structure" of the flood narrative was "quite unmistakeable," and Skinner
announced triumphantly that "the resolution of the compound narrative into its constituent elements in this case is justly reckoned among
the most brilliant achievements of purely literary criticism." Skinner,
a minister of the Free Church of Scotland and since 1890 professor of
Hebrew and apologetics at Westminster College, Cambridge, the theological college of the Presbyterian Church of England, marveled that
the editor who compiled the narrative had done his job with such "care
and skill that it is still possible to restore the original order and recover
a succinct and consecutive narrative, of which little if anything appears
to be lost." Despite Skinner's excessive confidence about the results
of source criticism, he and Driver differed over the assignment of some
of the verses to their alleged sources.[4]

Samuel Rolles Driver (1846-1914), Regius Professor of Hebrew
and canon of Christ Church, Oxford, discussed scientific aspects of
the deluge in as much detail as any of the critics.[5] Driver knew that
there were too many animal species on the globe to have been saved
on the ark and understood that a universal deluge failed to explain the
geographical distribution of existing land animals, but he saw not the
smallest warrant in the text for calling miracles to the rescue. Nor did
he believe that local flood theories satisfied the Genesis narrative. He
contended that whatever geological events Dawson and Prestwich were
investigating probably could not be linked to the biblical flood. Any
flood that submerged both Egypt and Babylonia would have had to rise
at least two thousand feet above sea level, the height of the elevated
country between them. Anything less would have fallen short of what
the biblical writers described and "would not have accomplished what
is represented as having been the entire *raison d'être* of the Flood, the
destruction of all mankind." We are forced, said Driver, to conclude
"that the Flood, *as described by the Biblical writers*, is unhistorical."

Skinner went farther. He argued that even the view that the
deluge was coextensive with the primitive seat of mankind had almost
insuperable difficulties because scientific evidence for human antiquity

4. Skinner, *A Critical and Exegetical Commentary on Genesis*, International
Critical Commentary (New York: Scribner's, 1910); T. K. Cheyne, *Traditions and
Beliefs of Ancient Israel* (London: Adam & Charles Black, 1907); and Herbert E.
Ryle, *The Book of Genesis* (Cambridge: University Press, 1914). Ryle also con-
tributed *The Early Narratives of Genesis* (London: Macmillan, 1900).

5. See Driver, *The Book of Genesis*, Westminster Commentaries (London:
Methuen, 1904).

around the world showed that such an event must have taken place thousands of years before the time generally assigned to Noah. He considered it unreasonable to suppose that the traditions could have been preserved for so long and thus "impossible to suppose that the Hebrew oral tradition had preserved an independent recollection of the historical occurrence which may be assumed as the basis of fact underlying the Deluge tradition." Skinner, Driver, Ryle, and Cheyne all believed that the Hebrew narrative must have been "derived from" the Babylonian. Skinner suggested that "the most natural explanation of the Babylonian narrative is after all that it is based on the vague reminiscence of some memorable and devastating flood in the Euphrates valley." The biblical narrative, Driver concurred, presupposed a country like Babylonia that was prone to inundations and was developed from a Babylonian source by oral transmission and accommodated to the genius of Hebrew monotheism. T. K. Cheyne, the canon of Rochester and Oriel Professor of Interpretation of Holy Scripture at Oxford for thirty-three years, concurred that the biblical story had been developed from a Babylonian source and argued that in the process Israelite piety purged the Babylonian tradition of its "dross."

Driver suggested that the Babylonian inundation was embellished by popular imagination into a destruction of all mankind except those who escaped. The story found its way into Palestine and ultimately was incorporated into Genesis. Thus the biblical narrative was not a fiction but a current popular belief of long standing in Israel that was reported. Instead of being shocked and startled by that view, Driver believed that "we should rather marvel at the 'divinely-guided religious feeling and insight, by which an ancient legend has been made the vehicle of religious and spiritual truth.'" Driver and Skinner both agreed with Delitzsch and Dillmann's favorable assessment of the flood explanation of the "eminent" Eduard Suess.

Conservative Biblical Scholarship

For all their distress over the inroads of higher criticism, conservative scholars rarely disagreed with the critics concerning their use of extrabiblical data to discount a literal universal deluge. Ever since the days of Smith, Hitchcock, and Miller, conservatives had been just as eager as the critics to invoke geology to show that the text had to be meshed with a local flood interpretation. But while the critics uniformly heaped accolades on the Viennese scholar Suess for showing how a catastrophic Mesopotamian deluge might have occurred, English-speaking conservatives appear to have been less familiar with his views, which made it into English principally in the contexts of translations of the work of the German higher critics. Moreover, Suess's belief that the Babylonian tradition had a historical value equal to that of the biblical narrative may have predisposed conservatives to be dismissive. In any event, conservatives were not yet ready to constrict the flood to quite so small an area. They tended to appeal instead to the Caspian basin hypothesis or to the more recent views of Howorth, Dawson, or Prestwich.

The major issue separating critics and conservatives was the nature of the biblical account: Was the narrative a composite of sources, or was it the unified product of a single author, Moses? The critics blithely assumed the validity of their reconstructions and paid little attention to vigorous conservative assaults on their views. Leading the conservative charge were the scholars at Princeton Theological Seminary. Princeton's polemics against criticism are rightly associated by religious historians with Charles Hodge (1797-1878) and Benjamin B. Warfield (1851-1921), but the detailed rebuttal was offered by Princeton's Old Testament department.

Foremost among Princeton's Old Testament scholars was William Henry Green (1825-1900), longtime professor of Oriental and Old Testament literature and author of a major critique of the documentary hypothesis, *The Unity of the Book of Genesis*.[6] Green argued the unlikelihood that the so-called J (Yahwistic) and P (Priestly) documents represented two entirely distinct complete accounts of the deluge. For example, Genesis 6:8 (J) states that Noah found grace in the eyes of the LORD, implying that the reader of J was already acquainted with Noah, but J had not previously mentioned Noah. In Genesis 7:1, J records that God told Noah and his family to board the ark despite J's failure to mention either a family or an ark earlier. Green concluded that instead of a complete uninterrupted account, J had "several important gaps created purely by the critical partition; other chasms scantily bridged by scattered clauses torn from their context, in which they are indispensable, or attached to passages where they

---

6. Green was an instructor of Hebrew at Princeton Seminary from 1846 to 1849. Between 1851 and 1859 he was professor of biblical and Oriental literature, and from 1859 to 1900 he served as professor of Oriental and Old Testament literature. Green's primary works dealing with critical views are *The Unity of the Book of Genesis* (New York: Scribner's, 1895) and *The Higher Criticism of the Pentateuch* (New York: Scribner's, 1895).

are inappropriate; expressions which by critical rules cannot belong to J and require the assumption, which has no other basis than the exigencies of the hypothesis, that the text has been manipulated by the redactor; and discrepancies, so called, which are wholly due to the redactor's gratuitous interference." He also denied that the so-called P document was continuous.

Green attempted to rebut the standard criteria for source divisions. He asserted that there are "no superfluous repetitions" to warrant any separation of sources, and he was intrigued that the critics were not impressed by other repetitions in the text: the corruption and violence on the earth are mentioned four times in four successive clauses; the entry of the animals into the ark is repeated three times; God's establishment of a covenant with Noah is mentioned twice; and the rainbow is referred to as the token of the covenant several times. Yet in these repetitions critics recognized only one writer. A rule that is applied at the whim of the critic is a "very insecure dependence," he said.

Nor was Green impressed by the use of different names of God to assign documents to different sources. The deluge might be variously regarded as the act of the Creator who destroyed his perverted handiwork (Elohim) or regarded in relation to the work of redemption (Yahweh), and Green suggested that the writer alternated his use of the divine names "discriminatingly" throughout the whole account to reflect these emphases. Green further challenged ostensible differences in diction between P and J. As one example, he argued that the word *destroy*, assigned to P in the flood account, occurs outside the flood narrative only once in P whereas it occurs repeatedly in J. An alleged J word, *blot out*, occurs in J, E (Elohist), and P outside of the flood narrative. He was perplexed that a word could be assigned only to one source in the flood narrative but to another source elsewhere.

Green believed that similarities between the Mesopotamian and Hebrew versions indicates that a common event or tradition lies behind them. Like Dillmann, he doubted that the Jews of the exile would enshrine a foreign story "so variant in many particulars from their own style of thought." He complained against the readiness of some critics to grant high antiquity "to the productions and beliefs of other nations, often on the most slender grounds," while they assigned everything pertaining to Israel "to the latest possible period." Green maintained that Abraham brought the Hebrew deluge tradition into Canaan and hence that there was no need to assume "a post-Mosaic addition to Israel's creed." Abraham might have purged familiar flood traditions of their polytheism "by his own purer faith," but Green favored the idea that "a truer account free from mythological conceit was transmitted to him in the line of a pious ancestry."

Green's successor, John D. Davis (1854-1926), agreed that the Hebrew narrative had not been derived from the cuneiform account but that the two accounts were "*independently transmitted* traditions of the same event."[7] The Babylonian tale, he said, contained nothing incredible except for God's participation. As Suess had pointed out (Davis was one of the rare conservatives who acknowledged Suess's existence), the Babylonian tradition described a natural physical disturbance in Mesopotamia and narrated an escape that made sense. The ancient Semites regarded the flood story as historically true, and similar stories among other races confirmed the historical character of the Semitic tradition. Davis doubted that such an influential tale could have emerged without a real catastrophe as a basis.

Davis contended that the Hebrew story had been transmitted orally through the generations rather than given by direct revelation. In historical matters, direct revelation was contrary to the divine method, he argued, because human events needed no subsequent supernatural disclosure. Even the history of salvation had been handed down from father to son. He suggested that Abraham probably brought some form of the deluge tradition to the land of Canaan, because it would have been incredible that "an intelligent resident of Ur of the Chaldees should have been ignorant of an event which had already stamped itself indelibly on the geography, history, art, and religion of Babylonia." Davis also believed that the flood narrative shed light on the true view of the authorship of the Pentateuch. Moses had not witnessed every event he described but had used oral or written sources in compiling his account. Some of the stylistic peculiarities of Genesis could be traced to such facts. Davis thought that the story of the flood might have been repeated by the Israelites in many forms and literary styles. Only in its present form, however, and not as "parcelled out" to different sources, did the Hebrew record tell all the incidents of the flood known in ancient Israel. Only in its "composite" form did the

---

7. Davis, "The Babylonian Flood-Legend and the Hebrew Record of the Deluge," *Presbyterian Review* 10 (1889): 425. Davis studied at Princeton Theological Seminary and the Universities of Bonn and Leipzig. On two occasions he taught Hebrew at Princeton. From 1888 to 1892 he was professor of Hebrew and cognate languages. From 1892 to 1900 he was professor of Semitic philology and Old Testament history. Upon William Henry Green's death in 1900, Davis became professor of Oriental and Old Testament literature.

Hebrew narrative correspond incident by incident with the cuneiform account except on the matter of the rainbow.

During the same period, an extensive amount of predominantly American and British conservative biblical scholarship was published in monumental multivolume commentaries, compilations of sermon helps, and anthologies of comment. Conservatives who contributed to these efforts were uniformly insistent that the flood was historical. Deluge traditions, extensively reviewed by J. Cunningham Geikie, John Urquhart, and the author of the article "Deluge" in the *Cyclopedia of Biblical, Theological, and Ecclesiastical Literature,* were cited as corroboration.[8] Despite a commitment to the historicity of the deluge, conservatives continued acknowledging the difficulties of universality on the basis of extrabiblical considerations.

Geikie (1824-1906), a Presbyterian minister who served in both Canada and England, observed that Bagster's *Comprehensive Bible,* first published in 1827, had claimed that evidence for the flood's universality was "most incontestable" on the grounds of fossil "moose deer" found in Ireland, elephants in England, crocodiles in Germany, and whales in inland England. But he acknowledged that the situation had radically changed: "The least tincture of geological knowledge explodes this whole string of illustrations." The old theories from Burnet to Fairholme did not work, because any flood that left a leaf on an olive tree could not have formed beds of rock miles thick or deposited "successive types of animal and vegetable life, from the corals of the lowest rocks, through every upward stage, to the highest." All manner of arguments suggested a local deluge.

Geikie also recognized the difficulties associated with accounting for animal migration to and from the ark — a point on which he was joined by Robert S. MacArthur (1841-1923), pastor of New York City's Calvary Baptist Church for forty-one years and eventual president of the Baptist World Alliance, and Marcus Dods (1834-1909), a Free Church pastor in Glasgow who later became a controversial professor of New Testament theology at New College, Edinburgh. MacArthur perceptively asked whether Noah, not being a professor of zoology, would have understood the command to take onto the ark two animals of every kind to include such unfamiliar species as the

---

8. See Geikie, *Hours with the Bible* (New York: J. Pott, 1887), pp. 187-203; *Cyclopedia of Biblical, Theological, and Ecclesiastical Literature,* ed. J. M'Clintock and J. Strong, vol. 2 (New York: Harper, 1891), pp. 734-36; and Urquhart, *The New Biblical Guide* (Chicago: Blessing, n.d.), pp. 256-97.

armadillo, kangaroo, and polar bear. Conservatives also granted that the efforts of Ralegh and Buffon to find a place for the animals on the ark were inadequate in light of the vastly greater number of known species.[9] Writing in Ellicott's *Bible Commentary for English Readers*, R. Payne Smith (1818-1895) further diminished the ark's cargo by excluding the carnivores, claiming (1) that they were not mentioned in the text, (2) that it would have been impossible to store enough animals on board to feed them for a year, and (3) that they would have become tame enough during the period of the flood that they would have remained in the neighborhood after disembarking and devoured all the remaining animals since no others would have been available to eat.[10] The omission of carnivores from the ark implied a highly restricted deluge.

There were, among the conservatives, still commentators who unabashedly spun out fantastic scenes in which all the animals of the world inexorably trekked to the great boat. George Gilfillan (1813-1878), a longtime United Presbyterian pastor in Dundee, Scotland, who was well known for several critical editions of poetry, made the constraints of the text and the discoveries of biogeography secondary to rhetorical flourishes:

> The lion and the lionness come, loth, it would seem in a degree, to circumscribe their wild freedom and majesty, yet unable to resist the pressure of the power above. The tiger and his mate, like fiends chained, but the chains not seen; the rhinoceros, buffalo, and mammoth, causing the earth to groan beneath their tread; panthers and leopards swiftly advancing; the slow-moving bear and the "solemn" elephant; the bull, the stag, and the elk, with their flashing horns; the horse, the glory of his nostrils terrible still, although tamed somewhat in the shadow of his unseen rider, God; the antelope and the wolf met together; the fox and the lamb embracing each other, the hyaena, horrible even in his transient tameness;

9. See Geikie, *Hours with the Bible*, p. 216; MacArthur, *Bible Difficulties and Their Alleviative Interpretations* (New York: E. B. Treat, 1899); Marcus Dods, *The Book of Genesis*, Expositors Bible Commentary (New York: Armstrong, 1903); and Thomas Whitelaw, *The Book of Genesis*, Pulpit Commentary (New York: Funk & Wagnalls, n.d.). Strictly speaking, Dods should probably not be lumped with the conservatives, since some of his views on inspiration were rather controversial. However, in his comments on the flood, Dods shows no enthusiasm for the critical subdivision into sources.

10. Smith, in *A Bible Commentary for English Readers*, vol. 1, ed. Charles John Ellicott (London: Cassell, n.d.).

beside fifty more forms of brutal life, clean or unclean, beneath whose ranks you see thick streams of reptile-existence, from the serpent to the scorpion, from the boa-constrictor to the lizard, wriggling on their ark-ward way. And high overhead are flights of birds, here all oracular of doom, winging their courses — the earnest eagle, the gloom glowing raven, the reluctant vulture, the heavy kite, the fierce-eyed falcon, the high-soaring hawk, the lark with her lyric melody, the dove with her spotless plumage, the humming-bird with her sparkling gem-like shape, the nightingale with her sober plumage and melting song, the swallow with the dark-light glance and shivered beauty of her wing, and a hundred more of those skiey demons or angels now sweep past to their prepared nests in the ark, even as spirits from a thousand deaths on a battlefield their winged way to the "land of souls."[11]

Geikie, MacArthur, and Thomas Whitelaw (b. 1840), a prominent United Presbyterian and United Free Church pastor, wrote that the addition of a vast mass of water to the earth, eight times that present in the oceans, would have disturbed the earth's orbit (a phenomenon for which they could cite no evidence). Geikie, Whitelaw, and Smith repeated the classical argument against a global catastrophe based on the volcanoes of Auvergne. Various commentators doubted that life could have survived submergence for a year. Everything not on the ark would have perished, including fish exposed to water that was suddenly too salty or not salty enough. Perowne observed that great multitudes of marine animals lived at depths of less than fifty fathoms. If the land sank thousands of feet and was raised again in a few months then "the animals could not possibly have accommodated themselves to such vast and rapid changes. All the littoral animals, therefore, would have been killed." Coral reefs would have been destroyed by the pressure of the rising water, and freshwater fish and terrestrial plants would also have perished.

Despite the dominant conservative opinion that the flood failed to cover the globe's mountain ranges, a few like Gilfillan and the Metropolitan Tabernacle's great Calvinistic Baptist preacher Charles Haddon Spurgeon (1834-1892) paid no heed to scientific conclusions.[12] Gilfillan envisioned

11. Gilfillan, in *The Biblical Illustrator*, ed. Joseph S. Exell (Grand Rapids: Baker Book House, 1956), pp. 440-41.

12. For Spurgeon's views of science, see Colin A. Russell, *Cross-Currents: Interactions between Science and Faith* (Grand Rapids: William B. Eerdmans, 1985).

the Grampian range surmounted; and Ben Nevis sunk fathoms and fathoms more under the waves; the Pyrenees and the "infant Alps" or Apennines lost to view; the Cervin's sharp and precipitous horn seen to pierce the blue-black ether no more; the eye of Mont Blanc darkened; old "Taurus" blotted out; the first of Cotopaxi extinguished; the tremendous chasm of snow which yawns on the side of Chimborazo filled up with a sea of water; the hell of Hecla's burning entrails slaked, and the mountains of the Himalayah overtopt; till at last, the waves rolling over the summit of Mount Everest, and violating its last particle of virgin snow, have accomplished their task, have drowned a world![13]

Just two pages after this selection in Exell's anthology, an extensive quotation from Geikie underscores the extreme improbability of anything remotely resembling what Gilfillan had just so lavishly described.

Whitelaw noted that the discoveries of science had forced a closer investigation of the text. Like conservatives of the previous generation, Whitelaw's contemporaries adjusted their exegetical vision by focusing on the perspective of eyewitnesses to the deluge and often claiming that the flood narrative uses hyperbole in describing a more restricted event. Payne Smith spoke for most conservatives when he suggested that the mountains mentioned in the text were simply those of Noah's immediate ark-bound world.

Conservatives willingly held to a geographically restricted deluge, but they still insisted that the text demanded the destruction of all mankind. Anthropology was insufficiently developed by the 1880s to challenge their general confidence that prediluvian humanity was restricted to the Middle East. Although conservatives speculated on geological causes of the flood, they advanced little beyond the Lyell-Smith-Miller subsidence hypothesis until the ideas of Prestwich, Howorth, and Wright gained a following.[14] Apart from John D. Davis, conservatives paid little heed to Suess.

---

13. Gilfillan, in *The Biblical Illustrator*, p. 445.

14. See Urquhart, *The New Biblical Guide*, pp. 309-80. Another favorable appeal to Prestwich, Dawson, Howorth, and Wright was made by James Orr in his essay "The Early Narratives of Genesis," which appeared in *The Fundamentals* (Chicago: Testimony, 1910-1915), pp. 85-97. Orr (1844-1913) was an important conservative Scottish theologian who taught at the United Free Church College in Glasgow. For examples of the influence of Wright, see D. Gath Whitley, "Noah's Flood in the Light of Modern Science," *Bibliotheca Sacra* 64 (1907): 519-51; and H. W. Magoun, "The Glacial Epoch and the Noachian Deluge," *Bibliotheca Sacra* 66 (1909): 217-42, 431-57, and 67 (1910): 105-19, 204-29.

Whatever their position on the geological circumstances of the deluge, conservatives evidenced a stunning change in attitude during the nineteenth century with respect to their growing reluctance to appeal to miracle. Perowne observed that everywhere in Genesis we meet with no "setting aside of the laws of nature." MacArthur asserted that a universal flood required belief in stupendous "miracles as needless for the moral purpose for which the flood came as they would have been gigantic in themselves." In his view, commentators who made constant appeals to miracle produced a false view of God in doing so; he was astonished that some people thought they honored God and the Bible by taxing their readers' credulity to the utmost. He charged that such interpreters almost put God into the category of heathen deities, "delighting in vast displays of power, without necessity, without reason, and without wisdom," and almost reduced the Bible to the level of the senseless legends of barbaric gods and mythological deities. Payne Smith suggested that the invocation of unnecessary miracles was contrary to both the wisdom of God and the biblical teaching about the exercise of supernatural power. If miracles were invoked to obviate difficulties, it would have been far easier to save Noah and the denizens of the ark by one display of supernatural power. But the ark was the means provided by God, and it denigrated the sufficiency of his choice of this instrumentality to presume that numerous additional acts of omnipotence were necessary to secure its operation.

As earlier in the century, virtually no conservatives thought that Mount Ararat was the ark's landing site despite several nineteenth-century attempts to scale that massif. Some commentators specifically located the landing site in the Armenian or Gordyaean hills.

Analysis and Application

By the early part of the twentieth century, few biblical scholars any longer endorsed the notion of a universal or geologically significant flood. Conservatives had matured in their thinking about the implications of science. They maintained an intense commitment to an infallible Bible and to the historic Christian gospel, but they also took science seriously, dealt honestly with the data, and refused to make appeals to miracle to help them out of intellectual impasses. They recognized that a mounting volume of scientific evidence consistently indicated that no universal deluge had taken place. When they began to propose nontraditional ways of interpreting the deluge story that reflected this awareness, there were no cries of alarm that the Bible was being abandoned. Mature Christians could see in these new interpretations the expression of a faith that God's works are consistent with Scripture, that all truth is God's truth, and that believers have no need to fear or deny the conclusions of honest scientific inquiry.

13. Scientific Advances of the Early Twentieth Century

The early twentieth century was a crucial time for the church, especially in North America. Liberal theology had gained control in both academic and ecclesiastical centers of power. Exponents of source analysis of the biblical deluge story ignored conservative critiques and dogmatically continued to assert the conclusions of biblical higher criticism. Conservative orthodox theology and ecclesiastical life were fighting for survival. Conservatives lost cultural prestige and control over academic and ecclesiastical institutions and were increasingly consigned to ghettos of intellectual irrelevance.[1] They responded to this marginalization by themselves withdrawing from the rest of the academic world, seldom even attempting to make significant intellectual contributions outside the realm of theology. Several important scientific advances were made early in the century, but many of these are still alien to the evangelical community because of its relative isolation from the larger culture and because the few qualified Christian scholars have failed to keep conservatives informed.

---

1. For more thorough treatments of the decline of nineteenth-century conservative theology and its transformation into twentieth-century fundamentalism in North America, see George M. Marsden, *Fundamentalism and American Culture: The Shaping of Twentieth-Century Evangelicalism, 1870-1925* (New York: Oxford University Press, 1980), and Ernest R. Sandeen, *The Origins of Fundamentalism: Toward a Historical Interpretation* (Philadelphia: Fortress Press, 1968). Also relevant is George M. Marsden's essay "The Collapse of American Evangelical Academia," in *Faith and Rationality: Reason and Belief in God*, ed. Alvin Plantinga and Nicholas Wolterstorff (Notre Dame, Ind.: University of Notre Dame, 1983), pp. 219-64. Of related interest is Douglas Frank's *Less Than Conquerors: How Evangelicals Entered the Twentieth Century* (Grand Rapids: William B. Eerdmans, 1986).

Geological Developments

Sir Joseph Prestwich's assertion that the rubble drift provided evidence for a major regional submergence linked to the flood influenced George Frederick Wright and many subsequent Christians. References to rubble drift repeatedly surfaced in evangelical writings in support of the assertion that a major catastrophe had occurred — despite the fact that subsequent research invalidated Prestwich's views. Recent arctic explorations have included observation of geological processes near the margins of active glaciers. In one of these processes, known as solifluction, clay containing rock rubble derived from underlying bedrock slowly flows downslope when saturated with snowmelt. This process produces precisely the sort of angular fragments embedded in poorly stratified clay that appear in the rubble drift on British raised beaches. Geologists immediately recognized that British rubble drift is the product of slow local downslope movements that occurred during periods of much colder climate when glaciers were in the vicinity.[2] The great submergences that Wright and Prestwich imagined could not have produced the rubble drift as they imagined, and there is no other evidence to suggest that they ever occurred.

The Mammoths

Vast accumulations of mammoth tusks and bones as well as the partial fleshy remains of a few mammoths frozen in Siberian permafrost had long captured the imagination of explorers and scientists. As we have seen, they played a fairly sensational role in a number of catastrophe theories. Discovery of a nearly complete frozen mammoth on the banks of the Beresovka River in 1900 hardly discouraged such speculations despite the fact that knowledge gained from the Beresovka carcass alone quite clearly undercut those speculations. Some conservative writers continue to disseminate misinformation about mammoths in the face of reliable data to the contrary, however.

In 1926, Bassett Digby, a British journalist, explorer, and fellow of the Royal Geographical Society, published *The Mammoth and Mam-*

2. See H. G. Dines, S. E. Hollingworth, W. Edwards, S. Buchan, and F. B. A. Welch, "The Mapping of Head Deposits," *Geological Magazine* 77 (1940): 198-226. For a detailed description of geological deposits produced by solifluction along the British Devonshire coast, see D. H. Mottershead, "Coastal Head Deposits between Start Point and Hope Cove, Devon," *Field Studies* 3 (1971): 433-53.

moth-Hunting in North-east Siberia.[3] In an entertaining, popular style, Digby paints a picture of the frozen wastes of Siberia, provides accounts of exploration, and describes the icy cadavers. He appears to have taken perverse delight in demolishing the catastrophic schemes of people such as Howorth who contended that mammoths were not adapted to Siberian harshness. Some writers found it hard to believe that mammoths could survive the frigid Siberian winters and suggested that they "trekked south every autumn to winter in warmer surroundings" or left Siberia entirely. Digby counters that mammoth remains are very scarce a thousand miles south of the Arctic Ocean and hardly occur at all in the two thousand miles between Siberia and Central Asia. If there had been a seasonal migration from the Arctic tundra, mammoth skeletons with crumbling tusks, like those found in England, should have turned up throughout the migratory range.

Of those who believed that "sudden doom" dropped the Siberian mammoths in their tracks and promptly buried and froze them, Digby asks if they had never been impressed that "the sabre-toothed tiger, the bison, the cave bear, the giant stags, the reindeer" and such "smaller fry . . . as the hyenas, foxes, gluttons, and wolves" all lived alongside the mammoth and yet *"only the mammoth and two species of woolly rhinoceros have survived as perfect cold-storaged, flesh-and-blood carcasses."* Why had "The Doom" been so selective? Digby also thought it significant that only twenty frozen mammoths had ever been found, for "if sudden, swift, annihilating cold had descended over North Siberia the whole country would have been littered with frozen mammoths."

Poking fun at the "starvation school" who contended that a sudden climatic change killed off the vegetation the mammoths needed to survive, Digby asked why the mammoth would have been such a fool as to stick around to starve when the hypothesized cold descended. When fire or drought destroyed vegetation over a large African feeding ground, elephant herds did not "sit down with the docile resignation of a group of Hindu villagers in a famine and die." Instead they "girded up their physical loins and lumbered off until they found a district where there was food." If food had in fact been rendered more scarce by a change in climate, the mammoths would likewise have moved elsewhere.

Digby is especially critical of Howorth. "To read some authors

3. Digby, *The Mammoth and Mammoth-Hunting in North-east Siberia* (New York: D. Appleton, 1926).

of world-wide repute," he says, one might gain the impression "that frozen mammoths and woolly rhinos had been shaken all over Siberia from some monstrous pepper-pot." In a letter to *Nature* in 1889, Howorth had talked of the bodies being found on the "now bare and almost perpetually frozen tundra." Digby rejoined that most of the tundra is pretty bare of trees just as most of London is pretty bare of bread and butter. One could walk around London all day without noticing any bread and butter and yet never be more than a few minutes from a place where one could obtain all the bread and butter one could eat. Similarly there are plenty of patches in the Arctic with many evergreen trees. The mammoths stayed near the trees for food and for shelter from the piercing winds and blizzards. The frozen mammoths were not found on bare tracts of tundra but along timbered banks of rivers in soil that nearly always contained fragments of timber. Digby explains that the frozen animals were a very few "unfortunates" that probably fell into deep, snow-filled crevasses during blizzards. Having fallen, the animals dislodged more snow with their struggles and effectively buried themselves. Most of the frozen mammoths and woolly rhinos, Digby explains, were found on the sides of cliffs sloping down to rivers. He reports having found many deep crevasses in the cliffs and banks of Siberian rivers during his own expeditions. In southern Siberia, where no frozen mammoths have been found, snow disappears from the crevasses after the end of May. In the north, however, countless gullies remain full of snow for years on end.

Digby also includes excerpts from the diary of an excavator of the Beresovka River carcass in 1901.[4] "In my opinion," wrote Dr. Otto F. Hertz, leader of the expedition,

> the entire cliff region rests upon a glacier, which was disintegrating and in which there were deep crevasses. The whole was later covered with a layer of soil, upon which doubtless there developed a rich flora that served as excellent food for mammoths and other animals. Whether this flora was identical with the present flora can be determined only when the food fragments found in the mouth and stomach of the mammoth shall have been examined and compared

---

4. The expedition to recover the carcass of the Beresovka mammoth was headed by Dr. Otto F. Hertz, a zoologist at the museum of the Imperial Academy of Sciences in Petrograd. Hertz was accompanied by E. V. Pfizenmeyer, another zoologist who attempted to reconstruct the mammoth, and by a geologist named Sevastianov. Digby's book includes photographs of the Beresovka mammoth at its recovery site and in a museum.

with the plants I collected on the cliff. The upper layer of earth was at that time not yet everywhere firm enough to support the weight of mammoths. Probably our specimen fell through into a crevasse, which would account for his position and for the fracture of such heavy bones as the pelvis and the right fore-leg. After falling, the mammoth no doubt tried to crawl out, the position of both fore-legs being peculiarly like that of an animal making such an effort, but the injuries were so serious that his strength failed, and he soon perished.

Much has been learned about the food the animals ate in the years since excavation of the Beresovka carcass. Digby reports that remains of cones and branches of fir, larch, and pine, as well as sedges, wild thyme, Alpine poppy, buttercup, two kinds of moss, and other flora have been recovered from the teeth and stomachs of frozen Siberian mammoths. Several of these plants, still native to the region, were found in the teeth and stomach of the Beresovka mammoth, indicating that the Siberian climate has not changed substantially since the animal perished. Since most of the undigested remains in the Beresovka mammoth's stomach had seeds attached, the great beast probably died in the autumn, consistent with the contention that the frozen mammoths were those which had fallen into "the soft snow of riparian crevasses that had been hidden by an early autumn snowfall, and were then preserved and buried by the subsequent succession of autumn frosts and snowfalls."

A more technical report by I. P. Tolmachoff details the circumstances of thirty-nine recorded discoveries of carcasses of mammoths and rhinoceroses commencing with the 1692 Ides expedition.[5] Tolmachoff observes that the Beresovka mammoth "was found in the best imaginable condition and comparatively little spoiled by wild animals." The position of the animal indicated that it was "trying with its last strength to go out of some trap into which it had happened to fall." Tolmachoff believed that the mammoth died of a combination of suffocation and injuries received when the beast plunged into soft ground. The pelvis, a forefoot, and some ribs had been broken, and there was "indication of a strong hemorrhage." Suffocation was "proved by the erected male genital, a condition inexplicable in any other way." The carcass had been found within a

5. Tolmachoff, "The Carcasses of the Mammoth and Rhinoceros Found in the Frozen Ground of Siberia," *Transaction of the American Philosophical Society*, n.s., 23 (1933): 11-74.

landslide caused by the thawing of rock ice beneath the tundra of a high terrace along the river bank.

While acknowledging that in the past forests had extended farther north than they do now, Tolmachoff chides Howorth for his greatly exaggerated claim that northern Siberia once had a climate similar to that of modern-day Lithuania. He counters that "the shifting of the forest limits could be measured only through a few degrees of latitude, and subfossil forest flora found in the ground of the recent tundra is represented by Arctic and Subarctic flora, not by that of more moderate regions." Any hypotheses about a milder climate in that time should "be accepted only with great reservations." Tolmachoff instructs his readers that northern Siberia, despite its severe climate, did have the world's northernmost forest limit, extending beyond latitude 72° N.

Tolmachoff also reinforces Digby's conclusions about mammoth feeding habits. In summertime, he states, the Beresovka mammoth was a grass eater who had no difficulty picking up the lowest tundra grass with its trunk and probably never attempted to "graze close to the tundra like oxen" as Howorth had suggested. If the Siberian forests had retreated, the mammoth neither needed nor would have enjoyed a milder climate and probably would have suffered no dietary privations, "because in nearly all cases of carcasses of mammoth discovered, they belonged to well fed and often fat animals, of robust health." Tolmachoff recognized that between the moment of death and transformation into a frozen carcass a mammoth would suffer some decay despite the fact that "current opinion attributes to the meat of a mammoth an almost absolute freshness." Such a degree of freshness was fiction. Although the flesh was bright red and avidly devoured by dogs and wild animals, one adventurous scientist found the same meat absolutely unpalatable. Published stories about a dinner in St. Petersburg at which meat of the Beresovka mammoth was served were "a hundred per cent invention." In fact, Tolmachoff reports that the carcasses had such an "intolerable putrid smell" that scientists had often been unable to examine the mammoth flesh until a year or two after discovery. Although the stench had been attributed to putrefaction after the exposure of a carcass, Tolmachoff points out that a strong smell also emanated from the ground in which mammoth remnants were still concealed and firmly frozen. The smell in the ground resulted from partial putrefaction that began "immediately after the death of an animal, before it became permanently frozen." Tolmachoff suggests that some of the animals might have been buried in mud streams caused by the thawing of frozen ground, rock, and ice. Or they may have drowned in rivers or lakes during winter or early spring, frozen at the bottom, and been buried in drift on the very spot or drifted downstream to be later buried in river deltas.

In any event, Tolmachoff presented ample data to lay to rest the notion that Siberian mammoths had perished in a vast cataclysm accompanied by a radical climatic change. Despite the writing of Digby, Tolmachoff, and others, however, conservative Christians have persisted in giving credence to discredited notions that the deep-frozen mammoths count as important evidence for the biblical deluge.

Radiometric Dating

Decades of detailed stratigraphic studies had made it crystal clear by the early nineteenth century that the secondary and tertiary fossiliferous sedimentary formations had been deposited, turned to stone, and variously deformed long before the advent of human beings on the earth. Stratigraphic investigation throughout the nineteenth century did nothing to alter that conviction. By the early twentieth century, geologists had improved their ability to recognize the rocks as deposits formed in marine, glacial, lacustrine, fluvial, deltaic, and eolian environments, each totally incompatible with a global deluge. Geologists were also learning to recognize deposits and landforms that were probably produced by large regional catastrophic floods, a fact frequently overlooked by those who claim that uniformitarian geology has no room for great cataclysms.[6] The channeled scablands of eastern Wash-

6. Geologist J Harlem Bretz contributed several articles to the *Journal of Geology* and other professional publications over a period of several decades but especially during the 1920s in which he contended that the area from western Montana to eastern Washington bore evidences of large-scale catastrophic flooding. He believed that a gigantic lake, Lake Missoula, was formed when Clark's Fork River was dammed by glacial ice, and when the ice dam collapsed, the water spilled out catastrophically, sweeping out to cover northern Idaho and eastern Washington in a matter of days, devastating the landscape and producing what is now known as the channeled scablands. He argued that several features such as the coulees and the dry falls area of central Washington were results of the great flood. Geologists were skeptical of Bretz's hypothesis at first, perhaps in reaction to older catastrophic theories, but the geological community now accepts his hypothesis. During the late nineteenth century, geologist Grove Karl Gilbert similarly detailed physical evidence in northern Utah indicating that the Great Salt Lake was once much larger and that from time to time it had experienced very rapid outflow to the north into the Snake River valley.

ington and gravel deposits and shorelines on mountainsides in western Montana are all evidences of the catastrophic collapse of a huge glacial lake in the distant past, and they are very different from the materials and landforms that were once cited as evidence of flooding by Buckland. At long last geologists were able to recognize genuine flood effects that clearly predated the biblical era.

Prior to the twentieth century, absolute measurement of the age of various rock strata was not possible. In the absence of any reliable, precise means for making such determinations, the ages of events and deposits could only be estimated. The major time divisions of the standard geological time scale had been worked out, but any assignments of absolute age remained questionable.[7] While nineteenth-century geologists could confidently assert that a Triassic rock was younger than a Permian rock, they could only estimate how long ago a Triassic rock had been deposited. Nor did geologists have a clear conception of the age of the planet. They suspected that the earth was at least hundreds of millions of years old because estimates could be made on the basis of assumed rates of sediment deposition and thicknesses of sedimentary rock sequences, but such estimates were susceptible to serious error. In addition, the esteemed physicist Lord Kelvin (1824-1907), professor of natural history in the University of Glasgow, was convinced from his analysis of known energy sources that the sun and earth could be no more than a few tens of millions of years old. Geologists rethought their assumptions to bring their estimates in line with Kelvin's conclusions. As eminent a geologist as Clarence King (1842-1901), director of the United States Geological Exploration of the Fortieth Parallel and later the first director of the United States Geological Survey, suggested that the earth might be only 24 million years old.[8]

All the sophisticated guesswork changed with the Nobel prize–winning discovery of radioactivity by French physicist Henri Becquerel (1852-1908) in 1896. Physicists soon recognized that radioactive decay was a process that occurred at a measurable rate. During his stay at

7. For a description of the development of the geological time scale, see William B. N. Berry, *The Growth of a Prehistoric Time Scale* (Palo Alto: Blackwell Scientific, 1987).

8. For the detailed story of Lord Kelvin's thinking about the age of the earth and his influence on contemporary scientists, see Joe D. Burchfield, *Lord Kelvin and the Age of the Earth* (New York: Science History, 1975). On Clarence King, see Thurman Wilkins, *Clarence King: A Biography* (Albuquerque: University of New Mexico Press, 1988).

McGill University, Ernest Rutherford (1871-1937) worked out the mathematical equations for radioactive decay and recognized helium as a by-product of the radioactive decay of uranium and thorium. Both Rutherford and R. J. Strutt (1875-1947) of the Imperial College, London, then calculated "helium ages" by measuring the quantities of helium in several uranium-bearing minerals from deposits whose relative age was known from their stratigraphic relationships. They discovered that the "helium ages" ranged up to several hundreds of millions of years. The minerals considered to be oldest on the basis of their stratigraphic position generally yielded the highest absolute radioactive ages.[9]

Bertram Boltwood (1870-1927), a professor of physics at Yale, suggested that lead found in radioactive ores might be an end product of the decay of uranium. He developed methods for measuring the abundance of lead in uranium minerals and calculated ages as great as 2.2 billion years. Eventually it was recognized that a given chemical element in a mineral will contain various different isotopes, some radioactive and some not, and that the different radioactive isotopes have different rates of decay. Thus, in order to achieve an accurate estimation of the age of a sample on the basis of radioactive decay, it is necessary to perform a more sophisticated analysis of the relative percentages of the various isotopes within the sample. As investigators developed these more sophisticated analytical techniques, radiometric dating became far more precise and reliable.[10] The determination of the ages of the rocks provided by such studies has added one more major line of evidence indicating that the earth's stratified fossiliferous rocks formed long before the arrival of human beings on the earth.

9. For a detailed description of the earliest efforts to determine the ages of minerals by means of radioactive decay, see chap. 6 of Burchfield's *Lord Kelvin and the Age of the Earth*.

10. The earliest methods involving helium were eventually abandoned as improved methods were developed. Current testing focuses on the decay of uranium and thorium isotopes into different isotopes of lead, the decay of potassium 40 into argon 40, rubidium 87 into strontium 87, and samarium 147 into neodymium 143. All of these methods provide reliable measurements of the ages of minerals that are millions to billions of years old. For objects only a few hundreds or thousands of years old, the radiocarbon method, based on the decay of carbon 14, has become an extremely valuable tool in the field of archeology. For a detailed discussion of the various radiometric methods, see Gunter Faure, *Isotope Geology*, 2d ed. (New York: John Wiley, 1986).

Archeology and Anthropology

Not all scientific developments of the period relevant to the deluge were limited to geology. Following the investigations of George Smith, much new archeological material pertaining to Mesopotamian flood legends was discovered, translated, and published. After discovering the Izdubar (Gilgamesh) epic, Smith himself went on in 1875 to unearth tablets featuring part of the "story of Atarpi" (Atrahasis), which contains several lines of a deluge story. In 1898, French Assyriologist Jean Vincent Scheil published fragments of another flood story from the reign of King Ammisaduqa, and Theophilus G. Pinches (1856-1934), lecturer in Assyrian at University College, London, published a version of a story of the creation of man. A couple of years later, Heinrich Zimmern (1862-1931), professor of Assyriology at the University of Leipzig, showed that the fragments of Scheil and Pinches were part of the story of Atarpi (Atrahasis). Translations of a third Akkadian deluge tradition were published in 1902 by Leonard W. King (1869-1919), assistant keeper of Egyptian and Assyrian antiquities at the British Museum, professor at the University of London, and subsequently author of massive volumes on the history of Sumer and Akkad and the history of Babylon.

Tablets containing portions of Babylonian flood traditions were discovered at Nippur and Sippar. Fragments of Sumerian deluge traditions were also found in the ruins of Nippur by Arno Poebel (b. 1881) under the auspices of the Museum of the University of Pennsylvania. In this version, the hero's name was Ziusudra. Also found were Sumerian king lists that mentioned prediluvian cities and kings, the flood itself, and the reestablishment of the monarchy after the deluge.[11] The discovery and analysis of these traditions from different periods in Mesopotamian history led to the realization that the deluge story had a complex tradition history and was originally independent of the story of Gilgamesh into which it was later incorporated.[12]

In the meantime, a general understanding of the development of city building, metalworking, and the development of agriculture in the ancient Near East was arising out of wide-ranging archeological

11. For a review of many of the Mesopotamian deluge fragments, see Daniel Hammerly-Dupuy, "Some Observations on the Assyro-Babylonian and Sumerian Flood Stories," *Andrews University Seminary Studies* 6 (1968): 1-18.

12. For an exhaustive analysis of the development of the Gilgamesh epic and of the deluge tradition contained within it, see Jeffrey H. Tigay, *The Evolution of the Gilgamesh Epic* (Philadelphia: University of Pennsylvania, 1982).

investigations. Since Genesis 4 indicates that prediluvian human communities were raising crops, living in cities, and working metal, these investigations provided biblical scholars with an additional means by which to constrain the timing of the catastrophe. Moreover, the discovery of approximate dates for the reign of the Sumerian king Gilgamesh helped narrow the period during which the deluge that gave birth to both the biblical and Mesopotamian traditions could have taken place. The archeological evidence alone (prior to the development of radiocarbon dating) suggested that the deluge might have occurred as recently as 4000-3500 B.C.

Anthropologists of the early twentieth century also built on the work of Lenormant and others by evaluating as many flood traditions as could be found. The most comprehensive collection appears in *Folklore in the Old Testament* (1918), written by British anthropologist-folklorist James George Frazer (1854-1941).[13] Frazer relates hundreds of traditions in detail. Although recognizing that many traditions are interrelated by diffusion from one group of people to another, Frazer suggests that many others may have arisen independently among different groups of peoples. In Frazer's view, myths "developed during savagery, which explained why so many 'savage' peoples possessed the same myths."[14] This view contradicts the argument long popular among conservative theologians that the global distribution of deluge traditions constitutes prima facie evidence of a single devastating flood of worldwide dimensions that was seared into the memory of a few survivors and passed down through the generations with greater or lesser accuracy.

Frazer suggests that several flood traditions such as those of the Lolos of southwestern China, the Kamars in central India, and some South American Indians may have been strongly tainted by Christian missionary influence. In other localities, such as the Tahitian island group, he contends, the tradition was probably based on local marine inundations of low-lying areas. Like the Innuits, native Tahitians cited fossil remains embedded in rocks as evidence of a deluge. Frazer attributes the legends of still other regions to significant local river flooding. He concludes that the view that all of these traditions are

13. On Frazer, see Robert Ackerman, *J. G. Frazer: His Life and Work* (Cambridge: Cambridge University Press, 1987).

14. *The Flood Myth*, ed. Alan Dundes (Berkeley and Los Angeles: University of California Press, 1988), pp. 113-16. This volume is an anthology of material dealing with numerous flood traditions from around the world and is a valuable resource for anyone interested in deluge traditions.

"corrupt and apocryphal" versions of the biblical tradition "can hardly be maintained any longer." While recognizing the relatedness of Near Eastern traditions, he argues that "there is little evidence to prove that the ancient Indian and Greek legends of a flood are derived from the corresponding Babylonian tradition." Frazer does grant that many of the North American stories share certain features and might be variants of an original tradition, that several of the Polynesian traditions might have a common source, and so on, but he maintains that it is not possible that all of the world's deluge traditions could have derived from a single source.

Frazer was not surprised that purely local traditions would have taken on an aura of universality. He could see how "the memory of a similar catastrophe, orally transmitted" could easily grow in just a few generations "into the legend of a universal deluge, from which only a handful of favored individuals had continued in one way or another to escape." When all was said and done, it made sense to him "that some and probably many diluvial traditions are merely exaggerated reports of floods which actually occurred, whether as the result of heavy rain, earthquake-waves, or other causes. All such traditions, therefore, are partly legendary and partly mythical." In the face of anthropological studies of this sort, few scholars any longer gave much weight to the worldwide distribution of flood traditions as evidence for a universal deluge.

Analysis and Application

For centuries Christians had valued the significance of extrabiblical knowledge and had used it to improve their understanding of Scripture. During the nineteenth century, the church courageously dealt with geological and biogeographical evidence that undercut the notion of a global deluge. On the whole, conservative biblical scholars were willing to rethink their exegesis in view of scientific insights. And, oblivious to the implications their work may have had for biblical exegesis, scientists continued to accumulate relevant extrabiblical knowledge on many fronts. The firmly grounded awareness of the considerable antiquity of the earth and the conviction that the biblical deluge could not have been universal both received further corroboration with the development of radiometric dating techniques. Investigation of such ancillary matters as the fate of the frozen mammoths likewise further served to undercut sensational catastrophic deluge theories. And anthropological analysis of global deluge traditions indicated that they offered no substantial evidence of the occurrence of a global flood.

The case against a Woodwardian global deluge was more firmly established than ever by the early decades of the twentieth century. Faced with this growing body of evidence, some conservative Christians elected to depart from the strategy that their ideological predecessors had employed for more than a century. Rather than working to refine their understanding of the flood narrative in the light of the best science of the day, they began to ignore that science, to refute it, or to assemble various poor substitutes for it in an effort to support their readings of Scripture. Beleaguered by what they perceived as modernist attacks on the integrity of the Bible, some twentieth-century Christian fundamentalists began to reject extrabiblical knowledge on the grounds that it constituted a threat to theological orthodoxy. In doing so, however, they weakened their cause by turning away from truth (the truth about the natural world that was being painstakingly accumulated by the scientific community) and embracing a kind of untruth (pseudoscience) that told them what they wanted to hear. If conservative orthodox theology is to remain vital and relevant to a world in need of the Christian gospel, conservative theologians will have to abandon their flirtation with flood geology and other forms of pseudo-science, reacquaint themselves with genuine scientific knowledge, and incorporate that knowledge into their thinking, secure in the realization that genuine insight into God's creation, whether discovered by Christians or heathens, is still a gift of God to be treasured.

14. Mesopotamian Flood Deposits

The Excavations

For decades the critical school speculated that the biblical flood tradition could be traced to a strictly Mesopotamian event that disrupted civilization and spawned several traditions that exaggerated or universalized the disaster. Although Eduard Suess provided a scientific explanation for an event that might have given birth to the legends, early archeological work found no concrete evidence for major floods in Mesopotamia. That changed in the 1930s. British archeologist C. Leonard Woolley (1880-1960) began excavation at Ur in 1922 for the Museum of the University of Pennsylvania and the British Museum. He was convinced that Mesopotamian flooding formed the basis for flood traditions and Sumerian king lists. In 1928 he wrote that references to antediluvian kings and cities signified that Sumerian occupation of Mesopotamia predated the great disaster. "However much tradition may have magnified and coloured the account," Woolley observed, "it would be absurd to deny the ultimately historical character of a story which bears on itself the stamp of truth." In his view the details of the traditions meshed perfectly with the local conditions of the delta. Floods were common in Lower Mesopotamia, and "it only requires just such a combination of these causes acting simultaneously as is actually described in the legend for an inundation to take almost the proportions attributed to the Deluge of Noah's day." Even so, Woolley denied that all the inhabitants of the delta would have been destroyed. He maintained that some antediluvian cities would have survived but that enough damage would have been done "to

216

make a landmark in history and to define an epoch."[1] Given Woolley's strong belief in the event, it is hardly surprising to note that the very next year he announced that he had found physical remains of the inundation.

Woolley had already discovered the remarkable treasures of the graves of the First Dynasty of Ur. In October 1929 he reported on his efforts during the preceding year to dig more deeply.[2] He described his discovery of a deposit of stratified rubbish below which were about 3.7 meters of "perfectly clean water-laid clay." Beneath that layer were about 1.2 meters of ashes and rubbish containing masses of pottery, including painted wares. Finally, below the ash and rubbish layer was the virgin soil on which the original settlement of Ur was built. At another locality within Ur he found 2.7 meters of clean water-laid clay beneath the stratified rubbish and then a thin layer containing painted pottery. In a third pit, Woolley encountered 1.7 meters of the clean clay. Only one agency, he insisted — namely, "a flood of dimensions unparalleled in Mesopotamian history" — could account for the layer of clay. Citing evidence from excavations at nearby Al 'Ubaid, Woolley claimed that the people who had used the painted pottery "lived in open villages built of reed or wattle huts." According to the Sumerian flood legend, the presumably non-Sumerian town of Shuruppak that was destroyed by the flood was constructed of reed huts. Woolley believed that the Ur deposits provided evidence for a flood that was potent enough to have destroyed the reed hut villages of the painted pottery people but restricted enough to have spared the Sumerians and allowed them to spread north.

Hoping to reinforce the newfound evidence, the renowned archeologist returned for another season of excavation at Ur with a party including his wife, Max Mallowan, and Eric Burrows. After digging through several layers of house ruins and shattered pottery, Woolley's team ultimately penetrated a three-meter thick stratum of clean water-laid sand that rested on a layer of refuse from human occupation. Some graves had been dug into the sand layer. Woolley counted this to be adequate confirmation. In the meantime, L. C. Watelin and Stephen Langdon (1876-1937) of Oxford also encountered a diluvial stratum north of Ur at Kish.[3] They wondered if that stratum might represent

1. Woolley, *The Sumerians* (Oxford: Clarendon Press, 1928).

2. Woolley, "Excavations at Ur, 1928-9," *Antiquaries Journal* 9 (1929): 305-48.

3. See Watelin and Langdon, *Excavations at Kish* (Oxford: Oxford University Press, 1925-30).

the flood of Sumerian legend. Which group had really encountered strata of *the* flood? Woolley, of course, knew the answer. The Kish stratum, about eighteen inches thick, was dated by Watelin and Langdon between about 3400 and 3200 B.C. and occurred continuously above cemetery remains dated at 3400 to 4000 B.C. Woolley contended that the Ur flood layer was separated from the Kish flood stratum by eight different cultural strata so that the two floods could not be the same. He argued that Ur contained the sediments deposited by the *real* flood.[4]

One of Woolley's coworkers at Ur for a few seasons, Jesuit scholar Eric Burrows (1882-1938), agreed that the Ur flood "overwhelmed, to all appearance, the primitive civilization of the Euphrates valley. It is obvious to identify this with the Great Flood of the native tradition."[5] Noting that the Sumerian documents indicated that the flood began at Shuruppak and that kingship resumed at Kish, north of Sumer, Burrows concluded that the flood had devastated the southern land of Sumer of which Ur was a part. He believed that the break in Sumerian cultural tradition was not complete, however, on the grounds that archeological evidence indicated that the "Deluge overwhelmed a primitive culture which was partly Sumerian, but civilization was reconstructed without loss of continuity in its Sumerian elements." Burrows joined Woolley in holding that the culture of the painted pottery people, preserved only beneath the flood stratum, was extinguished by the flood in Sumer but survived toward the north in Akkad. He postulated that northern populations unaffected by the deluge might have absorbed refugees from reed-hut cities like Shuruppak. Struck by the prominence of the reed hut in the principal native tradition of the deluge, Burrows suggested that "the men of the reed-hut village who built the famous Deluge-ship probably belonged to part of the population which had a special traditional skill in all matters of boat-craft."

Burrows reasoned that the deluge hero must have been one of the reed-hut, painted pottery people who later came into contact with the Hurrians to the north. He further suggested that the Genesis narrative had a Hurrian source, nicely agreeing with the likely location of Noah's vineyards toward the north, possibly as far as Armenia

---

4. Woolley, "Excavations at Ur, 1929-30," *Antiquaries Journal* 10 (1930): 315-43.

5. Burrows, "The Discovery of the Deluge," *Dublin Review* 186 (1930): 1-20.

(Urartu). He doubted, however, that the ark could have floated to that area "on water fifteen cubits high above the mountains" if it had in fact been launched at Shuruppak on the lower Euphrates. He argued that the reference to the mountains of Armenia may have been "used quite vaguely" inasmuch as "ancient Syriac and Aramaic (Targum) versions interpreted it of the Kurdish country, which is approximately the region of the Mt. Nisir of the original native tradition." He believed such an interpretation posed "little difficulty."

Orientalist Harold Peake (1867-1946) took immediate advantage of the discoveries of Woolley and Langdon.[6] He accepted the results of the documentary hypothesis, agreed that the biblical narrative was ultimately dependent upon the Babylonian account, and maintained that the latter was a legend based on a genuine historical event of which Mesopotamian archeology had found the remains. Peake claimed not only that Woolley's stratum of clean clay at Ur had been deposited by the legendary flood but also that it should be correlated with the lowermost flood layer at Kish. He suggested that the antediluvians of lower Mesopotamia were not Sumerians, however. He believed that Sumerians were a sea-faring people who arrived at the head of the Persian Gulf from elsewhere and warned Xisuthros, the king of Shuruppak, to escape in a boat at the time of the flood. He further asserted that all of the pre-Elamites were wiped out and their cities devastated by the deluge. After the flood, he said, the Sumerians reoccupied all the cities of Mesopotamia and established the early dynasties of Kish, Erech, and Ur.

Assessment of Claims

Understandably, these claims were subjected to critical review by archeologists and biblical scholars. For example, John Bright (b. 1908), Old Testament theologian at Richmond's Union Theological Seminary, answered the question of whether archeology had found evidence of the flood with a resounding No. Excavations at Jericho indicated more or less continuous occupation since between 8000 and 5000 B.C., he noted, and the ruins showed no evidence of a flood. Likewise, other thoroughly investigated Palestinian and Syrian sites displayed no shred

6. See Peake, *The Flood: New Light on an Old Story* (New York: R. M. McBride, 1930).

of evidence of flooding during the course of five thousand years of occupation.

Bright granted that researchers had uncovered clear evidence of flooding in Mesopotamia, at Ur and Kish as well as Fara and Nineveh. Archeologists had produced unquestionable evidence that a deluge had interrupted occupation at Ur during the fourth millennium, for example — but that flood had not even disturbed the entire city, much less the whole region. Further analysis of deposits at Kish led to the conclusion that they were centuries younger than deposits at Ur. The sediments at Fara indicated an inundation earlier than the one at Kish but later than the one at Ur. Nineveh's flooding may have been temporally close to that of Ur. Bright concluded that none of these represented the flood of Genesis. Even at Ur the deposits before and after the flood indicated the same general civilization. Bright concluded that the Mesopotamian flood strata simply represented local inundations of the type that still occur from time to time. "Either Mesopotamian archeology has yielded no trace of Noah's Flood," he wrote, "or else the Genesis narrative is but an exaggeration of a flood of purely local significance."[7] The latter alternative was difficult for him to accept because he believed that the flood tradition had been widely diffused. On the other hand, any proposal to date the flood in the fourth millennium B.C. ruled out the possibility that it could have been dispersed globally in light of the developing consensus that early settlement of the Western Hemisphere via the Bering Strait probably took place over a long period of time prior to 5000 B.C. Since archeology had provided no traces of the flood that Bright found convincing, he felt safe in assigning it a date far back in the Stone Age; he was unwilling to view the flood narrative as pure myth.

André Parrot (b. 1901), a French archeologist who had extensively excavated at Mari and Lagash, also reviewed the archeology of the flood. He asserted that a flood disaster would certainly have "left traces in the soil of Mesopotamia. One ought to find there the thick deposits of alluvium which would be left by the unleashing of great masses of water."[8] Noting that both Langdon and Woolley had succumbed to the temptation to identify their sterile strata with the flood, Parrot, too, pointed out that the deposits were of differing ages. He noted that a five-foot-thick stratum found at Uruk had been deposited

7. Bright, "Has Archaeology Found Evidence of the Flood?" *Biblical Archaeologist* 5 (1942): 58.
8. See Parrot, *The Flood and Noah's Ark* (London: SCM Press, 1955).

around 2800 B.C. and that a similar layer had been found at Fara (Shuruppak). He considered the sterile layer at Lagash (Tello) to be a subfoundation of packed soil prepared for subsequent building rather than a flood deposit. An excavation at Nineveh had turned up a six-foot-thick layer consisting of thirteen layers of alternating muds and river sands. The stratigraphy at Nineveh appeared to correlate approximately with the Ur stratum. Parrot suggested that the several strata probably represented deposits left by a number of more or less violent overflowings of the Tigris or Euphrates, that archeology had furnished evidence of several floods. Disagreeing with Bright, however, Parrot suggested that one of these cataclysms had been "accompanied by destruction on such a scale, and made such an impression, that it became one of the themes of cuneiform literature." Declining to indicate which of these deposits was left by *the* flood, Parrot simply stated that one was the result of that event, "of which legend has no doubt exaggerated the violence and the destruction, whereas archeology indicates that not all the cities suffered equally." Flooding of greater than average violence could easily have swept away human habitation in such a flat area, he said; Westerners had no idea how incredibly intense rainstorms in the area could be, and there was always the Suessian possibility of a tsunami as well.

The great British archeologist Max Mallowan (b. 1904), Woolley's early associate at Ur and later an excavator at Nineveh, Calah, Nimrud, and other Mesopotamian tells, concurred with nearly everyone else that the flood stories of the Bible and of Mesopotamia were recorded by those who had in mind a definite historical event that made such an overwhelming impression on its survivors that the story was written down "as soon as the Sumerians were sufficiently literary to commit the story to clay."[9] Heavy rainstorms, said Mallowan, were common in Mesopotamia. During his own work he observed that "there was hardly a season either in the spring or in the autumn when the desert did not, at least for a few days, assume the appearance of a lake." He agreed with Parrot and University of Chicago Orientalist Alexander Heidel (b. 1907) that the cuneiform records in no way suggested a marine inundation and that the expression "fountains of the great deep" could be applied to such an inundation only with a great stretch of the imagination. In the face of near consensus, however,

9. Mallowan, "Noah's Flood Reconsidered," *Iraq* 26 (1964): 63. One of the helpful features of Mallowan's article is a table showing important correlations between major Mesopotamian sites.

he speculated that Mount Nisir of the Gilgamesh epic must have been located in southern Mesopotamia, because the traditional view of a northern landing site would involve the boat drifting against a rushing tide.

Mallowan attempted to date the flood. The legendary Gilgamesh, a Sumerian king known from inscriptions, probably lived around 2700 to 2600 B.C. Because Gilgamesh sought out Utnapishtim, the immortal survivor of the flood, the flood must have occurred before 2650 B.C. On the basis of the Sumerian king lists, Mallowan suggested that Ziusudra, the Sumerian Noah, should be placed no more than a couple of centuries earlier than 2650 B.C. This date corresponded with the first or possibly the second Early Dynastic period as ascertained from tell stratigraphy. The king associated with the flood was a king of Shuruppak (Fara).

Acknowledging that the Ur "flood deposits" he had helped excavate in earlier years were probably fluvial, Mallowan suggested that more work on the geology was still necessary to establish that they were not marine, eolian, or estuarine. If the "flood stratum" proved to be marine, that would rule out any association with the Noachic flood which, he insisted, was not a marine event. He asserted that the lack of flood deposits at nearby Eridu called into question but did not rule out the claim that biblical deluge deposits occurred at Ur. The alleged flood stratum at Ur did not result in a complete break in civilization. Given its stratigraphic position, Mallowan suspected that the Ur stratum was much too early to be associated with Early Dynastic period I.

Noting that several flood strata had also been found at Kish, Mallowan concurred with Watelin's rejection of the top stratum as a deposit of *the* flood (even though it was the thickest), because Watelin had found Gilgamesh's name in material below that deposit. The earlier deposits at Kish were associated with Early Dynastic period I and might possibly be related to the flood. Moreover, at Kish the Early Dynastic period I levels contained innovations in ceramics, seals, and architecture that "no doubt corresponded with a widespread social disturbance throughout Babylonia" (p. 79). At Fara (Shuruppak), Mallowan noted, a yellow dirt layer separated Jemdat Nasr remains from Early Dynastic period I remains. Although there was evidently a continuity of civilization at Fara, Mallowan suggested that "it is possible that the inundation deposit at Fara was contemporary with the earliest observed Flood stratum at Kish" (p. 80).

Mallowan concluded that the Old Testament flood account "was based on a real event which may have occurred in about 2900 B.C., or perhaps a century or more after, at the beginning of the Early Dynastic period" (p. 81). He suspected that traces of that flood had been found at Shuruppak (Fara) and possibly among the earliest deposits at Kish. Departing from his mentor's earlier claims, he now suggested that the Ur flood was too ancient to be identified with Noah's flood. He also decided that there was "no reason to suppose that traces of this catastrophic Flood would have been left everywhere" (p. 81). Flood debris would likely often have been cleared away by later inhabitants. Flood waters, too, may well have by-passed some cities "because obstructive barriers protected them, or because parts of them were sufficiently elevated from the level of the plain and sufficiently remote from the river to avoid the main impact of the Flood" (p. 81). He significantly concluded that "no flood was ever of sufficient magnitude to interrupt the continuity of Mesopotamian civilization," despite the fact that as a direct consequence of the Ur flood there was evidence for "a powerful impetus on the arts and crafts which underwent significant changes and developments" (p. 81). He suggested that "one of the most important historical consequences of the Flood may have been a social upheaval which eventually facilitated the rise to power of Akkadian rulers bearing Semitic names" (pp. 81-82).

Adding to the Sumerian version of the flood and the flood reference in the Sumerian king list, the University of Pennsylvania's professor of Assyriology Samuel Noah Kramer (b. 1897) translated two new tablets that both began with references to a great flood.[10] Kramer claimed that the corpus of Sumerian literature justified the conclusion "that the Mesopotamian minstrels and poets knew of a catastrophic Deluge that had done immense damage to the land and its people, but from which it eventually recovered." This disaster "inspired them to create and develop over the centuries a universal Flood-myth that was appealing, entertaining, and in accord with their religious world view." He corroborated the testimony of Parrot and Mallowan that torrential floods are endemic to the area, noting that an overflow of the Tigris in 1954 submerged the low-lying plain for hundreds of miles, threatening Baghdad with destruction.

The date of the flood depended on the assignment of a date to Ziusudra. A recently discovered version of "The Instructions of Shurup-

10. Kramer, "Reflections on the Mesopotamian Flood: The Cuneiform Data New and Old," *Expedition*, 1967, pp. 12-18. For information on Kramer himself, see his autobiography, *In the World of Sumer* (Detroit: Wayne State University Press, 1986).

pak," a document referring to the flooded city of which Ziusudra was king, had been dated to 2500 B.C. From this document, Kramer concluded that "Ziusudra had become a venerable figure in literary tradition by the middle of the third millennium B.C." The flood, he estimated in general agreement with Mallowan, must have occurred in the early third millennium B.C. He agreed that Woolley's Ur flood was too old to be identified with the Ziusudra deluge. The Kish flood was a more plausible candidate. The Shuruppak flood evidence was the most intriguing. "All in all," he concluded, both the Mesopotamian and Old Testament flood stories were "inspired by an actual catastrophic but by no means universal disaster that took place, not as Woolley claimed, immediately after the Ubaid period, but some time about 3000 B.C." Its traces were left in Kish, Shuruppak, and "probably at a good many other places yet to be discovered."

Another review of the evidence by R. L. Raikes reiterated the point that the various deposits were not contemporaneous. Raikes insisted that a lack of knowledge about the specific levels of the various strata and about their absolute levels relative to the floodplain level at the time when they had been deposited rendered correlation extremely difficult.[11] He emphasized that flood deposits would have been made in standing water but not from water flowing rapidly toward the Persian Gulf. Exceedingly heavy rains for seven days, let alone forty, superimposed on a floodplain already submerged by exceptional overflow would produce a rush toward the Gulf. Such a flood would be unable to deposit great thicknesses of silt, and any ark or primitive raft would have been swept into the Persian Gulf. Noting the work of Lees and Falcon on the instability of the Mesopotamian basin,[12] Raikes suggested that subsidence could have led to large bodies of standing water that might have contributed huge silt deposits. He proposed the importance of studying the flooding of the

11. Raikes, "The Physical Evidence for Noah's Flood," *Iraq* 28 (1966): 52-63.

12. G. M. Lees and N. L. Falcon, "The Geographical History of the Mesopotamian Plains," *Geographical Journal* 118 (1952): 24-39. Lees and Falcon wrote that the Mesopotamian basin had experienced considerable subsidence during the past few thousands of years. The rivers were discharging their sediment load into a tectonic basin that had already received thousands of feet of sediment. They said they could "visualize a whole sequence of 'floods,' not necessarily catastrophic in pace, but certainly catastrophic in eventual result." They further speculated that subsidence of the bottom of the Persian Gulf combined with a rise in sea level could have buried the remains of many cities beneath river-borne sediments or else below the waters of the Gulf.

rivers as a problem in its own right and urged an investigation of floodplain profiles away from the ancient sites.[13]

Analysis and Application

The excavation of various flood deposits at Mesopotamian sites provided the first compelling evidence for ancient flooding that might really have something to do with the Genesis flood, despite the fact that sediments from *the* flood itself cannot yet be unequivocally identified. Woolley's optimistic claims to have found the Genesis flood record are very probably unjustified. Nevertheless, the stratigraphy of some of the Mesopotamian flood deposits, literature pertaining to Gilgamesh and ancient Sumerian cities, the Near Eastern setting of the biblical account, and the obvious affinities of the biblical and Mesopotamian flood traditions all converge to suggest that there may very well have been a catastrophic deluge in the Tigris and Euphrates River valleys that severely disrupted the civilization of that area — a civilization that represented the world to the biblical writer — and it may be that this is what the biblical story is all about.

Efforts to find physical evidence outside that part of the world have completely failed in spite of the application of some of the most capable, diligent, and devoted Christian minds and hands in the search. Woodward failed. Buckland failed. Prestwich failed. Wright failed. It is clear now that the evidence they were searching for simply does not exist. Those who believe that extrabiblical information can be helpful in securing a proper understanding of the biblical message and are eager to find evidence for the deluge would do well to abandon efforts to find that evidence in North America or eastern Asia and focus their efforts on the archeology and anthropology of the ancient Near East. If the evidence is to be found anywhere, this is where it will lie.

---

13. For a recent review of the relevant evidence, see David MacDonald, "The Flood: Mesopotamian Archaeological Evidence," *Creation/Evolution* 23 (1988): 14-20. MacDonald accuses scientific creationists of failing to pay any attention to the Mesopotamian flood deposits. He also chides those with a broader outlook, including liberal theologians, for putting too much stock in them. After reviewing the evidence provided by Woolley, Watelin, Mallowan, Raikes, and Schmidt at Fara, MacDonald joins the others in pointing out that the deposits were not coeval and asserts that there "are no compelling reasons to identify any of the floods at Ur, Kish, or Shuruppak — with the Flood of Mesopotamian literature and the Bible."

15. *Recent Developments in Science and Biblical Studies*

New Dating Techniques

Before examining later twentieth-century theological treatments of the deluge story, we would do well to review some developments in the areas of geology, paleontology, anthropology, archeology, and biblical studies that are relevant to our understanding of Genesis 6–9 and that have not yet been appreciated by many Christian theologians. Although tentative dating of events of the past several thousand years had long been possible on paleontological and stratigraphic grounds, no definitive means existed for absolute dating apart from written documents. Thus many Mesopotamian and Egyptian sites were reasonably well dated, but the same could not be said for North American sites or for such very old sites as Shanidar Cave in northeastern Iraq.[1] The radiometric methods that were so valuable in dating ancient rocks were of little help in dating events of the past few thousand years because of the slow rates of radioactive decay. In the absence of reliable means for absolute dating of recent deposits, the significance of presumed flood deposits and other geological formations could not always be determined on the basis of their age. Prestwich, for example, had assumed that widely scattered rubble-drift deposits were essentially

1. Shanidar Cave is located in the Zagros Mountains close to the area where Turkey, Iran, and Iraq meet. The cave contains several occupation layers, some with remains of Neanderthals. The deposits have now been dated by radiocarbon methods. Exploration of the cave began in 1951.

contemporaneous and might therefore have been produced by a single event. Howorth assumed that all mammoths had been exterminated in a single catastrophe. At the turn of the century, there was no dating procedure to test these assumptions, but in recent decades dating methods have been developed that undercut the claims of Howorth and Prestwich.

Easily the most important means for dating artifacts of the last few tens of thousands of years is the radiocarbon dating method developed during the late 1940s by Willard Libby (1908-1980), professor of chemistry at the Institute for Nuclear Studies of the University of Chicago, and subsequently improved by several scholars.[2] The radiocarbon method has been calibrated against the rings of very old trees such as the bristlecone pine. Once corrections were made for the fact that variations in the earth's magnetic field affect the cosmic ray production of carbon 14, and once improved determinations of the rate of decay of carbon 14 were made, remarkably good agreement between radiocarbon dates and the dates determined from tree ring counts was obtained. Careful sample collection from uncontaminated sites is, of course, important for accurate determination.[3] But over the years, thousands of reliable dates have been assigned to recent geological and archeological sites.[4] A young evangelical geochemist named J. Laurence Kulp was one of the first to recognize that results gathered from the use of the radiocarbon dating method poked serious holes in the theories of the twentieth-century flood geology movement.[5]

Other important new methods that are capable of yielding reasonably reliable ages include the obsidian hydration rim, thermoluminescence, and fission track methods. The obsidian hydration rim method has yielded satisfactory dates on hand-tooled artifacts from sites lacking uncontaminated organic material suitable for radiocarbon dating. Thermoluminescence and fission track dating have proved valuable for age analysis of glass and ceramics. Any

2. See Libby, *Radiocarbon Dating* (Chicago: University of Chicago, 1952).

3. For a concise summary of the details of radiocarbon dating, see chap. 3 of Stuart Fleming's *Dating in Archaeology* (New York: St. Martin's Press, 1976), or chap. 22 of Gunter Faure's *Isotope Geology*, 2d ed. (New York: John Wiley, 1986).

4. New radiocarbon dates and articles on new methods and analytical techniques regularly appear in the journal *Radiocarbon*.

5. See Kulp, "The Carbon 14 Method of Age Determination," *Scientific Monthly* 75 (1952): 259-67. See also Ronald L. Numbers, "Creationism in Twentieth-Century America," *Science* 218 (1982): 538-44, and *The Creationists* (New York: Alfred A. Knopf, 1992).

modern program of archeological dating seeks a combination of methods for a given site.[6]

Applications of Dating — the Mammoths

Radiocarbon dating has been successfully applied to several frozen Siberian mammoth carcasses.[7] One of the most exciting discoveries, made in 1977, was that of an entire frozen six-month-old mammoth named "Dima."[8] Frozen bison were recovered from Siberia and Alaska in 1951, and a bison carcass named "Blue Babe" was discovered north of Fairbanks in 1979.[9] Woolly rhinoceros, ground squirrel, vole, horse, pony, and wolverine carcasses have also been discovered since the beginning of the century.[10] Radiocarbon dating indicates that most of these animals died between 40,000 and 10,000 years ago.[11] The Beresovka mammoth was dated at more than 39,000 years old, and the Adams mammoth discovered on the banks of the Lena River in 1799 is about 37,000 years old. Skin of baby "Dima" yields a 40,000 year date, but the age is problematical as the carcass was surrounded by wood dated at 10,000 years old. A woolly rhinoceros from the Indigirka River is 38,000 years old. A Siberian pony dates somewhere between 39,000 and 35,000 years. The Taimyr Peninsula mammoth is 11,500 years old, and the Yuribei mammoth is 9,700 years old. Hair from an Alaskan mammoth is about 33,000 years old. Two bison are 31,000 and 36,000 years old, while a musk ox is 17,000 years old. The range

6. For detailed summaries of the methods of obsidian hydration rim, fission track, and thermoluminescence dating as well as other methods with potential value, see Fleming, *Dating in Archaeology*, and R. E. Taylor, "Dating Techniques in Archaeology and Paleoanthropology," *Analytical Chemistry* 59 (1987): 317-28.

7. Much new information about the frozen mammoths and associated animals can be found in chap. 9 of Antony J. Sutcliffe's *On the Track of Ice Age Mammals* (Cambridge: Harvard University Press, 1985).

8. See John Massey Stewart, "The Not-So-Fast Frozen Mammoths, Including an Intact Baby, Which Are Being Recovered from the Permafrost of Siberia," *Smithsonian* 8 (1977): 60-69.

9. On the subject of these frozen animals generally, see R. Dale Guthrie, *Frozen Fauna of the Mammoth Steppe: The Story of Blue Babe* (Chicago: University of Chicago Press, 1990).

10. See Sutcliffe, *On the Track of Ice Age Mammals*.

11. See Sutcliffe, *On the Track of Ice Age Mammals*; Guthrie, *Frozen Fauna of the Mammoth Steppe*; and N. K. Vereshchagin and G. F. Baryshnikov, "Quaternary Mammalian Extinctions in Northern Eurasia," in *Quaternary Extinctions*, ed. Paul S. Martin and Richard G. Klein (Tucson: University of Arizona, 1984).

of these dates reinforces the conclusion that the frozen mammoths were not exterminated in a single catastrophic event. Although several major events might have killed these animals, the evidence suggests that they died unspectacularly over a long period of time. The most recent mammoth deaths in Europe and Siberia, for example, fall in the general range of 13,900 to 9,780 years ago, suggesting that the mammoth only gradually became extinct on that continent.[12] Even if the last mammoths had been killed in a single catastrophic event, it would have to have occurred around 9000 B.C., a date much too early to correlate with the biblical flood, inasmuch as the Bible indicates that Near Eastern civilization had already developed prior to the flood, and we know that that civilization did not arise until around 8000 B.C.

Much has recently been learned about the diet and habits of the mammoth. Ice age expert Antony Sutcliffe reiterated that "macroscopic plant remains from the Beresovka mammoth included predominantly grasses and sedges, with rare buttercup, poppy and other herbs." Fragments of larch, birch, and alder bark were discovered beneath the carcass. The stomach and teeth of the Shandrin mammoth "included abundant mosses and *Sphagnum* together with occasional woody fragments of bilberry and willow and needles of larch." Some of the pollen extracted from mammoth stomachs may have been wind-borne and hence not indigenous to the mammoth feeding places, but overall evidence suggests "a diet of predominantly herbs, though with a great proportion of grasses and sedges in the Beresovka mammoth and more mosses in the Shandrin mammoth." The mammoth's habitat was probably varied, since the various plant remains recovered with the animals are "characteristic of a dry steppe-like environment, others of slightly wet conditions, others of swampy conditions and a few arctic-alpine plants." The most typical mammoth habitat was likely "meadow-like with swampy areas and more sparsely growing trees." Sutcliffe's observation that "most of the plants represented in the mammoth stomachs and in the sediment surrounding the carcasses are of species that still grow locally or within a few hundred kilometres of the finding places at the present-day" is especially telling against catastrophic theories.[13]

Recent studies have indicated that the mammoths probably did not all die the same way. The Shandrin mammoth was an old animal

---

12. Vereshchagin and Baryshnikov, "Quaternary Mammalian Extinctions in Northern Eurasia."

13. See Sutcliffe, *On the Track of Ice Age Mammals*.

lying on its stomach with its legs in front, a position characteristic of dying elephants. Other mammoths may have died by falling through ice or into permafrost collapse pits. E. V. Pfizenmayer believed that the Beresovka mammoth fell down a steep river bank and was buried by landslides and snow drifts, although later investigations suggested that it was buried in river deposits. Sutcliffe suggested that slow downslope movements of frozen soil trapped some of the mammoths and may have been the major cause of burial and freezing. Most carcasses had partly decomposed and some were mutilated by predators prior to burial. Chemical alteration of the tissues of the Beresovka mammoth had begun prior to freezing.

William Farrand, pointing out that marine fossils never accompanied the frozen mammoths, cogently argued that if a world-wide flood had been responsible for the mammoth carcasses, then oceanic fossils would be found associated with mammoths somewhere.[14] He believed that the physique of mammoth and rhinoceros contributed to their preservation. "The low-slung rhinoceros," he said, "would have trouble negotiating marshy ground and snow drifts" as would the mammoth "with his stiff-legged mode of locomotion." Once it had fallen into a snow-filled gully or become mired in boggy ground, a mammoth could extricate itself only with extreme difficulty. And certainly the mammoth's great weight would be "a dangerous attribute if the animal happened to graze too near the edge of a river bluff which had been softened by the summer sun." There simply are no grounds for asserting that mammoths died in a catastrophe linked to the biblical deluge.

Applications of Dating — Other Animals

An unimaginably vast array of data on other late Pleistocene and Holocene animals has been collected during the past century with a strong bearing on the flood question.[15] Although a wealth of evidence had long ago ruled out the possibility of a globally devastating flood, new data with which to test that notion further have continued to accumulate at an accelerating pace. One body of data has been gleaned

14. Farrand, "Frozen Mammoths and Modern Geology," *Science* 133 (1961): 729-35.

15. The term *Holocene* refers to the geologically very recent past — namely, the few thousand years since the end of the last glaciation.

from North American caves. An illustrative example is Baker Bluff Cave near Kingsport, Tennessee, which has been investigated since 1968.[16] The floor of this cave is underlain by about ten feet of yellow clay that was washed in by downslope movements. The clay is not stratified, and there is no evidence of interruption by flooding. Remains of organisms have been collected at half foot intervals through the thickness of clay, and 186 animal species have been recovered. Some were present at all or most levels; others were selectively preserved.

Of particular significance is the fact that all the remains are animals restricted to the Americas. Most of the species are still native to the area, but the range of some animals (e.g., the thirteen-lined ground squirrel, the tapir, and the magpie) has since diminished.[17] The cave contains abundant remains of *Crotalus horridus*, the timber rattlesnake, at virtually all levels, various shrews and moles, and many other species. The list presents us with an updated version of the biogeographical problem. If a global flood destroyed all life except for one pair of each kind of animal, then the timber rattlesnake, the shrews, moles, and the other animals indigenous solely to North America that were found in Baker Bluff Cave would have had to migrate from North America to the site of the ark and, having survived the flood on the ark, would then have had to migrate back to North America. But there is no fossil record of these species outside of North America and no indication of their presence anywhere between the Middle East and North America. Moreover, these species are incapable of covering huge distances overland. Snakes and shrews are slow movers that also have specific habitat and food requirements. There are no rattlesnakes in Alaska today, and the western rattlesnake *Crotalus viridens* barely extends its range into southern Canada. Timber rattlesnakes do not exist at all in the western states or western Canada. How then could a timber rattlesnake survive the rigors of the mountainous, frigid Canadian Northwest and Alaska on its way to the Bering land bridge? How could *Condylura cristata*, the star-nosed mole, which cannot survive outside boggy and marshy terrain, have made its way to the ark and back?

16. See John E. Guilday, Harold W. Hamilton, Elaine Anderson, and Paul W. Parmalee, "The Baker Bluff Cave Deposit, Tennessee, and the Late Pleistocene Faunal Gradient," *Bulletin of Carnegie Museum of Natural History*, no. 11 (1978): 3-67.

17. The thirteen-lined ground squirrel is still widespread throughout the United States but is no longer found in the southeast; it is primarily a midwestern species. The magpie is largely restricted to the arid intermountain regions of the west. The tapir is now restricted to South America.

To make matters more difficult, the radiocarbon dates at Baker Bluff Cave become greater for materials sampled at successively deeper levels in the cave. Material at the 9-10 foot level is about 19,000 years old, and material at the 6-7 foot level yielded dates of about 10,560 and 11,640 years. If the flood occurred within the last 19,000 years, there is no evidence at this site of the event. Not only does the site contain no flood deposits, but to the contrary there is every evidence of continuous occupation of the area by a wide variety of species, many of which survive there to the present day.

If it is argued that the flood must then have occurred more than 19,000 years ago, other problems arise. Prior to that time, the globe was populated by a vast array of large Pleistocene animals that did not become extinct until around 11,000 years ago. If the flood occurred earlier than the time of their extinction, we would have to assume that God preserved pairs of all these large animals on the ark along with all the others. The ark would thus have had to contain not only familiar African elephants, lions, and kangaroos but also pairs of mammoths, mastodons, Irish elk, giant beaver, Shasta ground sloth, megalonyx, megatherium, dire wolf, saber-toothed cat, cave bear, short-faced bear, long-horned bison, woolly rhinoceros, and many other exotic and now-extinct species. Could Noah really have managed to corral and feed all of these animals for a year? Could he have accumulated enough tundra vegetation to feed even just one pair of Siberian woolly mammoths for a whole year?

Applications of Dating — Anthropology and Archeology

Physical anthropologists and archeologists have added the new absolute dating techniques to their repertoire of traditional relative dating methods based on stratigraphy, pottery and artifacts, and written documents, and the newer techniques have confirmed that agriculture and animal domestication in the ancient Near East began around 7000-8000 B.C., earlier than anywhere else in the world. Metalworking began around 6000-7000 B.C.[18] Since Genesis 4 indicates that prediluvial human beings had mastered both agriculture and metalworking, a literal reading of the biblical text would demand that the flood took

18. For an introduction to the archeology of the Neolithic revolution in the Near East, see Charles Burney, *From Village to Empire* (Oxford: Phaidon, 1977), and James Mellaart, *The Neolithic of the Near East* (New York: Scribner's, 1975).

place sometime after 6000 B.C. (which, as it happens, is consistent with the reign of Mesopotamian king Gilgamesh). Nevertheless, despite extensive investigation of such very old Near Eastern cities as Jericho and Catal Hüyük outside Mesopotamia, archeologists have not found any signs of very extensive flooding.

Moreover, human fossils and artifacts have been discovered in considerable quantities all around the globe, and these relics clearly indicate that human beings had covered the world long before 8000 B.C. They also show that there was no worldwide extermination of the human race at any point in the past and that the human race did not spread outward from the Near East within the past few thousand years. Moreover, the racial characteristics of ancient humans suggest that they could not all have descended from the three sons of Noah. Native Americans, for example, who are related to the peoples of eastern Asia, have been in North America for at least 12,000 years.[19]

An irrefutable association between a carefully flaked stone dart or spear point and the remains of an extinct *Bison antiquus* was established in a fossil bone bed near Folsom, New Mexico, in 1926. The existence of similar stone points in association with mammoth remains near Clovis, New Mexico, was subsequently established. According to anthropologist Roger C. Owen of Queens College, New York, "the Clovis find led to the definition of a hemisphere-wide cultural complex associated with elephant hunters." The widespread evidences of the Clovis complex have been dated very accurately to between 11,500 and 11,000 years ago. The Folsom cultural complex is typically associated with extinct bison remains and is generally younger than the Clovis complex. The Folsom complex was followed by the Plano Complex around 9,500 to 7,500 years ago.[20]

On the basis of this sort of physical evidence, a solid consensus has emerged that human beings have been in North America continuously for the past 12,000 years; some scholars maintain that they have been here even longer than that. Owen has suggested that humans

19. See C. Vance Haynes Jr., "Carbon-14 Dates and Early Man in the New World," in *Pleistocene Extinctions: The Search for a Cause*, ed. Paul S. Martin and Harold E. Wright Jr. (New Haven: Yale University Press, 1967), pp. 267-86. For an extensive popular treatment of the population of the Americas, see Brian M. Fagan, *The Great Journey* (London: Thames & Hudson, 1987).

20. See Roger C. Owen, "The Americas: The Case against an Ice-Age Human Population," in *The Origins of Modern Humans: A World Survey of the Fossil Evidence*, ed. Fred H. Smith and Frank Spencer (New York: Alan R. Liss, 1984), pp. 517-63.

may have crossed the Bering land bridge from Siberia as much as 20,000 years ago in pursuit of game and gradually moved southeast as climatological changes reduced the range of the steppe tundra and the large Pleistocene mammals that depended on it. Ultimately, he says, around 12,000 years ago the ancient hunters moved south of the ice sheets and "burst into the northern plains of North America," where they found abundant, easy prey. A fluted point characteristic of the Clovis people that was discovered at Fell's Cave at the tip of South America has been dated to around 9000 B.C. — just 500 years after the earliest known date for the Clovis culture in the north.

Across North America, from California to Pennsylvania, many stratified sites have yielded evidence making it possible to reconstruct the ancient Clovis culture.[21] C. Vance Haynes of the University of Arizona has shown that the evidences of human occupation increase in number and spread across the continent through time, which indicates that the continent has been continuously occupied from the time of the original entry.

No physical evidence exists of a catastrophe that obliterated human beings in North America during the last 12,000 years. Nor is there clear evidence for a later wave of immigrants who might have arrived after such a catastrophe. In other words, archeology indicates that humans have been in North America for at least 12,000 years and that no flood wiped them out during that time. Those who claim that the flood was anthropologically universal thus have to assume that it occurred more than 12,000 years ago — but that conflicts with the conclusion based on biblical references to prediluvial agriculture and metalworking that the flood could not have occurred more than 10,000 years ago.

Other distinct human racial groupings pose similar if not more intractable problems for proponents of an anthropologically universal flood. Archeological and anthropological evidence indicates that the Australian aboriginals have been isolated on Australia for the past 30,000 to 40,000 years, for instance.[22] And in addition to the issue of the geographical isolation and continuity of such populations, their genetic uniqueness clearly establishes the point that they could not all

21. See Owen, "The Americas."
22. For information on Australian fossils, see Rhys Jones, "East of Wallace's Line: Issues and Problems in the Colonization of the Australian Continent," in The Human Revolution, ed. Paul Mellars and Chris Stringer (Princeton: Princeton University Press, 1989). Also of interest is Peter Bellwood, Man's Conquest of the Pacific (New York: Oxford University Press, 1979).

have descended from the three sons of Noah at any point in recent human history.

Biblical Studies

Significant advances have continued apace in Near Eastern studies as well. Critical editions of the Atrahasis epic have been published by British Orientalists W. G. Lambert and Alan R. Millard.[23] Tikva Frymer-Kensky, professor of Near Eastern studies at Wayne State University, has drawn a comparison between the structure of the Atrahasis epic (a primeval history of humanity from the creation until the flood) and the early chapters of Genesis supporting the assertion that the biblical material forms a theological unity, a point most welcome to theologically conservative Christians who had long emphasized unity in Scripture and had lamented the tendency of critical scholars to fragment the Bible. Frymer-Kensky contends that the author of Genesis used a historical framework at least as old as Atrahasis (viz., Creation-Problem-Flood-Solution) and reinterpreted the ancient tradition in order to illuminate the fundamental Israelite and biblical ideals that "law and the 'sanctity of human life' are the prerequisites of human existence upon the earth."[24]

More recently, Jeffrey Tigay, professor of Hebrew and Semitic languages and literatures at the University of Pennsylvania, has examined the development of the Gilgamesh epic in detail.[25] In contrast to source critics, who have no extrabiblical texts on which to base their reconstructions of biblical textual history, Tigay demonstrates from a wealth of Mesopotamian texts the possible ways in which the late Akkadian version of the Gilgamesh epic might have developed. Tigay claims that the flood story of Tablet XI of the epic was not in the earliest Old Babylonian fragments and was probably a later addition. He suggests that the story was inspired by a specific flood in southern Mesopotamia around 2900 B.C. The flood story became popular in the Near East, he says, as indicated by the appearance of the Atrahasis

23. Lambert and Millard, *Atrahasis: The Babylonian Story of the Flood* (Oxford: Oxford University Press, 1969). See also A. R. Millard, "A New Babylonian 'Genesis' Story," *Tyndale Bulletin* 18 (1967): 3-18.

24. Frymer-Kensky, "The Atrahasis Epic and Its Significance for Our Understanding of Genesis 1–9," *Biblical Archeologist* 40 (1977): 147-55.

25. Tigay, *The Evolution of the Gilgamesh Epic* (Philadelphia: University of Pennsylvania Press, 1982).

epic, which has been dated at least as far back as the Old Babylonian period, and the Sumerian deluge story. It reached Ras Shamra by the Middle Babylonian period and was eventually incorporated into the Gilgamesh epic and later still in Berossus's version during the Hellenistic period.

Tigay asserts that there is "no question" that the Atrahasis epic served as the source for Tablet XI of the Gilgamesh epic. First, several lines from Gilgamesh and the various recensions of Atrahasis are virtually identical. Second, the flood story was integral to the plot of Atrahasis as far back as the Old Babylonian period but did not enter Gilgamesh until later versions. Third, the list of gods that opens the Gilgamesh flood account is the same as that in Atrahasis, suggesting "that the editor of the *Gilgamesh* flood story simply took the list over bodily from *Atrahasis*." Lastly, on one occasion the Gilgamesh epic refers to Utnapishtim, the flood survivor, as Atrahasis. This is not to say that the Gilgamesh epic simply echoes the Atrahasis epic, however; it expands upon and abridges parts of the earlier work and also introduces theological and stylistic changes in keeping with the theme of Gilgamesh's search for immortality. *Utnapishtim* ("he found life") is an old Babylonian translation of *Ziusudra* ("life of long days"), the name of the Sumerian flood hero. Tigay concludes that "the *Atrahasis* flood story has thus been incorporated into *The Gilgamesh Epic* in a form which differs considerably, in wording, style, content, and apparently ideology, from the Old Babylonian version of that story." Yet other materials incorporated into the Gilgamesh epic were subjected to far more drastic changes than was the material taken from the Atrahasis epic.

According to Tigay the deluge story was added to the Gilgamesh epic by a late editor who took relatively little liberty with his source material. "Prior to its appearance in *Gilgamesh*, this was already a story about the survivor of the flood who tells it to Gilgamesh. Hence the story needed relatively little modification to render it suitable for its new context in *The Gilgamesh Epic*." Tigay's masterly study demonstrates that ancient authors did combine oral tales and written sources and exercised some freedom in composing their own versions of the tales, but at the same time, some material survived in written form for centuries with few modifications.

While Tigay's work on the tradition history of the Gilgamesh epic had considerable empirical control because it was based on a wealth of textual materials from various periods in Mesopotamian history, the reconstructions of Pentateuchal transmission history have always lacked that control, based as they are solely on the final text as we now have it. Source critics have never seen differing versions of the alleged sources from different periods in Israel's history. Keenly aware of that lack of extrabiblical evidence, Tigay notes with refreshing honesty the tentative, hypothetical nature of much Pentateuchal criticism. He has sensed some validity in the challenges to the documentary hypothesis by conservatives.[26] Nevertheless Tigay suggests in a significant recent work that there exist several empirical models in ancient literature against which various Old Testament source critical hypotheses can be tested. If by no means proving their correctness, he says, "many of the central hypotheses of biblical criticism are realistic."[27]

In recent years, some critical scholars have called into question the traditionally accepted grounds for postulating diverse sources for the flood narrative. No less an Old Testament scholar than the University of Heidelberg's Claus Westermann has argued that criteria such as differing names of God, doublets, and linguistic variants are inadequate for discerning distinctive literary sources.[28] Indeed, some scholars employing the methods of literary criticism have been struck by evidences of striking unity and careful craftsmanship in the biblical texts. The flood narrative has come under close scrutiny in this regard.

For example, Martin Kessler (b. 1927) of the State University of New York at Albany has pointed out that the biblical text may be examined via the "genetic" or "diachronic" approach (which seeks to

---

26. Among the more significant conservative works since William Henry Green and John Davis that have taken issue with the documentary hypothesis are James Orr, *The Problem of the Old Testament Considered with Reference to Recent Criticism* (New York: Scribner's, 1906); Robert Dick Wilson, *A Scientific Investigation of the Old Testament* (Philadelphia: Sunday School Times, 1926); Oswald T. Allis, *The Five Books of Moses* (Philadelphia: Presbyterian & Reformed, 1943); Edward J. Young, *An Introduction to the Old Testament* (Grand Rapids: William B. Eerdmans, 1949); and Umberto Cassuto, *The Documentary Hypothesis and the Composition of the Pentateuch* (Jerusalem: Magnes Press, 1961). For some archeological arguments against the documentary hypothesis, see Kenneth A. Kitchen, *Ancient Orient and Old Testament* (London: Tyndale, 1966), and Derek Kidner, *Genesis* (London: Tyndale, 1967).

27. Tigay, "Summary and Conclusions," in *Empirical Models for Biblical Criticism*, ed. Jeffrey H. Tigay (Philadelphia: University of Pennsylvania Press, 1985), p. 239. Tigay also contributed an introduction and a chapter entitled "The Evolution of the Pentateuchal Narratives in the Light of the Evolution of the *Gilgamesh Epic*" to this volume.

28. Westermann, *Genesis 1-11* (Minneapolis: Augsburg Press, 1984). The chapter on the flood in this valuable commentary is useful not only for its exegetical insights but also for its extensive bibliography.

determine how the text achieved its present form) or the "teleological" or "synchronic" approach (which deals with the text as it now stands).[29] Kessler charges Pentateuchal scholars with being "excessively preoccupied" with the "genetic" approach. He prefers to examine the present text of Genesis using rhetorical criticism. While maintaining dialogue with "diachronic" source criticism, Kessler does not hesitate to challenge its monotonous analysis of the flood story. He suggests that "the obvious duplication, viz. the execution of the divine command and the description of the flood may be suggestive of the narrator's 'framing' method." After comparing ostensibly parallel J and P sections in Genesis 7, Kessler concludes that the argument that the two accounts are contradictory is unconvincing. A writer who wanted to provide a duplicate account might compose "two verbally identical accounts (which biblical writers generally avoid), or he could create 'variation by design,' in other words, write an alternate, duplicating materially synonymous account." In the case of the flood story, Kessler opts for the latter.

The narrative displays "considerable artistic sophistication," he says, in which every detail serves a formal and material purpose. He maintains that the source critics have inconsistently used duplications for source divisions into J and P and that many approximately synonymous terms are distributed between the two sources. He concludes that "the criteria whereby sources are isolated are at least problematic in Gen 7" and that the evidence is stronger that the repetitions are a "deliberate device" to emphasize key features in the story. "There are no 'seams' in Gen 7," he says; "the garment is of one piece and if materials should be of different provenance, their joining has been executed with such artistry that they have been dissolved in the whole." Kessler insists that source criticism has vastly underrated the quality of the biblical literature. "Genetic criticism will have to find other ways and design different criteria from those set forth in the 19th century by the creators of the documentary hypothesis."

Along other lines, British evangelical scholar Gordon Wenham has made a case for the coherence and unity of the flood narrative on the basis of a perceived extended palistrophic or chiastic structure in which the first item matches the final item, the second item corresponds to the penultimate item, and so on, so that the second half of the story is a

29. Kessler, "Rhetorical Criticism of Gen 7," in *Rhetorical Criticism: Essays in Honor of J. Muilenburg*, ed. Jared Judd Jackson and Martin Kessler (Pittsburgh: Pickwick Press, 1974), pp. 1-17.

mirror image of the first half.[30] According to Wenham, the flood narrative (Genesis 6:10–9:19) contains a total of thirty-one elements, half of which appear before the center of the narrative at 8:1 ("God remembered Noah") and half of which appear after (see p. 240). He argues that there are "certain features in the story which reflect the large element of contrivance in casting the whole tale into this form."

First, although the central section, from the command to enter the ark to the command to leave, fits a palistrophic structure naturally, the same is not true of the section dealing with the prediluvial situation and the closing scene. Yet the author mirrored such terms as Shem, Ham, and Japheth, the ark, the flood, the covenant, and food in reverse order to the opening scene. Second, some of the time spans may have been mentioned specifically to achieve symmetry. Wenham claims, for example, that even though the passengers entered the ark only one week before embarking, the period of seven days is mentioned twice to maintain "literary balance with the two weeks of waiting in the ark at the end of the flood." The third contrived feature is the forty days of flood, a part of the 150 days of prevailing, which maintain literary balance with the forty days mentioned in Genesis 8:6. Wenham suggests that "some of the references to time in the flood appear to have as much a literary as a chronological function. They underlie the symmetry of the flood's rise and fall, thereby enhancing the structure of the palistrophe."

Despite the contrivances, the writer skillfully produced a self-consistent, coherent tale "when read as a straightforward narration." But the writer also paid close attention to chronology for theological reasons. Both the work of creation in Genesis 1 and the "uncreation" of the flood narrative begin on Sunday and end on Friday, so that "even the chronology of the flood story becomes a vehicle for expressing theological ideas." Furthermore the chronology embraces the whole story and not just parts of it. Wenham argues that "the evidence of chronology corroborates that of syntax and literary structure, that the Genesis flood story is a coherent unity."

Wenham points out that at least seventeen features appeared in both the biblical narrative and the Gilgamesh flood story, generally in the same order. When considered separately, the hypothesized J

30. Wenham, "The Coherence of the Flood Narrative," *Vetus Testamentum* 28 (1978): 336-48. Wenham's views on the flood are very favorably received by Isaac M. Kikiwada and Arthur Quinn in *Before Abraham Was: The Unity of Genesis 1–11* (Nashville: Abingdon Press, 1985).

G. Wenham's Proposed Flood Narrative Chiasm

A   Noah (6:10a)
B   Shem, Ham, and Japheth (10b)
C   Ark to be built (14-16)
D   Flood announced (17)
E   Covenant with Noah (18-20)
F   Food in the ark (21)
G   Command to enter ark (7:1-3)
H   7 days waiting for flood (4-5)
I   7 days waiting for flood (7-10)
J   Entry to ark (11-15)
K   Yahweh shuts Noah in (16)
L   40 days flood (17a)
M   Waters increase (17b-18)
N   Mountains covered (19-20)
O   150 days waters prevail (21-24)
P   GOD REMEMBERS NOAH (8:1)
O'   150 days waters abate (3)
N'   Mountain tops visible (4-5)
M'   Waters abate (5)
L'   40 days (end of) (6a)
K'   Noah opens window of ark (6b)
J'   Raven and dove leave ark (7-9)
I'   7 days waiting for waters to subside (10-11)
H'   7 days waiting for waters to subside (12-13)
G'   Command to leave ark (15-17 [22])
F'   Food outside ark (9:1-4)
E'   Covenant with all flesh (8-10)
D'   No flood in future (11-17)
C'   Ark (18a)
B'   Shem, Ham, and Japheth (18b)
A'   Noah (19)

---

document displays only twelve points in common with the Gilgamesh epic, and the hypothesized P document only ten. Wenham considers it strange "that two accounts of the flood so different as J and P, circulating in ancient Israel, should have been combined to give our present story which has many more resemblances to the Gilgamesh version than the postulated sources." The J and P versions in their original form might have been more similar, he suggests, or perhaps only one source similar to the Mesopotamian flood story was used by the writer of Genesis. Whichever solution one adopts, says Wenham, the argument from parallels with Gilgamesh reinforces the idea "that the Genesis flood story is a coherent narrative within the conventions of Hebrew story-telling." He maintains that syntax, literary structure, chronology, and Mesopotamian parallels all point to the unity and coherence of the Genesis account. Skeptical of the presumption of an ingenious and thorough redactor who blended J and P into a marvelous and coherent unity, Wenham favors the more economical hypothesis of one epic source reworked by a later priestly editor.

Wenham's intriguing case for unity has not gone unchallenged. Lloyd Bailey (b. 1936), professor of Old Testament at Duke University Divinity School, concedes that the documentary hypothesis would be in deep trouble if the entire flood story had a palistrophic structure, but he doubts that Wenham has shown that it does.[31] He notes that the corresponding elements in Wenham's scheme are highly unbalanced. For example, element D consists of just one verse, while D' consists of seven verses. Genesis 6:11-13 and 9:5-7 are omitted entirely. Bailey also maintains that since there is an obvious "return" between Genesis 6:5-8 (where God plans to destroy humanity because of its wickedness) and 8:20-23 (where God announces that he will never again do so), the palistrophic structure should begin at Genesis 6:5 and cite 8:20-23 as its parallel. But these verses play no role in Wenham's palistrophe. In Bailey's opinion, this flaw alone is "sufficient to demolish the entire proposed palistrophic hypothesis for the flood story." Discussion about the structure and unity of the flood narrative has entered a potentially vigorous and stimulating phase.

Analysis and Application

The development of new techniques for dating archeological materials, especially the radiocarbon method, has given us a much more detailed understanding of the structure of human and animal history during the past few tens of thousands of years. Archeology and paleontology

---

31. Bailey, *Noah: The Person and the Story in History and Tradition* (Columbia, S.C.: University of South Carolina Press, 1989). See also J. A. Emerton, "An Examination of Some Attempts to Defend the Unity of the Flood Narrative in Genesis," *Vetus Testamentum* 37 (1987): 401-20.

are sufficiently constrained by well-documented chronological data to have established beyond a reasonable doubt that there is no known physical or paleontological evidence for a global deluge. It is manifestly clear that mammoths and their contemporaries did not die in such a catastrophe, and, if we accept the biblical testimony that human beings had mastered the arts of agriculture and metalworking prior to the flood, it is also clear that the mammoths died out long before the flood could have occurred in any case. In addition, the fossil record of North American caves provides another compelling line of evidence against the concept of worldwide animal migration to the ark.

Archeology has firmly demonstrated that the civilization described in Genesis 4 was in place by at least 6000 B.C., thus constraining the biblical deluge to a date more recent than that, and evidence associated with the Gilgamesh epic seems to imply that the biblical deluge would have to have occurred closer to 3000 B.C. Archeological evidence rules out the occurrence of a widespread deluge ten or twenty thousand years ago. Most of those who support the notion that a deluge occurred at that more distant date are seeking to establish the viability of an event that, even if confined to the Near East, could have destroyed the whole human race. But archeological investigations have established the presence of human beings in the Americas, Australia, and southeastern Asia long before the advent of the sort of Near Eastern civilization described in the Bible and thus long before the biblical deluge could have taken place. In the light of a wealth of mutually supportive evidence from a variety of disciplines and sources, it is simply no longer tenable to insist that a deluge drowned every human on the face of the globe except Noah's family.

Some Christians find this conclusion very unwelcome and have reacted to it by denying the validity of the growing mountain of evidence along with the techniques used to gather it, including radiocarbon dating. This strategy is shortsighted and self-defeating. How can one hope to defend one category of truth by suppressing or disparaging another? All the relevant evidence from the created order tells us that the flood was neither geographically nor anthropologically universal. Surely we will do better in the long run to grapple with this fact and seek to determine its implications for our interpretations of the text of Scripture than to turn our backs on it and on the people who in good conscience have worked to gather, refine, and test the evidence supporting it.

In the realm of biblical studies, on the other hand, while the extrabiblical evidence is provocative, it has as yet yielded no evidence to establish the history of the biblical text conclusively. Scholars have not yet located J, P, or an ancient Hebrew flood text buried in some Palestinian tell. All reconstructions of the text's history have been based solely on internal evidence and hence remain tentative and speculative. There is no external corroboration for the classical critical source hypothesis and hence no empirical support for the assertion that the biblical text is merely a product of Israel's religious consciousness and not a divine revelation.

16. Twentieth-Century Flood Geology

Adjusting to the vast accumulation of geological evidence strongly indicating the earth's great antiquity and demonstrating that the fossiliferous strata were not the result of the flood, orthodox Christians of the late nineteenth century accepted the notion of a very extensive deluge that covered much of central Asia and perhaps large regions of other continents, while critical scholars decided that the deluge was confined to Mesopotamia. Even though data acquired throughout the twentieth century reinforced the conceptions of earth's antiquity and the nondiluvial origin of rock layers, many Christians resisted the directions being taken by science and theology. Sensing a loss of respect for biblical authority associated with the changing understanding of the meaning of the early chapters of Genesis, they tenaciously clung to a very literal view of this material and reinforced the view with vigorous appeals to extrabiblical data. But in order to establish extrabiblical support for their view, they have had to reject the findings of established science and in essence develop their own science, typically along the lines of Woodward's or Penn's flood geology but cloaked in the trappings of twentieth-century scientific language. Their interpretations of the data, however, tend to be highly selective and confused. Cut off from mainstream intellectual centers, writers who espouse the reactionary science are typically self-taught and lack the requisite qualifications for discussing geology. In spite of that, twentieth-century flood geology has exercised a profound influence on modern evangelicalism, especially in North America.[1] Significantly, the literalist flood

1. For an overview of the growth of this movement in this century, see Ronald L. Numbers, "Creationism in Twentieth-Century America," *Science* 218

geology school has not rejected extrabiblical data. Indeed, the literalists have depended more heavily on extrabiblical physical substantiation of biblical statements than have other Christians. The problem with this strategy is that they have improperly interpreted and generally failed to grasp the significance of the extrabiblical data to which they have appealed.

George McCready Price

The modern flood geology movement sprang out of Seventh-day Adventism through the efforts of the self-taught George McCready Price (1870-1963). Historian of science Ronald L. Numbers has established that Price became convinced of the validity of flood geology and the error of evolutionism through reading the writings of Ellen Gould White (1827-1915), founding "prophetess" of Seventh-day Adventism. Specifically, Price seems to have been impressed by White's claim of "divine inspiration for her view that the Noachian flood accounted for the fossil record on which evolutionists based their theory."[2] Earlier British and American flood geology had died out by the mid-nineteenth century, so it is clear that modern flood geology stems from this reintroduction by White; under her influence, Price committed his life to the espousal of strict creationism.[3]

Price wrote several books on geology with sufficient style and sophistication that readers untrained in geology are generally unable to detect the flaws. All his writings challenge accepted notions of earth history. One early salvo accused standard geology of being speculative, full of metaphysics, and more concerned with theory than with true

---

(1982): 538-44. Numbers has also completed a comprehensive study of creationism in which he discusses the major figures of the movement, their educational attainments, and their influence. See Numbers, *The Creationists* (New York: Alfred A. Knopf, 1992). For an informative and very sympathetic treatment of creationism and flood geology, see Henry M. Morris, *History of Modern Creationism* (San Diego: Master Book, 1984).

2. Numbers, "Creationism in Twentieth-Century America," p. 539.

3. In many ways modern flood geology is a descendant of the thought of the "scriptural geologists" of the early nineteenth century such as Penn, Fairholme, Bugg, and Young, and of such later nineteenth-century authors as the Lords and Isaac Newton Vail. Price was a prolific writer who not only penned several influential books but also published in such prestigious journals as the *Princeton Theological Review*. Price's career is reviewed in detail in chap. 5 of Numbers's *The Creationists*.

induction from facts.[4] Price complained about the biological "onion-coat" theory of fossils and denied the global applicability of the British succession of fossils. Paradoxically Price argued in uniformitarian fashion that there should have been various faunal and floral provinces in the past as there are today. There was no a priori reason why trilobites and mammals should not have occupied different provinces or ecological niches simultaneously in the past, he argued, so one could not legitimately draw conclusions about temporal successions of organisms from fossil successions in rocks.

Price argued that genuine progress in geology requires the recognition of five basic facts:

1. Rocks of any assigned geological age can actually be found lying directly on basement rocks somewhere. Cambrian trilobite-bearing rocks rest on basement at many localities, but Tertiary mammal-bearing rocks or Jurassic ammonite-bearing strata lie on basement rocks elsewhere. This phenomenon implies that trilobites, ammonites, and mammals all lived at the same time.
2. "Any formation whatever may rest conformably upon any other 'older' fossiliferous formation." Price provided several examples. He argued that mainstream geologists were identifying time breaks between geological formations solely on the basis of

---

4. Price, *The Fundamentals of Geology* (Mountain View, Calif.: Pacific Press, 1913). This book is an expanded version of a pamphlet that Price had released under the title *Illogical Geology* in 1906. Still earlier Price had written *Outlines of Modern Christianity and Modern Science* (1902) in which he similarly challenged the claims of orthodox science. Like other flood geologists, Price constantly attacks "uniformitarianism," by which they mean an approach to geology, supposedly first advanced by Charles Lyell, that rules out the influence of major catastrophes in the development of geological features and instead attributes all such features to very slow, gradual processes analogous to those in operation today. This is a major distortion of the understanding of uniformitarianism in the mainstream discipline of geology, however. For careful discussions of the standard understanding of uniformitarianism, see Martin J. S. Rudwick, "Uniformity and Progression: Reflections on the Structure of Geological Theory in the Age of Lyell," in *Perspectives in the History of Science and Technology*, ed. Duane H. D. Roller (Norman, Okla.: University of Oklahoma, 1971), pp. 209-27; Stephen Jay Gould, "Toward the Vindication of Punctuational Change," in *Catastrophes and Earth History* (Princeton: Princeton University Press, 1984); Reijer Hooykaas, *Natural Law and Divine Miracle: The Principle of Uniformity in Geology, Biology and Theology* (Leiden: E. H. Brill, 1963); and *Philosophy of Geohistory, 1785-1970*, ed. Claude C. Albritton (Stroudsburg, Pa.: Dowden, Hutchinson, & Ross, 1975). For Charles Lyell's original views, see his three-volume masterwork, *Principles of Geology* (London: John Murray, 1833).

differences in the fossil content of the formations, which they presumed (incorrectly he believed) to have been deposited in different ages. Price asserted that if the evidence were taken at face value — that is, without the theory of biological succession imposed upon it — no one would conclude that there were any time breaks between the formations.

3. The mainstream geological notion of the thrust faulting of older rocks over younger rocks is an illusion.[5] Price noted several instances in which what mainstream geologists identify as ancient rocks (e.g., Cambrian limestones) lay on top of what they identify as comparatively young rocks (e.g., Cretaceous shales) over areas of hundreds of square miles. Price argued that there is nothing exceptional about such formations to suggest that an older layer had been thrust over a younger layer. He maintained that the whole idea of overthrusting was devised by geologists simply to salvage the dogma of fossil succession.

4. The evidence from the action of rivers flowing over rock clearly suggested to Price both that all rock formations are the same age and that the rivers of the world "began sawing at them all at the same time."

5. There are gaps in the mainstream geological assignments of specific time ranges to specific fossil organisms, said Price. For example, a given animal might exist in Paleozoic rocks, disappear in Mesozoic rocks, and reappear in Tertiary rocks. Price also spoke of documented cases of fauna presumed extinct from the fossil record that have nonetheless been discovered alive.

---

5. Overthrust faults involve one large block of rock being superimposed over another along nearly horizontal fault planes. The existence of an overthrust is often disclosed by mapping of rocks on a regional scale, but physical evidence for faulting is common along the fault planes. Rock in the fault plane is typically granulated and sheared, and small-scale distortions of thinly layered rocks within or adjacent to the fault are common. In some cases, metamorphosed rocks are positioned above rocks that are not metamorphosed. Overthrust faults are confined to mountain belts where all manner of rock deformation exists. In many though not all cases, older rock has been thrust on top of younger rocks. Among the most impressive overthrusts in the world are the Glarus thrust of the Swiss Alps, the McConnell thrust in the Canadian Rockies near Banff, Alberta, the Lewis thrust at Glacier National Park, Montana, and the Great Smoky fault in the vicinity of Great Smoky Mountains National Park, Tennessee. For more detailed discussion of overthrusts, see any text on structural geology — e.g., John Suppe, *Principles of Structural Geology* (Englewood Cliffs, N.J.: Prentice-Hall, 1985), and George H. Davis, *Structural Geology of Rocks and Regions* (New York: John Wiley, 1984).

Price was firmly convinced that mainstream geologists had no means of accounting for these five facts because they remained dedicated to the "fantasy" of an evolutionary development of life. He was certain that true and unbiased induction would inevitably lead to the conclusion that the world had "witnessed an awful aqueous catastrophe" back of which lay "a direct and real Creation as the only possible origin of things." Price asserted that his strictly inductive study of the facts marvelously confirmed the literal interpretation of the first chapters of Genesis. So much for critics who had consigned Genesis to the realm of fable!

Price proceeded to present his evidence for the "awful aqueous catastrophe." Considerably influenced by Howorth and Prestwich, he argued that the appearance of huge quantities of fossils of several "ages" gathered together in common "graveyards" could be explained only by the fact that they had been buried suddenly rather than over a long period. Moreover, the fact that there was no evidence that such graveyards were being formed anywhere in the world today indicated that uniformitarian geology could not account for them. According to Price, the fossil evidence indicated that prior to the flood, the world enjoyed a uniformly temperate climate. Specifically, the fossil evidence gave "proofs of an almost eternal spring's having prevailed in the arctic regions, and semitropical conditions in north temperate latitudes; in short, give us proofs of a singular uniformity of climate over the globe which we can hardly conceive possible, let alone account for." Fossil corals, coal deposits, and mammoth remains, all of which Price believed to be indicative of temperate or tropical climates, can all be found at high latitudes. This point proved especially compelling to Price's early readers, since mainstream geologists had not as yet provided a satisfactory account of the distribution of fossilized temperate organisms throughout the world, and many people were not yet familiar with Fleming's reasons for believing that mammoths had in fact been adapted to the cold.[6]

Price also claimed that fossil evidence indicated that prediluvial plants and animals were generally larger than their nearest modern counterparts. He characterized modern organisms as "degenerate" varieties of the earlier forms. He contended that the fossil record of

---

6. The existence of tropical fossils in rocks at high latitudes remained a problem during the early twentieth century. Not until later was it demonstrated that global plate tectonics provides the explanation. Several continental land masses have drifted from more temperate regions to higher latitudes.

humans extends far enough back to establish the point that mankind witnessed many catastrophic events including large mountain uplifts and subsidences. He was convinced that the world of rocks and fossils reflects an older state of the world the ruins of which have been preserved as a unit but that geological changes indicated by the fossils must have occurred since man was on the earth. What mainstream geologists have identified as the geological series of fossils, said Price, is in fact simply a record of the organisms that lived simultaneously in an Eden-like world that was transformed by a sudden catastrophe into a wholly different modern world. He also asserted that forces and changes now in operation are insufficient to explain the disappearance of animals and the uplift of great mountains. "Is it in any way transgressing the bounds of true inductive science," asked Price, "to correlate this event with the Deluge of the Hebrew Scripture and of the traditions of every race on earth?"

A decade later Price put a more sophisticated face on his flood geology by issuing a textbook entitled *The New Geology*. Published in an attractive format with excellent photographs, the volume treats the standard topics of traditional texts such as physiographic, structural, dynamic, stratigraphical, and theoretical geology. A lay reader sees no obvious indications that the book is not a competent exposition of the essentials of geology. Indeed, many descriptive aspects of the work are quite in line with mainstream geology. Embedded within the text, however, is a cleverly updated presentation of the diluvialism that had been discredited a century and a half earlier.

In a chapter on the earth's organic features complete with high-quality illustrations of various extinct organisms, Price alludes to the disappearance of the fossil horse, noting that "elephants, rhinoceroses, camels, megatheriums, and glyptodonts, the three first mentioned being identical with the kinds now living in the Old World, also lived here in North America alongside these fossil horses."[7] So far, so good. But then he proceeds to say, "The huge dinosaurs may also have been contemporary" (p. 60) — an assertion that no mainstream geologist would admit as a possibility. And then, sliding past this glaring misinterpretation of the fossil record, he asks how such an assemblage of animals could all have become extinct together. Diluvialism is his answer.

In discussing stratigraphical geology, Price asserts that the main-

---

7. Price, *The New Geology* (Mountain View, Calif.: Pacific Press, 1923), p. 60.

stream geological understanding of the sequence of organisms through time is only a theory that has in fact been "definitely disproved by a large number of recently discovered facts" (p. 280). He states that all animals in the fossil record "probably *lived contemporaneously in an older state of our world*" (p. 280). There is no valid evidence, he says, to suggest that any given fossil plant or animal lived before any other kind of plant or animal or even before humans were on the earth.

Price cites such Pleistocene phenomena as Prestwich's raised beaches, rubble drift, and the ossiferous fissures at Palermo, Howorth's Siberian mammoth mummies, and relic lakes as evidence of a sudden and permanent change of climate. Unaware of the firsthand reports, Price repeats the fable that frozen mammoth meat had proved fresh enough for humans to eat. "Occasionally one of these ancient animals comes to light with the flesh in such a state of preservation that the dogs and wolves are greedy to eat the meat, and a party of scientists even had a meal off this ancient meat which has been kept in cold storage so many millenniums" (p. 581).

As in his earlier book, Price provides several examples of what he calls "deceptive conformity" and challenges the concept of the thrust fault. He felt that after a study of the facts, his readers would conclude "that this theory of 'thrusts' is rather a pitiful example of the hypnotizing power of a false theory in the presence of the very plainest facts" (pp. 627-29). Mainstream geologists had identified fault contacts of the Lewis thrust near Glacier National Park, the McConnell thrust at Banff National Park, and several thrust faults in the Appalachians, but Price dismisses this characterization in each case, affirming to the contrary that each contact is marked by perfect conformity and cannot be distinguished from an ordinary depositional contact.

According to Price, virtually all of the geologic record can be attributed to the effects of the deluge. He maintains that during the course of the flood enormous thicknesses of soft sediments were piled onto foundations with unequal stability. Where basement rocks were unable to support a mile or more of overlying load, the still unconsolidated strata settled, while in other large areas they remained nearly horizontal. The upper strata near the edges of depressions became tilted where large volumes of strata settled in this way. Where settling was extensive, the tilting of the strata led to "very marked contortion" or distinct rupturing of surface rocks. In this way great folded rock layers would be produced around the world. And where strong currents of water surged across the still soft strata, immense amounts of erosion occurred in a very short time.

If erosion removed much of the strata exposed in a deeply cut canyon before the strata were consolidated, says Price, the pile left standing would necessarily settle, because "nothing but firmly consolidated rocks at the bottom could possibly support a weight of a mile or more of superincumbent rocks" (p. 690). With lateral support removed, the pile of strata would settle or collapse, producing folded structures. Price appears not to have been aware of the fact that folding in layered rocks is generally unrelated to nearby valleys.

Repeating the discredited claim of Fairholme, Price concludes that geological formations everywhere present "the clearest evidence that most of the folding and tilting of the rocks occurred while the beds composing them were *still soft*" (p. 691). He accuses mainstream geologists of ignoring the clear physical evidence out of sheer prejudice. Caught up in biases of his own, Price failed to mention the considerably larger body of physical evidence that counted against his position.

Price's Successors

Byron Nelson (1893-1972), a Norwegian Lutheran Synod pastor who was profoundly influenced by both Price and the conservative Lutheran view of the early chapters of Genesis, soon took up the defense of flood geology through a number of books in which he expressed his opposition to the theory of evolution and through activity in various creationist organizations.[8] In *The Deluge Story in Stone*, Nelson presents a survey of the history of views of the flood from Tertullian to the present.[9] He provides considerable material on Steno, Burnet, Woodward, Catcott, and their critics. He notes that flood geology was most widely accepted during the eighteenth century but that support for it began to wane during the first half of the nineteenth century. He cites Cuvier, Buckland, and Silliman approvingly as flood geologists of a newer catastrophic school while granting that they were not full-fledged flood geologists after the fashion of Granville Penn, William Kirby, George Fairholme, and George Young. Yet Nelson failed to appreciate the radical difference between Buckland's empirically based catastrophism and the ungrounded speculations of Granville Penn and the

---

8. For an overview of Nelson's career, see chap. 6 of Numbers's *The Creationists*.

9. Nelson, *The Deluge Story in Stone* (Minneapolis: Augsburg Press, 1931).

other scriptural geologists. As the nineteenth century advanced, says Nelson, flood geology fell on hard times as

> the control of education in Europe and America passed gradually out of the hands of such men into the hands of men more or less lacking in religious convictions, and even into the hands of men secretly or openly hostile to the Bible. The result was that the theory of uniformity, which had come down from the ancients and had been advocated to some extent in the sixteenth and seventeenth centuries, gained the upper hand and the Flood theory fell into the background.[10]

Even so, flood catastrophism was not silenced entirely, for in the latter part of the nineteenth century individuals such as Howorth and Price gave it new credence. Nelson dismisses as futile George F. Wright's novel attempt to combine theories of the flood and modern geology, but he reserves his harshest criticism for what he characterizes as the anticatastrophic theories of modern geology, and he argues for a return to diluvialism.

In Great Britain the creationist publication *Transactions of the Victoria Institute* provided a forum for the presentation of even the most bizarre flood geology scenarios.[11] In America, too, antievolutionists began to organize in the hopes of winning America over to creation and deluge geology.[12] The Religion and Science Association was founded in 1935 through the efforts of California rancher Dudley J. Whitney (1883-1964), Price, and Nelson. Internal problems led to the collapse of the group, but the Creation-Deluge Society arose out of its ashes in 1938. More successful than its predecessor, the Society published several issues of the *Bulletin of Deluge Geology and Related Sciences*. One important player in these organizations was the formidable Seventh-day Adventist flood geologist Harold Clark (1891-1986), a professor of biology at Pacific Union College in California and protégé

---

10. Nelson failed to explain why he chose to ignore the Christian commitment of such geologists as Fleming, Hitchcock, Miller, and others who were very critical of the old flood theories.

11. A not unrepresentative article by Philip J. Le Riche ("Scientific Proofs of a Universal Deluge," *Journal of the Transactions of the Victoria Institute* 61 [1929]: 86-117) indulges in such hyperactive speculation that even seventeenth-century cosmogonists might have been puzzled and amused. In the United States, *Bibliotheca Sacra* continued its tradition of publishing articles on the deluge.

12. For surveys of various creationist organizations and their histories, see chaps. 6 and 7 of Numbers's *The Creationists*.

of Price who had far more field experience than his mentor.[13] Clark's book *The New Diluvialism* (1946) offers what is without doubt the most competent twentieth-century endorsement of flood geology. In diametric opposition to the first three facts of Price's *Fundamentals of Geology*, Clark took great pains to demonstrate that the stratigraphic sequences worked out by mainstream geologists must be considered valid. He also considered the paleontological correlation of sequences to be legitimate. In accepting the standard geological succession, the fossil basis for that succession, and the correlations, Clark differed sharply from virtually all other twentieth-century flood geologists. He also accepted the mainstream geological understanding of the nature of overthrusts. He recognized that such great faults are generally detected on the basis of regional mapping, the physical characteristics of the rocks involved, and physical deformation at or near the fault planes. In granting the validity of these standard geological findings, Clark displayed far more sophistication and awareness of geological data than Price ever did.

Despite the fact that he began from these mainstream premises, however, Clark still interpreted the geological record in terms of catastrophe. He rejected mainstream estimates of the antiquity of the rocks and insisted on interpreting the stratigraphic and paleontological sequences in terms of Price's principle of ecological zonation. In essence, he maintained that the fossiliferous strata formed when flood waters surged across continents destroying successive ecological zones. Like every other flood scheme, Clark's hypothesis of ecological zonation presumes that all the sediments remained unconsolidated until the entire catastrophe had run its course, despite a wealth of compelling evidence to the contrary. Perhaps because Clark's work was more technical and detailed and was never published in the attractive format of Price's books, he didn't have the sort of impact on the conservative evangelical community that Price did.

Although some Lutherans, such as Theodore Graebner (1876-1950) of Concordia Theological Seminary in St. Louis, were suspicious of flood geology, most Lutherans (and particularly those in the Lutheran

13. Seventh-day Adventism has long been a stronghold of flood geology. *The Seventh-day Adventist Bible Commentary,* especially the first edition (ed. Francis D. Nichol, 7 vols. [Washington: Review & Herald Publishing Association, 1953-1957]), includes extensive arguments for a global flood. The Geoscience Institute at Loma Linda University in California and Andrews University, both Adventist institutions, generally favor some form of flood geology. On the life and views of Harold Clark, see chap. 7 of Numbers's *The Creationists.*

Church–Missouri Synod) embraced it warmly.[14] The major flood geology book of mid-century, *The Flood in the Light of the Bible, Geology, and Archaeology* (1951), was written by Alfred M. Rehwinkel (b. 1887), a Missouri Synod Old Testament theologian at Concordia Seminary. Like all members of the flood geology movement, Rehwinkel was greatly concerned about perceived attacks on the historicity of the creation and flood stories. He observed that scientists generally agreed with the biblical teachings about creation and the flood until about 125 years ago, when evolutionary geology began to dominate the intellectual scene. Rehwinkel bemoaned the fact that college students were being confronted with views hostile to traditional readings of the Bible and that as a result their faith was crumbling and disappearing. Again and again, he lamented, "a pious Christian youth has gained a glittering world of pseudo learning but has lost his own immortal soul." Rehwinkel wrote his book to help students withstand such temptation. His fundamental premise was that "to countless millions of all ages this book has been and still is the inspired Word of God, and therefore correct in every detail, also when dealing with natural phenomena and scientific facts."

Following Luther, Rehwinkel believed that the original perfect world contained no thorns, thistles, deserts, bleak hills, Arctic wastes, or disease-breeding tropical heat. The fall into sin introduced subtle changes in the natural world, although it remained a paradise by today's standards. Mountains were not so high then as they are today, for example. The soil was better, natural resources were distributed more equitably, and a uniformly mild climate prevailed, as demonstrated by the fossil record. This warm climate, most satisfactorily explained by a "vapor canopy," promoted the development of gigantic animals such as the dinosaurs and the sort of luxuriant plant life that is preserved in coal beds.

This original world lasted 1,656 years, stated Rehwinkel, working from the genealogy of Genesis 5. Because of generally good health, a population of more than two billion covered the world, he said, as

---

14. Lutherans from the time of Luther himself have commonly held to more conservative positions on the relationship between science and the Bible. As we have seen, Keil and Hävernick held to a universal flood and cited outdated geological information. In more recent times, Herbert C. Leupold and Leander S. Keyser held to a global flood. Walter Lang of the Bible-Science Association is a Lutheran, as are such creationist writers as Paul Zimmerman, John Klotz, and Wilbert Rusch. On Lutheranism and young-earth creationism, see chapter 15 of Numbers's *The Creationists.*

evidenced by the human remains found associated with the remains of mammoths around the world. These antediluvians were not savages, for Genesis 4 speaks of an advanced culture, but this advanced civilization was infected by a moral degeneracy so extreme that the flood became necessary. Rehwinkel insisted on a global deluge. Genesis being God's infallible record, he insisted that no other interpretation was possible.

Rehwinkel believed that the ark could adequately contain representatives of all the world's animals. Noting that estimates of the total number of species ran from five hundred thousand to three million, he suggested that large animals on the ark were comparatively few, apparently having forgotten that on his understanding of geology dinosaurs and other fossilized large animals should have been aboard. He contended that the animals, prompted by divine instinct, made their way to the ark of their own accord. He did try to solve some of the difficulties of animal migration by suggesting that there "were no arctics and no deserts in that world, no high mountain barriers to separate one region from another, and this uniform climate also made possible a more uniform distribution of animals over the entire face of the earth." Migration to the ark might have taken place over many generations, he suggested, and there might have been land bridges that are no longer present to assist in that migration. Still, he acknowledged that the problems of animal migration could not be solved completely, and in the end he appealed to what he identified as the miraculous element in the narrative. He gave no satisfactory answer to the question of how plant life could have survived the deluge.

Rehwinkel dismissed the problems associated with the collection and storage of food for the animals on the ark by saying that "the Flood as a whole was a stupendous, miraculous interference with the laws governing the entire universe; a temporary suspension of the laws governing the routine and habits of a select group of animals for one year is but an insignificant detail in comparison." One is left to wonder why Rehwinkel expended so much effort trying to give natural explanations for so many features of the account while glibly resorting to miracle each time he found something he couldn't explain.

He also had difficulty accounting for the source of the flood water and the means by which it was removed at the end of the ordeal. Rehwinkel claimed that we don't know the answer to that problem because we don't know the conditions of the antediluvian atmosphere. He concluded somewhat enigmatically that "it was therefore a divine interference with the regular and established laws of nature, and yet the forces by which this judgment was carried out and the destruction of the world was wrought were latent in nature. Even in the Deluge the laws of nature were operating, but on a scale unprecedented in the entire history of the universe."

Rehwinkel asserted that the fountains of the great deep included ocean water and cataclysmic fountains from the interior. "Heaven and earth were thrown into a furious and terrible revolution," he wrote, with a rhetoric fully the match of Gilfillan's.

> The lightning flashed without ceasing, and the thunders rolled from pole to pole throughout the heavens. These were the trumpets and bugle calls of God announcing that the day of judgment had come. The earth heaved and trembled in its very foundations. Its writhing convulsions encircled the earth. Volcanoes belched forth fire, water, steam, and brimstone, to add more horrors to this terrifying spectacle of divine judgment. This is not a mere fancy of the imagination.

Thus fancied Rehwinkel's imagination. He bemoaned the fact that standard geology refused to acknowledge this universal catastrophe. He mentioned Dawson, Suess, and Price as lone voices crying in the wilderness of geology, apparently unaware of the extreme difference between Price and the other two geologists, not to mention the significantly different conceptions of the flood entertained by Suess and Dawson.

Rehwinkel contended that the damage done by the catastrophe could be envisioned by multiplying the New Madrid earthquakes ten thousand times ten thousand.[15] There were probably also "10,000 and more Krakatoas, Mount Pelees, and Vesuviuses shaking and tearing at the foundation of the earth," he wrote, "roaring their incessant thunders as a terrible funeral dirge, belching forth dust and steam and lava and boulders, and illuminating the death struggles of a perishing world with their terrifying and lurid volcanic fires." As fantastic as such an apocalyptic tumult might seem, Rehwinkel believed that the rocks bore evidence of such events. The tops of the mountains were composed of fossiliferous strata obviously laid down in water, he said, and the size of the present oceans made it plain that enough water existed to have covered them.

Curiously, Rehwinkel also invoked Mesopotamian archeology to

15. The New Madrid earthquakes, several of which were very destructive, occurred in 1811 and 1812 in southeastern Missouri and environs.

support the biblical flood. In a clear appeal to extrabiblical evidence, Rehwinkel noted the work of the excavators of Ur who reported that they had uncovered evidence of the biblical flood and stated that "when scholars and churchmen refuse to accept divine revelation and are ashamed to give honor to Almighty God, the stones and the material remains of generations and things that have been must cry out." Apparently he failed to detect the internal incoherence of his appeal to both geology and the Ur deposits as deluge evidence: the Mesopotamian cities were constructed on top of alluvial sediments that in turn overlie the fossiliferous stratified rocks to which he also appealed as evidence of the flood. He also failed to recognize that Ur's flood deposits do not cover the whole city and that the various Mesopotamian deposits are not contemporary.

Rehwinkel was perplexed that the greatest opposition to a global flood was coming from the geologists, because they used to believe in a worldwide flood. He attributed their change in view to the ascendancy of rationalism rather than any compelling geological discovery. He insisted that a vast array of geological evidence (including Prestwich's rubble drift, ossiferous fissures, and bone deposits) clearly supported the flood. He cited Wright as having suggested that the Great Lakes, Lake Baikal, and the Great Salt Lake are remnants of the floodwaters. Of course, both Prestwich and Wright would have opposed Rehwinkel's Pricean contention that coal beds were formed by vast accumulations of floating plant material.

In sum, Rehwinkel built his case by appealing to various phenomena that had been claimed as flood evidence by one scientist or another, oblivious to the fact that many of his "evidences" supported mutually exclusive theories. Despite his desire to heed the testimony of extrabiblical data, Rehwinkel did not understand those data well enough to construct a coherent deluge hypothesis.

The Genesis Flood

Rehwinkel's failure did not discourage others from following in his train. Although equally flawed, unquestionably the most influential twentieth-century treatment from any perspective was *The Genesis Flood* by John C. Whitcomb (b. 1924) and Henry M. Morris (b. 1918). This impressive work owed its success to the collaboration of a theologian and an engineer with scientific training. When they joined forces, Whitcomb was an Old Testament scholar at Grace Theological Seminary in Winona Lake, Indiana, and Morris was a Baptist civil engineer at Virginia Polytechnic Institute (he later gained further fame at the Institute for Creation Research in California). The seismic waves generated by the arrival of this volume in the evangelical world triggered a stunning tsunami of flood geology, catalyzed a vigorous "creationist" movement that has dominated evangelicalism during the latter half of the twentieth century, and in general greatly influenced evangelical thought. Such creationist organizations and institutions as the Creation Research Society and the Institute for Creation Research owe their existence at least indirectly to *The Genesis Flood*.[16] The book is more comprehensive than the works of Price and Rehwinkel and manages to avoid some of Rehwinkel's faulty logic while nonetheless introducing some of its own. The basic thesis of the book is Pricean, but it updates Price's positions in light of newer geological data.

In many respects *The Genesis Flood* is an attempt to refute the ideas of two evangelical scholars, Bernard Ramm and J. Laurence Kulp. In 1954, Ramm (1916-1992), a Baptist theologian at Baylor University, wrote *The Christian View of Science and Scripture*, a powerful theological and scientific critique of fundamentalist science from an evangelical perspective. Ramm had been advised on the scientific issues by J. Laurence Kulp (b. 1921) of Columbia University, a geochemist who had exposed the scientific flaws of flood geology in the *Journal of the American Scientific Affiliation*.[17] *The Genesis Flood* begins with an extended argument for a universal flood that includes an assessment of the biblical chronology of the flood, calculations of the size of the ark, a review of the New Testament testimony to the event, and an assertion that all of humanity except the passengers on the ark was destroyed. Presuming an increased fecundity and longevity of early humanity, Whitcomb and Morris contend that a great population was destroyed by the flood, and they cite the fact that fossilized human remains have been found far from Mesopotamia as evidence that human beings had spread over the whole earth, necessitating a global deluge.

Whitcomb and Morris are among the few evangelical writers to acknowledge the existence of anthropological arguments against a universal flood, although they vigorously disagree with them. Ramm had

16. For a more detailed look at the genesis and impact of *The Genesis Flood*, see chap. 10 of Numbers's *The Creationists*.
17. Kulp, "Deluge Geology," *Journal of the American Scientific Affiliation* 2 (1950): 1-15.

argued against an anthropologically universal flood on the grounds of the problems raised by the presence of human beings in North America prior to the flood and on the grounds that the various races could not all have descended from the three sons of Noah. Taking up the matter of human beings in North America, Whitcomb and Morris correctly observe that evidence in the Genesis account of the flood and in its Near Eastern parallels indicates that it could not have occurred as early as 10,000 B.C., the date by which the mainstream scientific community says that human beings had established a foothold in North America. They respond by arguing that no human beings had made it to North America by that early date, that the means anthropologists have used to date the arrival of people in the New World is flawed. Specifically, they argue that radiocarbon dating cannot accurately be applied to remote periods because the biblical deluge implies "a non-uniformitarian history of the earth's atmosphere and thus of cosmic-ray activity and radiocarbon concentrations." Because the assumptions of all radiometric dating methods are "clearly contradicted by the testimony of God's Word (e.g., II Pet. 3:3-7)," say Whitcomb and Morris, we can safely conclude that human beings in fact migrated to North America only after "the confusion of tongues at Babel, even though the Flood occurred after 10,000 B.C."

Ramm also suggested that since Mongoloid and Negroid peoples are not mentioned in the table of nations of Genesis 10, they are not descendants of Noah. That argument from silence failed to impress Whitcomb and Morris. Nor do they approve of James Frazer's efforts to attribute some flood traditions to local conditions or his assertions that missionaries might have influenced some of the traditions. They endorse the traditional notion that Noah's descendants carried the story throughout the world.

Whitcomb and Morris also challenge exegetical attempts to limit the universal terms in the flood story. The ark was big enough to hold representatives of all the world's animals, they argue, and Noah could have cared for them all, inasmuch as the supernatural and the natural worked side by side. The lack of marsupial fossils in Asia does not prove that the animals never lived there, they say; there is no fossil evidence that the lion ever lived in Palestine, and yet the Bible clearly indicates that it did. On that reasoning, it follows that there is no reason why all the animals might not originally have lived near the ark. Moreover, there is nothing to say that the ark had to be built in the same place where it landed. And furthermore, world geography might have been very different in the past. Finally, Whitcomb and

Morris insist that animals could have migrated very quickly to their present locales from the ark.

In a review of the history of ideas about the flood, Whitcomb and Morris dispute the views of Buckland and Lyell, object to the rise of uniformitarian theory, dismiss the "tranquil flood" notion, discount John Pye Smith's local flood theory, and reject the idea that the flood strata at Ur and Kish represent the biblical deluge. Turning to the geological implications of the biblical record, they contend that the deluge rains would have had to come from a source other than clouds, that the rainfall would have caused tremendous erosion, and that the event would have been accompanied by the enlargement of the ocean basins, volcanic and seismic upheavals, and unprecedented sedimentary activity — in short, ideal conditions for the formation of fossils. Moreover, they maintain that the biblical record undermines the uniformitarian philosophy that controls mainstream geological thinking and that the geological record actually supports their inferences from the Bible. Sedimentary phenomena, volcanic activity, and fossils, they argue, are readily explicable in terms of the flood, whereas the standard orthodox uniformitarian view of the world is inadequate to account for fossilization and sedimentary rocks.[18] They also assert that mainstream geology is unable to account for fossils and whole geological formations that allegedly violate the integrity of the established stratigraphic sequence or for the discovery of living animals that were previously considered extinct on the basis of the fossil record. Building on Price and ignoring Clark, they criticize the thrust-fault hypothesis and the mainstream geological explanation of paraconformities.[19] They denounce standard uniformitarian geology as "a pseudoscience composed . . . of a patchwork of circular reasoning, Procrustean interpretations, pure speculation and dogmatic authoritarianism — a system purporting to expound the entire evolutionary history of the earth and

18. According to Whitcomb and Morris, uniformitarians assume that all fossils were formed very slowly. In fact, like flood geologists generally, they fail to recognize that mainstream geologists most often explain fossil formation in terms of rapid burial under such local "catastrophic" conditions as storms, floods, or mass kills.

19. Paraconformities (what Price calls "deceptive conformities") are boundaries between layers of sedimentary rock that are interpreted as erosional surfaces because the rocks above the surface are much younger than those below. Although on any given outcrop the boundary may look like any ordinary bedding plane and give no indication of being an erosional surface, the existence of paraconformities is almost always verified on a regional scale, where rocks of the "missing" time period can usually be found sandwiched in between the rock layers exposed at the paraconformity.

its inhabitants, yet all the while filled with innumerable gaps and contradictions."[20]

Whitcomb and Morris place these views in what they characterize as a genuine biblical framework, which according to them also entails such things as the notion of a mature creation and radical changes at the time of the fall. They contend, for example, that the antediluvian climate was uniformly warm and equable, and on that ground they dismiss all geological evidences for pre-Pleistocene glaciations. They state that a "vapor canopy" established on the second day of creation produced a greenhouse effect that generated the pleasant climate and that the canopy collapsed at the time of the flood, producing a staggering amount of erosion and depositing sediments and fossils in Woodwardian fashion. To account for the distribution of fossils (e.g., the restriction of mammal fossils to the highest strata), Whitcomb and Morris adopt a modified ecological zonation scheme, arguing that the more mobile animals were able to escape the rising flood waters for a longer time than slower ones.

They argue that raised river terraces, pluvial lakes, and incised canyons were formed when floodwaters drained into depressed ocean basins. To explain the sedimentary rock record in terms of the flood, Whitcomb and Morris needed to discredit standard geological methods of age dating. They dismiss radiometric dating by claiming that God put just the right amounts of radioactive and daughter elements in the rocks at the time of creation so that they would have an appearance of age. But just to be on the safe side they also employ the additional (and contradictory) approach of disputing the validity of the methods by finding as many faults with them as they can. They also try to discredit other dating methods based on the rate of infall of meteoritic dust or tektites, on the abundance of salts in the sea, and on crustal accretion rates. They discount archeological findings in order to compress recent human history into just a few thousands of years. They discount the significance of such geological phenomena as evaporites, varved deposits, volcanic fossil forests, coral reefs, deep-sea sediments, and cave deposits, the formation of all of which implies the passage of considerable amounts of time. In sum they attempt to explain virtually the entire sedimentary rock record by the action of the flood. Although more consistent in their command of evidence than Rehwinkel, Whitcomb and Morris have failed to convince mainstream

20. Whitcomb and Morris, *The Genesis Flood* (Philadelphia: Presbyterian & Reformed, 1961), p. 212.

geologists of the validity of their theory because of the highly prejudicial manner in which they handle the data. They simply dismiss a mountain of evidence detrimental to their hypothesis.

After *The Genesis Flood*

Although *The Genesis Flood* was vastly influential in the evangelical community, it was by no means the last word on the subject of flood geology books. Just five years after its publication, Donald Patten produced *The Biblical Flood and the Ice Epoch* (1966), in which he says he hopes "to achieve the most critical, penetrating, systematic, analytical, and synthetical examination of the uniformitarianism which has been accomplished to date" and once and for all bring this modern "sacred cow . . . into the arena of test and trial."[21] He begins with the assumption that uniformitarian geologists have an a priori prejudice against major catastrophes (a false assumption, as demonstrated recently by the emerging consensus among ostensibly uniformitarian geologists that a catastrophic meteorite impact in Central America led to the global extinction of the dinosaurs). Like other flood geologists, Patten views uniformitarianism as a product of humanism and contrasts it with a catastrophism that he believes is integral to Christianity. He cites James Hutton, Charles Lyell, and Charles Darwin as examples of uniformitarians and Henry Howorth, Hugh Miller, and Isaac Newton Vail as catastrophists — despite the fact that Hugh Miller would have nothing to do with flood geology and Howorth differed radically from Vail.[22]

Patten was a throwback to Whiston and Halley in attributing terrestrial catastrophes to astronomical causes. He cites the planetary opposition of Neptune and Pluto, lunar perturbations, the development of Saturn's rings, the fragmentation of the asteroids, the cratering of the moon, and the existence of comets as evidence of past catastrophes in the solar system, and he specifically attributes the deluge to the visitation of an "astral visitor."

Unlike most other catastrophists, Patten proposes that the "Ice

---

21. Patten, *The Biblical Flood and the Ice Epoch* (Seattle: Pacific Meridian, 1966), p. 3.

22. Vail was a Quaker who wrote a number of catastrophe books during the late nineteenth and early twentieth centuries, including such titles as *Waters above the Firmament* and *The Earth's Annular System*.

Epoch" and the flood were "one and the same catastrophe." He argues that the ice age resulted not from snow falling over vast spans of time but from a single catastrophic ice dump that froze "millions" of mammoths in their tracks and preserved them so effectively that their carcasses had fed sled dogs in Alaska and Siberia. "In fact," taking a local joke seriously, Patten reports that "mammoth steaks have even been featured on restaurant menus in Fairbanks." Patten asserts that "the mammoths died suddenly, in intense cold, and in great numbers." He rightly recognizes that "death came so quickly that the swallowed vegetation is yet undigested in their stomachs and their mouths," but he uncritically assumes that all the animals died at the same time. Totally ignoring published technical literature, Patten speculates that if ice particles at -200° F had been dumped on the earth by an icy asteroid,

> this could produce a great, icy avalanche of supercooled ice, possibly reproducing the supercooled conditions under which the mammoths so suddenly met their death. Under these conditions, even a huge, wooly mammoth would immediately perish, not to mention sheep, camels, rhinoceroses, bison, and other animals which have similarly been found encased in ice. They perished immediately by asphyxiation because, at these temperatures, their lungs were frozen solid. They dropped immediately, and death ensued very shortly.[23]

Patten vastly overestimates the number of frozen animal remains that had been found, he fails to acknowledge the mainstream explanations of the remains forwarded by Tolmachoff and Farrand, and he confidently but incorrectly asserts that "concerning the perishing of the mammoths, the uniformitarian approach has been non-plussed, and has had no explanation" (p. 107). In a further display of his unfamiliarity with recent literature, Patten asserts that "several studies" — he fails to identify which — "indicate that mammoths were not especially designed for the Arctic; nor did they live in Arctic conditions. The Indian elephant, which is a close relative of the mammoth . . . has to have several hundred pounds of food daily just to survive. But, for more than six months of the year, there is nothing for any such creature to eat on the Arctic tundra. Yet there were tens of thousands of mammoths" (p. 106).

Patten claims that around 2800 B.C., a small icy asteroid was

---

23. Patten, *The Biblical Flood and the Ice Epoch,* p. 106.

captured by the earth's gravitational pull and passed over the earth's surface twice at a height of 15,000 and 30,000 miles. Its speed and proximity were just adequate to prevent it from being captured by the earth's gravity but not adequate to prevent a portion of its material from being drawn off. According to Patten, this supercold ice collapsed onto the earth's polar regions and initiated the ice age. He further contends that gravitational instability associated with the passage of the asteroid caused the elevation of mountain systems, great volcanic eruptions, the collapse of the vapor canopy, and tidal flooding for 150 days that swept the ark upstream and produced widespread sedimentation.

To this day, flood catastrophism continues alive and well. Articles on the flood appear regularly in *Creation Research Society Quarterly*, for example. For the most part the proposals lack empirical control and fail to engage or test the hypotheses of other flood geologists.[24] Flood geology has proved to be a marvelous illustration of the unlimited human capacity both to offer and embrace unchecked speculation.

Analysis and Application

One might expect that those who endorse a strict literalistic interpretation of the flood narrative (involving the complete destruction of human and animal life not preserved on the ark and the significant reordering of the earth's surface features) would be inclined simply to reject the relevance of extrabiblical data, given the fact that such data seem clearly and overwhelmingly to deny that such a planet-altering flood ever took place. One might expect that such individuals would instead make appeals solely to the Word of God as the complete and final authority in all such matters and that they would denounce extrabiblical evidence as superfluous and misleading. And yet the proponents of flood geology have moved in the opposite direction, not only showing a substantial interest in extrabiblical evidence but actually elevating it to the status of apologetic proof. The issue for flood geologists is not whether extrabiblical evidence is relevant to biblical interpretation but rather how to interpret that evidence. Having already

---

24. See, e.g., D. Russell Humphreys, "Is the Earth's Core Water?" *Creation Research Society Quarterly* 15 (1978): 141-47; David W. Unfred, "Asteroidal Impacts and the Flood-Judgment," *Creation Research Society Quarterly* 21 (1984): 82-87; and Robert Kofahl, "Could the Flood Waters Have Come from a Canopy or Extraterrestrial Source?" *Creation Research Society Quarterly* 13 (1977): 202-6.

employed, without benefit of external evidence, a hermeneutic that demands literal interpretation of the Bible, flood geologists are prepared to do anything but accept the mainstream scientific evidence that flatly refutes their claims that the earth is geologically young and that a global deluge deposited the fossiliferous strata. They have thus been forced either to appeal to miracles or to construct elaborate theories that manipulate the extrabiblical data to fit their view of what must be true.

The appeals to miracle have been made mostly in the context of arguments for a young earth (e.g., in claims that God created the world in such a way that it simply has the *appearance* of great age). The flood theories themselves have been characterized more by speculation ungrounded in valid data or by the selective use and mishandling of "the real facts of science." The typical twentieth-century flood geologist has paid great attention to the ark, to deluge traditions, and to stratigraphy and paleontology but has largely ignored the overwhelming contrary evidence from anthropology, comparative mythology, archeology, biogeography, petrology, and geochemistry. Among their ranks, only Whitcomb and Morris have attempted to address the serious problems posed by biogeography and anthropology. The few flood geologists who have sought to deal with stratigraphic and paleontological evidence have on the whole been poorly informed in those fields. Most have lacked substantial experience in field geology, have not been well acquainted with relevant scientific literature, and have generally tended to view geological data in a fragmented fashion, isolated from the larger context of regional geology.[25] Their work is broadly characterized by untested or untestable speculations that have a more solid grounding in the imagination than in God's creation. They assert confidently but without support that these speculations are the "real facts of science," and then they propose that these "real facts" constitute an apologetic for the Bible literally interpreted.[26] In the process, they effectively divorce the Word of God from any connection to God's actual created handiwork.

25. See Howard J. Van Till, Davis A. Young, and Clarence Menninga, *Science Held Hostage: What's Wrong with Creation Science and Evolutionism* (Downers Grove, Ill.: InterVarsity Press, 1988), especially chap. 6, "Making Mysteries out of Missing Rock," which explores the failures of flood geologists to deal adequately with regional geology and geological literature, using the Grand Canyon as a case study.

26. See James R. Moore, "Interpreting the New Creationism," *Michigan Quarterly Review* 22 (1983): 321-34.

In recent decades, the flood geologists have devoted more energy than any other group to discussion of the biblical flood. Because most flood geologists have expressed a commitment to the infallibility of the Bible, God's revelation, and salvation through Christ alone, conserva- tive twentieth-century evangelicals (who are already isolated from the broader academic community and a bit suspicious of higher intellectual endeavors) have generally been receptive to their pronouncements on scientific matters as well, especially since the alternatives have seemed implicitly to threaten their understanding of Scripture. And since main- stream evangelical scientists have done relatively little to educate the laity about the degree to which flood geologists have failed in both their understanding and their treatment of scientific data and technical literature, the latter have been able to exert an unwarranted force in evangelical thinking. This has established a vicious circle: in following the flood geologists and divorcing themselves from the mainstream scientific community, evangelicals have further cut themselves off from important sources of information that might have served to correct the errors. If flood geologists and evangelicals really want to be serious about heeding extrabiblical evidence, they will have to exercise more scientific competence, sophistication, and integrity than they have displayed thus far in the twentieth century.

17. Recent Theories of the Flood

Flood geology has powerfully influenced twentieth-century evangelical-ism. Modern flood geologists are not deficient in imagination when it comes to constructing scenarios of how the flood came about, nor has their energy or zeal flagged in the effort to discover physical evidence of the remains of the flood or even of the ark. At the opposite end of the theological spectrum, biblical critics have largely settled on the notion that the flood narrative has a historical core involving a local flood or set of floods that devastated Mesopotamia and temporarily interfered with civilization. During this century, moderating views of the Genesis flood story have been in the minority and have generally had little impact. Most of these views have come from evangelicals sensitive to the flaws of flood geology. We will review a few of these ideas here.

In 1936 an intriguing paper was delivered before the Victoria Institute by Lt. Col. F. A. Molony.[1] He maintained that the name *Ararat* was applied in ancient times to the district south of Lake Van toward Mesopotamia.[2] Molony favored a Mesopotamian flood of which Lake Van might have been the source. He suggested that the lake could have been blocked by lava or glaciers during the ice age when such blockages might have been commonplace. It was probable, he claimed, that glaciers were in the vicinity of Lake Van in Noah's day, and the raised beaches around the lake are evidence of blockages that tem-

1. For the text, see Molony, "The Noachian Deluge and Its Probable Connection with Lake Van," *Journal of the Transactions of the Victoria Institute* 68 (1936): 43-65.
2. Lake Van is located approximately one hundred miles southwest of Mt. Ararat.

porarily raised the lake level. If the lake had risen a hundred feet above its current level and all the excess water had been released at once, Molony calculated, there would have been at least thirty cubic miles of floodwater. Sixty miles to the northwest of Mosul (Nineveh) are many low, rounded hills that looked to Molony as though they had been deposited by some tremendous flood. If the ark was built at Shuruppak as the Gilgamesh epic says, a flood from Lake Van would have emerged from the mountains about 430 miles from the ancient "dry dock," said Molony, and the waters would have spread out before reaching the ark.

Molony argued that the huge spreading sheet of water would have produced an immense amount of evaporation and, by raising the atmosphere thirty or forty feet (his estimated depth of the floodwaters), would have caused further atmospheric disturbances. As the flood passed any given point, Molony maintained, winds would have stirred, clouds would have formed, and drizzle and rain would have fallen, all within twenty-four hours. The continued evaporation would have caused the rain to last for many days.

The ark might have grounded on one of the higher mounds in the Mesopotamian plain. But why wouldn't it have floated into the Persian Gulf if the flood had come from the north? Noah would naturally have wanted to avoid that possibility, said Molony, so he might have equipped the ark with masts and sails and dropped anchor when winds blew out of the north. Because the Mesopotamian plain has such an imperceptible gradient and because some winds would blow from the southeast, Molony was not surprised that it took so long for the floodwater to drain. For supporting evidence, he cited a report that the Tigris River once rose by 22.5 feet and a full month elapsed before people could ride beyond their walls. Predictably, Molony's paper triggered plenty of discussion and disagreement. And predictably, the scholarly world has not embraced Molony's hypothesis with great enthusiasm.

In 1960, Rhodes Fairbridge (b. 1914), a Columbia University professor writing as a professional geologist with no apologetic motives for defending the biblical narrative, postulated a completely new explanation for the various deluge traditions.[3] He suggested that sea level rises of a few feet per decade might have "profound effects upon the way of life and the imagination of those who experienced it." Had the

    3. See Fairbridge, "The Changing Level of the Sea," *Scientific American* 202 (1960): 70-79.

sea level kept rising generation after generation with only occasional retreats, Fairbridge speculated, floods would have become incorporated into legends all over the world. Major climate changes that brought about increased rainfall and snow melts could have made calamitous river floods common. "If the two kinds of flood had occurred together, they could easily have been recorded as a deluge."

After summarizing data on the effect of melting glacial ice caps on sea level changes, Fairbridge suggested that ice has been melting and sea level has generally been rising ever since the maximum advance of the most recent ice sheets about 17,000 years ago. He further stated that "the greatest and fastest rise yet discovered in the geological record reached its crest about 6,000 years ago." Low-lying coastal lands were flooded by the sea in every part of the world. "This," proposed Fairbridge, "was the deluge that drowned the homes and troubled the legends of the ancients." The flood, said Fairbridge, represented the last traces of the North American and Scandinavian glaciers. His hypothesis failed to win the day, because such gradual, imperceptible rises in sea level, however significant their cumulative effects, would not have been likely to make such a dramatic impression on peoples everywhere. Why would it have been necessary for "survivors" to have escaped on a boat when civilization would have had ample time to move out of the way of the encroaching sea?

Perhaps the most comprehensive effort since the days of George Frederick Wright to explain the flood apart from "flood geology" has been that of British evangelical Frederick A. Filby. He begins by rejecting views that dismiss the Genesis account as legend growing out of a local flood or that treat the account as a myth designed to teach mankind useful lessons and sets out to demonstrate that a vast flood "swept across a very large area of Europe and Asia, and possibly beyond, at a date which lies somewhere between the end of the Glacial Period and the rise of the great Empires of the Middle East."[4]

He addresses three issues: the fact of floods in ancient times, possible causes for such floods, and the probable extent and date of Noah's flood. Citing experts on Quaternary geology, Filby considers it an established fact that "great risings and fallings of huge areas of land took place during and after the end of the Ice Age." That being the case, he contends that the Genesis flood fits very naturally into such a period of rapid and violent upheaval. Plainly influenced by Howorth, Prestwich, Dawson, and Wright, Filby contends that the

---

4. Filby, *The Flood Reconsidered* (Grand Rapids: Zondervan, 1970).

Flandrian Transgression in Europe, great changes in the Sahara, the biblical flood in the Middle East, and "the sudden coming of the Great Cold to Siberia" that led to "the extinction of the mammoth and literally a hundred million other creatures" were either "a series of catastrophes" that caused the disappearance of the early races of man "or they all belong to one event." Regarding the flood's cause, Filby felt that the oceans must have been involved, because the ark moved inland. He liked Patten's idea of an astronomical cause, but he thought that Patten's digressions on evolution and uniformitarian geology marred his overall argument. Concerning the extent of the deluge, Filby notes that great floods on the Yangtse and Yellow Rivers and in the Zuider Zee had probably exceeded any Tigris and Euphrates floods. From written records, Filby dates the rise of the Babylonian and Egyptian empires to around 3000 to 2500 B.C. He believed that the flood could not have occurred too much earlier than that and suggested that a date of 4000 to 3500 B.C. was perhaps more reasonable than 8000 B.C.

While disputing assertions that thousands of species were preserved on the ark, Filby nonetheless endorses the idea that the deluge covered a very large area and had a significant impact on global climate, sea levels, humanity, and animal and plant life. Filby contends that abandoned dry river beds in the Sahara, dry wadis in Arabia and Egypt, creeks in the Atacama Desert, fish remains in the Sahara, and dry waterfalls all provide evidence of a dramatic climatic change somewhere between 6000 and 5000 B.C. He believed these climatic changes were also linked to the Flandrian Transgression, the breaking of the land connection between Britain and France, the filling of the Caspian and Aral Seas, and the beginnings of the Neolithic period. Filby maintained, as Dawson had, that there was a distinct break between Paleolithic and Neolithic civilizations and that the latter spread outward from a center in the Caspian–North Persian area. Finally, Filby thought there was evidence for the sudden death of a large number of creatures, including the woolly mammoth, at about the same time. Giving credence to the outmoded notions of Howorth rather than the findings of Digby, Tolmachoff, and Farrand, Filby argues that the Siberian mammoth evidence indicates a major climatic change. "Examination shows that some died of sudden shock with eyes and blood vessels violently distended," he says. "Experts estimate that they were suddenly struck with extreme cold of the order of -150° F. which froze these huge beasts before decomposition could set in." Was Patten the expert to whom Filby is referring? Clearly it was no one publishing in the mainstream technical journals. Filby was also impressed by reports of "numerous" other animals frozen in Alaska's muck as well as masses of piled up smashed trees in Siberia, evidence that he interprets as pointing toward something like Patten's explanation. Finally, Filby repeats Prestwich's argument about the ossiferous fissures at Santenay, Palermo, and Gibraltar.

Filby overconfidently concludes that these various evidences are of a piece. Setting aside his earlier suggestion that a series of catastrophes might also be implied by the evidence, in the end he argues that the data fit "a pattern of one single astronomical or geological event, which caused the flooding within a very *short* space of time, of a vast area stretching from Western Europe through the Middle East and Siberia to Alaska."[5] He maintains that archeological findings confirm this scenario. He claims, for example, that the lowest layers at Ur and Nineveh are remnants of a flood that predated Woolley's Ur flood and that the earlier flood swept some pots from an unknown neighboring site and deposited them in the bottom muds. When the flood withdrew, he says, the land rose slightly, and the mud hardened. People once more built huts, and a new civilization developed long before the eleven-foot silt layer was deposited. In sum, Filby successfully avoids the excesses of flood geology but does not manage to get much beyond the exploded ideas of Howorth, Prestwich, and Wright. Much of his extrabiblical information is out-of-date and inaccurate.

5. Filby sums up his thesis as follows: "Some time after the end of the Ice Age, and before the rise of the great dynasties, a great flood, caused either by the close approach of some heavenly body, or by the movement of the continents, or both, swept from the Atlantic, the Mediterranean, and the Indian Oceans over much of Europe and Asia to Alaska and even beyond. During that period Palaeolithic man disappeared, the entire climate of Siberia was radically changed, herds of mammoths were completely eliminated, some being apparently almost instantaneously frozen to death by unprecedented cold, and the sabre-toothed tiger, the woolly rhinoceros and a hundred million other creatures perished. Herds of animals in Europe and Western Asia were trapped by rising water and many were dashed to pieces, their bones being swept into great cracks which had appeared in the earth. Lesser risings and fallings of certain local areas have continued, giving rise to raised beaches, shifting levels of fens in England, or various flood levels in Mesopotamia, but these are obviously small compared with the event which drowned a hundred million animals and exterminated an ancient race of men. That great oceanic tide, accompanied in the Middle East by torrential rain, and in Siberia by intensely frozen snow, capable of floating and indeed of driving a 10,000 ton wooden barge, probably from Mesopotamia to the regions of Ararat . . . that Flood which Genesis describes so minutely, was surely unique in history, and, by the promise of God, was not to be repeated — and in fact, never has been" (*The Flood Reconsidered*, pp. 31-32).

Shortly after Filby's book appeared, long-time British Bible-science enthusiast Robert E. D. Clark (1906-1984) suggested that evidence for Noah's flood might be detected in the Black Sea.[6] He reported that more than sixty cores taken from the bottom of the Black Sea by the ship *Atlantis II* showed three distinct horizons of which the middle one was a very dark sapropel zone rich in organic matter that had been radiocarbon dated around 7,140 to 6,740 years old. Clark was tempted to correlate this layer with the biblical flood on the grounds that after the biblical devastation "the bordering land must have been covered with decaying organic matter and this would naturally and slowly find its way into bordering lakes and seas. Under the reducing conditions obtaining in the Black Sea its preservation would be ensured."

Like Filby, Clark thought the flood could be explained by one of the sudden sea level rises of the Pleistocene. He argued that such rises and falls might be readily accounted for by supposing that large chunks of the Antarctic ice cap broke off into the sea as a result of a meteorite impact or volcanic eruption under the ice. Clark calculated that "a complete breakaway of the ice from the underlying land in the Antarctic would raise the sea level by 60 meters or more." Clark wanted to put Noah's flood at about 5000 B.C., about the age of the sapropel layer. But even if the flood occurred one or two thousand years earlier, he surmised that evidence should be obtainable from Black Sea cores. A rise in sea level at that time would have been catastrophic, he said, and already in Denmark and Finland thick sediment layers of that age had been found. Clark wisely avoided dogmatism on the matter, however. His proposal has been greeted with absolute silence.

I also addressed the topic of the flood in an earlier book entitled *Creation and the Flood* (1977). My convictions about the nature of the deluge have changed considerably during the years since the publication of that volume, but it may still be worthwhile to consider its content briefly to get a sense of one more balancing perspective to have come out of the evangelical community during this period.

My intent in the book was not to offer or endorse a specific theory of the flood, but I did take the opportunity to summarize some important geological evidences against common flood geology claims. I suggested that the biblical data favor an essentially global flood (a

6. See Clark, "The Black Sea and Noah's Flood," *Faith and Thought* 100 (1972): 174-79.

position I now consider doubtful) but denied that acceptance of a global flood requires adherence to any particular flood theory. Just because the Bible mentions a great flood does not mean that its focus is on geology. There are any number of geological events, some perhaps even more momentous than the flood, that are not mentioned in the Bible because they played no particular role in redemptive history. Just as the Bible's focus on Israel because of its redemptive significance carries no implication that Israel was therefore the predominant nation in the ancient world culturally, economically, or politically, so, too, the Bible's mention of a flood because of its significance in the history of redemption carries no implication that the biblical flood was the predominant geological event of ancient times.

I concluded that a great flood could have produced ephemeral silt and gravel deposits that might have been eroded away quickly. In general, I suggested, "remnants of flood deposits scattered around the world would be extremely difficult to correlate stratigraphically or geochronologically." I went on to criticize the flood geology of Whitcomb and Morris, introducing some still valid geological arguments that had not previously appeared in discussions of the deluge.

1. I argued that known rates of heat flow from bodies of crystallizing magma pose problems for those who contend that all fossil-bearing rocks were laid down during the single year of the biblical flood. On the New Jersey side of the Hudson River opposite Manhattan, there is a geological formation known as the Palisades sill, a thick sheet of rock of igneous origin that intruded into red sandstones and shales. Flood geologists of the Whitcomb-Morris school hold that the sandstones and shales were laid down during the course of the flood, and hence they would logically have to assert that the magma was injected into this material during the course of the flood, cooled, hardened, tilted, and eroded before the other flood sediments settled atop it. But this would not have been possible. We know on the basis of heat flow considerations and the thickness of the sill that it would have taken several hundred years to cool and crystallize in the way it now appears. Indeed, many other much larger igneous rock bodies would have required thousands to hundreds of thousands of years to lose their heat in order to crystallize. Flood geologists have made little attempt to refute this line of evidence.

2. Radiometric dating of igneous formations of the sort mentioned above — formations that according to the Whitcomb-Morris theory must have been produced within the space of a single year — suggest that they are in fact millions of years old. These figures are

consistent with ages predicted on the basis of stratigraphical relationships with the intruded rocks. Similar examples can be multiplied many times over.

3. The phenomena of *metamorphism* also pose problems for flood geology. In some localities, fossils are found in rocks that also bear evidence of having undergone significant changes (metamorphism) as a result of having been exposed to very high temperatures and pressures. The problem for flood geologists is to show how a sedimentary rock, which they contend was formed at the surface of the earth during the course of the flood, could have been buried and heated fast enough to metamorphose. Both heat flow theory and known rates of chemical reactions indicate that such rocks could not possibly have undergone the observed metamorphism within a single year.

4. A wealth of evidence associated with modern discoveries about continental drift and sea floor spreading indicate that various kinds of rocks — including varieties that the flood geologists maintain were formed during the course of the flood — must have been formed both before and after the separation of continents. If the flood geologists are right, this would imply that the continents must have been drifting apart substantially during the course of the flood. But thousands of miles of continental drift within the space of a few months is completely inconsistent with any known rates of drift.

I concluded the book with a look at Scripture, arguing that the biblical data (Gen. 2 in particular) suggest that pre-flood geography was fundamentally the same as post-flood geography, which precludes the possibility of a global deluge involving a wholesale reorganization of terrestrial surface features. I also affirmed my belief that the biblical flood was in fact a historical event and not merely myth or legend. It was my intent to show how Christians could endorse the idea of a historical flood without having to commit themselves to a flood geology theory that is thoroughly in conflict with the data of creation.

Another recent discussion appeared in *The Genesis Debate*, a volume in which several controversial issues arising from Genesis 1–9 are addressed by scholars with opposing points of view. On the issue of whether the flood covered the entire globe, Steven A. Austin of the Institute for Creation Research argues in the affirmative, and Donald Boardman, longtime chairman of Wheaton College's geology department, argues in the negative.[7]

---

7. Boardman, "Did Noah's Flood Cover the Entire World? — No," in *The Genesis Debate*, ed. R. Youngblood (Nashville: Thomas Nelson, 1986), pp. 210-29.

Boardman claims that a proper understanding of the story requires taking into account both scientific and textual considerations. On the basis of stratigraphy, he suggests that if the flood had been universal we should be able to find distinctive flood strata that could be consistently dated back to a given point, but no such strata are evident. Moreover, he asserts that the draining of such huge quantities of floodwater would have left distinctive erosion patterns, and yet close scrutiny of the earth's great canyons fails to indicate such rapid erosion. Citing a general consensus that the flood probably occurred "after the retreat of the last Pleistocene glacier," Boardman notes that "examination of the glacial deposits makes it apparent that they have not been eroded by a universal flood." Moreover, the volcanic cinder cones of Auvergne, along with similarly ancient cones near such localities as Flagstaff, Arizona, are still intact and bear no marks of having been subjected to wave or stream erosion, let alone a universal flood, which would surely have destroyed them altogether.

Boardman also notes problems associated with a literal reading of that portion of the biblical account dealing with the preservation of the world's animal population. First he asserts that the ark could not have accommodated two of all species of animals then in existence. He also points out the fact that there was an abundant animal population on every continent for millions of years before the ice age and that there is no evidence of mass destruction of North or South American animals since the last glacial advance. Some animals such as the mastodon and mammoth have become extinct, but other species have been continuously present in various isolated habitats for millennia. Boardman also offers the traditional argument against universality based on the improbability of the migration of kangaroos and other species from great distances. He also presses the environmental argument. Salmon live part of their lives in fresh water, he notes, migrate to the salt ocean, and later return to fresh water to spawn. Other animals live in estuaries and lagoons and are at home in either fresh or salt water. Most animals are confined to one environment. Ships accumulate barnacles in the ocean and then move into fresh water as an effective means of killing them. Whatever the mineral content of the floodwaters, says Boardman, "it seems probable that those animals whose tolerance for other than their natural environment is small would probably die." A limited flood, on the other hand, need not have adversely affected the overall animal population.

Boardman sums up by noting that the text can be interpreted as indicating that the flood was not worldwide, particularly if the word *eretz* is translated as "land" rather than "earth." If that translation had been used in the first place, he suggests, there might not have been any controversy. Unlike Filby, Boardman makes no attempt to construct his own theory of the flood.

Analysis and Application

Some evangelical writers have been sufficiently versed in the relevant extrabiblical evidence to recognize that flood geology is completely unviable and to realize that some reinterpretation of Scripture may be necessary. However, the failure of many opponents of flood geology to construct a positive scientific theory of the deluge or an acceptable alternate interpretation of the biblical narrative may have worked against their gaining much of a following. British theories like those of Molony and Clark are probably too inaccessible and brief to capture any audience in North America. Filby's ideas depend too much on the outdated conceptions and discarded data of Wright and Howorth. Fairbridge, writing in a scientific publication without any apologetic interests, has made no impact on the churches. Thus, lacking any serious competition from proponents of coherent and comprehensive scientific and theological theories of the deluge, flood geologists continue to exert a powerful force on late twentieth-century evangelicalism. If conservative Christians are going to remain committed to the validity of extrabiblical information in biblical interpretation, it is essential that they seek to avoid inaccurate formulations of that information — not least the glaring conceptual and empirical flaws of flood geology. The evangelical community urgently needs to cultivate and acknowledge the work of intellectual descendants of Smith, Hitchcock, and Miller in the spheres of geology, anthropology, paleontology, and archeology.

18. Recent Commentary on the Flood

The Critical School

We will conclude our survey of Christian interpretations of the flood narrative in light of extrabiblical data with a look at the Bible dictionaries, Bible encyclopedias, study Bibles, Old Testament introductions, and commentaries on Genesis in common use among pastors and serious Bible students. The theologically liberal clientele continues to be addressed by commentaries that accept the source divisions advanced by earlier critics. Although the claims of source criticism have been challenged by developments in the field of literary criticism, allegiance to P and J continues unabated. Claus Westermann concludes his invaluable commentary on Genesis 1–11 by pointing out that the traditional criteria for the separation of sources are not quite so ironclad as generally thought,[1] but, despite his reservations, neither he nor a

---

1. See Westermann, *Genesis 1–11* (Minneapolis: Augsburg Press, 1984). Westermann is by no means alone in challenging the standard documentary hypothesis; a number of authors, not all theologically conservative, have recently expressed their own concerns on this point. See, e.g., Rolf Rendtorff, *The Old Testament: An Introduction* (Philadelphia: Fortress Press, 1986); Isaac M. Kikiwada and Arthur Quinn, *Before Abraham Was: The Unity of Genesis 1–11* (Nashville: Abingdon Press, 1985); Gary A. Rendsburg, *The Redaction of Genesis* (Winona Lake, Ind.: Eisenbrauns, 1986); Sven Tengstrom, *Die Hexateucher-zahlung: Eine Literaturgeschichtliche Studie* (Lund: Gleerup, 1976); and Y. T. Radday and H. Shore, *Genesis: An Authorship Study in Computer-Assisted Statistical Analysis*, Analecta Biblica (Rome: Biblical Institute, 1985). Conservatives who have been objecting to the idea of multiple sources for more than a century

host of modern critics including John C. L. Gibson, Robert Davidson, C. A. Simpson, Bruce Vawter, Gerhard von Rad, E. A. Speiser, Terence Fretheim, James King West, G. Henton Davies, or Ralph Elliott has shown any inclination to abandon P and J.[2] These source critics hold a wide spectrum of theological opinion from the more conservative Baptist pastor-theologian Ralph Elliott of Southern Baptist Theological Seminary in Louisville, Kentucky, who maintains that too much attention has been paid to the differences between J and P, to the more dogmatically liberal views of Church of Scotland theologian John C. L. Gibson of New College, Edinburgh, who flatly asserts that the biblical story is not interested in history.

Recent source critics have so confidently distanced themselves from older conceptions of the flood that they have felt little need to invoke new data to discredit a historical global catastrophe. Some have been content simply to state that a local flood lies behind the biblical account. Many critical scholars have confined themselves to exegesis and ignored matters of scientific relevance. Of those cautious scholars who venture into the realm of extrabiblical material, some talk only about the relationship of the biblical narrative to archeology or deluge traditions, leaving the scientific concerns of geology and paleontology virtually untouched. Gerhard von Rad (1901-1971) of the University of Göttingen, for example, notes with refreshing candor that "as for the natural and historical aspect of the Flood problem, theology is not competent to express an independent opinion." The monumental commentary of Claus Westermann, including one of the longest sections on the flood since that of Martin Luther, is also noteworthy for its striking omission of talk about science.

---

are, of course, delighted to see critical scholars themselves finding flaws in source criticism.

2. Among the more important critical commentaries of recent decades are the following: John C. L. Gibson, *Genesis* (Philadelphia: Westminster Press, 1981); Robert Davidson, *Genesis 1–11* (Cambridge: Cambridge University Press, 1973); Cuthbert A. Simpson, *The Book of Genesis*, Interpreter's Bible, vol. 1 (New York: Abingdon Press, 1952); Bruce Vawter, *On Genesis* (Garden City, N.Y.: Doubleday, 1977); Gerhard von Rad, *Genesis* (Philadelphia: Westminster Press, 1961); Ephraim A. Speiser, *Genesis* (Garden City, N.Y.: Doubleday, 1964); Terence E. Fretheim, *Creation, Fall, and Flood* (Minneapolis: Augsburg Press, 1969); James King West, *Introduction to the Old Testament* (New York: Macmillan, 1981); G. Henton Davies, *Genesis*, Broadman Bible Commentary, vol. 1 (Nashville: Broadman Press, 1969); Ralph H. Elliott, *The Message of Genesis* (Nashville: Broadman Press, 1961); R. E. Brown, J. A. Fitzmyer, and R. E. Murphy, *The Jerome Biblical Commentary* (Englewood Cliffs, N.J.: Prentice-Hall, 1968); and Westermann, *Genesis 1–11*.

None of these critical scholars entertains the thought of a global deluge for a moment. Many dismiss universality without argumentation from either the text or extrabiblical considerations. Cuthbert A. Simpson, for example, simply asserts that a universal flood of the sort described by J or P would be a physical impossibility. Terence Fretheim of Luther Northwest Theological Seminary in St. Paul, Minnesota, agrees and adds that Noah's family "could never have collected nor could the ark have contained a pair of every existing species of animal and creeping thing." Most critics doubt that the worldwide distribution of diluvial legends can be traced to a single event, although von Rad questions the conclusion that the worldwide flood legends all arose from local flood catastrophes. He contends that the widespread distribution and "remarkable uniformity" of the deluge saga requires an "actual cosmic experience." He suggests that a clouded recollection of the original event was in many cases "brought to new life and revised only later by local floods." Nevertheless, Roman Catholic scholar Bruce Vawter probably speaks for many when he says that the wealth of flood stories should not be surprising in view of the powerful impression made on people by the common natural phenomenon of flooding.

Virtually all of the critics maintain that the Israelite flood tradition was derived from Mesopotamia, possibly by way of the Canaanites, and most agree that a major Mesopotamian catastrophe lies behind the Near Eastern traditions. This helps explain the interest among critical scholars in Mesopotamian archeological excavations. Davidson, West, Gibson, and Jewish scholar Nahum Sarna all note the various investigations in which deluge deposits have been discovered and explain the popularity of deluge accounts in the ancient Near East as a result of the common experience of local flooding in the area. None, however, makes the claim that the remains of Noah's flood have been located. Modern critical writers generally pay less attention to extrabiblical data than those of a century earlier. Such comments as they do make in this regard, however, tend to be essentially accurate, reflecting an adequate understanding of bodies of knowledge external to Scripture.

Modern Evangelical Commentaries

Theological conservatives have traditionally been suspicious of the work of critical scholars and have avoided it in favor of the vast body of evangelical scholarship. Overall, evangelical writers of the latter twentieth century have devoted far more attention to extrabiblical concerns than have the critics. This continuing phenomenon remains somewhat ironic, given the intense evangelical devotion to the preeminent authority and inerrancy of the biblical text. Some very recent commentaries (e.g., those of Allen Ross, Gordon Wenham, John Sailhamer, and Victor Hamilton) do focus almost exclusively on the text and show far more concern with the questions of textual interpretation raised by source and rhetorical criticism than with questions raised by science, but such works are distinctly in the minority amid evangelical literature.[3] Evangelical laity consulting various representative works in the field are almost certain to be exposed to ideas about the effects of the deluge.

Recent conservative scholars have almost unanimously characterized the flood narrative as the record of a literal, historical event. British exegete Wenham is one of the rare exceptions to the rule.[4] The majority insist on both geographical and anthropological universality. Some lay out the alternatives on the extent of the deluge without committing themselves. A few favor a geographically local but anthropologically universal flood. Very few entertain the notion of a flood that was less than anthropologically universal.

Writers Favoring a Universal Deluge

A host of recent conservatives has used the familiar arguments for geographical and anthropological universality. John C. Whitcomb has

3. Ross, *Creation and Blessing: A Guide to the Study and Exposition of the Book of Genesis* (Grand Rapids: Baker Book House, 1988); Wenham, *Genesis 1–15* (Waco, Tex.: Word Books, 1987); Hamilton, *The Book of Genesis: Chapters 1–17,* New International Commentary on the Old Testament (Grand Rapids: William B. Eerdmans, 1990); and Sailhamer, *Genesis,* Expositor's Bible Commentary, ed. Frank E. Gaebelein, vol. 2 (Grand Rapids: Zondervan, 1990). Merrill Unger's articles on the flood in *Unger's Bible Dictionary* (Chicago: Moody Press, 1957) and the *New Unger's Bible Dictionary* (Chicago: Moody Press, 1988) also generally avoid scientific questions and are concerned primarily with Near Eastern parallels to the biblical text.

4. Wenham addresses the question of the historicity of the narrative in his discussion of Genesis 2 and 3. He notes that much of the material deals with events that took place before there were written records, so deep in the past that the term *prehistory* does not adequately describe it. He argues that Genesis, like the Atrahasis epic, relates stories about God/gods and men "sequentially and in terms of cause and effect." Since the "obviously mythical features have been eliminated" from Genesis (unlike the Atrahasis epic), he believes the biblical narrative might better be characterized as "proto-historical."

espoused his distinctive understanding of the flood in various Christian encyclopedias. Merrill Unger of Dallas Theological Seminary presents a very similar view in his commentary on the Old Testament. Baptist Old Testament theologian Stephen Schrader of Liberty University has defended a universal deluge, as has Methodist Lee Haines, office editor of Wesleyan Methodist Sunday School literature, Kyle Yates of Golden Gate Baptist Seminary, Presbyterian pastor and radio Bible expositor Donald Grey Barnhouse of Philadelphia's Tenth Presbyterian Church, Presbyterian Harold Stigers, Gordon Talbot, and several other authors whose ideas we will explore more closely below.[5] Although not all would insist, as radio evangelist J. Vernon McGee did, that "to attempt to make a case for a local flood is actually, in the long run, to reject the Word of God," they fully agree that "the Bible makes it very clear that it was a universal flood."

Conservatives have pressed the case for universality on both textual and scientific grounds. The textual grounds include the depth of water mentioned in Genesis 7:19, the emphasis of Genesis 6:17 that everything would die in the impending flood, the seemingly universal wickedness described in Genesis 6:5-7, and the New Testament witness, particularly that of 2 Peter 3. Many agree with James Burton Coffman's assessment that the historical truth of the deluge event is "categorically affirmed by the words of both Christ and His apostles." The global extent of the flood is a "necessary deduction" from the fact that Christ used it as a type of the final judgment and Peter made the deliverance of Noah and his family a type of the church's salvation expressed in baptism (1 Pet. 3:21).

Many writers favor universality because of perceived difficulties engendered by a local flood concept. Some argue that God's promise never again to flood the earth precludes a local flood, for instance. Some view the elaborateness of Noah's preparations and the size of

---

5. Articles on the flood by Whitcomb can be found in the *Encyclopedia of Christianity* (ed. Philip E. Hughes, vol. 4 [Wilmington, Del.: National Foundation for Christian Education, 1972], pp. 298-314) and the *Wycliffe Bible Encyclopedia* (ed. Charles F. Pfeiffer, Howard F. Vos, and John Rea, vol. 1 [Chicago: Moody Press, 1975], pp. 613-17). See also Unger, *Unger's Commentary on the Old Testament* (Chicago: Moody Press, 1981); Schrader, "Genesis," in *The Liberty Bible Commentary*, ed. E. E. Hindson and W. M. Kroll (Nashville: Thomas Nelson, 1983); Lee Haines, "Genesis," in *The Wesleyan Bible Commentary*, ed. C. W. Carter (Peabody, Mass.: Hendrickson, 1979); Yates, "Genesis," in *Wycliffe Bible Commentary*, ed. Charles F. Pfeiffer and Everett F. Harrison (Chicago: Moody Press, 1962); and Donald Grey Barnhouse, *Genesis: A Devotional Commentary* (Grand Rapids: Zondervan, 1970).

the ark as inconsistent with a mere river inundation, and they presume that no local flood could have lasted for a full year. Some argue that a deep local flood would necessarily have become universal over a long period of time anyway, on the grounds that water seeks its own level. And some have argued that a local flood would not have required the preservation of either man or beast, since a devastated valley or region would soon have been reinhabited from the outside. Various authors from a variety of theological traditions supplement these arguments with what they consider to be supporting evidence from science.

Lutherans

We have already seen that flood geology has been strongly supported within Lutheranism. Herbert C. Leupold (b. 1892), professor of Old Testament exegesis at Evangelical University Seminary in Columbus, Ohio, is a representative Lutheran advocate of diluvial universality. His definition of universality does not extend to a presumption that the floodwaters covered every last mountaintop on the globe; he excepts a few of the highest peaks such as the Himalayas from total submergence, citing Keil's assertion that these amount to "no more than a few pinpoints on a globe, and are disregarded because of the limited horizon of the ancients."[6] Leupold does hold that the flood was universal in the sense of destroying all the world's animal populations, however, with the exception of the beasts preserved on the ark. He contends that the construction of a craft adequate to the task fell well within the range of the "other huge enterprises carried through by men of antiquity" (p. 273).

Leupold dismisses the discomfiting capacity and migration problems by insisting that nobody knows how widely diversified species were at the time of the flood, and "since no one can prove anything on this question either pro or con, the question may well be left to rest. Untenable claims," he charges, have been made by those "who seek to invalidate Scripture testimony but without proof" (p. 277). Indeed, there might never be any data available on this matter, so "why question the possibility or the consistency of this matter in an account where everything else is so simple and consistent? Had we actually seen how this matter was adjusted, we might marvel at the stupidity of our question" (p. 277). Leupold sweeps aside the classic difficulty

6. Herbert C. Leupold, *Exposition of Genesis* (Columbus, Ohio: Wartburg Press, 1942), p. 302.

of kangaroo migration from Australia with the assertion that there is absolutely no way to tell how the continents were formed or "whether they were more intimately connected with one another prior to the Flood and immediately thereafter" (p. 303). He characterizes as "merely an assumption" the idea that Australia was formerly isolated as it is now. Besides, he says, we do not even know how the animals of Australia took a foothold there.

With respect to geological evidence, Leupold states that in "an earlier age . . . a climate uniformly tropical prevailed also in the arctic region" (p. 340), but the flood altered that situation. The flood occurred, he says, when vast subterranean eruptions caused a rush of huge waves that deposited geological formations of every kind and drowned mammoth and trilobite alike. Assuming the evidence of the great disruption to be both universally and immediately apparent, Leupold asks, "When will geologists begin to notice these basic facts?" (p. 301).

A more recent Lutheran representative is Fred Kramer, professor of theology at the Lutheran Church–Missouri Synod's Concordia Theological Seminary in St. Louis. Unlike Leupold, Kramer wisely refrains from rash assertions about geology to support his belief in universality. He comments that modern believers in the biblical flood story who are better schooled in geology have avoided the obvious mistakes and speculations of earlier generations of flood geologists. In refreshing contrast to most proponents of a global deluge, Kramer follows the Bible's lead in refusing to "identify certain specific geological phenomena as the results of the Flood."[7] Scripture does not speak about strata formation, he notes; it speaks to the purpose rather than the mechanism of the deluge.

Despite his general caution, however, Kramer ultimately falls into the trap of speculation by postulating that the deluge waters came from and returned to the ocean. He assumes that major physical changes that Scripture does not describe and that he does not pretend to understand must have taken place to account for the rapid subsiding of the great flood. Noting that geologists have been unable to identify evidence of the flood with any certainty, Kramer finally states that "the Noachian flood was an act of God which is not susceptible to our research and verification. Christians believe it, because the Bible, which they revere as God's Word, teaches it" (p. 191).

---

7. Kramer, "The Biblical Account of the Flood," in *Rock Strata and the Bible Record*, ed. P. A. Zimmerman (St. Louis: Concordia Publishing House, 1970), p. 188.

Presbyterians

Several Presbyterians have endorsed diluvial universality. Gleason Archer (b. 1916), an Old Testament scholar who served at Fuller Theological Seminary and Trinity Evangelical Divinity School, updated Wilkins's calculations of the ark's capacity. "There are only 290 main species of land animal larger than sheep in size," he states; "there are 757 more species ranging in size from sheep to rats, and there are 1,358 smaller than rats."[8] He asserts that the ark could easily have handled two of each of these species and still have had plenty of room for fodder. He does recognize the difficulties associated with maintaining a large number of animals for so many months, but he considers none of them insuperable. He does grant that the difficulty of accounting for the migration of animals from Australia to the ark and back is especially "acute," but that is as far as he goes. He rehearses the arguments of Prestwich and Wright concerning ossiferous fissures as evidence of an overwhelming flood (although he puts a modern spin on things by deferring to radiometric dating for a determination of whether the deposits are sufficiently recent to warrant identification with Noah's flood). He also points to the frozen Arctic cadavers as evidence of an extensive and sudden inundation.

Archer cannot quite bring himself to believe that the Bible does not demand a flood that killed all of humanity. He recognizes that Genesis 10 does not permit "easy identification with the remoter races who lived in the lower reaches of Africa, Far East Asia, Australia, and the Americas" (p. 197), but on the other hand he insists that the worldwide nature of the deluge traditions seems to imply the "inclusion of all human races in the descendants of Noah, rather than excepting some of the populations of Africa, India, China, and America" (p. 199). Archer repeatedly invokes the inundation of Mount Ararat as evidence undercutting a local flood hypothesis. It would take water to a depth of 17,000 feet to cover the peak of Ararat, he says, and such a quantity of water could scarcely have remained purely local for a whole year. Even though he clearly favors a universal flood, however, Archer admits to being impressed by the scientific and textual problems with such a reading and on the whole charitably engages the arguments for a local flood.

Francis Schaeffer (1912-1984), self-styled Presbyterian evangelist to students and founder of L'Abri Fellowship in Switzerland, wrote

---

8. Archer, *A Survey of Old Testament Introduction* (Chicago: Moody Press, 1964), p. 200.

voluminously on apologetic and philosophical topics. Even his book on Genesis bears an apologetic flavor.[9] Among the evidence he cites there to substantiate the universality of the flood is the case of the Siberian mammoths, which he characterizes as a mystery that nobody has been able to explain. He also seeks to bolster the case for a catastrophic flood by attacking uniformitarianism. "Modern man believes in a uniformity of natural causes in a closed system, and therefore such a thing as a catastrophe in the sense of an abrupt change is not considered possible" (p. 137). According to Schaeffer, John Woodward introduced the catastrophist explanation of the nature of fossils, but his superior insights were set aside by later geologists who were blinded to the truth by their uniformitarian bias. Apparently unaware of Fleming's earlier views on uniformity, Schaeffer lays the blame for the modern misreading of the biblical creation and flood accounts at the feet of uniformitarian Charles Lyell. Schaeffer happily reports, however, that geologists are now finding it necessary to revert to the concept of catastrophe in their theories, "for they have not been able to demonstrate that everything (in the order of events we know today) flows in a simple cause-and-effect line" (p. 138). His meaning here is not entirely clear, but we can at least say the following: while contemporary geologists have become more aware of large-scale catastrophes in earth history, that increased awareness has not undermined their traditional search for related causes and effects or their use of traditional methodologies in reconstructing earth history, nor, more specifically, has this increased awareness of the role of catastrophic events led to greater acceptance on the part of modern geologists of the hypothesis that a global deluge produced all (or any) of the world's fossiliferous stratified rocks.

Schaeffer was so wedded to the belief that Scripture teaches an anthropologically universal flood that he was willing to date the flood before 20,000 B.C. in order to set aside the problem of accounting for the presence of human beings in North America after that date. (And this despite the fact that he had earlier linked the deluge to the extermination of the mammoths around 10,000 B.C.) "Because the Indians were descendants of Noah and his sons," says Schaeffer, "the flood would have had to be prior to this time" (p. 135). Predictably, he found it compelling that both North and South American Indians have flood myths.

9. Schaeffer, *Genesis in Space and Time* (Downers Grove, Ill.: InterVarsity Press, 1972).

J. Vernon McGee (b. 1904), long-time Presbyterian pastor of Los Angeles's Church of the Open Door and prominent radio Bible preacher, was an avid diluvial universalist who minced no words in his admiration for Whitcomb and Morris and highly recommended the "very scholarly book" *The Genesis Flood* by these two "thoroughly qualified" men. In contrast to that eminent work, McGee laments that "there have recently come from the press several books by men whom I consider to be pseudointellectuals and pseudotheologians."[10] Included among those who earned McGee's opprobrium were any who suggested that the flood had been confined to the Tigris-Euphrates valley.

McGee held that the frozen mammoths alone should be sufficient to convince anyone of the universality of the deluge. Failing to distinguish between frozen carcasses and isolated bones, he approvingly quotes a writer who states that the mammoths were "found in herds on the higher ground not bogged in marshes, hundreds of thousands in number" (p. 45). McGee notes that it has been determined that the frozen mammoths died of asphyxiation, but he jumps inaccurately to the conclusion that they must therefore have drowned. "If they had just gotten bogged down," he says, "they would have died of starvation" (p. 45). McGee also incorrectly deduces from descriptions of the food remains found in the mammoths' stomachs that the Siberian climate must have changed drastically following their death.

Donald Barnhouse's most recent successor at Philadelphia's Tenth Presbyterian Church is James Boice (b. 1938), a prolific and widely respected writer and speaker. Boice's extensive commentary on the flood addresses a host of extrabiblical issues.[11] He contends that the ark was spacious enough to have carried a full complement of passengers safely through the global deluge. He accepts biologist Ernst Mayr's tabulation of 1,072,300 extant animal species, but he argues that the fishes, tunicates, echinoderms, mollusks, coelenterates, sponges, protozoans, most arthropods, and most worms could have survived outside the ark, and, setting their numbers aside, he estimates that only about 35,000 to 70,000 individuals, mostly small, need have been on the ark. He completely overlooks the fact that a global flood would presumably have violated the very restricted temperature and salinity tolerances of virtually all of the aquatic species he lists. Boice

10. McGee, *Thru the Bible with J. Vernon McGee,* vol. 1 (Nashville: Thomas Nelson, 1981), p. 42.

11. Boice, *Genesis: An Expositional Commentary* (Grand Rapids: Zondervan, 1982).

pleads ignorance as to how various animals arrived at Noah's ark from a distance, saying only that "animals do seem to get across vast bodies of water, and in most cases the water involved was not all that vast" (p. 278). He also suggests that there would have been plenty of time for migrations if Noah spent 120 years to build the ark. "It is not impossible," he concludes, "that any animal could have reached Noah from anywhere on the earth in that period" (p. 278).

Borrowing from Prestwich, Wright, and Howorth, Boice points to Lake Baikal, glacial Lake Agassiz, bone-bearing fissures, and frozen mammoths as geological evidence for the flood. Then, borrowing from flood geologists, he asserts that coal beds and oil fields were also produced by the flood. He even speculates about a connection between the deluge and the dramatic rise in sea level mentioned by Rhodes Fairbridge. Concluding that geology neither proves nor disproves the flood, he optimistically suggests that geology "actually discloses quite a few items that might best be explained by a flood of world-wide dimensions" (p. 294). Boice also cites flood traditions as prime evidence of universality.

Baptists

Evangelist John R. Rice (1896-1980), longtime editor of the *Sword of the Lord*, has been characterized by historian George Marsden as the most influential fundamentalist publicist of his day. It is regrettable that his popular commentary on Genesis flays science beyond recognition.[12] Rice plays fast and loose with biology, for instance, by arguing that the ark would have needed only one pair of dogs and one pair of horses from which their varieties might descend, and perhaps only one pair of cats would have been required to produce subsequent generations of lions, tigers, leopards, and mountain lions. He seems oblivious to the fact that this would have entailed an unimaginably furious rate of biological evolution — no small irony in light of the fact that Rice was a determined opponent of all forms of evolutionary theory. Perhaps sensing the weakness of his reasoning, in the end he asserts that "however God wanted to handle it He did" (p. 197).

Apparently unaware that only a few dozen frozen mammoths have ever been found, Rice states that "there were many, many thousands of these carcasses found frozen solid" (p. 171). He also erroneously asserts that "undigested tropical plants and flowers that now

12. Rice, *In the Beginning* (Murfreesboro, Tenn.: Sword of the Lord, 1975).

never grow within a thousand miles of that frozen area" have been discovered in the mouths and stomachs of the pachyderms, and on this basis he paints pictures of tropical plants and weather in Siberia and millions of mammoths feeding on tropical vegetation "around the earth" before the deluge (p. 171). The animals all perished, he says, when the vapor canopy collapsed, exposing the earth's poles to the cold of outer space. He also contends that before its collapse, the vapor canopy filtered out infrared rays that accelerate the human aging process and that the remains of mammoths, saber-toothed cats, and dinosaurs prove that animals grew to much larger sizes in the antediluvian world.

Rice explains that the diluvial convulsion broke all the natural boundaries of oceans and seas: mountains rose, volcanoes spewed out lava covering thousands of square miles, sea bottoms rose and fell, and tidal waves around the earth washed across the highest mountains, covering vast forests and the bodies of slain animals with great layers of earth.

> If tidal waves again and again went round the earth, surely the sand, the silt, the carcasses of animals, the uprooted forests would be carried, and then dropped, and then covered by succeeding tides. And then the giant inland seas would begin to break through the soft layers, and so the Grand Canyon would have been formed in the first few years or centuries after the flood. Then volcanic action and internal pressures and changes in the earth could raise the mountain systems as they are today with some of the layers and fossils of sea shells and other fauna, high above their original position. (P. 46)

Like many other proponents of flood geology, Rice believed that his view had been held by prominent scientists of the past, but he failed to comprehend the vast gulf between Silliman and Cuvier's conception of the deluge and that of Penn or Woodward. Following in the line of such modern "men of science" as Nelson, Rehwinkel, Price, and "perhaps best of all" Whitcomb and Morris, Rice not only attributed rock layers to the washing back and forth of tidal waves but also envisioned rock deformation as the result of the flood:

> We suppose these layers in the ground would have been laid approximately level but with the sinking of ocean basins and the rising of mountains and with the earthquakes and convulsions, sometimes the ground would be squeezed together, raising mountains,

and those layers would be curved. For example, on Highway I-24 between Murfreesboro and Nashville, the highway cuts through some hills. The layers are arched. When these layers of mud and soft dirt were pressed together in waves, they then hardened into stone and the waves are still there. (Pp. 217-18)

As the flood drew to a close, says Rice, the ocean basin sank, giant ranges of mountains reared their heads, the mighty tidal waves were stopped, and the water drained into the ocean. The ark was left stranded on modern Mount Ararat.

Seventh-day Adventists

Seventh-day Adventism has distinct links and affinities with conservative Protestant evangelicalism, and because evangelicals have been much influenced by Adventist thought on the topic of the flood, we would do well to take a brief look at Adventist views.

The first edition of *The Seventh-day Adventist Bible Commentary* was pure George McCready Price in claiming that mainstream geology's "serial arrangement" of fossil remains is based on circular reasoning. This should be no surprise, inasmuch as Price wrote the section on the flood. Virtually all fossils are treated as organisms killed by the flood. The *Commentary* states that the Adventist "believes that the trilobites, dinosaurs, and mastodons were all contemporary, or living in the same age of the world's history; and that they were all destroyed together at approximately the same time."[13] The *Commentary* cites some key diluvial evidences from George F. Wright, including frozen carcasses, the remains of trees in the Arctic, ossiferous fissures, and rubble drift.

The second edition of the *Commentary* (1978) gives evidence that significant changes had occurred over a generation, for Price's views had been replaced with those of Harold Clark. The new commentary accepts many standard geological conceptions such as the paleontological sequence and the reality of thrust faults, although these data are interpreted as supporting an ecological zonation theory of a universal flood.

13. *The Seventh-day Adventist Bible Commentary*, ed. Francis D. Nichol, 7 vols. (Washington: Review & Herald Publishing Association, 1953-1957), 1:81. For a comparison of the first and second editions of the *Commentary* on the topic of the flood, see W. W. Hughes, "Shifts in Adventist Creationism," *Spectrum* 16 (1985): 47-51.

Other Writers

The author of numerous introductory volumes on scriptural matters, John Phillips (b. 1927) presents a particularly dramatic and idiosyncratic account of the flood in a work entitled *Exploring Genesis*. He offers a variation on the notion of an antediluvian water canopy, arguing that the earth was in fact surrounded by a sphere of ice. The flood resulted, he says, when an explosion tore this ice canopy apart, dropping immense quantities of ice and water to the earth below and thereby sweeping all evidences of antediluvian civilization into the depths of the ocean. "The bolts of heaven fell," he writes, "avalanches of water came down, the ocean deeps were rent asunder and heaved up boiling maelstroms of destruction. The hungry floods scoured the very mountain tops, searching out the sinner's hiding place."[14] The intense cold accompanying this catastrophe froze some animals in their tracks, he says, where they are found to this day in a remarkable state of preservation.

Phillips speculates that towering Mount Ararat might have been "the last resort of earth's fleeing multitudes, hurrying, panic-stricken up its slopes pursued by the relentless rising tides" (p. 87). And he goes on to say that this great peak, standing "midway between Gibraltar and the Caspian Sea and midway between the Cape of Good Hope and the Bering Strait" later served as "a new pivot from which the races of mankind were to radiate to repopulate the globe," after the passengers of the ark descended its slopes (p. 87).

John Jefferson Davis, a systematic theologian at Gordon-Conwell Theological Seminary in Wenham, Massachusetts, appeals to miracle to account for the migration of the animals to the ark but offers more natural explanations of the means by which they managed to survive aboard the ark during the flood's duration. For example, he suggests that a combination of lack of exercise and hibernation reduced their appetites enough to resolve the problems associated with space requirements for food. Acknowledging a debt to Whitcomb and Morris, he affirms that a universal flood would necessarily have had catastrophic geological effects, and he laments the fact that the identification of those effects has hardly begun, "because geology has been dominated by uniformitarian concepts. As experts have begun to analyze earth history," he says, "it has become more and more evident that uniformitarian presuppositions are inadequate."[15]

14. Phillips, *Exploring Genesis* (Chicago: Moody Press, 1980), p. 84.
15. Davis, *Paradise to Prison* (Grand Rapids: Baker Book House, 1975), p. 126.

James Burton Coffman, a Church of Christ pastor in Houston who has written several Bible commentaries, maintains that the flood was an epic catastrophe in which the Adamic curse on the ground was extended. In dealing with extrabiblical evidence, he begins by dismissing the findings of professional geologists on the grounds that they either know nothing or are hiding from the evidence. In fact, he seems to suggest that it would do no good to examine geological evidence in any event, because in the end it cannot tell us what went on in the distant past. He flatly states that "the appearance of marine fossils upon all continents at elevations of very great height cannot be explained apart from what is written" in Genesis and emphatically asserts that the frozen Siberian mammoths are a great mystery that nobody has been able to explain. He expresses his own amazement that these "tropical creatures" froze so quickly that "the plants found in their mouths, neither spit out nor swallowed, were still *in the process of being eaten!*"[16]

He contends that any geological evidences of great floods must surely have been "disturbed, rearranged, and scrambled" by untold subsequent geological disturbances, and "the theory that the present status of the continents would necessarily preserve any readable record of the events in this chapter is unfounded" (p. 117). He chides "geologists who seek in vain for the confirmation of the Flood in the present structure of the earth" for overlooking "the catastrophic changes which we *know* have occurred *since* the events recorded here" (p. 120). In fact, he suggests that the failure of geologists is not merely philosophical but also moral in nature. "Human conceit being what it is," he writes, "it is very difficult for unregenerated man to believe anything that he does not think he can explain! Well, there is *no way* to explain all of this Deluge. Just as that event was a moral test for Noah's generation, it is still a moral test for our own generation. Faith in what is written here cannot be produced by intellectual understanding of it" (pp. 120-21). This is not to say that he dismisses all scientists as incompetent or heterodox, however. "A scientific community that has no explanation whatever for how marine fossils are found at elevations above the snowline in the Cordilleras and the Himalayas are not at all convincing in their shouted denials that what is recorded here is a record of what really happened. However, it should be noted that faith in the Bible is confidently affirmed by some of the greatest scientists"

16. Coffman, *Commentary on Genesis* (Abilene: Abilene Christian University Press, 1985), pp. 106-7.

(p. 121). One is left to wonder how he would categorize some of the nineteenth century's greatest geologists, such as Silliman, Dana, and Dawson, who professed a conservative evangelical faith but also offered coherent explanations for the fossils that Coffman is referring to apart from any sort of flood geology.

Coffman rejects any connection between the archeological findings in lower Mesopotamia and the biblical flood on the grounds that none of the evidence indicates flooding of the huge scope described in Genesis. He affirms that either Greater or Lesser Ararat, the twin summits of the massif, might have been the landing place for the ark. And he registers his amazement that scholars cannot imagine that animals could have descended through the snows from a high peak. Such difficulties, he says, come not from the Bible "but from the interpretations that men have imported into it" (p. 125).

For the most part, evangelicals favoring the concept of a universal flood have seriously distorted scientific evidence to prop up their view. Discussions of the frozen mammoths are symptomatic of their failure to treat the paleontological record adequately. The false claims that thousands of frozen mammoths have been found, that tropical vegetation has been recovered from their stomachs, that they were killed during a radical climatic change, or that they were suddenly overwhelmed by a deluge surface repeatedly. The numerous appeals to the mammoth evidence by twentieth-century evangelicals demonstrate that on the whole they tend to see nothing wrong with using extrabiblical information in biblical interpretation, but far too many of them have flagrantly violated the allegiance to truth that has historically characterized their faith tradition by failing to obtain accurate information in this regard. Some writers have compounded their abuse of the available data with wild speculations or suggestions that scientists are ignorant of many matters that were established long ago. The arrogance and laziness of such commentators is an affront to knowledgeable scientists and puts a stumbling block in the way of those who might otherwise be won to Christianity.

Many proponents of a universal flood have dismissed the findings of mainstream geology by claiming that they are based on a fallacious philosophical position called uniformitarianism. They understand uniformitarianism as a dogmatic a priori insistence that all past geological processes were analogous to those of the present and occurred only slowly and gradually. They contend that uniformitarians refuse to believe in the occurrence of geologically catastrophic events solely on the basis of anti-theistic prejudices. They are simply working with a definition of uniformitarianism that doesn't apply to the professional scientific community. Mainstream geologists have always acknowledged the role of catastrophe as well as more gradual physical processes in the production of geological phenomena. Uniformitarianism as they understand it is the assertion that the basic laws governing change operate the same way in different time periods. Moreover, the professional scientific community assesses the validity of these laws (and judges the likelihood that any given phenomenon, either catastrophic or gradual, produced a given result) on evidential grounds, not because of a priori commitments.

Writers Agnostic about the Extent of the Deluge

Many scholars have concluded that the biblical text is noncommittal about the extent of the deluge.[17] Some of those who remain agnostic in this fashion nonetheless lean toward universality, such as Old Testament theologian Gerhard Charles Aalders (b. 1880) of the Free University of Amsterdam.[18] Although charitable to local flood views, his charity failed to preserve him from scientific gaffes. He speculated that the earth might not have been fully populated with animals at the time of the flood so that all animal species could easily have gotten to the ark. He also speculated that an ice mass in space might have dumped vast quantities of rain on the earth. Aalders dated the flood before 4000 B.C. because the civilizations of Babylon, Egypt, and Ur could all be traced well into the fourth millennium B.C.

Oswald T. Allis (1880-1973), an Old Testament scholar at Princeton and Westminster theological seminaries, also leaned toward universality without insisting on it. He, too, was misinformed about mammoths, suggesting that their condition indicated sudden destruction and climatic change "perhaps due to a sudden shifting of the polar axis."[19] To account for the sudden inundation of the land, Allis speculated that earthquakes and volcanic eruptions may have caused a sudden elevation of the sea floor, or perhaps giant meteorites fell into

17. See, e.g., Meredith G. Kline, "Genesis," in *New Bible Commentary*, ed. D. Guthrie and J. A. Motyer, rev. ed. (Grand Rapids: William B. Eerdmans, 1970); and John T. Willis, *Genesis* (Austin: Sweet, 1979).

18. See Aalders, *Genesis*, trans. William Heynen (Grand Rapids: Zondervan, 1981).

19. See Allis, *God Spake by Moses* (Philadelphia: Presbyterian & Reformed, 1951), p. 24.

the sea. Allis saw no warrant for identifying the Ur deposits with the Noachian flood.

Howard Vos (b. 1925) of The King's College in New York has forwarded the idea that the biblical "kinds" were roughly equivalent to the modern taxonomic families rather than species, which would greatly have reduced the space requirements for the animals aboard the ark. He suggests that only basic types like dog, cat, and cow may have been on the ark (curiously, the examples he mentions are all species). Yet Vos is no adherent of flood geology, for he also notes a lack of evidence "of any general and cataclysmic alteration of the earth's crust at a given time in the past,"[20] and he notes that radiocarbon dating of some wood recovered from Mount Ararat indicates that it did not come from a five-thousand-year-old source.

Vos rules out both the Ur and Kish floods as candidates for the biblical flood on the grounds that there is no evidence of a major break in Middle Eastern culture after the sixth or fifth millennium B.C.; indeed, he notes that undisturbed remains date back to the eighth millennium B.C. at Jericho and Jarmo. He also believes that human beings probably arrived in North America well before 20,000 B.C., a point that further complicates efforts to account for an anthropologically universal flood within a time frame that accords with other evidence suggesting a more recent event. In the end, Vos does not commit himself to any theory.

In a contribution to the *Zondervan Pictorial Encyclopedia of the Bible*, Wayne Ault (b. 1923), a geochemist at The King's College at the time he wrote the article, contends that the text allows for no firm decision on the extent of the deluge, although he leans toward a local deluge. He has probably handled relevant extrabiblical data as accurately as any recent evangelical. Observing that "there are presently about 4500 species of living mammals and 8650 species of living birds" and that comparatively few species have become extinct in the last few thousand years, Ault maintains that it is not credible to suppose that all those animals could have been squeezed onto the ark.[21] He is virtually the only recent evangelical to get the facts about mammoths straight. He notes that mammoths were native to colder latitudes, lays to rest the myth that the recovered frozen mammoth meat was fresh,

20. Vos, "Flood (Genesis)," in the *International Standard Bible Encyclopedia*, ed. Geoffrey W. Bromiley, 2d ed., vol. 2 (Grand Rapids: William B. Eerdmans, 1979), p. 317.

21. Ault, "Flood (Genesis)," in *Zondervan Pictorial Encyclopedia of the Bible* (Grand Rapids: Zondervan, 1975), p. 352.

explains their probable manner of death, and points out that the various individuals did not die simultaneously. "Each death and burial," he says, can be attributed to "normal accidents such as falling over a cliff or into a crevass," or being "caught in a blizzard or a mud flow, etc. in situations where they were quickly frozen and preserved" (p. 559). Radiocarbon dating of recovered mammoth carcasses indicates that they died at various times between 11,450 and 39,000 years ago — which also constitutes strong evidence, he says, "that the north tundra regions of the earth have remained frozen and therefore have not been covered by a flood during this time" (p. 559).

Ault discusses geology with a degree of detail and confidence that theologians cannot. He points out the untenability of appeals to terrace gravels and unconsolidated sediments as evidence of the flood because these deposits cannot be correlated and are too old. He disputes the claim that the elevations of major surface features of the earth were significantly different before the flood, and he confidently asserts that there was no adequate source of subterranean water for the flood. Rightly insisting that the best view of the flood should be one that strikes the best agreement between Scripture *and* scientific information, Ault argues that theories disregarding basic knowledge or consisting of conjecture with little basis in fact should be dismissed as "science fiction." Speculations about an antediluvian "vapor canopy," icy comets, and the like as sources of the floodwaters are groundless in their own right and in any case inconsistent with evidence now available: any such huge infusion of fresh water would greatly have diluted the world's oceans, and yet oxygen isotope measurements indicate that there has been no such dilution in recent times. The vapor canopy theory is also problematic on other grounds, notes Ault. It assumes that the earth underwent an abrupt change from a subtropical to an ice age climate, whereas a wealth of data from a variety of sources indicates that the continental glaciers of the ice age built up, advanced, and retreated over long periods of time. Ault grants that the planet did indeed experience periods of widespread subtropical conditions in the distant past, but he cautions that "one cannot at random claim one of these as evidence and ignore the time aspect of when such conditions prevailed" (p. 557). He is willing to entertain Fairbridge's idea that a rise in sea levels at the end of the ice age might have helped produce the various deluge traditions, but he rejects the theory that the ocean floor was uplifted while continental land masses sank, and he notes that the deposits once categorized as "diluvial" have been shown to be unrelated to the flood.

Ault also effectively counters the complaints about uniformitarianism common among flood geologists and defends orthodox conceptions of the geological record. He concludes by saying that "the predominance of qualified Christian scholarship appears to favor a local flood interpretation because of the lack of evidence for and the problems attendant on a universal flood. . . . The serious Bible student will not seek to support the physical aspects of Bible history with pseudo-science. In the final analysis the true interpretation of the Biblical flood account will fully accord with true science" (p. 563).

Writers Favoring a Local Deluge

The New International Study Bible recognizes that some scholars believe that the flood was universal "only from the standpoint of Moses' geographic knowledge."[22] Among those endorsing the idea that the flood was a local event are Albertus Pieters, Derek Kidner, and Ronald Youngblood. Youngblood and Kidner contend that an event as extraordinary as the flood would naturally call forth hyperbolic description. Appealing to the hyperbole in Colossians 1:23, Kidner observes that "the concern of the story is to record the judgment which man brought on his whole world, not to dilate on geography," and he reminds his readers that the Bible commonly uses universal language for limited events.[23]

Albertus Pieters (1869-1955), a Reformed Church of America theologian at Western Theological Seminary in Holland, Michigan, asserted that it is a violation of the text to think of the Rocky Mountains as being submerged and thought it silly to envision kangaroos and other animals migrating to the ark from far distant lands.[24] Pieters claimed that the Mesopotamian discoveries suggest but do not prove the historicity of the flood, inasmuch as the flood deposits at Ur probably do not belong to Noah's time. He was content not to attach himself to any particular scientific theory of the flood.

Baptist scholar Ronald Youngblood of Bethel Theological Seminary counters several textual arguments that have traditionally been used to support the notion that the flood was universal. He argues that

22. *The NIV Study Bible*, ed. Kenneth Barker (Grand Rapids: Zondervan, 1985), p. 15.
23. Kidner, *Genesis* (Chicago: InterVarsity Press, 1967), p. 91.
24. Pieters, *Notes on Genesis* (Grand Rapids: William B. Eerdmans, 1943).

if every mountain had been covered, the runoff rate at the conclusion of the flood would have produced such spectacular erosion that it would have been years before cultivation would have been possible. He observes that 2 Peter 3:6 uses the term *kosmos* in distinguishing the "world" from the "heavens and the earth" of verses 5 and 7, and argues on this basis that the author is referring to the "world of mankind" rather than the geographical world. The biblical writer is thus underscoring the point that the purpose of the flood was to destroy all people, says Youngblood. He goes on to say that "it cannot be proved that the writer had in mind anyone other than the inhabitants of the ancient Near East,"[25] which would seem to suggest that he questions whether the flood was even anthropologically universal. After citing various other aspects of the issue, including problems of animal migration to and from the ark, he notes that "most Christian geologists insist that although there is evidence for extensive local flooding in ancient times, no geological evidence whatever exists to prove the universal flood theory" (p. 131).

Youngblood is one of the rare evangelicals who think that the deposits at Ur might be correlated with the biblical flood. He suggests that the flood may have occurred about 3500 B.C., the most recent date proposed by an evangelical. He doubts that the world's deluge traditions were all derived from Noah's flood, given the local setting of many of the traditions and heroes: none of the legends characterizes the flood as having occurred at some distant location. He also suggests that some of the stories might have been brought to the natives by missionaries.

According to archeologist Derek Kidner, warden of Tyndale House, Cambridge, little doubt remains that "the events of Genesis 6–8 must have taken place within a limited though indeed a vast area, covering not the entire globe but the scene of the human story of the previous chapters."[26] Moreover, unless the world's "population was drawn back into the vicinity of Mesopotamia before the flood, or unless the palaeontological data need drastic reinterpretation, it seems to follow that the destruction of life was, like the inundation of the earth, complete in the relative and not the absolute sense" (p. 94). By relative he means restricted to the area of immediate interest to the Old Testament.

On the basis of the evidence of the table of nations, Kidner

25. See Youngblood, *How It All Began* (Ventura, Calif.: GL Regal Books, 1980), p. 134.
26. Kidner, *Genesis*, p. 94.

concludes that the flood must have occurred a few millennia prior to the Babylonian floods. Like Youngblood, he is skeptical that all flood traditions can be related back to the Noachic deluge. Some of them may have been so derived, he concedes, but he reminds his readers that floods "are not the rarest of disasters, and survivors' experiences will have much in common" (p. 96). Moreover, the similarities between Genesis and many other traditions are utterly outweighed by the differences, and "it is only the Babylonian legend that shows any close resemblances to the story of Noah" (p. 96).

Roland K. Harrison of Wycliffe College, University of Toronto, suggests that if the deluge was comparatively local, then the "natural concern of Noah and his family would be for the preservation of only the most immediate fauna of the neighborhood in the ark, thus precluding some of the fanciful interpretations of the situation as furnished by artists and others."[27] He recognizes the absence of any certain geological evidence of the flood and sees no basis for the belief that the Genesis deluge covered the entire world. He notes that much of the evidence adduced in support of a global deluge can be explained in terms of the history of mountain structure or as the vestiges of glacial activity during the ice age.

Harrison argues that the flood deposits at Ur, Kish, Lagash, Uruk, and Shuruppak were left by different events and none can be definitively associated with the Genesis flood. Cataclysmic floods were commonplace in Mesopotamia, he notes, and he suggests "that the deluge recorded in Genesis constituted one such flood of major proportions that occurred in a comparatively localized area" (p. 99). He acknowledges that the cuneiform deluge accounts exhibit points of contact with the biblical story that can be explained "by common reference to an actual original or historical event, or by the fact that a standard method of escaping from the worst effects of the devastating flash-floods of Mesopotamia was being described in mythological or epic fashion" (p. 557). He dismisses efforts to locate the ark as pointless because "there is very little likelihood that the ark has survived in any form to the present day, and even if traces of an ancient vessel were recovered from a probable site, there would be no means of knowing with certainty whether or not the fragments were in fact part of the original ark" (p. 100).

Relatively few conservatives are willing to accept the view that

27. Harrison, *Introduction to the Old Testament* (Grand Rapids: William B. Eerdmans, 1969), p. 558.

the flood was less than anthropologically universal. Although Baptist theologian Bernard Ramm expresses an openness to an anthropologically restricted deluge in his landmark book *The Christian View of Science and Scripture,* one finds relatively little commitment to that view in the standard Bible helps. A major exception can be found in the first edition of the Harper Study Bible, which grants that extrabiblical evidence seems to refute a universal flood. After listing three views of the flood's extent, editor Harold Lindsell leans toward the option that the flood was both geographically and ethnologically local on the grounds that "the genealogies of chapter 10 make no reference to the Negroid and Mongoloid races, which leads one to suppose that these races were not included in the flood."[28]

Analysis and Application

Evangelical conservatives of the twentieth century are generally to be applauded for recognizing that extrabiblical data are important and should, in principle, agree with the Bible's story of the flood. Relatively few writers have avoided such data: none of them has argued that extrabiblical information is irrelevant, and virtually all of them have sought external corroboration for their positions. But while it is commendable that external data are being addressed, far too many recent evangelicals, especially those who favor a universal flood, have handled those data very poorly.

Faced with an increasing burden of physical evidence against their position, recent proponents of a universal flood have adopted a number of strategies for supporting their case. The first of these involves appeals to miracle — most typically to a large number of separate miracles in the areas of animal migration, animal behavior aboard the ark, the proliferation of species following the flood, and the like — to circumvent problems in a more straightforward explanation of the

---

28. Lindsell's annotations have been attached to various standard translations of the Bible (e.g., RSV, KJV, NASB) and published separately under the title *Harper Study Bible* (first by Harper & Row and later by Zondervan). In the first edition of the annotations (which first went to press in 1964), a note on Gen. 6:17 reads, in part, "Extrabiblical evidence appears to be against a universal flood." In Lindsell's substantial revision of the annotations, first published in 1991, he completely reverses his position on both geographical and anthropological aspects of the flood. In his revised note on Gen. 6:17 he states that "recent evidence of a gigantic catyclysm [sic] in all parts of the world clearly suggests a universal flood."

event. This strategy is problematic in the extent to which it imports a presumption of immediate divine activity into the biblical account. The Bible clearly testifies to miraculous divine activity on many occasions. The miracle of the virgin birth and the resurrection of Jesus constitute the very foundation of the Christian faith. But these miracles are clearly presented as such in the text of the Bible. The biblical account of the flood makes no such presentation; to the contrary, it gives every evidence of attributing the deluge to terrestrial mechanisms — the bursting of the fountains of the deep and the opening of the floodgates of the sky. Appeals to miracle in this context seem most frequently to be made in an effort to protect a hermeneutical position — namely, the presumption of the universality of the flood — rather than to approach the text on its own terms.

Another tactic that has surfaced frequently in recent discussions of the flood by evangelicals is what amounts to an appeal to ignorance. For example, some individuals who have encountered scientific challenges to their interpretation of the flood narrative have claimed that scientists can do no more than speculate about what happened in the distant past, that they cannot make any certain pronouncements about it. Some of those who adopt this sort of strategy are themselves ignorant about the relevant scientific data and project their own ignorance onto the scientific world. Some dismiss the validity of scientific findings on the presumption that any line of investigation that reaches conclusions they consider unacceptable must for that reason be essentially flawed. Whatever the motivation for making such assumptions, the willingness of Christian scholars to characterize experts in disciplines other than their own as ignorant is at best presumptuous and at worst arrogant and unethical. Pastors and theologians who write commentaries should think twice about summarily dismissing any body of truth that has been assembled painstakingly and in good conscience.

A third strategy that has recently been adopted by a large number of evangelicals entails the presentation of distorted or outdated scientific findings and indulgence in unsubstantiated speculation in support of given interpretations of the biblical flood narrative. We have noted the considerable number of scholars who have cited the frozen mammoths as evidence of a catastrophic deluge, for instance, despite the fact that a considerable amount of compelling evidence against such a position has been accumulating for the last century. Are these scholars simply unaware of the evidence? Like other professional scholars, theologians will understandably have limited expertise in fields outside of their main interest and hence will have to rely on trustworthy experts in those other fields. But, that being the case, they are obliged to choose their experts carefully. Unfortunately the evangelical community has been too willing to assess the credibility of its experts on the basis of the conclusions they reach rather than on the basis of the means by which they have reached them. Again and again conservative exegetes have turned to the work of catastrophists such as Price, Rehwinkel, and Whitcomb and Morris because their findings are compatible with a literal reading of the Bible and heedless of the fact that their research methods, such as they are, fall outside the canon of acceptable scientific procedure. In fact, few flood geologists can lay claim to any significant expertise in geology, paleontology, anthropology, or biogeography. Evangelicals are compromising the integrity of their biblical scholarship to the extent that they base their exegesis on this sort of questionable secondary scholarship.

All of these strategies constitute a retreat of some sort from the admittedly difficult task of studying and assessing both God's written Word and his created order in an open, honest, and diligent way to see what each has to say to us. We cannot conclude that such a task is impossible, because conservative scholars of earlier generations undertook it with some considerable success. Indeed, the departure of evangelicals during this century from a familiarity with and an appreciation of mainstream science constitutes a lapse in a commendable heritage. Modern biblical scholars would do well to return to the work and the example of Miller and Hitchcock and seek to return to the higher intellectual ground occupied by their predecessors a century ago.

Epilogue

I want to conclude this survey of the church's thinking about the flood narrative with a few observations addressed to those Christians who question the propriety of using extrabiblical sources in biblical interpretation or are nervous about the influence of those sources.

1. *Throughout church history a majority of biblical commentators across the theological spectrum have incorporated relevant extrabiblical information into their interpretations of the deluge account.*

If the interpretation of the flood story is typical, the church, as represented by its finest theological thinkers and not a few of its lesser minds, has from its inception considered extrabiblical information to be of great importance. Christian thinkers have always wanted their understanding of the deluge narrative to be in agreement with the character of reality as they have understood it. The nature of the extrabiblical material to which they have appealed has inevitably varied as the knowledge of the world has expanded throughout the Christian era. At first, reports of remains of the ark and other flood traditions were accorded major significance. The known deluge traditions were typically divorced from the biblical tradition. Some attention was given to the size of the ark and its ability to transport representatives of all of the world's known animals. A few writers linked fossil remains to the effects of the deluge, and Augustine wondered about the problems associated with the dispersal of the animals after the flood.

Centuries later, the discovery of North America provided a wealth of new information that created conceptual problems for biblical exegetes. Christians felt compelled to account for how the ark could have held the vastly larger number of known species and how the animals, many of great size, could have traveled from various remote and isolated parts of the world to the ark and back. The discovery of new human groups raised similar problems regarding the dispersal of humankind after the deluge and additional problems concerning the relationship of these newly encountered peoples to the sons of Noah. Indigenous deluge traditions, however, were seen as strong evidence for a global deluge.

The study of fossiliferous rock strata from the seventeenth into the early nineteenth century eventually made it clear that neither the rocks nor the fossils had been formed by the flood. Moreover, the fossil record revealed a number of species yet more vast than those surviving today. Those who persisted in arguing that the flood produced the fossils were faced with the prospect of explaining either how all these additional animals could have been preserved on the ark or why they failed to survive the flood along with all the species we know today. Efforts to identify the deluge with mammal-bearing surficial gravels in the northern hemisphere also failed once the glacial origin of the gravels was established. And during the past two centuries commentators have had to cope with the implications of the discoveries of several Near Eastern deluge legends, Mesopotamian flood deposits, archeological evidence, and human remains.

The main point, however, is that those who deny the propriety of using extrabiblical evidence as a tool in understanding the flood story fly in the face of the general tendency of church history. In rejecting such evidence, they implicitly condemn the approach of many of the church's premier minds from Augustine through Luther, Archibald Alexander, and Keil to Bernard Ramm.

2. *Some commentators have avoided addressing extrabiblical information in their discussions of the deluge.*

A number of scholars have elected not to engage external evidence in relation to the deluge without explicitly condemning the use of such evidence. John Calvin, Robert Candlish, Matthew Henry, and others simply focused exclusively on the practical and devotional aspects of the flood story. Perhaps all these individuals should be commended for avoiding discussion of matters in which they lacked competence. Some commentators who have themselves steered clear of external information have nonetheless referred their readers to other commentators who do interact with pertinent data. It is noteworthy that those who have avoided using extrabiblical knowledge have uniformly refrained from criticizing other scholars for invoking that knowledge and typically refrained from making scientifically untenable assertions on purely textual grounds.

While there is unquestionably a proper place for the strictly devotional, practical, or textual commentary that ignores the scientific implications of the deluge, the church would suffer immeasurably if everyone avoided dealing with extrabiblical data. Fortunately the majority have not avoided those data. By interacting with other bodies of knowledge, exegetes have been forced to probe the biblical text more deeply and with greater critical skill than they ever would have had they studied it in isolation from knowledge of the world. As Hugh Miller so astutely observed in the nineteenth century, the church can ill afford to ignore science when the enemies of scriptural truth are eagerly employing science in their arsenal against Christianity.

3. Those Christians who have interacted with extrabiblical data have responded in contrasting ways.

One response to extrabiblical data came from the rationalistic borders of Christendom. Many scholars of a skeptical bent cited extrabiblical information as a reason to jettison various aspects of traditional orthodoxy, perhaps most notably a high view of the Bible. From such early church critics as Celsus to La Peyrère to the more radical higher critics of recent centuries, many scholars have undertaken to reconstruct Scripture, variously consigning it to the realm of unreliable fable or denying its uniquely divine origin. While external evidence exerts a powerful force of its own, as the handiwork of God inevitably must, the attitudes, worldviews, and faith commitments of scholars have also played a profound role in determining how that evidence is used. I hold it as a point of faith, however, that the evidence itself, coming as it does from the God who created and sustains the heavens and the earth, can in no way undermine Christian faith.

It is worthy of note, too, that higher critics have often been inconsistent in the employment of extrabiblical evidence. Some scholars have accused traditional exegetes of being unable to support their reading with appropriate biological or geological evidence but have themselves proceeded to endorse speculative reconstructions of presumed textual sources without any support whatever from extrabiblical texts.

Many conservative Christians have reacted to rationalistic challenges to their reading of the flood story by marshaling their own bodies of extrabiblical evidence for essentially apologetic purposes, to confirm their own preestablished beliefs or to establish the reliability of the biblical text. During the early church era, Christians uncritically assumed the straightforward historical character of the Genesis narratives, and they took it for granted that any extrabiblical knowledge would automatically concur with the church's understanding of a literal creation, fall, flood, and genealogical descent. Reports of ark remains and even fossils were held to provide clear-cut corroboration of the literal historicity of the Bible. This same approach is evident in many conservative twentieth-century treatments of the deluge. The flood geology movement, for example, believes that the "real facts of science" amply support the occurrence of a catastrophic global deluge. Unfortunately, these apologists have not hesitated to contort or ignore relevant evidence for ideological purposes.

Another group of Christians confronting the difficulties of harmonizing the growing body of external evidence with traditional interpretations of the flood story has sought out new ways of understanding the biblical narrative that do not violate the integrity of either source of truth. Scholars from Bishop Stillingfleet to Hugh Miller to Bernard Ramm have approached the issue eager to maintain a high view of Scripture and full commitment to historic Christian orthodoxy but also eager to do full justice to tested scientific findings. Faced with the growing incompatibility between the notion of a universal deluge and evidence from a host of disciplines, they demonstrated a readiness to adjust their interpretation of the narrative. Admittedly their reinterpretations of the biblical text have not always proved fully satisfactory. On occasion they have been guilty of distorting the scriptural data in their zeal to bring the Bible into agreement with scientific data. But on the whole they have properly supported the principle that extrabiblical information should serve as a check to constrain the interpreter from indulging in exegeses that can no longer be credibly sustained and as a stimulus to intensified probing of the text in order to elucidate an interpretation that is faithful to the text. Indeed, they have considered that extrabiblical evidence provides a marvelous opportunity for achieving an improved understanding of the Word of God.

4. *Commentators seeking to defend traditional ideas of the flood have been far too eager to appeal to miracles.*

God is omnipotent. There is no question for the Christian that God is able to do as he wishes and that he is hardly constrained by his normal modes of operation, which we are accustomed to describing as "laws of nature." Christians freely confess the miraculous — for example, the virgin birth and resurrection of Jesus, the healing acts of Christ, and predictive prophecy. Miracle typically attests to the redemptive work of God.

Our belief in miracle, however, warrants neither the postulation of miracles unattested by the biblical text nor the invocation of miracles to avoid scientific difficulties. There is no doubt that God acted in marvelously providential ways during the deluge. The text, however, requires no miraculous "suspension of natural laws." The water was neither miraculously created nor destroyed: the sources are mentioned. The textual statement that the animals came to Noah no more requires a miracle than the statement that God sends the rain. The fact that animals and Noah's family had to be on the ark to avoid drowning suggests no suspension of God's normal method of operating. Suggestions of miracles in connection with the deluge are inevitably arbitrary.

Moreover, suggestions of miracles have generally been made to escape profound scientific difficulties. The weakness of global deluge theories is evident in the extent to which their proponents will claim as much scientific support as possible for their views and then appeal to miracle at those points where their explanations break down. Christians need to develop a more biblical view of miracles, a vision of miracles as more than arbitrary acts of divine omnipotence or props to support simplistic readings of the biblical text or means for evading the force of the evidence abounding in the created order.

5. *While implicitly acknowledging the importance of extrabiblical information to biblical interpretation, biblical scholars have frequently employed inaccurate or obsolete information.*

The path of church history is strewn with incorrect, misinterpreted, and misrepresented data and theory. Christian writers have not always been thoroughly up-to-date in their understanding of the scientific data. After the discovery of the New World, some commentators continued to write about the flood as if that discovery had never been made. Again, in the early nineteenth century, many commentators ignored the growing evidence of the earth's antiquity and espoused views that had been discredited a century earlier. They continued to promote the theories of such individuals as Woodward and Whiston despite the fact that they had been rejected on the basis of sound evidence by the generation of Cuvier and Buckland. The lucid, logical, and orthodox popular scientific writing of Hugh Miller and Edward Hitchcock in widely respected theological journals helped commentators of the later nineteenth century gain a much clearer grasp of scientific matters, but many twentieth-century Christians have elected to turn their backs on this and subsequent research and return to the exploded hypotheses of the past century. Because of the relative isolation of conservative theology from the broader academic community, much contemporary thinking about the deluge is seriously flawed by woefully inadequate handling of scientific data and concepts.

In essence, the church has wanted to pay due heed to important sources of knowledge but has not always done so very effectively. This weakness is understandable, especially in the modern era. Biblical scholars cannot be expected to be expert in scientific fields. Few have the training and time to understand the primary scientific literature. The temptation to accept the validity of inaccurate or obsolete extrabiblical information is especially acute for those who are committed to the notion of a global deluge. But clearly biblical commentators have a special obligation to secure the truth concerning matters of geology, archeology, anthropology, and the like from qualified scholars if they intend to discuss such things. The Christian community can ill afford to produce slipshod scholarship or dogmatic and unsubstantiated theorizing.

6. Because of new extrabiblical evidence, new interpretations of Scripture have challenged older views that had been established for a very long period of church history.

The church almost unanimously held to a universal flood until the mid-seventeenth century. By the mid-nineteenth century, however, a very large segment of the church no longer viewed a universal deluge as credible. Scientific evidence provided by the rapidly developing disciplines of professional geology and biogeography had provided the impetus for this shift in interpretation.

Systematic theologian John M. Frame of Westminster Theological Seminary in California has written that "Scripture does often correct our *interpretation* of general revelation, but the reverse is also true. All of our interpretations are subordinate to every form of divine revelation." Frame acknowledges that extrabiblical knowledge may in principle correct a faulty interpretation of the Bible, but he also introduces what he calls an "important asymmetry":

> We must believe Scripture even when it appears to contradict information available from other sources. We are not to accept information apparently derived from other sources which seems to us to contradict Scripture. Or to put it more concisely: what we interpret as the teaching of Scripture must prevail, in event of conflict, over what we interpret as the teaching of general revelation. I am, of course, talking about *settled* interpretations; certainly information derived from general revelation can correct our interpretation of Scripture, as I have said earlier. But once we are convinced that Scripture teaches x, we must believe it, even if general revelation appears to teach not-x.[1]

Frame is undoubtedly anxious to safeguard the major teachings of the Bible that have long been confessed by the church from scientific or philosophical challenges, but perhaps he has overstated his case. Frame is right to wish to protect, for example, the doctrine of the Trinity, the doctrine of providence, the two natures of Christ, and the concept of God's saving grace in Christ. Indeed, the church should always adhere to such teachings and many others — no matter what — simply because Scripture teaches them. Perhaps the church's confessions provide a guide to the kind of teachings that Frame is especially concerned about. Certainly the confessions serve to remind us that a "settled" interpretation is arrived at not by the deliberation of any one individual but by the collective Spirit-directed wisdom of the church.[2] Setting aside the unlikely prospect that general revelation could contradict Scripture on a settled confessional matter, does Frame really want to insist on accepting a traditional interpretation of the Bible in the face of a mass of conflicting extrabiblical evidence when the issue is a matter of a more historical, geographical, or scientific character? I suggest that such an approach cannot be sustained forever. As we

---

1. Frame, "Rationality and Scripture," in *Rationality in the Calvinian Tradition,* ed. Hendrik Hart, Johan Van Der Hoeven, and Nicholas Wolterstorff (Lanham, Md.: University Press of America, 1983), p. 300.

2. The issue of who decides what is a settled interpretation is crucial and requires extended discussion. Given the multiplicity of denominations and confessions, what one church denomination considers settled may be a mild heresy to another. Perhaps no interpretations are truly settled except those that have been endorsed by the church universally, such as the affirmation of such ecumenical confessions as the Apostles' and Nicene creeds. Even here, there is disagreement between the Orthodox churches and the West over the filioque clause concerning the nature of the Holy Spirit. In any event, it seems clear that the mantle of settled interpretation does not extend to cover peripheral issues that continue to be debated by Christians of good conscience on the basis of established extrabiblical evidence.

have seen, the idea of a universal deluge was the settled interpretation
of the church for nearly seventeen centuries, but that changed as a
body of compelling evidence undercutting that interpretation gradually
accumulated. The cumulative pressure of general revelation can be
ignored only so long. Christians must always be ready to reexamine
even settled interpretations when a wealth of external data call these
interpretations into question. God may be trying to tell us something!

This case study of the flood suggests the need for more humility
and less dogmatism in interpretation. The arrogant attitude displayed
by some commentators who have lacked appropriate scientific knowledge, especially in this century, is appalling. Christians must also be
cautious in using extrabiblical data for apologetic purposes, since their
data may eventually be supplanted by better information that demands
a different interpretation. There is danger in basing an apologetic for
our interpretations on a presumed agreement of the Bible with science.

7. *The church is too often overly cautious and reactionary in handling
extrabiblical information and desperately needs to develop an attitude
and a hermeneutic that eagerly embrace the discoveries that are made
in God's world.*

In response to the growing body of evidence regarding the flood, many
Christian scholars seem to have waited until the last possible moment
to accept the idea of a local flood. Indeed, a large segment of the church
still seeks to support a belief in a global flood by resisting, distorting,
or misinterpreting relevant extrabiblical evidence. It is, of course, easy
to find fault in hindsight. And as the church has been singed from
time to time by overeager scholars who have rushed to construct the
most tenuous hypotheses on the slenderest threads of evidence, some
caution is understandable. It is also understandable that long-held
traditional ways of interpreting the Bible may easily become equated
with what God is actually saying, and, of course, the church is reluctant
to part with what it thinks God is saying! And yet many Christians
have come to dread all scientific evaluations of the created world
because they perceive in them a threat to the authority of the Bible
and the certainty of personal salvation.

A large segment of the church has unfortunately locked itself
into a biblical hermeneutic that requires a global flood and a recent
six-day creation and that prevents it from dealing responsibly with
God's creative work. I submit that there is something inherently flawed
in any hermeneutic that prevents us from reading God's handiwork

properly and that repeatedly puts us at odds with the established conclusions of a scientific community that is composed not just of opponents of Christianity but also of confessing Christians. Some Christians delight in contrasting the infallible Word of God (that is to say, the Word of God infallibly interpreted by them) with the fallible ideas of sinful human beings and on that basis reject scientific conclusions they do not like. Scripture does oppose purely human philosophies, human pride, and human sin. But does the Bible oppose everything human? Science is a human endeavor that requires the input of fallible humans, but that hardly means that it is anti-Christian, and it certainly does not prevent Christians from accepting and using the results of science. Even the most doctrinaire advocates of a literal reading of Genesis 1–11 are selective in their objections to the findings of the scientific community. How many of them deny that the earth orbits the sun rather than the other way around, for example? How many object to the science that made high-tech electronics, manned missions to the moon, or modern drugs possible? When so many scientists of such a diverse array of worldviews are able to achieve a virtual consensus regarding a given body of evidence, we had better pay attention. When for the past two centuries thousands of geologists from around the world, including numerous Bible-believing Christians, insist from a lifetime of experience in looking at fossiliferous rocks that those rocks are extremely old and had nothing to do with a global deluge, then the church must listen. Commentators who dismiss or disparage that body of geological knowledge solely on the grounds of their commitment to a principle of interpretation might do well to question their commitment to truth in a larger sense. Is it likely that they will arrive at a sound understanding of what God is saying in the biblical text if they reject a sound understanding of what God is saying in the created order? The extrabiblical data pertaining to the flood have been pushing the church to develop a better approach to the flood story and indeed to all the early chapters of Genesis.

Just what are those extrabiblical data? In summary, several centuries of effort to locate physical remnants of the biblical deluge have completely failed. Any physical evidence that has been claimed to support a global flood has eventually been demonstrated to have a different explanation. The idea that the flood deposited the world's stratified rocks has been thoroughly discredited by numerous lines of evidence. Many of the individual strata give evidence of having been deposited in such non-flood environments as rivers, beaches, deltas, lakes, glaciers, deserts, and shallow oceanic platforms. Many strata, such as lake deposits and fossil reefs, contain abundant indicators of very slow deposition under environmentally sensitive conditions quite incompatible with a catastrophic deluge. Many strata are overlain by fossil soils and separated from higher strata by erosional breaks that could only have been produced over extensive lengths of time. The fossils themselves are arrayed in progressive order in the geologic column. Many of the organisms lived in environments utterly unlike flooded terrains. Radiometric dating of volcanic ash or lava flows interbedded with fossiliferous strata show that they are millions of years old. Some large masses of igneous rocks injected into the strata took hundreds of thousands of years to cool and crystallize. Many fossiliferous rocks have been metamorphosed, indicating extreme burial that could not possibly have occurred during a year-long deluge. All the evidence of the rocks tells us that they were not produced or arranged by a flood. The views of earth history offered by Woodward, Catcott, Price, Whitcomb and Morris, and John R. Rice are simply and obviously incorrect.

The evidence is also arrayed against views that confine the action of the flood to the globe's surface features. Most of the gravels, sands, boulders, smoothed U-shaped valleys, and surface grooves and scratches have been amply demonstrated to be the result of continental ice sheets rather than a flood. We now know that the frozen mammoths and their friends did not perish in a major catastrophe only a few thousand years ago involving a radical climatic change. These animals were well adapted to life on the harsh tundra and died individually over a period of thousands of years in accidents that were catastrophic only to them. The rubble-drift deposits of southern England and the Mediterranean (and scarcely evident at all in the Middle East) are most likely the result of downslope soil movements during the ice age. The views of the deluge propounded by Buckland, Sedgwick, Prestwich, and Wright are also incorrect.

In addition to the wealth of geological evidence opposing the possibility of a global deluge, a variety of biogeographical evidence also counts conclusively against such an event. For one thing, there is no evidence whatsoever to indicate that human or animal populations were ever disrupted by a catastrophic global flood at any point in the past. Indeed, all the evidence indicates continuous occupation by these populations of points around the globe into the exceedingly distant past. Human beings have been in North America for at least twelve thousand years and in Australia for at least thirty or forty thousand years, long before the biblical deluge could have occurred by any consistent reading of the textual evidence of the Bible. Furthermore, a literal reading of the flood narrative requires us to presume that representatives of tens of thousands of different species left their natural habitats and restricted supplies of food, made their way from all the distant and isolated parts of the globe, crossing oceans, arctic wastes, and any number of hostile environments to arrive at the ark, that these vast numbers of creatures somehow all boarded the craft, which (presumably) already held enough food to sustain them for a year, and then after the retreat of the floodwaters all made the journey back to their respective habitats to replenish the earth. Commentators who maintain that fossils were laid down in the flood must apparently also assume that representatives of all the species in the fossil record, including dozens of species of dinosaurs, were also aboard the ark. Is a literal reading of the flood narrative really so sacrosanct as to induce us to entertain such bizarre scenarios?

We need to find an interpretation of the text that does not commit us to a globe-covering catastrophe. Surely the text itself provides clues to a better understanding. Doesn't the fact that the text suggests that Mesopotamian geography was not rearranged by the flood nor the topsoil displaced suggest that it was not a globally catastrophic event? Given the frequency with which the Bible uses universal language to describe local events of great significance such as the famine or the plagues in Egypt, is it unreasonable to suppose that the flood account uses hyperbolic language to describe an event that devastated or disrupted Mesopotamian civilization — that is to say, the whole world of the Semites? I do not consider it a violation of the integrity of the biblical text to suppose that the biblical flood account uses a major Mesopotamian event in order to make vital theological points concerning human depravity, faith, and obedience and divine judgment, grace, and mercy.

The church serves no good end by clinging to failed interpretations of the Bible and refusing to explore new directions. Christian scholars have an obligation to lead the way toward a renewed reverence for God's truth wherever it can be found. Conservative scholars must develop a more aggressive attitude toward creation and encourage the church's youth to enter not only the pastorate, mission work, and theology but also such fields as the natural sciences, archeology, anthropology, and the social sciences. If anything, Christians should be preeminently motivated to investigate the intricacies of God's created order, confident that a better grasp of both God's Word and God's works will be forthcoming. If the fruits of that improved understanding are to be communicated to the Christians in the pew, their preachers will have to do the communicating. And this means that the theologians and commentators who educate the preachers have an obligation to consult more frequently with Christian scholars in other disciplines before making pronouncements on matters in those areas. What marvelous insights into Scripture might await the church if from now on the theologians and exegetes would work side by side with biologists, archeologists, anthropologists, geologists, linguists, astronomers, sociologists, and paleontologists! In a world of burgeoning knowledge about ancient literature, languages, civilizations, culture, and customs as well as about the workings of God's creation, biblical scholars must engage in dialogue with other representatives of the intellectual world they profess to want to influence with the good news — "the gospel he promised beforehand through his prophets in the Holy Scriptures regarding his Son, who as to his human nature was a descendant of David, and who through the Spirit of holiness was declared with power to be the Son of God by his resurrection from the dead: Jesus Christ our Lord" (Rom. 1:2-4).

Appendix: Arkeology

Since Noah's ark would plainly be a major piece of extrabiblical evidence, a brief overview of searches for the ark is in order. One major source of support for the biblical flood story in early Christian times was a variety of unverified reports that remnants of the ark had been recovered. The most widely held view was that the ark was probably stranded on Jabal Judi in the Gordyaean mountains. Not until the Middle Ages did attention focus on Agri Dagh, modern Mount Ararat. Travelers in that era including Marco Polo and John Mandeville reported having spotted something near the top of that mountain, brought reports from local citizens that the ark remained up there, or recounted what they had read in travelogues of earlier explorers. At least three seventeenth-century travelers referred to Ararat.[1] One of them, Jans Janszoon Struys, tried to climb the mountain in 1670 but concluded that "you cannot survive on this uninhabitable mountain." He claimed to have visited a hermit who gave him a little cross made from a piece of the ark. John Chardin traveled through Armenia at the end of the seventeenth century and considered it a miracle that anyone should climb so high because the upper half of Ararat was always covered with snow.

Surprisingly, during the nineteenth century neither the biblical commentators nor the geologists we have reviewed talked of looking for the ark, and few thought that Mount Ararat was the landing site.

---

1. See John Warwick Montgomery, *The Quest for Noah's Ark* (Minneapolis: Bethany Fellowship, 1972). Montgomery, a Lutheran theologian, not only provides detailed summaries of earlier searches for the ark on Ararat but also includes an account of his own ascent.

Several expeditions were undertaken, however. The first modern effort to climb the mountain was undertaken in 1829 by J. J. Friedrich W. Parrot, a professor of natural history at the University of Dorpat.[2] On his third attempt, Parrot erected a large cross during his ascent with his party of five. Upon reaching the summit, he erected another cross.[3] He contended that the summit would have been an adequate resting place for the ark in terms of level space. Moreover, he wrote, "it is obvious that on the top of Ararat there may be easily a sufficient depth of ice to cover the Ark."

In 1834 Spassky Aftonomof climbed the peak, and Hermann Abich (1806-1886), a professor of mineralogy at the University of Dorpat, finally succeeded in reaching the summit in 1845 after bad weather had repeatedly frustrated his efforts the preceding summer. Abich also planted wooden crosses on the mountain. Five years later, Col. Khodzko and a team of sixty Russian soldiers scaled the mountain to carry out scientific tests and to triangulate the Transcaucasian region precisely. Khodzko's team encountered "upright and well into the ground, the Cross which one of Abich's men had planted there in 1845." Upon attaining the summit, the Russian party also erected a cross.

Robert Stuart and a British party successfully challenged Ararat in 1856. He also reported finding Abich's large oak cross "on a rocky spot, about 1200 feet from the summit." Weathering had so softened the wood's surface that it could be scraped off with a fingernail to a depth of an eighth of an inch. Twenty years later, in 1876, Ararat was ascended by James Bryce (1838-1922), a prominent English statesman, jurist, and author. Although Bryce recognized that the biblical account referred only to the mountains of Ararat, he was so awed by the great volcano's dominant bulk that he said that "one could hardly doubt that if the Biblical writer had any particular mountain present to his mind, it must have been our Mount Ararat. No one who had ever seen it could have any doubt that if the Ark rested anywhere in that part of the world, it rested upon that particular summit." It was "just the place where an ark ought to rest." Bryce reported that above 13,000 feet he saw "lying on the loose blocks, a piece of wood about four feet long and five inches thick, evidently cut by some tool, and so far above the limit of trees that it could by no possibility be a natural fragment."

2. For his own account of the expedition, see Parrot, *Journey to Ararat* (London: Longman, Brown, Green, & Longmans, 1845).

3. This according to Tim F. La Haye and John D. Morris in *The Ark on Ararat* (Nashville: Thomas Nelson, 1976).

Bryce cut off a piece with his ice axe and brought it back with him in order to submit it "to the inspection of the curious." The wood, he suggested, met all the requirements for ark remains; the argument for its being a genuine relic was "exceptionally strong."[4]

E. de Markoff climbed the mountain in 1888 and found a marker pole left by a previous expedition above 13,600 feet. The pole, which Markoff's party burned in order to make tea, contained the initials of two Russian explorers who had attempted to reach the summit a few years earlier. Markoff suspected that the pole had been planted on the summit by Abich in 1845 and subsequently carried down by avalanches. In 1902, the Ivangouloff expedition made an ascent and placed a small wooden instrument box at the summit. During the next few years the box was torn from its base by hurricane-force winds and "lay half hidden in the ice, with the instruments it was to protect" until it was encountered eight years later by the next expedition.

Many climbers have also been to the top of Ararat in the twentieth century. Nineteenth-century expeditions were generally undertaken for scientific reasons or a mountaineering challenge. Not until the twentieth century did the mountain become the object of an intense search for the ark.[5] Many of those interested in finding Noah's craft were Seventh-day Adventists or associates of the flood geology movement hoping to find the ark in order to prove the truthfulness of the biblical account, establish a global deluge, and undermine the "myth" of evolution.

Some of the most spectacular claims were made by a French industrialist named Fernand Navarra. Navarra's adventures on the mountain with his young son during the 1950s attracted attention because of his claim to have recovered large hand-tooled beams of wood from under the ice at the 13,500 foot level.[6] A large dark structure from which much of the wood could not be extracted was said to be under the ice. Navarra believed he had found part of the ark and was anxious to have his claims tested by submitting samples of the wood for laboratory analysis. A preliminary investigation of the darkened and very dense wood led some to estimate that the beams might be

---

4. See Bryce, *Transcaucasia and Ararat* (London: Macmillan, 1878).

5. Among those who report having climbed Ararat this century to search for the ark are Prince John Joseph Nouri, Eryl Cummings, Bud Crawford, Clifford Burdick, Hardwicke Knight, and former astronaut James Irwin.

6. See Navarra, *Noah's Ark: I Touched It* (Plainfield, N.J.: Logos International, 1974). Navarra climbed Ararat several times during the 1950s. He reported having found the hand-tooled beams in 1955.

around five thousand years old, but later radiocarbon analysis called such an old date into question. The entire matter was thoroughly reviewed by Lloyd R. Bailey, who has kept a close watch on "arkeological" developments in recent years.[7] Bailey noted that at least eight different sites had been proposed as the landing place of the ark, and that Mount Ararat does not appear to have been widely regarded as the landing place until the eleventh or twelfth century. Bailey also stressed that wood high above the treeline on Mount Ararat was not unexpected given the number of climbs and the fact that "a considerable amount of wood has been carried *up* it in recent times as well!"

The reports of wood fragments, Bailey commented, had varied considerably as to their specific location, the color of the wood (variously reported as red, brown, green, blue, and black), and its hardness (variously described as soft and soggy and so hard that a bullet or dagger could not penetrate it). Wood experts informed Bailey that tests based on density change and discoloration were very unreliable. Such tests were highly dependent on precise identification of the wood species. All analysts of Navarra's wood agreed that his beam was oak, but different labs differed as to the exact species. That identification itself cast some doubt on whether the wood could have come from the ark, for if the author of Genesis wanted to identify the ark's timbers as oak he had well-known Hebrew words at hand. Radiocarbon analyses published by five different laboratories dated the wood from A.D. 720 to 790. One other laboratory dated the wood to about A.D. 260 but reported that the submitted sample was too small to yield a meaningful date. Specimens collected by Navarra on a 1969 expedition were tested by two labs and yielded radiocarbon ages around A.D. 620-640. At the very least these analyses conclusively showed that Navarra's beams could not have been part of any ship constructed in the third or fourth millennium B.C.

Linked with many of the ark searches have been a host of purported sightings of a barge-like object high on the mountain, partially embedded in glacial ice. A barrage of literature describing these sightings is now on the market.[8] These fascinating descriptions include the deathbed account of Haji Yearam, who claimed to have entered

---

7. See Bailey, "Wood from 'Mount Ararat': Noah's Ark?" *Biblical Archeologist* 40 (1977): 137-46.

8. See, e.g., Dave Balsiger and Charles E. Sellier, *In Search of Noah's Ark* (Los Angeles: Sun Classic Books, 1976); Violet M. Cummings, *Noah's Ark: Fact or Fable?* (San Diego: Creation Science Research Center, 1972); Charles Berlitz, *The Lost Ship of Noah* (New York: G. P. Putnam, 1987); and La Haye and Morris, *The Ark on Ararat.*

the ark as a boy; the tale of Georgie Hagopian, who was allegedly taken by his uncle to visit the relic twice; a famous apocryphal story of Russian aviators who spotted the ark from the air during World War I and the Russian soldiers who purportedly made a follow-up expedition that culminated with an entry into the ancient ship; and the story of George Greene, an oil pipeline engineer in eastern Turkey who is said to have spotted the ark from a helicopter 13,000 feet high on Mount Ararat and photographed the vessel protruding from a melting glacier.

In *Where Is Noah's Ark?* Bailey reviews these and other claims regarding the ark and explicitly points out the discrepancies and improbabilities of the various accounts. For example, Bryce, Navarra, and Knight claimed to have found the wood easy to cut, but Hagopian's uncle claimed it was so hard that bullets bounced from its surface. Hagopian said the ark was held together with dowels, while Prince Nouri said it was nails. Hagopian made no mention of a great hole in the side as others did or of a great door lying beside the ark as Haji Yearam had. Bailey concluded that the evidence was extremely tenuous. Sources are typically third- and fourth-hand. Original photographs and documents cannot be found. Alleged eye-witnesses have died and can no longer verify reports attributed to them. In short, the various reports are filled with substantial discrepancies.[9]

David Fasold, another "arkeologist" (or "arkologist," as he styles himself), believes that everyone has been looking in the wrong place.[10] He believes that he has found and investigated the ark on a much lower hill to the south of Mount Ararat. Fasold's "ark" was first recognized by satellite imagery in the late 1950s, and *Life* magazine published aerial photographs of the large, canoe-shaped structure the dimensions of which approximately matched those recorded in Genesis.[11] A ground-based exploration team headed up by Seventh-day Adventist preacher George Vandeman and veteran ark explorer Rene Noorbergen investigated the structure and concluded that it was only a geological formation.[12]

9. See Bailey, *Where Is Noah's Ark? Mystery on Mount Ararat* (Nashville: Abingdon Press, 1978). See also Rene Noorbergen, *The Ark File* (Mountain View, Calif.: Pacific Press, 1974). Although Noorbergen is a firm believer in the ark, he has carefully followed up many leads and has shown fine critical sense in doubting a large number of alleged sightings and finds.

10. See Fasold, *The Ark of Noah* (New York: Wynwood, 1988).

11. Photos and an article on the ark appeared in the 5 September 1960 issue of *Life* magazine.

12. See Noorbergen, *The Ark File*, pp. 114-29.

Fasold began work on the structure in the early 1980s. He was allowed to carry out surface surveys using metal detectors, but he was not permitted to do any excavating. He reported that his metal detector readings showed exceptionally high iron content at regularly spaced intervals. He also reported seeing lumpy protrusions on the surface and theorized that they were the remains of support beams. In a daring proposal, he suggested that the ark was not a wood structure but a vessel constructed of reeds that were packed together with some kind of cement. He claimed that a reed vessel would be more consistent with Mesopotamian flood legends. The Turkish government has prohibited Fasold from doing further work on the structure and has set it aside as a tourist site. Much more work is needed if the scholarly world is to be convinced that Fasold has really been working on an ancient ship. His intriguing photographs, which show several layers of folded stratified rock in the immediate vicinity, suggest that the structure may in fact simply be a small syncline — a natural geological formation of folded rock that is shaped like a trough or a canoe. The photographs also clearly show stratification within what Fasold claims to be the walls of the ship. Any geologist could determine in short order whether the "walls" of this "ark" are in fact composed of an ordinary rock type. Fasold supplied no information of that sort one way or the other, nor did a geophysicist who accompanied him on the investigation.

To date no one has provided compelling evidence for the existence of remains of Noah's ark anywhere.

Index

Documentary hypothesis, 155,
189, 190-91, 219, 237-38, 241.
See also Criticism
Dods, Marcus, 197
Driver, Samuel Rolles, 191-93
Duns, John, 161, 163-64

Ecological zonation theory, 246,
253, 261, 289
Evangelicals. *See* Conservatives
Evidences of the flood: bone caves,
105-7, 110, 117, 145, 180-81,
184; boulders, 100-102, 106-7,
109, 115, 118-19, 133, 144,
311; fossils, 18, 26-29, 31, 34,
39-42, 45-46, 48, 71-73, 75-77,
83, 93, 95, 99, 127, 133, 166,
244-45, 248-49, 256, 260-61,
288-89, 291, 302-3, 305, 312;
gravel deposits, 88, 95, 100,
102, 104-7, 109, 112-14, 116-
19, 139, 144, 149, 187, 295,
303, 311; loess, 180, 184, 186;
ossiferous fissures, 145, 180-81,
183, 186-87, 250, 257, 271,
284, 287, 289; rock strata, 42,
71-72, 75, 77, 83-84, 95, 97-99,
116, 122-23, 127, 133, 142,
188, 244, 250-51, 256, 260-61,
265, 275, 285, 288, 303, 310;
rubble drift, 179-81, 183-84, 186-
87, 204, 226, 250, 257, 289,
311; shape of continents, 94; valleys, 88, 100, 102, 104, 107-9,
112-13, 117-18, 144, 311
Evolution, biological, 29, 182, 245,
248, 251-52, 270, 287, 316

Fairbridge, Rhodes, 268-69, 276,
287, 295
Fairholme, George, 125, 127-28,
140, 142-43, 197, 251-52
Farrand, William, 230, 263, 270
Fasold, David, 318-19
Filby, Frederick, 269-72, 276
Fixity of species, 96

Fleming, John, 109-13, 116, 133,
149, 161-62, 248, 285
Flood: date of, 101-2, 104, 106,
114-15, 128-29, 186, 213, 218,
220, 222-24, 229, 232, 234,
242, 255, 259, 270, 272, 285,
293, 297-98; extent of, 11-12,
19, 25-27, 50-56, 147-48, 163,
270, 280, 293-96. *See also* Anthropological universality of the
flood; Evidences of the flood;
Flood geology; Flood narrative;
Flood traditions; Local flood; Universal flood
Flood geology, 124, 136, 188, 215,
244-45, 251-54, 258, 262, 264-
67, 269, 271-74, 276, 283, 287-
88, 294, 296, 301, 316
Flood narrative: composite nature
of, 154, 159-60, 189-92, 194-95,
237-38, 277-78; literal historicity of, 11-12, 14-15, 18, 45, 49,
55-56, 60-61, 70, 77, 79, 125,
129, 139, 153, 158-59, 162, 196-
97, 221, 244, 248, 254, 264-65,
274, 280-81, 305; unhistorical
nature of, 156, 158, 192, 278;
unity of, 194-96, 237-39, 241;
written from perspective of observer, 148-49, 158, 163, 185,
200
Flood traditions, 11, 18, 28, 36,
45, 47, 49, 52, 54, 62, 77, 82,
114, 132, 139, 142, 147, 158,
161-62, 166, 169-73, 177, 182,
188, 190, 197, 213-14, 216,
220, 259, 265, 268, 278-79,
284, 287, 295, 297-98, 302-3;
American, 37, 50, 55, 62, 77,
171-72, 214, 285; of Berossus, 5-
6, 12, 18, 55, 169, 182; Greco-
Roman, 6-8, 12, 15, 18-20, 26,
62, 171, 191, 214; Hindu, 8,
171-72, 214; Mesopotamian, 5-
6, 9, 12, 15, 62, 169, 182, 186,
191, 193-96, 212, 214, 216,